The Bahá'í Faith and African American History

The Bahá'í Faith and African American History

Creating Racial and Religious Diversity

Edited by Loni Bramson

Introduction by Loni Bramson

LEXINGTON BOOKS
Lanham • Boulder • New York • London

Published by Lexington Books
An imprint of The Rowman & Littlefield Publishing Group, Inc.
4501 Forbes Boulevard, Suite 200, Lanham, Maryland 20706
www.rowman.com

6 Tinworth Street, London SE11 5AL, United Kingdom

Chapter 7 "Race, Place, and Clusters: Current Vision and Possible Strategies" was previously published as an article, "Race, Place, and Clusters: Vision and Possible Strategies," in The Journal of Bahá'í Studies 27.3, 2017, and is used by permission of the author.

British Library Cataloguing in Publication Information Available

The hardback edition of this book was previously catalogued by the Library of Congress as follows:

Library of Congress Cataloging-in-Publication Data

Names: Bramson, Loni, editor.
Title: The Bahá'í faith and African American history : creating racial and religious diversity / edited by Loni Bramson.
Description: Lanham : Lexington Books, [2019] | Includes bibliographical references and index.
Identifiers: LCCN 2018044215 (print) | LCCN 2018050479 (ebook) | ISBN 9781498570039 (Electronic) | ISBN 9781498570022 (cloth) | ISBN 9781498570046 (pbk.)
Subjects: LCSH: African American Bahais. | Bahai Faith—United States—History. | Bahai Faith and social problems—United States. | African Americans—Religion. | Race relations—Religious aspects—Bahai Faith. | African Americans—Segregation. | United States—Race relations.
Classification: LCC BP350 (ebook) | LCC BP350 .B34 2019 (print) | DDC 297.9/308996073—dc23
LC record available at https://lccn.loc.gov/2018044215

Contents

List of Figures

Introduction

Loni Bramson

When the American Academy of Religion launched a new Bahá'í Studies Unit in 2016, the unit's steering committee decided that the obvious subject choice for an inaugural panel discussion at the Academy's subsequent annual meeting in San Antonio was "The Most Challenging Issue: Race and Religion in the Bahá'í Community."[1]

At the heart of the doctrines, practices, and theology of the Bahá'í Faith is the principle of the oneness of humanity. The religion's essential aim, enunciated by its founder, Bahá'u'lláh, in the second half of the nineteenth century, is the establishment of a just and peaceful global civilization characterized by universal human rights and freedom from prejudices of all kinds. Within the Bahá'í doctrine of the oneness of humanity, racism is considered to be a baneful evil.[2] Virtually since the moment of its arrival in North America around 1900, a major theme in the development of the Bahá'í Faith in the United States has been the confrontation of a new world religion explicitly grounded in human equality and solidarity with the ideologies, structures, and practices of white supremacy. Therefore, this was a logical topic for the first panel discussion, and in the context of the United States' continuing racial conflict, an all too timely one with which to start.

Unfortunately, not all those who were interested in participating were able to make it to San Antonio. In addition, two excellent papers that were delivered at the panel were, for logistical reasons, not ready for publication. This volume, then, includes versions of three papers from the panel plus a number of others that are thematically related but were assembled afterwards. The authors hope that this book will help both to crystallize the place of the Bahá'í Faith in the broader scholarship on race and religion in modern America and to spur further research on the many intersections between Bahá'í and African American history.

THE BAHÁ'Í FAITH: ORIGINS AND SCOPE

Although a comprehensive overview of the Bahá'í Faith is outside the purview of this volume, some background information needs to be provided at the onset for readers who are new to its study. Bahá'í history starts with Sayyid 'Ali Muhammad Shirázi (1819–1850), who took the title of the Báb.[3] He declared himself a messenger or manifestation of God[4] in Iran in 1844, a controversial claim that soon resulted in a massive effort on the part of the government and religious leaders in Iran to exterminate his religion. The Báb's teachings were revolutionary in Persia because he abrogated Islamic law and prophesied another manifestation of God would soon follow. The Báb was executed and his followers viciously persecuted.

Among the Báb's followers was Mírzá Ḥusayn-'Alí Núrí (1817–1892), who came to be called Bahá'u'lláh.[5] He was born into a family of nobility and wealth in Iran. Although born in luxury, Bahá'u'lláh chose to become a follower of the Báb despite the risks involved. Iranian religious and government leaders considered the Bábí religion a threat to their power, and when there was an attempt on the life of the Shah, Bahá'u'lláh became a victim of the pogrom that followed and that engulfed the real and perceived opponents of the Shah. Bahá'u'lláh was thrown into a notorious prison and weighed down in chains for months. When he was freed, it was on condition of agreeing to an exile to Baghdad; Bahá'u'lláh and his family were sent there on foot. This exile was the first of several that finally ended in the prison-city of Akko (in present-day Israel). Bahá'u'lláh is buried in the compound of the house where he died, now a place of pilgrimage for Bahá'ís.

The Báb and Bahá'u'lláh were born and raised in a violent world in which slavery and other forms of forced labor, the oppression of women, and despotism were commonplace. Yet, their writings hold out a startling vision of spiritual and social transformation in which justice, equity, and kindness become the ruling principles in human affairs. While the Báb did not explicitly forbid slavery during his short ministry, when Bahá'u'lláh wrote his book of laws (around 1873), he firmly declared that slavery was wrong.[6] Further in his book of laws, he likens humanity to a human body, "Be ye as the fingers of one hand, the members of one body."[7] In a letter he sent to Napoleon III, Bahá'u'lláh wrote, "He Who is your Lord, the All-Merciful, cherisheth in His heart the desire of beholding the entire human race as one soul and one body."[8] One of his most well-known statements is "Ye are all the leaves of one tree and the drops of one ocean."[9]

The third central figure in the Bahá'í Faith is 'Abdu'l-Bahá (1844–1921), Bahá'u'lláh's eldest son, whom he appointed as his successor and head of the Bahá'í community in his Will and Testament (Kitáb-i-'Ahd).[10] 'Abdu'l-Bahá has a particularly important place in this volume because it was during the period of his leadership that the religion arrived in the United States and developed its initial stance toward American racism. His earliest years were spent in privilege, but once his father became a follower of the Bábí religion, 'Abdu'l-Bahá's life quickly turned to one of hardship. When describing his childhood, 'Abdu'l-Bahá recalls being chased and bullied because of his Bábí connections, and later he shared Bahá'u'lláh's imprisonment and exile. This suffering helped mold him into a man of compassion and loving-kindness. As an adult, 'Abdu'l-Bahá became his father's most important assistant. Bahá'ís consider him to be the perfect exemplar of Bahá'í teachings and doctrines, and of how to live a Bahá'í life.[11]

'Abdu'l-Bahá did not hold a prophetic station. Rather, he was the "center" of the covenant established by Bahá'u'lláh with his followers. In this capacity, 'Abdu'l-Bahá had the authority to interpret the religion's scriptures, protect the unity of the community, and provide for its growth and establishment around the world. A major goal for 'Abdu'l-Bahá was the initial development of democratically elected lay councils, as the Bahá'í Faith has no clergy. 'Abdu'l-Bahá also worked to deepen the Bahá'ís' understanding of Bahá'u'lláh's teachings on the oneness of humanity and its profound implications, primarily through voluminous correspondence to followers explaining the Bahá'í teachings, interacting with pilgrims who visited him in Akko and Haifa, and sending erudite Persian Bahá'ís where needed to clarify key concepts. In this way, 'Abdu'l-Bahá helped the Bahá'ís better understand Bahá'u'lláh's teachings on race relations.

'Abdu'l-Bahá's most memorable elaborations of the Bahá'í approach to race relations came during an eight-month visit to the United States, part of a three-year extended journey to Egypt, Europe, and North America, which he undertook after being released from prison in Akko following the Young Turk Revolution in 1908. It was during his time in the United States that 'Abdu'l-Bahá was able to elaborate in detail the Bahá'í approach to race relations. His visit in the United States came at an important moment in African American history, what the Howard University historian Rayford Logan later famously termed the "Nadir of the Negro." Across the South, where the vast majority of African Americans lived, Reconstruction was a dead letter, and the Jim Crow system severely restricted blacks' social, political, economic, and educational opportunities. When they fled the South, first as a trickle and then a flood with the outbreak of World War I, discrimination and mob violence frequently greeted them. In academia and in popular culture, on the street and in the halls of Congress, white supremacy was the order of the day. The NAACP had been founded in 1909, and the National Urban League, in 1910, shortly before 'Abdu'l-Bahá's visit. The year after his visit, ironically, the fiftieth anniversary of the Emancipation Proclamation, President Woodrow Wilson officially segregated federal workplaces. In 1915, the Ku Klux

Klan was reborn in response to D. W. Griffith's *The Birth of a Nation*. The contrast could not have been sharper.

While in the United States, 'Abdu'l-Bahá did not just talk about race amity. He made a point of demonstrating what he thought it should look like in public and private interactions and in the press. This included holding integrated meetings in such rigidly segregated cities as Chicago and Washington, DC. 'Abdu'l-Bahá directly contradicted the reigning ideology of white racial superiority; openly promoted interracial marriage; and demonstrated such uncommon courtesy and love toward individual African Americans that they and their white counterparts were astonished.

Considerably more research is needed on how 'Abdu'l-Bahá's visit may have affected the course of American race relations. Memoirs of the people who met 'Abdu'l-Bahá are still being explored to fully understand how he helped the American Bahá'ís better understand the importance of interracial harmony. Two important ones were written by women mentioned in this book, Agnes Parsons and Juliet Thompson.[12] An important collection of his talks while in North America, *The Promulgation of Universal Peace*, clearly shows his consistent thematic emphasis on the oneness of humanity.[13] Even a cursory review of press coverage and of his interactions with prominent African Americans indicates that the visit is a significant and under-studied event in early twentieth-century race relations.[14]

Deep academic analysis is still not available related to how 'Abdu'l-Bahá affected the course of race relations through his letters and visiting pilgrims. His approach was to promote personal, social, and spiritual transformation through the teachings of his father. Buck's chapter, "The Bahá'í 'Pupil of the Eye' Metaphor," discusses this, as does Mike McMullen's, "Race Unity Efforts among American Bahá'ís: Institutionalized Tools and Empirical Evidence." Gwen Etter-Lewis's chapter, "The Most Challenging Issue Revisited: Black Women's Perspectives on Race and Gender in the Bahá'í Faith," also analyzes this.

'Abdu'l-Bahá's writings and the record of his public talks are replete with references to the oneness of humanity, including the imperative need to abandon all prejudices and to establish justice. For example, he wrote, "In every Dispensation . . . the light of Divine Guidance has been focused on one central theme. . . . In this wondrous Revelation, this glorious century, the foundation of the Faith of God, and the distinguishing feature of His Law, is the consciousness of the oneness of mankind."[15] To accomplish this, 'Abdu'l-Bahá continually advised the whites and blacks in the United States to associate together, remove mistrust and apprehension, and cooperate for the common good: "Endeavor that the black and the white may gather in one meeting place, and with the utmost love, fraternally associate with each other, so that quarrels and strife may vanish from among the white and the black."[16] Similarly, 'Abdu'l-Bahá counseled, "If it be possible, gather together these two races—black and white—into one Assembly, and create such a love in the hearts that they shall not only unite, but blend into one reality. Know thou of a certainty that as a result differences and disputes between black and white will be totally abolished."[17]

'Abdu'l-Bahá's successor as head of the Bahá'í Faith was Shoghi Effendi Rabbaní (1897–1957), his eldest grandson. In his Will and Testament, 'Abdu'l-Bahá appointed Shoghi Effendi, as he is known, Guardian of the Bahá'í Faith.[18] Shoghi Effendi was a wide-ranging traveler during his lifetime: in the Middle East, Europe, and Africa. His writings demonstrate political astuteness and a passion for uniting the races. Based on the terms in the writings of Bahá'u'lláh and 'Abdu'l-Bahá, he further developed the handful of nascent Bahá'í administrative bodies into a worldwide system of elected local and national councils (termed spiritual assemblies).

Once the basic administrative system was in place, Shoghi Effendi introduced a series of multi-year plans to expand the geographic scope and to diversify the ethnic and racial makeup of the Bahá'í community. He spearheaded the Bahá'í Faith's expansion into all parts of North America, Latin America, and the Caribbean. Loni Bramson's chapter, "'The Most Vital and Challenging Issue': The Bahá'í Faith's Efforts to Improve Race Relations, 1922–1936," advances analysis on how Shoghi Effendi guided Bahá'ís and Bahá'í institutions in the United States to improve race relations within the Bahá'í community, further diversify its membership, and attempt to influence public discourse on race. After World War II, Shoghi Effendi detailed plans to the take the Bahá'í Faith further into Europe and Africa. He established a massive Ten Year Crusade (1953–1963) to spread the religion to the remaining countries of the world. From the beginning of the Bahá'í Faith until 1921, Bahá'ís resided in thirty-five countries and territories. By 1957, that number had increased to more than 200. Shoghi Effendi kept track of the numbers of different races and ethnic groups from around the world included in the Bahá'í community, and any others that had been contacted. He joyfully shared the news with the Bahá'ís when there was an increase in the number of racial and ethnic groups represented within Bahá'í membership.[19] He used *The Bahá'í World*, a series of volumes detailing the progress of the Bahá'í Faith, telegrams, and letters to describe to the Bahá'ís his pride in their achievements and explain why such diversity and global diffusion was important. For Shoghi Effendi, each increase in the Bahá'í community's diversity was a further step in a world-historical process in which all peoples would contribute to the building of a new global civilization.

TERMS OF REFERENCE: SHOGHI EFFENDI AND *THE ADVENT OF DIVINE JUSTICE*

In 1931, Shoghi Effendi wrote to all Bahá'ís in a letter eventually called "The Goal of a New World Order":

> Let there be no mistake. The principle of the Oneness of Mankind—the pivot round which all the teachings of Bahá'u'lláh revolve—is no mere outburst of ignorant emotionalism or an expression of vague and pious hope. Its appeal is not to be merely identified with a reawakening of the spirit of brotherhood and good-will among men. . . . It implies an organic change in the structure of present-day society.[20]

While the importance of promoting interracial fellowship figured prominently in Shoghi Effendi's guidance to the North American Bahá'í's from early on in his tenure as Guardian of the Bahá'í Faith, his seminal treatment of the subject came in 1938 with a book-length letter published as *The Advent of Divine Justice*. Due to its enduring importance in shaping the American Bahá'í community's stance toward race, it is frequently cited by the authors of this volume. For ease of reference, a summary is provided here. The pertinent section of the book begins with:

> As to racial prejudice, the corrosion of which, for well-nigh a century, has bitten into the fiber, and attacked the whole social structure of American society, it should be regarded as constituting the most vital and challenging issue confronting the Bahá'í community at the present stage of its evolution.[21]

Shoghi Effendi calls the Bahá'ís to action and clearly indicates that he is not satisfied with how they have been working for race unity up to that point:

> The ceaseless exertions which this issue of paramount importance calls for, the sacrifices it must impose, the care and vigilance it demands, the moral courage and fortitude it requires, the tact and sympathy it necessitates, invest this problem, which the American believers are still far from having satisfactorily resolved, with an urgency and importance that cannot be overestimated.[22]

Shoghi Effendi states that both blacks and whites must actively participate in the effort to achieve racial harmony. Both races are responsible to ensure its implementation. Referring to the first Seven Year Plan for the religion's diffusion throughout the Western Hemisphere, he indicates that no success is possible without progress in this field of endeavor:

> White and Negro, high and low, young and old, whether newly converted to the Faith or not, all who stand identified with it must participate in, and lend their

> assistance, each according to his or her capacity, experience, and opportunities, to the common task of fulfilling the instructions, realizing the hopes, and following the example, of 'Abdu'l-Bahá. Whether colored or noncolored, neither race has the right, or can conscientiously claim, to be regarded as absolved from such an obligation, as having realized such hopes, or having faithfully followed such an example. A long and thorny road, beset with pitfalls, still remains untraveled, both by the white and the Negro exponents of the redeeming Faith of Bahá'u'lláh. On the distance they cover, and the manner in which they travel that road, must depend, to an extent which few among them can imagine, the operation of those intangible influences which are indispensable to the spiritual triumph of the American believers and the material success of their newly launched enterprise.[23]

Shoghi Effendi continues by reminding the Bahá'ís of 'Abdu'l-Bahá, who through his very being demonstrated how one should think, act, and behave in order to implement interracial harmony. The Bahá'í standard is high and grounded in love for everyone. However, this love is to be demonstrated through personal actions:

> Let them call to mind, fearlessly and determinedly, the example and conduct of 'Abdu'l-Bahá while in their midst. Let them remember His courage, His genuine love, His informal and indiscriminating fellowship, His contempt for and impatience of criticism, tempered by His tact and wisdom. Let them revive and perpetuate the memory of those unforgettable and historic episodes and occasions on which He so strikingly demonstrated His keen sense of justice, His spontaneous sympathy for the downtrodden, His ever-abiding sense of the oneness of the human race, His overflowing love for its members, and His displeasure with those who dared to flout His wishes, to deride His methods, to challenge His principles, or to nullify His acts.[24]

Shoghi Effendi then, in some of the strongest language in the Bahá'í writings, clearly states that to be a Bahá'í means to actively work to eliminate prejudice, discrimination, all forms of injustice, and to resist all social and public pressures:

> To discriminate against any race, on the ground of its being socially backward, politically immature, and numerically in a minority, is a flagrant violation of the spirit that animates the Faith of Bahá'u'lláh. The consciousness of any division or cleavage in its ranks is alien to its very purpose, principles, and ideals. Once its members have fully recognized the claim of its Author, and, by identifying themselves with its Administrative Order, accepted unreservedly the principles and laws embodied in its teachings, every differentiation of class, creed, or color must automatically be obliterated, and never be allowed, under any pretext, and however great the pressure of events or of public opinion, to reassert itself.[25]

The only discrimination allowed, Shoghi Effendi continues, is what can be called the Bahá'í version of affirmative action. Still today, when there are elections for Bahá'í spiritual assemblies, guidelines based on the following section of the extract from *The Advent of Divine Justice* are used to encourage the broadest possible representation on Bahá'í elected and appointed bodies in order to encourage minorities, enable them to contribute fully to the community's governance, and serve as an example of solidarity and unity to the world. What is also interesting in this passage is the call for the Bahá'ís to pay attention so that those individuals from a minority who are already qualified are elected and appointed to various positions. Diversity at all levels is in the best interest of society:

> If any discrimination is at all to be tolerated, it should be a discrimination not against, but rather in favor of the minority, be it racial or otherwise. Unlike the nations and peoples of the earth, be they of the East or of the West, democratic or authoritarian, communist or capitalist, whether belonging to the Old World or the New, who either ignore, trample upon, or extirpate, the racial, religious, or political minorities within the sphere of their jurisdiction, every organized community enlisted under the banner of Bahá'u'lláh should feel it to be its first and inescapable obligation to nurture, encourage, and safeguard every minority belonging to any faith, race, class, or nation within it. So great and vital is this principle that in such circumstances, as when an equal number of ballots have been cast in an election, or where the qualifications for any office are balanced as between the various races, faiths or nationalities within the community, priority should unhesitatingly be accorded the party representing the minority, and this for no other reason except to stimulate and encourage it, and afford it an opportunity to further the interests of the community. In the light of this principle, and bearing in mind the extreme desirability of having the minority elements participate and share responsibility in the conduct of Bahá'í activity, it should be the duty of every Bahá'í community so to arrange its affairs that in cases where individuals belonging to the divers minority elements within it are already qualified and fulfill the necessary requirements, Bahá'í representative institutions, be they Assemblies, conventions, conferences, or committees, may have represented on them as many of these divers elements, racial or otherwise, as possible. The adoption of such a course, and faithful adherence to it, would not only be a source of inspiration and encouragement to those elements that are numerically small and inadequately represented, but would demonstrate to the world at large the universality and representative character of the Faith of Bahá'u'lláh, and the freedom of His followers from the taint of those prejudices which have already wrought such havoc in the domestic affairs, as well as the foreign relationships, of the nations.[26]

Beyond the specific composition of the Bahá'í community's administrative bodies, Shoghi Effendi counsels the Bahá'ís to demonstrate freedom from prejudice in every aspect of their lives, both individually and collectively, among themselves and in their interactions with society at large. In the context of widespread racial segregation in housing, schools, and public service facilities of all kinds, he says that they should actively cultivate interracial fellowship and cooperation, whatever their backgrounds or personal inclinations, and in all parts of the country.

> Freedom from racial prejudice, in any of its forms, should, at such a time as this when an increasingly large section of the human race is falling a victim to its devastating ferocity, be adopted as the watchword of the entire body of the American believers, in whichever state they reside, in whatever circles they move, whatever their age, traditions, tastes, and habits. It should be consistently demonstrated in every phase of their activity and life, whether in the Bahá'í community or outside it, in public or in private, formally as well as informally, individually as well as in their official capacity as organized groups, committees and Assemblies. It should be deliberately cultivated through the various and everyday opportunities, no matter how insignificant, that present themselves, whether in their homes, their business offices, their schools and colleges, their social parties and recreation grounds, their Bahá'í meetings, conferences, conventions, summer schools and Assemblies. It should, above all else, become the keynote of the policy of that august body which, in its capacity as the national representative, and the director and coordinator of the affairs of the community, must set the example, and facilitate the application of such a vital principle to the lives and activities of those whose interests it safeguards and represents.[27]

Shoghi Effendi did not underestimate the difficulties inherent in attempting the eradication of prejudice from all aspects of one's life, the effort to break free from the ideologies and structures of white supremacy, and the creation of an alternative social space along completely different lines from what existed in society. He makes it clear that Bahá'ís have no choice, and repeats 'Abdu'l-Bahá's warning that the fate of the nation rests in no small part on their efforts. Racism is evil:

> A tremendous effort is required by both races if their outlook, their manners, and conduct are to reflect, in this darkened age, the spirit and teachings of the Faith of Bahá'u'lláh. Casting away once and for all the fallacious doctrine of racial superiority, with all its attendant evils, confusion, and miseries, and welcoming and encouraging the intermixture of races, and tearing down the barriers that now divide them, they should each endeavor, day and night, to fulfill their particular responsibilities in the common task which so urgently faces them. Let them, while each is attempting to contribute its share to the solution of this perplexing problem, call to mind the warnings of 'Abdu'l-Bahá, and visualize, while there is yet time, the dire consequences that must follow if this challenging and unhappy situation that faces the entire American nation is not definitely remedied.[28]

Shoghi Effendi ends this section in *The Advent of Divine Justice* on racism and how to eliminate it with specific instructions for whites and blacks, based on their respective positions in an unjust social order. He explains that ultimately it is their joint responsibilities to build an interracial religious fellowship such as the country has never before seen:

> Let the white make a supreme effort in their resolve to contribute their share to the solution of this problem, to abandon once for all their usually inherent and at times subconscious sense of superiority, to correct their tendency towards revealing a patronizing attitude towards the members of the other race, to persuade them through their intimate, spontaneous and informal association with them of the genuineness of their friendship and the sincerity of their intentions, and to master their impatience of any lack of responsiveness on the part of a people who have received, for so long a period, such grievous and slow-healing wounds. Let the Negroes, through a corresponding effort on their part, show by every means in their power the warmth of their response, their readiness to forget the past, and their ability to wipe out every trace of suspicion that may still linger in their hearts and minds. Let neither think that the solution of so vast a problem is a matter that exclusively concerns the other. Let neither think that such a problem can either easily or immediately be resolved. Let neither think that they can wait confidently for the solution of this problem until the initiative has been taken, and the favorable circumstances created, by agencies that stand outside the orbit of their Faith. Let neither think that anything short of genuine love, extreme patience, true humility, consummate tact, sound initiative, mature wisdom, and deliberate, persistent, and prayerful effort, can succeed in blotting out the stain which this patent evil has left on the fair name of their common country. Let them rather believe, and be firmly convinced, that on their mutual understanding, their amity, and sustained cooperation, must depend, more than on any other force or organization operating outside the circle of their Faith, the deflection of that dangerous course so greatly feared by 'Abdu'l-Bahá, and the materialization of the hopes He cherished for their joint contribution to the fulfillment of that country's glorious destiny.[29]

CONTEMPORARY CONCERNS

When Shoghi Effendi died in 1957, the Bahá'í community had nearly completed the effort necessary to establish the Universal House of Justice, the international governing council that Bahá'u'lláh had ordained and upon which 'Abdu'l-Bahá had elaborated as the supreme authority in the Bahá'í Faith. Since 1963, this worldwide administrative body of the Bahá'í Faith is elected by the members of the National Spiritual Assemblies around the world, without nominations or campaigning, and is headquartered in Haifa,

Israel. Virtually since its establishment, the Universal House of Justice has continued Shoghi Effendi's pattern of global propagation plans. Beginning with a Nine Year Plan (1964–1973), these plans resulted in dramatic growth of the worldwide Bahá'í population, especially in Africa, Latin America, Asia, and the Pacific region.[30] At the same time, the Universal House of Justice also continued Shoghi Effendi's emphasis on establishing interracial harmony. In 1985, for example, it wrote a widely distributed open letter to the peoples of the world entitled *The Promise of World Peace*. In it the House of Justice identifies racism as an impediment to global peace and justice:

> Racism, one of the most baneful and persistent evils, is a major barrier to peace. Its practice perpetrates too outrageous a violation of the dignity of human beings to be countenanced under any pretext. Racism retards the unfoldment of the boundless potentialities of its victims, corrupts its perpetrators, and blights human progress. Recognition of the oneness of mankind, implemented by appropriate legal measures, must be universally upheld if this problem is to be overcome.[31]

In the mid-1990s, following decades of experimentation in diverse parts of the world where the Bahá'í Faith had experienced large-scale growth, the Universal House of Justice formalized a system of grassroots community education called the "training institute." Its goal is to empower growing contingents of people to become protagonists of the spiritual, social, and intellectual development of their communities. Through the study of a series of books that foster learning through action, individuals develop the skills, knowledge, and spiritual insights to engage in personal and social transformation, hold devotional meetings, and organize children's classes focused on moral and spiritual development. Another realm of service is mentoring middle schoolers through junior youth groups that raise, through study and acts of service, the participants' understanding of community service, their leadership skills, their ability in verbal and written expression, and their capacity to be agents of change. A process of study, consultation, action, and reflection helps individuals and communities advance systematically, to learn step by step within the reality of their own circumstances, to overcome obstacles that arise, and to increase their unity of vision.[32] The Universal House of Justice explains that when these training and community-building activities are highly advanced, they "will directly combat and eventually eradicate the forces of corruption, of moral laxity, and of ingrained prejudice eating away at the vitals of society."[33] June Manning Thomas's chapter, "Race, Place, and Clusters: Current Vision and Possible Strategies," using Detroit as an example, examines how this new Bahá'í framework for action can confront patterns of race and class segregation and discrimination in United States' cities.

ORGANIZATION OF THE BOOK

The chapters in this book span much of the Bahá'í history described above. The first chapter by Christopher Buck, "The Bahá'í 'Pupil of the Eye' Metaphor: Promoting Ideal Race Relations in Jim Crow America," focuses on the Bahá'í metaphor used by Bahá'u'lláh that black people are like the pupil of the eye; as the pupil channels the light of the sun, people of African descent channel the light of the spirit. Buck describes the people who received letters from 'Abdu'l-Bahá in which he employed this metaphor and analyzes its spiritual significance. This provides initial insight into how African Americans were accepted in the emerging American Bahá'í community at the turn of the twentieth century.

The second chapter, Loni Bramson's "'The Most Vital and Challenging Issue': The Bahá'í Faith's Efforts to Improve Race Relations, 1922–1936," helps to provide the context for Alain Locke's philosophy by exploring Bahá'í race relations work during the period when Locke was formulating his theories. She examines the efforts of the early American Bahá'ís to understand the Bahá'í Faith's teachings on the elimination of prejudices, and their sometimes audacious and radical efforts to implement them. While the chapter does not directly examine Locke, a prominent African American philosopher known as the "dean" of the Harlem Renaissance, it does explore the Bahá'í efforts to improve race relations in which he was involved. This provides important context for understanding Locke's philosophy. Locke was actively involved in the Bahá'í "race amity" efforts, and to not include this as a direct influence in the analysis of his philosophy is curious.

In the third chapter of the book, "Alain Locke on Race, Religion, and the Bahá'í Faith," Christopher Buck examines Locke and his work more directly. The bulk of the scholarship on Locke ignores the fact that he was an active member of the Bahá'í Faith. Buck examines Locke's views on race and religion, and on the Bahá'í Faith in this context. He concludes that one cannot understand Locke's position on democracy without understanding his Bahá'í conviction.

The fourth chapter, "The Most Challenging Issue Revisited: African American Bahá'í Women and the Advancement of Race and Gender Equality, 1899–1943," by Gwen Etter-Lewis, specifically focuses on Bahá'í African American women. She examines intersectionality in the context of religion, race, and gender. Etter-Lewis discusses how these Bahá'í women's religious belief helped them navigate racism and sexism. Her chapter helps bring forth activism that has not yet been recognized. Along with the first chapter by Buck and the one by Mike McMullen, Etter-Lewis's chapter provides direct analysis of 'Abdu'l-Bahá's approach to fostering interracial unity and justice.

The fifth chapter, Louis Venters's "Hand in Hand: Race, Identity, and Community Development among South Carolina's Bahá'ís, 1973–1979," adapted from a forthcoming monograph, examines the challenges and opportunities that presented themselves when thousands of people, mostly rural African Americans, embraced the new religion in South Carolina during the 1970s. Venters posits that the growth in South Carolina, part of the general shift in Bahá'í population toward the global South beginning in the 1960s, increasingly brought African Americans to the forefront of Bahá'í education, administration, and culture in the state. At the same time, it precipitated important changes in the structure and priorities of the Bahá'í community at the national level, representing a significant advance in implementing Shoghi Effendi's guidance in *The Advent of Divine Justice*.[34]

The sixth chapter, "Race Unity Efforts among American Bahá'ís: Institutionalized Tools and Empirical Evidence" by Mike McMullen, provides persuasive evidence that the many decades of Bahá'í involvement in improving race relations has borne fruit, at least within their own local communities. That data upon which the chapter draws comes from McMullen's role as the Bahá'í lead sociologist for the Faith Communities Today project, the goal of which is to study the reality of religious life in a wide variety of congregations in multiple religious faith traditions. McMullen also notes the continuing influence of 'Abdu'l-Bahá's visit to the United States on contemporary Bahá'í efforts to combat white supremacy and eliminate prejudice from their personal and collective lives.

June Manning Thomas's chapter, "Race, Place, and Clusters: Current Vision and Possible Strategies," previously published in the *Journal of Bahá'í Studies*, examines how the Bahá'ís have divided the planet into "clusters," a system of small, manageable units for growth and transformation, and how the training institute works within a cluster to overcome racism. The courses of the training institute each help develop capacity in individuals to take charge of their own development and, collaboratively, that of their environment.[35] She reviews current understanding of the importance of place-based community building for Bahá'ís and their friends, in neighborhoods and villages, and then describes one potential barrier for a religion devoted to racial unity: the racially segmented geography of many metropolitan areas. As Thomas points out, the Universal House of Justice sees the training institute as a sturdy solution to many problems including racial unity, and this chapter explains how this might be possible, even in a context of hyper-segregated metropolitan areas. Purposeful "homefront pioneering," for example, such as having whites move into black neighborhoods, can help initiate the training institute process. The study circles of the training institute and the process by which the courses are offered are "only the first step in what the Universal House of Justice sees as a serious process of community development starting with spiritual empowerment and moral education, extending to social action at a small scale, and ultimately expanding to include progressively complex community-building projects."[36] The article of Thomas is among the first research to examine the implications of the path on which the Universal House of Justice has set the Bahá'í community in regards to race relations. With McMullen's and Thomas's chapters, this volume engages the latest, ongoing phase of the American Bahá'ís' more than one century-long effort at interracial community building.

The chapters in this book are important for launching new research into the history of African Americans and the Bahá'í Faith. Of course, important work has already been done, but it is the tip of the iceberg of what still needs to be accomplished. For example, archives, both national and local, for the Bahá'í Faith, the National Urban League and the NAACP have barely been touched. The chapters presented in this publication raise more questions than they answer. One of the more obvious gaps is research into the connections between Bahá'ís and the civil rights movement of the 1960s. This is not because such connections were few. Rather, it is simply that academic research on this is still to be done. The authors of this book hope that their efforts inspire others to continue their research and improve upon it.

NOTES

1. Not everyone who attended the panel discussion was a member of the Bahá'í Faith, but due to circumstances, all the authors in this book are.

2. See, Universal House of Justice, *The Promise of World Peace*, http://www.bahai.org/library/authoritative-texts/the-universal-house-of-justice/messages/19851001_001/19851001_001.pdf.

3. The Báb means the Gate. For more on the Báb and the Bábí religion, see Peter Smith, *The Babí and Baha'í Religions: From Messianic Shi'ism to a World Religion* (Cambridge: Cambridge University Press, 1987), and Abbas Amanat, *Resurrection and Renewal: The Making of the Babi Movement in Iran, 1844–1850* (Ithaca, NY: Cornell University Press, 1989).

4. For Bahá'ís, manifestations of God are more than a human being as they release into the world divine forces to renew society and provide guidance to humanity from God. Some manifestations in Bahá'í texts are Abraham, Krishna, Zoroaster, Moses, Buddha, Jesus, Muhammad, the Báb, and Bahá'u'lláh.

5. Bahá'u'lláh means the Glory of God. For a biography of Bahá'u'lláh, see Moojan Momen, *Bahá'u'lláh: A Short Biography* (Oxford: Oneworld Publications, 2007) and Hasan Balyuzi, *Bahá'u'lláh: The King of Glory* (Oxford: George Ronald, 1991).

6. Bahá'u'lláh, *The Kitáb-i-Aqdas: The Most Holy Book* (Haifa: Bahá'í World Centre, 1992), 45.

7. Ibid., 40.

8. Bahá'u'lláh, *The Summons of the Lord of Hosts* (Haifa: Bahá'í World Centre, 2002), 81. This letter to Napoleon III is part of a series of letters that Bahá'u'lláh wrote to political and religious leaders. These are available in the abovementioned book.

9. Bahá'u'lláh, *Tablets of Bahá'u'lláh: Revealed after the Kitáb-i-Aqdas* (Haifa: Bahá'í World Centre, 1978), 27.

10. For more on 'Abdu'l-Bahá, see Hasan Balyuzi, *'Abdu'l-Bahá: The Centre of the Covenant of Bahá'u'lláh* (London: George Ronald, 1971). See Bahá'u'lláh, *Tablets of Bahá'u'lláh*, 219–223.

11. Shoghi Effendi, "The Dispensation of Bahá'u'lláh," in *The World Order of Bahá'u'lláh* (Wilmette, IL: Bahá'í Publishing Trust, 1974), 134.

12. The two best known memoirs are Richard Hollinger, ed., *'Abdu'l-Bahá in America: Agnes Parsons' Diary* (Los Angeles: Kalimát Press, 1996) and Juliet Thompson, *The Diary of Juliet Thompson* (Los Angeles: Kalimát Press, 1983).

13. 'Abdu'l-Bahá, *The Promulgation of Universal Peace: Talks Delivered by 'Abdu'l-Bahá during His Visit to the United States and Canada in 1912*, 2nd ed. (Wilmette, IL: Bahá'í Publishing Trust, 1982).

14. For a recent treatment of the influence of 'Abdu'l-Bahá's visit, see Negar Mottahedeh, ed., *'Abdu'l-Bahá's Journey West: The Course of Human Solidarity* (New York: Palgrave McMillan, 2013).

15. 'Abdu'l-Bahá, quoted in Shoghi Effendi, *The Promised Day Is Come*, rev. ed. (Wilmette, IL: Bahá'í Publishing Trust, 1980), 119.

16. *The Power of Unity: Beyond Prejudice and Racism*, compiled by Bonnie J. Taylor and National Race Unity Committee (Wilmette, IL: Bahá'í Publishing Trust, 1986), 69.

17. *The Power of Unity*, 68.

18. For a biography of Shoghi Effendi, see Rúḥíyyih Rabbaní, *The Priceless Pearl* (London: Bahá'í Publishing Trust, 1969). See 'Abdu'l-Bahá, *The Will and Testament of 'Abdu'l-Bahá*, http://www.bahai.org/library/authoritative-texts/abdul-baha/will-testament-abdul-baha.

19. These are listed in, Hands of the Cause Residing in the Holy Land, comp., *The Bahá'í Faith, 1844–1963: Information Statistical and Comparative, Including the Achievements of the Ten Year International Bahá'í Teaching and Consolidation Plan, 1953–1963* (N.p.: n.p., n.d.), 9–11, 15–20.

20. Shoghi Effendi, *The World Order of Bahá'u'lláh*, 42–43.

21. Shoghi Effendi, *The Advent of Divine Justice* (Wilmette, IL: Bahá'í Publishing Trust, 1984), 33–34.

22. Ibid., 34.

23. Ibid.

24. Ibid., 34–35.

25. Ibid., 35.

26. Ibid., 35–36.

27. Ibid., 36–37.

28. Ibid., 39–40.

29. Ibid., 40–41.

30. The letters of the Universal House of Justice about the Nine Year Plan are available online, for example the letter entitled "Teaching the Masses." Universal

House of Justice, letter "Teaching the Masses," July 13, 1964, http://www.bahai.org/library/authoritative-texts/the-universal-house-of-justice/messages/19640713_001/19640713_001.pdf.

31. Universal House of Justice, *The Promise of World Peace* (Haifa, Israel: Bahá'í World Centre, 1985), 10. For an account of the administrative transition from Shoghi Effendi to the Universal House of Justice, see Universal House of Justice, *The Ministry of the Custodians, 1957–1963: An Account of the Stewardship of the Hands of the Cause*, rev. ed. (Haifa, Israel: Bahá'í World Centre, 1997). Hands of the Cause of God were advisory leaders appointed by Bahá'u'lláh, 'Abdu'l-Bahá, and Shoghi Effendi.

32. Universal House of Justice messages between 1996 and 2006 reflect its evolving guidance as the training institute process developed and grew in complexity around the world. Universal House of Justice, *Turning Point: Selected Messages of the Universal House of Justice and Supplementary Material, 1996–2006* (West Palm Beach, FL: Palabra Publications, 2006).

33. Universal House of Justice, letter dated March 26, 2016, http://www.bahai.org/library/authoritative-texts/the-universal-house-of-justice/messages/20160326_002/20160326_002.pdf.

34. The first part of the study is Louis Venters, *No Jim Crow Church: The Origins of South Carolina's Bahá'í Community* (Gainsville, FL: University of Florida Press, 2015).

35. The list of books used by the training institute are available here: http://palabrapublications.com/publication-category/section/training-institute-materials. For the junior youth groups, the list of books is available here: http://palabrapublications.com/publication-category/section/publications-junior-youth-activities.

36. June Manning Thomas, 403 (in this book).

BIBLIOGRAPHY

'Abdu'l-Bahá. *The Promulgation of Universal Peace: Talks Delivered by 'Abdu'l-Bahá during His Visit to the United States and Canada in 1912*. 2nd ed. Wilmette, IL: Bahá'í Publishing Trust, 1982. Also available at http://www.bahai.org/library/authoritative-texts/abdul-baha/promulgation-universal-peace.

'Abdu'l-Bahá. *The Will and Testament of 'Abdu'l-Bahá*. http://www.bahai.org/library/authoritative-texts/abdul-baha/will-testament-abdul-baha.

Amanat, Abbas. *Resurrection and Renewal: The Making of the Babi Movement in Iran, 1844–1850*. Ithaca, NY: Cornell University Press, 1989.

Bahá'u'lláh. *Gleanings from the Writings of Bahá'u'lláh*. 2nd ed. Wilmette, IL: Bahá'í Publishing Trust, 1976. Also available at http://www.bahai.org/library/authoritative-texts/bahaullah/gleanings-writings-bahaullah.

Bahá'u'lláh. *Kitáb-i-Aqdas: The Most Holy Book*. Haifa: Bahá'í World Centre, 1992. Also available at http://www.bahai.org/library/authoritative-texts/bahaullah/kitab-i-aqdas.

Bahá'u'lláh. *The Summons of the Lord of Hosts: Tablets of Bahá'u'lláh*. Haifa: Bahá'í World Centre, 2002. Also available at http://www.bahai.org/library/authoritative-texts/bahaullah/summons-lord-hosts.

Bahá'u'lláh. *Tablets of Bahá'u'lláh: Revealed after the Kitáb-i-Aqdas*. Haifa: Bahá'í World Centre, 1978. Also available at http://www.bahai.org/library/authoritative-texts/bahaullah/tablets-bahaullah.

Balyuzi, Hasan. *'Abdu'l-Bahá: The Centre of the Covenant of Bahá'u'lláh*. London: George Ronald, 1971.

Balyuzi, Hasan. *Bahá'u'lláh: The King of Glory*. Oxford: George Ronald, 1991.

Hands of the Cause Residing in the Holy Land, comp. *The Bahá'í Faith, 1844–1963: Information Statistical and Comparative, Including the Achievements of the Ten Year International Bahá'í Teaching and Consolidation Plan, 1953–1963*. N.p.: n.p., n.d. Also available at https://bahai-library.com/handscause_statistics_1953–63.

Hollinger, Richard, ed. *'Abdu'l-Bahá in America: Agnes Parsons' Diary*. Los Angeles: Kalimát Press, 1996.

Momen, Moojan. *Bahá'u'lláh: A Short Biography*. Oxford: Oneworld Publications, 2007.

Mottahedeh, Negar, ed. *'Abdu'l-Bahá's Journey West: The Course of Human Solidarity*. New York: Palgrave McMillan, 2013.

Power of Unity: Beyond Prejudice and Racism. Compiled by Bonnie J. Taylor and National Race Unity Committee. Wilmette, IL: Bahá'í Publishing Trust, 1986. Also available at https://bahai-library.com/taylor_power_unity.

Rabbaní, Rúḥíyyih. *The Priceless Pearl*. London: Bahá'í Publishing Trust, 1969. Also available at https://bahai-library.com/khanum_priceless_pearl.

Shoghi Effendi. *The Advent of Divine Justice*. Wilmette, IL: Bahá'í Publishing Trust, 1984. Also available at http://www.bahai.org/library/authoritative-texts/shoghi-effendi/world-order-bahaullah.

Shoghi Effendi. *The Promised Day Is Come*. Rev. ed. Wilmette, IL: Bahá'í Publishing Trust, 1980). Also available at http://www.bahai.org/library/authoritative-texts/shoghi-effendi/promised-day-come.

Shoghi Effendi. *The World Order of Bahá'u'lláh*. Wilmette, IL: Bahá'í Publishing Trust, 1974. http://www.bahai.org/library/authoritative-texts/shoghi-effendi/world-order-bahaullah.

Smith, Peter. *The Babí and Baha'í Religions: From Messianic Shi'ism to a World Religion*. Cambridge: Cambridge University Press, 1987.

Thompson, Juliet. *The Diary of Juliet Thompson*. Los Angeles: Kalimát Press, 1983.

Universal House of Justice. *The Ministry of the Custodians, 1957–1963: An Account of the Stewardship of the Hands of the Cause*. Rev. ed. Haifa: Bahá'í World Centre, 1997.

Universal House of Justice. *The Promise of World Peace*. Haifa, Israel: Bahá'í World Centre, 1985. Also available at http://www.bahai.org/documents/the-universal-house-of-justice/promise-world-peace.

Universal House of Justice. *Turning Point: Selected Messages of the Universal House of Justice and Supplementary Material, 1996–2006*. West Palm Beach, FL: Palabra Publications, 2006. Also available at http://www.bahai.org/library/other-literature/periodicals-supplementary-materials/turning-point.

Venters, Louis. *No Jim Crow Church: The Origins of South Carolina's Bahá'í Community*. Gainesville: University of Florida Press, 2015.

Chapter 1

The Bahá'í "Pupil of the Eye" Metaphor

Promoting Ideal Race Relations in Jim Crow America

Christopher Buck

This chapter focuses on a notable contribution to promoting ideal race relations in Jim Crow America by a new religion, which, though small in number, was socially significant in its concerted efforts to foster and advance harmony between the races (primarily black and white at the time). The *Oxford English Dictionary* defines "race relations" (q.v. "race, n. 6," compounds) as "the interactions and degree of concord between racial groups within a particular area." Therefore, for the purposes of this chapter, the term "ideal race relations" is conceived as "socially amicable, reciprocal, and ameliorative interactions and an optimal degree of concord between racial groups within a particular area."

The Bahá'í religion (today known as the "Bahá'í Faith") was brought to the United States during the Jim Crow era of forced legal segregation under the *Plessy v. Ferguson* (1896) "separate but equal" doctrine.[1] During this time, 'Abdu'l-Bahá was keenly alive to the racial problem in America, which he saw firsthand in 1912 during his speaking tour in the United States and Canada.[2] "Bahá'u'lláh," 'Abdu'l-Bahá recalled, "once compared the colored people to the black pupil of the eye surrounded by the white. In this black pupil is seen the reflection of that which is before it, and through it the light of the spirit shineth forth."[3] This chapter, therefore, focuses on the role that Bahá'u'lláh's "pupil of the eye" metaphor played in Bahá'í efforts to promote ideal race relations, which, far from being "empty rhetoric," was figurative public discourse aimed at countering racial prejudice—individually and interpersonally.

The Bahá'í message of interracial harmony attracted the notice of the Black intelligentsia, which has been discussed in previous studies.[4] As a further contribution to the literature, this chapter is the first published survey of the Bahá'í pupil of the eye texts and reported statements that, all told, have so powerfully and definitively shaped and steeled the self-identity and group identity of African American Bahá'ís. The texts, though few, are poignant and, given their historical context in Jim Crow America, offered a remarkable and effective psychological antidote to the prevailing racial stereotypes of that era.

The chapter continues from where a previous study, on the same theme, left off. Richard W. Thomas, Professor Emeritus of History, Michigan State University, in 2006, published "The 'Pupil of the Eye': African-Americans and the Making of the American Bahá'í Community,"[5] later republished in a Palgrave Macmillan multi-author work that same year.[6] In "The 'Pupil of the Eye': African-Americans and the Making of the American Bahá'í Community," Thomas notes the impact of the Bahá'í pupil of the eye racial metaphor on the spiritual self-identity of African American Bahá'ís, down to the present:

> [T]he Bahá'í teachings on the spiritual qualities of Black people and their role in the growth and expansion of the Bahá'í Faith contributed to the formation of a new racial identity among Black Bahá'ís throughout the Bahá'í world. The "pupil of the eye" became the spiritual image which not only united Blacks in their service to their Faith, but also provided Bahá'ís of other racial and cultural backgrounds with a new way of looking at their Black coreligionists. Freed from the traditional anti-Black racist stereotypes, Bahá'ís could move forward in building a truly united multiracial religious community.[7]

After discussing the origin of the Bahá'í pupil of the eye metaphor, this chapter presents seven pupil of the eye tablets (letters by 'Abdu'l-Bahá):[8] (1) 'Abdu'l-Bahá's tablet to Sarah Farmer (1902); (2) Abdu'l-Bahá's tablet to Alma S. Knobloch (1906); (3) 'Abdu'l-Bahá's tablet to Pocahontas Pope (1906); (4) 'Abdu'l-Bahá's tablet to Robert Turner (c. 1909); (5) 'Abdu'l-Bahá's tablet to Ali-Kuli Khan (1909, regarding Robert Turner); (6) 'Abdu'l-Bahá's tablet to Louise Washington (1910); and (7) 'Abdu'l-Bahá's tablet to George A. Anderson (1914). Biographical highlights of the recipients of these tablets are offered. These pupil of the eye tablets are then placed within the wider context in Bahá'í history: first, with Bahá'u'lláh's contributions to emancipation and abolition, and then by 'Abdu'l-Bahá's public statements on ideal race relations.

ORIGIN OF THE BAHÁ'Í PUPIL OF THE EYE METAPHOR; BAHÁ'U'LLÁH'S STATEMENTS (PRE-1893)

What was the origin of the Bahá'í pupil of the eye racial metaphor? When was it first coined, and by whom? There is good evidence that traces this dignifying racial trope back to Bahá'u'lláh. In *The Advent of Divine Justice*, a lengthy letter dated December 25, 1938, written to the Bahá'ís of North America, Shoghi Effendi documents the following reported statements by Bahá'u'lláh on the issue of race:

> "O ye discerning ones!" Bahá'u'lláh has written, "Verily, the words which have descended from the heaven of the Will of God are the source of unity and harmony for the world. Close your eyes to racial differences, and welcome all with the light of oneness." "We desire but the good of the world and the happiness of the nations," He proclaims "... that all nations should become one in faith and all men as brothers; that the bonds of affection and unity between the sons of men should be strengthened; that diversity of religion should cease, and differences of race be annulled." "Bahá'u'lláh hath said," writes 'Abdu'l-Bahá, "that the various races of humankind lend a composite harmony and beauty of color to the whole. Let all associate, therefore, in this great human garden even as flowers grow and blend together side by side without discord or disagreement between them." "Bahá'u'lláh," 'Abdu'l-Bahá moreover has said, "once compared the colored people to the black pupil of the eye surrounded by the white. In this black pupil is seen the reflection of that which is before it, and through it the light of the spirit shineth forth."[9]

To better understand how African Americans likely understood and appreciated Bahá'u'lláh's pupil of the eye simile and its metaphorical implications, these insights by linguist Christina Alm-Arvius may well apply in stating that "the qualities that are foregrounded in a metaphorical application are comparatively often attitudinal rather than factually descriptive. So the meaning features that dominate in many metaphors seem merely connotative."[10] Obviously, there is little resemblance between a person of African descent and the pupil of an eye, except for the "black" color that is a shared feature. Alm-Arvius speaks of a "metaphorical relaxation" that takes place when "peripheral meaning qualities in the source" are cognitively understood as a reflex of metaphorical competence (i.e., ability to "decode" figurative language).[11]

Alm-Arvius claims that "metaphorisation is an imaginative widening or generalisation of the semantic contents of some word(s) or longer stretch(es) of language use."[12] She further explains that such meaning is a "type of figurative extension" that "involves the suppression of ordinarily quite central characteristics in the source contents," thereby resulting in "a live, transparent [obvious] metaphor that spans both the basic, literal understanding and the metaphorical generalisation at the same time."[13] Here, the pupil of the eye involves a "metaphorical widening,"[14] whereby not only is the color (i.e., appearance) of the pupil significant, but, even more importantly, also its visual function.

Bahá'u'lláh's pupil of the eye image creates associative links of perceived similarity between the source—the black color of the pupil ("surrounded by the white" [race])—and the metaphor target, "the colored peoples." The transfer of qualities of sight (i.e., insight into the human condition) from the source image (pupil of the eye) to African Americans in the Jim Crow context by way of "reflected meaning"[15] was an effective rhetorical strategy then, and remains so today in the eyes of African American Bahá'ís, as Richard W. Thomas has clearly pointed out. The pupil of the eye metaphor was expressive and rich in associative potential.

To put Bahá'u'lláh's reported statement in historical context, 'Abdu'l-Bahá recalled it in remarks at a gathering of Theosophists in London in September, 1911:

> A COLOURED man from South Africa who was visiting 'Abdu'l-Bahá, said that even now no white people really cared very much for the black man.
>
> 'Abdu'l-Bahá replies: Compare the present time and the feeling towards the coloured people now, with the state of feeling two or three hundred years ago, and see how much better it is at present. In a short time the relationship between the coloured and white people will still further improve, and bye and bye no difference will be felt between them. White doves and purple doves exist, but both kinds are doves.
>
> Bahá'u'lláh once compared the coloured people to the black pupil of the eye surrounded by the white. In this black pupil you see the reflection of that which is before it, and through it the light of the Spirit shines forth.
>
> In the sight of God colour makes no difference at all, He looks at the hearts of men. That which God desires from men is the heart. A black man with a good character is far superior to a white man with a character that is less good.[16]

The fact that 'Abdu'l-Bahá was responding to a question posed by a South African demonstrates that Bahá'u'lláh's pupil of the eye metaphor applies to all peoples of African descent in general, and not only to African Americans in particular. This is the source that historians point to in support of the proposition that the pupil of the eye metaphor originates with Bahá'u'lláh himself. Here, 'Abdu'l-Bahá reported a statement sometime prior to May 29, 1892, the date of Bahá'u'lláh's death.

For historical purposes, although the reported statements may not be 'Abdu'l-Bahá's words verbatim as no Persian original has been found, the historical gist is nevertheless regarded as reliable. Further, it was widely distributed at the time, first by the British publication, and then through its publication in the United States with the Bahá'í Publishing Society of Chicago in 1921. In 1953, Shoghi Effendi stated this directly, in the African context: "I am reminded, on this historic occasion, of the significant words uttered by Bahá'u'lláh Himself, Who as attested by the Center of the Covenant ('Abdu'l-Bahá), in His Writings, 'compared the colored people to the black pupil of the eye,' through which 'the light of the spirit shineth forth.'"[17]

As for the statement, "Bahá'u'lláh once compared the coloured people to the black pupil of the eye" in which is seen "the reflection of that which is before it, and through it the light of the Spirit shines forth,"[18] a more familiar example is readily available. The English etymology for pupil is parallel to that of Arabic and Persian. According to the *Oxford English Dictionary* (*OED*), "pupil, n. 2" derives from the Middle French, *pupille*, for the "opening in the iris through which light passes into the eye." The *OED* entry further explains, "its etymon classical Latin *pūpilla* in same sense, transferred use of *pūpilla*, female child, also doll (feminine form corresponding to *pūpillus*), so called on account of the small reflected image seen when looking into someone's pupil." Here, "the small reflected image seen when looking into someone's pupil" as explained in the *OED* parallels Bahá'u'lláh's reported statement that in "the black pupil of the eye" is seen "the reflection of that which is before it."[19] What is "reflected" is not only the collective image of people of African descent, but also their legacy of oppression, first under slavery, and then, after abolition, of the after-effects of slavery, from violent racism to subtle racist attitudes, or "polite prejudice." In other words, the racially ennobling pupil of the eye metaphor rhetorically affirms the unique perspective of peoples of African descent in the historical experience of slavery and colonialism that they collectively suffered. While a rhetorical analysis of 'Abdu'l-Bahá's discourses on race awaits a full study, a natural place to begin is his pupil of the eye metaphor found in seven tablets to American (mostly African American) Bahá'ís, examined in roughly chronological order.

'ABDU'L-BAHÁ'S TABLET TO SARAH FARMER (1902)

Sarah Jane Farmer (1844–1916) is best known as the founder of the Green Acre Bahá'í School in Eliot, Maine.[20] Such was the magnitude of her contributions to the establishment of the Bahá'í Faith in the United States that she was posthumously named by Shoghi Effendi as one of the nineteen "Disciples of 'Abdu'l-Bahá."[21] Farmer received several tablets from 'Abdu'l-Bahá, mostly in Arabic, among which is the first of the several pupil of the eye tablets surveyed in this chapter. The pertinent extract from this tablet is:

> As to (Robert, Alice) and (Louise), verily the faces of these [the members of the black race] are as the pupil of the eye; although the pupil is created black, yet it is the source of light. I hope God will make these black ones the glory of the white ones and as the wellspring of the light of love of God. And I ask God to assist them under all circumstances, that they may be encompassed with the favors of their Loving Lord throughout centuries and ages.[22]

Both in the originally published translation[23] and in the more recent translation[24] when first published, the three bracketed names were deleted. They conspicuously appear in digital scans of the original manuscript translation: "Robert, Alice and Louise."[25] Instead of the names, the bracketed information, "[the members of the black race]," was inserted in the translation when first published. These three names may well refer to the following early African American Bahá'ís: Robert Turner, Alice Ashton, and Louise Washington. The identification of Alice Ashton seems quite probable, since she helped at the Green Acre school: "The Ashton family became believers and devoted adherents of the Bahá'í Faith in 1913. . . . Also for four or five summers Mrs. Ashton served the friends at Green Acre."[26] In a tablet dated August 3, 1921, 'Abdu'l-Baha wrote:

> Extend my respectful greetings to Mr. and Mrs. Mann. I supplicate to the Divine Bounties and ask that they may daily become more attracted, become two lighted candles of the love of God, and that the White and the Colored may, in their meetings, fall into each other's arms. I also ask that Mr. and Mrs. Ashton may hold luminous meetings in their house and through thy help teach the Colored.[27]

That same year, in 1902, 'Abdu'l-Bahá addressed a tablet to Marie Botay, a member of the early Washington, DC, Bahá'í community, which further demonstrates his concern about race relations in the United States:

> O thou maid-servant of God!
>
> I have read thy letter which indicated thy straightforwardness in the love of God and thy desire in spreading this brilliant light among the offspring of the Africans. How good is the intention! And what an excellent aim this great aim is! Indeed the hearts of the Africans are as a blank scroll of paper upon which thou canst write any phrase; but thou must have patience and a heart as firm as a mountain, owing to the innumerable hardships that may intervene, which could be endured only by one who surrenders to grievous calamities.[28]

Given the American context, what is translated here as "Africans" clearly and primarily refers to African Americans. Although 'Abdu'l-Bahá is not explicit regarding racism, the reference to future hardships (i.e., "the innumerable hardships that may intervene") could presuppose that social context.

In 1906, in another tablet to Sarah Farmer, 'Abdu'l-Bahá includes ideal race relations as part and parcel of the Bahá'í Faith's grand vision of world unity:

> Consider thou how vast is the arena of the Kingdom—it hath environed the whole world. The splendor of Providence hath encircled all races, nations, communities and religions; the foundation of foreignness is swept away and the

basis of Oneness is established; love hath become universal and the spiritual ties are strengthened.[29]

Racism is predicated on differences negatively valued. "Race amity" values differences in the wider social goal of "unity in diversity," a basic Bahá'í principle.

'ABDU'L-BAHÁ'S TABLET TO ALMA S. KNOBLOCH (1906)

Alma S. Knobloch (1863–1943) taught the Bahá'í Faith to African Americans in its earliest days in America, prior to 'Abdu'l-Baha's historic visit to the United States and Canada in 1912. According to Moojan Momen, "most Bahá'í histories seem to regard Alma Knobloch as the real founder of the German Bahá'í community."[30] Of German-American ancestry, she became a Bahá'í in 1903. On July 17, 1907, she left America for Germany. In the years following, she helped establish the Bahá'í Faith in Austria and in Switzerland. In 1920, she returned to America, where she passed away on December 22, 1943.[31] In 1906, she received the following tablet from 'Abdu'l-Bahá:

> To Alma S. Knobloch.
>
> Blessed are you that to you the White and the Black are one. Whiteness is by the light of the heart and not the skin; and Blackness is the blackness of the heart and not the face. The reflection of a person is seen in the black pupil of the eye. How many there are who have black faces but their characters are white and illumined. I am most happy on account of this work which you have been doing; it is the cause of the whiteness and the illumination of your spirit. Abdu'l-Baha Abbas.[32]

This text needs to be read within the immediate social context of that day and age. "Whiteness" is shorthand for "light," and more importantly, for "enlightenment." Sunlight is often described as a "white" light. Therefore, this color is independent of race. "Blackness," by contrast, is simply the absence of light. It is, thus, also independent of race. "Light" simply serves as a physical metaphor for spiritual enlightenment.

'ABDU'L-BAHÁ'S TABLET TO POCAHONTAS POPE (1906)

Pocahontas Pope (c. 1865–1938) was the first African American Bahá'í of Washington, DC. A salt-of-the-earth former seamstress and simultaneous

Baptist, since membership in the Bahá'í community, at that time, did not require discontinuing other religious affiliations, Pope received a beautiful letter from 'Abdu'l-Bahá that drew upon Bahá'u'lláh's pupil of the eye metaphor in a racially uplifting way. Her family history and ancestry are difficult to reconstruct. Relying largely on the sources compiled and posted online by Paula Bidwell,[33] along with newspaper articles found by Steven Kolins,[34] and by the present writer's own research, Pope's North Carolina background can tentatively be reconstructed as follows:

Pocahontas Pope's mother was Mary Cha, born Mary Sanling. John Kay was Pope's natural father. John and Mary married on January 11, 1861.[35] According to the U.S. Census, 1900, Pocahontas Pope was born in June 1863.[36] On November 11, 1876, Mary (Cha) Kay married Lundy Grizzard, who then became Pope's stepfather.[37] Lundy and Mary Grizzard went on to raise several children of their own (Pope's step-siblings). Mary Grizzard died in May 1909.[38] In her will, she named her daughter, Pocahuntas [*sic*] Pope" as the heir to her personal effects.[39]

On December 26, 1883, John W. Pope (1857–1919), born and raised in Rich Square, North Carolina[40], and Pocahontas Grizzard were married in Northampton (or Halifax) County, North Carolina. John was twenty-six. Pocahontas was nineteen. As to "race," each is listed in the Halifax County Marriage Register as "colored." At that time, and for several years, Pocahontas' husband, "J. W. Pope," was first assistant, then vice principal, and finally during the 1886–1887 academic year was promoted to principal of the Scotland Neck Normal Select Graded School, which was under the auspices of the Eastern Baptist Association in Scotland Neck, Halifax County.[41] He was also one of three "managers" of the African Methodist Episcopal (AME) Church in Rich Square, North Carolina, in 1896–1897.[42] On June 12, 1887, in that AME church, Pocahontas Pope played the church organ and read an essay at the Children's Day exercises.[43] That same year, the Rev. ("Professor") John W. Pope commented on the state of race relations in his locality:

> A great many of our white friends at Jackson contributed money to our academy. We desire to return our thanks. The white people at Jackson are an open hearted, generous class of people. They believe in helping those who are willing to help themselves. I regret that I can't say that about some sections of the county.[44]

In the summer of 1898, John and Pocahontas moved to Washington, DC, where he worked for the U.S. Census Office.[45] Unfortunately, in early 1902, he was fired by Director Merriam, along with other "Negro clerks." John Pope landed a job in the U.S. Government Printing Office. In June 1902, he was elected first vice-president of the "Second Baptist Lyceum," one of the oldest African American congregations in Washington, DC, and Pocahontas Pope became the assistant recording secretary.[46] Pocahontas Pope was described as "intensely religious": "Even among our own race the woman with a past is intensely religious."[47] The Rev. John W. Pope died on March 30, 1918.[48]

Fast forwarding to 1920, according to the U.S. Census for that year, "Pocahontas Pope" is listed as "Widowed." For "Race," she is now "Mulatto."[49] According to the U.S. Census of 1930, "Pocahontas Pope" is classified as "Negro."[50] Pope died on November 11, 1938, in Hyattsville, Prince George's County, Maryland. She is buried in National Harmony Memorial Park Cemetery.[51]

Pocahontas Pope first learned about the Bahá'í Faith from Pauline Hannen, Alma Knobloch's sister.[52] The encounter took place in 1905, in Washington, DC. She became a Bahá'í in 1906. In the context of Jim Crow America, the story of how a white woman, Pauline Hannen, decided to reach out to African Americans, is extraordinary and worth retelling.

Alma Knobloch employed Pocahontas Pope as a seamstress. Then, as fate would have it, Pauline chanced upon this passage from Bahá'u'lláh:

> O Children of Men! Know ye not why We created you all from the same dust? That no one should exalt himself over the other. Ponder at all times in your hearts how ye were created. Since We have created you all from one same substance it is incumbent on you to be even as one soul, to walk with the same feet, eat with the same mouth and dwell in the same land, that from your inmost being, by your deeds and actions, the signs of oneness and the essence of detachment may be made manifest. Such is My counsel to you, O concourse of light! Heed ye this counsel that ye may obtain the fruit of holiness from the tree of wondrous glory.[53]

This passage struck Pauline in a lightning flash of sudden insight. After she realized the profound implications of Bahá'u'lláh's words regarding the oneness and equality of the human race—in the singular—this is what happened next:

> One snowy day, during the Thanksgiving season, Pauline came across a black woman trudging through the snow. Pauline noticed that the woman's shoelaces were untied. Arms full from the bundles she was carrying, the woman was unable to do anything about it. Inspired by this passage from *The Hidden Words*, Pauline knelt down in the snow to tie this woman's shoes for her. "She was astonished," Pauline recalled, "and those who saw it appeared to think I was crazy." That event marked a turning point for Pauline: she resolved to bring the Bahá'í message of unity to black people.[54]

In a letter dated May 1909, Pauline Hannen wrote: "I was the one who first gave the Message to Mrs. (Pocahontas) Pope":

> The work among the colored people was really started by my sainted Mother and Sister Alma (Knobloch,) though I was the one who first gave the Message to Mrs. (Pocahontas) Pope and Mrs. Turner. My Mother and Sister went to their home in this way, meeting others(,) giving the Message to quite a number and started Meetings. Then my sister left for Germany where she now teaches (propagates the Bahá'í Faith), I then took up the work. During the Winter of 1907 it became my great pleasure with the help of Rhoda Turner colored who opened her home for me . . . to arrange a number of very large and beautiful Meetings. Mrs. Lua Getsinger spoke to them here several times at Mrs. Pope's as Mirza Ali-Kuli Khan, Mr. (Howard) McNutt and Mr. Hooper Harris spoke in Mrs. Turner's home. Mr. (Hooper) Harris spoke at Mrs. Pope(')s (at) 12 N St. N.W. for my sister before his leaving on his trip to Acca and India. Mr. Hannen also spoke several times. My working to being to run around and arrange the meeting. At these Meetings we had from twenty to fourty [*sic*] colored people of the intellectual class.[55]

Pocahontas Pope was not famous, but a few newspaper articles mentioned her, such as the one calling her "intensely religious."[56] Here is an account, one that historians might call anecdotal:

> Mrs. J. W. Pope, who has been in the city [Washington DC] since Christmas, has returned to her home in Richsquare, N.C. [*sic*] for the summer. During her stay in Washington, Mrs. Pope has won many friends. Mrs. Pope was deeply interested in all matters of interests to the race and was an energetic worker in the Second Baptist Lyceum. Just before the close of the lyceum Mrs. Pope read a paper on race conditions, which met with unanimous indorsement and established herself as a lady of high literary attainments.[57]

This news story is a passing, albeit positive, notice of an African American citizen, whose dedication to church and racial amelioration is duly noted, and Pope's "high literary attainments" extolled. 'Abdu'l-Bahá wrote to her:

> He is God! O maidservant of God!
>
> Render thanks to the Lord that among that race thou art the first believer, that thou hast engaged in spreading sweet-scented breezes, and hast arisen to guide others. It is my hope that through the bounties and favours of the Abhá Beauty thy countenance may be illumined, thy disposition pleasing, and thy fragrance diffused, that thine eyes may be seeing, thine ears attentive, thy tongue eloquent, thy heart filled with supreme glad-tidings, and thy soul refreshed by divine fragrances, so that thou mayest arise among that race and occupy thyself with the

> edification of the people, and become filled with light. Although the pupil of the eye is black, it is the source of light. Thou shalt likewise be. The disposition should be bright, not the appearance. Therefore, with supreme confidence and certitude, say: "O God! Make me a radiant light, a shining lamp, and a brilliant star, so that I may illumine the hearts with an effulgent ray from Thy Kingdom of Abhá.[58]

"The first believer" of Pope's race is generally understood to mean the first African American of Washington, DC, to embrace the Bahá'í Faith, although there are other possible interpretations as well. Some have speculated that she was of Native American ancestry, partly on account of her first name, Pocahontas, and also due to the fact that the Haliwa-Saponi Indian Tribe lived nearby and frequently intermarried with local African Americans. As a brief commentary on the Persian and Arabic text, Nahzy Abadi Buck explains:

> In what is translated as "among that race" (میان آنقوم), Abdu'l-Bahá uses a different word for "race": قوم (*qaum*). The more common term is: جنس (*jins*), as in جنس بشر (*jins-i bashar*), the "human race"). The implication of this is that, by "قوم" (*qaum*), 'Abdu'Bahá may be referring to something other than "race," such as a "tribe" or "ethnicity."[59]

'ABDU'L-BAHÁ'S TABLET TO ROBERT TURNER (1909 OR BEFORE)

Robert C. Turner (1855–1909) was the faithful butler, for thirty-five years, to philanthropist Phoebe Apperson Hearst (1842–1919), and her son, William Randolph Hearst (1863–1951). The exact date of 'Abdu'l-Bahá's tablet to him is unknown. However, Turner died in 1909. Born on October 15, 1855, probably into slavery on a farm near Norfolk, Virginia,[60] Robert C. Turner was won over to the Bahá'í teachings in 1898 under the following circumstances:

> Turner's first exposure to the Bahá'í Faith occurred as he listened to an early American Bahá'í, Lua M. Getsinger, teach the Bahá'í Faith to his employer [Phoebe Hearst]. Turner was so affected by these teachings that he pursued opportunities to hear more. He learned more about the Bahá'í Faith and eventually became a firm believer sometime around late 1898.[61]

As for the tablet to Robert Turner, 'Abdu'l-Bahá wrote:

> O thou who art pure in heart, sanctified in spirit, peerless in character, beauteous in face! Thy photograph hath been received revealing thy physical frame in the

Figure 1.1 Robert Turner. *Source*: National Bahá'í Archives, United States. Courtesy of Lewis V. Walker, assistant archivist.

utmost grace and the best appearance. Thou art dark in countenance and bright in character. Thou art like unto the pupil of the eye which is dark in colour, yet it is the fount of light and the revealer of the contingent world.

I have not forgotten nor will I forget thee. I beseech God that He may graciously make thee the sign of His bounty amidst mankind, illumine thy face with the light of such blessings as are vouchsafed by the merciful Lord, single thee out for His love in this age which is distinguished among all the past ages and centuries.[62]

Nahzy Abadi Buck sheds further light on this pupil of the eye metaphor:

This tablet is in Arabic. The Arabic for "pupil of the eye": انسان العين. Fully voweled the Arabic is written as follows: إنْسان ال َعيْن . The English transliteration: *insān al-'ayn*. "*Insān*" means "man." *Insān al-'ayn* means "man of the eye"—because a person can see the reflection of his/her face in the pupil of another person's eye. "تصويرک الشّمسی" is an expression for "photograph," the second word of which literally means "sun-like" (*al-shamsī*). The phrase, اسمر الخلق ولكن ابيض الخلق (translated as "dark in countenance and bright in character") literally means: "darkest creature, yet brightest (most luminous) creature" (*asmar al-khalq wa-lakin abyāḍ al-khalq*).[63]

Further, Omid Ghaemmaghami, commenting on a similar Arabic expression found in 'Abdu'l-Bahá's 1902 tablet to Sarah Farmer, that is, "as the pupil of the eye" is كإنسان العين (*ka-insān al-'ayn*), notes that *insān al-'ayn* (literally, "human being of the eye") is a common one in Arabic for the pupil or darkest part of the eye, although *al-ḥadaqa* or *ḥadaqat al-'ayn* is more common today. The Persian, *mardumak-i chashm* (literally, "little people of the eye"), may be an old translation from Arabic or vice versa. As previously noted from the *OED*, the English "pupil of the eye" has a similar etymology, that is, the tiny image of the beholder that is seen when gazing into a mirror, for instance.[64]

This tablet appears to postdate Turner's 1898–1899 trip, when he accompanied Phoebe Hearst, who traveled to Palestine (Israel) to visit 'Abdu'l-Bahá, which was considered to be a pilgrimage by Bahá'ís. There were several pilgrim groups. Each one had different arrival and departure dates (from November 1898 to March 1899). Turner, along with Anne Apperson and Julia Pearson, arrived in Haifa on Monday, February 20, 1899. The three were received by 'Abdu'l-Bahá on the same day in Haifa.[65] May Maxwell, another member of the group, wrote an account of that encounter:

> On the morning of our arrival, after we had refreshed ourselves, the Master ['Abdu'l-Bahá] summoned us all to Him in a long room overlooking the Mediterranean. He sat in silence gazing out of the window, then looking up He asked if all were present. Seeing that one of the believers was absent, He said, "*Where is Robert?*" This was a coloured servant, whom one of the pilgrims in our party, in her [Phoebe Hearst] generosity, had sent to 'Akka. In a moment Robert's radiant face appeared in the doorway and the Master rose to greet him, bidding him be seated, and said, "*Robert, your Lord loves you. God gave you a black skin, but a heart white as snow.*"[66]

This reception must have deeply moved Mr. Turner, and stirred his heart to its very depths. Selena M. Crosson explains:

> 'Abdu'l Bahá, whose self-chosen title meant "servant of Glory," insisted on serving the pilgrims Himself, including Robert, in spite of the remonstrances

of those who insisted the butler should serve. On one occasion, in deference to them, He allowed Robert to *assist* him. The lesson was clear to May Maxwell and the rest of the pilgrims. When Phoebe Hearst returned to America, she sponsored a reception for prominent African-American educators in Washington, D.C., a city deeply divided by race.[67]

An archival translation of a tablet to Robert Turner evinces the deep and abiding regard that 'Abdu'l-Bahá had for Mr. Turner:

> O thou servant of God!
> Thank thou God that from the day of the meeting until now 'Abdu'l-Bahá has not forgotten thee. He remembers thee always. I ask of the Lord of the Kingdom that he make thee dear in this world and the world to come; crown thee with the love of God and make thee an ignited and enkindled candle among the colored race.[68]

Nahzy Abadi Buck comments:

- In the original Persian, the phrase translated as "colored race" is *jins-i siyāh*, or, literally, "black race."
- Consistent with the previous tablet to Robert Turner, 'Abdu'l-Bahá emphasizes light: "make thee an ignited and enkindled candle among the colored race."
- So, not only is Robert Turner "like unto the pupil of the eye which is dark in color, yet it is the fount of light and the revealer of the contingent world," he is a source of illumination for African Americans as well.[69]

Turner did not live to see this tablet, as the date of this translation, August 17, 1909, postdates his death. He remained steadfast as a Bahá'í until his death, even after Phoebe Hearst later became estranged from the Bahá'í movement.[70]

'ABDU'L-BAHÁ'S TABLET TO ALI-KULI KHAN (1909)

Marzieh Gail (1908–1993), a well-known Persian-American Bahá'í author, essayist, and translator, was the second daughter of the first Persian-American marriage in the United States Bahá'í community. Gail's father was Ali-Kuli Khan, the Persian (Iranian) consul in Washington, DC, and her mother was Florence Breed of Boston.[71] In her memoir, *Arches of the Years* (1991), Gail recounts finding, in her father's papers, an account of Robert Turner.

In the spring of 1909, Ali-Kuli Khan was a guest of Phoebe Hearst in her Pleasanton, California, hacienda. She told him that Robert Turner had taken ill, and encouraged Khan to call on him, which he did. Quite ill in bed, Turner recounted, "with great joy," his visit to Haifa and Akka in 1898–1899. Turner asked Khan to write to 'Abdu'l-Bahá, to send his love and ask for prayers. Faithful to his promise, Khan did so.[72] Back in Washington, DC, Khan received a tablet, in which 'Abdu'l-Bahá wrote four lines regarding Robert Turner, which Khan translated as follows:

> Convey wondrous Abha greetings to Mr Robert [Turner], the servant of that honorable lady, and say to him: "Be not grieved at your illness, for thou hast attained eternal life and hast found thy way to the World of the Kingdom. God willing, we shall meet one another with joy and fragrance in that Divine World, and I beg of God that you may also find rest in this material world."[73]

These words portend the inevitable, impending death of Turner, but with tender regard, evident fondness, and words of comfort, promising yet another joyful meeting in the afterlife. Turner died, whereupon Khan wrote a letter, dated June 22, 1909, to convey the sad news to 'Abdu'l-Bahá. Later that summer, while Khan was spending time with his family in Carmel, California, he received another tablet addressed to him. On the second page of this tablet, 'Abdu'l-Bahá conveyed the following eulogy of Robert Turner:

> As to Mr Robert (Turner), the news of his ascension saddened the hearts. He was in reality in the utmost sincerity. Glory be to God! What a shining candle was aflame in that black-colored lamp. Praise be to God that that lighted candle ascended from the earthly lamp to the Kingdom of Eternity and gleamed and became aflame in the Heavenly Assemblage. Praise be to God that you adorned his blessed finger with the ring bearing the inscription: "Verily I originated from God and returned unto Him" . . . This too is a proof of his sincerity and that in his last breath, he breathed the Alláh-u-Abhá,[74] whereby the hearts of those present were impressed.
>
> O Thou Creator! O Thou Forgiver! Glorify the precious Robert in Thy Kingdom and in the garden of the Paradise of Abha. Bring him in(to) intimate association with the birds of the celestial meadow. O Thou Knowing God! Although that sinless one was black in color, like unto the black pupil of the eye, he was a source of shining light. O Thou forgiving Lord! Cause that longing one to attain Thy meeting and cause that thirsty one to drink the water of life in abundance. Thou art the Forgiver, the Pardoner, the Compassionate . . ." (Signed) 'Ayn-'Ayn ('Abdu'l-Bahá)[75]

Here, Turner is described as "sinless", which is remarkable. Comparing him to "the black pupil of the eye," 'Abdu'l-Bahá acclaimed him as "a source of shining light." Redounding to his further honor and distinction, Robert Turner was named by Shoghi Effendi as one of the nineteen "Disciples of 'Abdu'l-Bahá."[76]

'ABDU'L-BAHÁ'S TABLET TO LOUISE WASHINGTON (1910)

Louise Washington was a member of the New York Bahá'í community. Little is known of her. She was African American, and an early American Bahá'í. As noted by Richard Hollinger, in 1910, Louise Washington lived in New York. She married in 1938 at age forty-four.[77] In 1912, she served on a committee for the "Clio Information Club" to organize a public meeting for 'Abdu'l-Bahá at that venue.[78] These are sketchy details, to be sure. According to the records kept at the U.S. National Bahá'í Archives, Louise Washington was on the Bahá'í membership lists for New York City. The important fact to be gleaned from this information is that Washington was an active Bahá'í, and she must have written to 'Abdu'l-Bahá, who, in reply, answered:

> HE IS GOD! O, thou beloved maid-servant of God! In thy letter thou hast intimated that thou art colored.[79]
>
> In the Kingdom of God no distinction is made as to the color of the skin, whether it be black or white; nay, rather the heart and soul are considered. If the spirit is pure, the face is illumined, although it be black. If the heart is stained, the face is dull and despondent, although it may be of the utmost beauty. The color of the pupils of the eye is black, yet they are the fountains of light.
>
> Although white is conspicuous, yet seven colors are hidden and concealed therein. Therefore whiteness and blackness have no importance; nay, rather true judgment is based upon the soul and heart.[80]

Four archival copies of an early translation of this tablet were consulted.[81] The pupil of the eye metaphor is offered in the plural: "The color of the pupils of the eye is black, yet they are the fountains of light."[82] Instantly, a racial correlation is implied, even though virtually all of humanity shares the same optical feature. Notwithstanding, 'Abdu'l-Bahá's use of this metaphor is consistent and recurrent. In this tablet, the metaphor contributes to the already edifying and uplifting discourse, in which race is both acknowledged, yet deconstructed in the larger scheme of race relations.

'ABDU'L-BAHÁ'S TABLET TO GEORGE A. ANDERSON (1914)

On October 31, 1910, the following tablet was addressed by 'Abdu'l-Bahá collectively to the Bahá'ís of Washington, DC, exhorting them, one and all, to overcome racial differences and to strive for social harmony:

> O, ye Dear Ones of 'Abdu'l-Bahá! In the world of existence the meeting is blessed when the white and colored meet together with infinite love and

Heavenly Harmony. When such meetings are established and the participants associate with each other with perfect united love and kindness, the Angels of the Kingdom of Abha praise them and the Beauty of Bahá'u'lláh addresses them: Blessed are you and again,

Blessed are you![83]

Further, 'Abdu'l-Bahá writes, "If it be possible, gather together these two races, black and white, into one Assembly and put such love into their hearts that they shall not only unite but even intermarry. . . ."[84] 'Abdu'l-Bahá's message to the Bahá'ís of Washington, DC, and to the individual believer encouraging interracial marriage provides further evidence for the importance that he placed on promoting ideal race relations. Later, additional evidence is provided by 'Abdu'l-Bahá's tablet to George A. Anderson (1914).

Three archival versions (not identical) of the original translation for the tablet to George A. Anderson were consulted by the present writer.[85] In the original manuscript translation of this pupil of the eye tablet, the recipient is said to be a certain "George A. Anderson." It is possible that the actual recipient was "Alan A. Anderson." They were father and son. Alan Anderson was a declared Bahá'í, whereas no record has yet been uncovered that George Anderson was an avowed Bahá'í, notwithstanding the fact that this tablet is said to have been intended for him. Since the identity of the recipient is not yet certain as to which person received the tablet, both individuals will be discussed.

Little is known about George A. Anderson, to whom 'Abdu'l-Bahá addressed the tablet. A story published in the *Washington Post* reveals the following biographical details regarding George Anderson: He served as a coachman during the administration of U.S. President Chester A. Arthur. Prior to that, Anderson "had been President James Garfield's doorman and bodyguard." While he was serving as a coachman, he and his wife, Jennie, lived in the "White House stables" on 17th Street (between "E" and "F" Streets). On June 18, 1883, their child was born. "President Arthur was so excited when he heard about the babe in the White House manger (a k a the White House stables . . .)," the article goes on to say, "that he wanted the child to be his namesake." "George and Jennie obliged by making the baby's middle name Arthur."[86]

The present writer had previously identified Alan A. Anderson as the recipient, as that was the information available at that time.[87] Alan Arthur Anderson had definitely become a Bahá'í in 1910. Details regarding his life have been published elsewhere.[88] On August 16, 1959, Anderson passed away in Spotsylvania, Virginia.[89] The problem of whether this tablet was written for Alan Anderson, or for his father, George (since archival documents clearly bear the name of "George A. Anderson"), cannot be resolved here. One solution may be that this tablet was sent through the father to the son, if the latter was the intended recipient. The tablet reads as follows:

> O thou (*ay ṣāḥib*) who hast an illumined heart (*qalb-i rushan*)! Thou art even as the pupil of the eye (*mardumak-i chashm*), the very wellspring of the light (*ma'dan-i nūr*), for God's love hath cast its rays upon thine inmost being and thou hast turned thy face toward the Kingdom of thy Lord.
>
> Intense is the hatred (*nafrat*), in America, between black and white (*sīyāh va sifīd*), but my hope is that the power of the Kingdom will bind these two in friendship, and serve them as a healing balm.
>
> Let them look not upon a man's colour (*rang*) but upon his heart (*qalb*). If the heart be filled with light, that man is nigh unto the threshold of his Lord (*agar qalb-i nūrānī ān muqarrab*); but if not, that man is careless of his Lord (*ghāfil az khudā*), be he white or be he black.[90]

The Persian original has been studied as well.[91] In reading the original Persian text, Nahzy Abadi Buck comments:

- In Persian, "pupil of the eye," مردمک چشم (*mardumak-i chashm*), literally means "small person of the eye" or "people-like [part] of the eye."
- When read as a whole, physical "color" (رنگ, *rang*) is not important, but the "heart" (قلب, *qalb*) matters—"If the heart be filled with light, that man is nigh unto the threshold of his Lord" (اگر قلب نورانی آن مقرّب).[92]

In contrast to prevailing social habits in Jim Crow America, 'Abdu'l-Bahá emphasizes character over characteristics. That is, one should not focus on another's extrinsic racial characteristics (color), but, rather, on that person's intrinsic character (heart) as a determinant of moral worth.

'ABDU'L-BAHÁ'S REMARKS TO LOUIS G. GREGORY (1911)

A graduate of the School of Law at Howard University (1902), Louis G. Gregory (1874–1951) practiced law for fifteen years. He first learned about the Bahá'í Faith in the latter part of 1907, when he was a federal employee in the Department of the Treasury. Through a colleague, Gregory attended a Bahá'í meeting. When he entered the room, Pauline Hannen warmly greeted him, and "told me that I would hear something very wonderful, though difficult," which "would afford me an opportunity similar to that which would have been mine had I lived on Earth as a contemporary of Jesus Christ." She gave him a copy of Bahá'u'lláh's *The Hidden Words*, and two other pieces of Bahá'í literature. The presenter for the evening then arrived, a "Mrs. Lua M. Getsinger, referred to as 'our teacher.'" "A little later," Gregory adds, "came two colored ladies, Miss Millie York and Miss Nelly Gray." Shortly after that first meeting, Pauline Hannen and her husband, Joseph H. Hannen, became "my sole connection with the Faith" for a period of time, with Joseph as Gregory's primary Bahá'í teacher. Then, when the Hannens "went on their pilgrimage to the Holy Land," Gregory learned (a "long time afterwards") that the Hannens "had kindly mentioned me to the Master ['Abdu'l-Bahá] who had instructed them to continue teaching me, assuring them that I would become a believer and an advocate of the teachings."[93]

'Abdu'l-Bahá's prediction came true. Gregory became a Bahá'í in June 1909. At the express wish of 'Abdu'l-Bahá (as indicated above), Gregory dedicated the rest of his life to promoting ideal race relations (referred to as "race amity" at that time) primarily through lecturing, in venues far and wide, on the Bahá'í principles of unity.[94] In 1909, in reply to Gregory's first letter to him, 'Abdu'l-Bahá wrote the following: "I hope that thou mayest become . . . the means whereby the white and colored people shall close their eyes to racial differences and behold the reality of humanity."[95] This empirically demonstrates 'Abdu'l-Bahá's awareness of the endemic racial problem in America at that time, and as early as 1902, as seen in 'Abdu'l-Bahá's tablet to Sarah Farmer. 'Abdu'l-Bahá explicitly states that Louis Gregory should strive to "become a herald of the Kingdom and a means whereby the white and colored people shall close their eyes to racial differences and behold the reality of humanity, which is the universal unity."[96] Further historical evidence indicates that 'Abdu'l-Bahá told Gregory, "Work for unity and harmony between the races."[97] Gregory championed this mission to inspire Americans of all persuasions to do their part, and their best, to eliminate racial prejudice, the bane and blight of American society. As such, a few words about this remarkable individual are in order. Of course, as discussed above, 'Abdu'l-Bahá's words to Louis Gregory, in particular, reflect the same mandate for American Bahá'ís in general. In the 1919 tablet quoted above, 'Abdu'l-Bahá gave, and still gives, American Bahá'ís a clear mission, a moral imperative, in fact, to do their part in ameliorating America's racial crisis, what Shoghi Effendi later characterized as America's "most challenging issue":

> As to racial prejudice, the corrosion of which, for well nigh a century, has bitten into the fiber, and attacked the whole social structure of American society, it should be regarded as constituting *the most vital and challenging issue confronting the Bahá'í community at the present stage of its evolution.* The ceaseless exertions which this issue of paramount importance calls for, the sacrifices it must impose, the care and vigilance it demands, the moral courage and fortitude it requires, the tact and sympathy it necessitates, invest this problem, which the

American believers are still far from having satisfactorily resolved, with an urgency and importance that cannot be overestimated.[98]

In early 1911, 'Abdu'l-Bahá invited Gregory to visit the Holy Land for a pilgrimage to the Bahá'í holy places in Haifa and 'Akka, in Ottoman Palestine. Gregory first traveled to Egypt, where 'Abdu'l-Bahá was residing at the time. Later that same year, Gregory recounted his experience:

> "How many are the colored believers?" asked 'Abdu'l-Bahá. As accurately as possible, an estimate was made of the number of those who had heard and accepted the Glad Tidings. He responded: "The Cause will advance among them. There are many good souls among them, and such people are my friends. You must continue to teach." "Do you remember My Tablet to you?" Gladly I announced that it was committed to memory. "I liken you to the pupil of the eye. You are black and it is black, yet it becomes the focus of light.[99]

How Gregory answered the question as to the number of African American Bahá'ís is not known. Today we know that at least forty African Americans embraced the Bahá'í Faith as their chosen religion during the years of Abdu'l-Baha's ministry (1892–1921):

> (1) Robert Turner (1898, Pleasanton, California); (2) Olive Jackson (1899, New York); (3) Pocahontas Pope (1906, Washington, DC); (4) Louis G. Gregory (1909, Washington, DC); (5) Mrs. Andrew J. Dyer (c. 1909, Washington, DC); (6) Alan A. Anderson, Sr. (1910, Washington, DC); (7) Louise Washington (1910, Washington, DC); (8) Harriet Gibbs-Marshall (c. 1910, Washington, DC); (9) Coralie Franklin Cook (c. 1910, Washington, DC)[100] (10) Millie York (c. 1910, Washington, DC); (11) Nellie Gray (c. 1910, Washington, DC); (12) Rhoda Turner (c. 1910, Washington, DC); (13) Edward J. Braithwaite (c. 1910, Washington, DC); (14) Alonzo Edgar Twine (1910, Charleston, South Carolina; (15) Susan C. Stewart (c. 1910, Richmond, Virginia); (16) Leila Y. Payne (1912, Pittsburgh, visiting Washington, DC); (17) Hallie Elvira Queen (c. 1913, Washington, DC); (18) Alexander H. Martin, Sr. (1913, Cleveland, Ohio); (19) Mary Brown Martin (1913, Cleveland); (20) Sarah Elizabeth Martin (1919, Cleveland, minor daughter (mentioned in a Tablet by 'Abdu'l-Bahá in 1919) later known as Dr. Sarah Elizabeth Martin Pereira); (21) Lydia Jayne Martin (1919, Cleveland, minor daughter also mentioned in the above Tablet); (22) Alice Ashton [Green] (1913, Washington, DC); (23) Elizabeth Ashton (Alice's mother, 1913, Washington, DC); (24) John R. Ashton (Alice's father, 1913, Washington, DC); (25) Mabry C. Oglesby (1914, Boston); (26) Sadie Oglesby (1914, Boston); (27) Beatrice Cannady-Franklin (Portland, OR, 1914); (28) William E. Gibson (Washington, DC, 1914); (29) Rosa L. Shaw (1915, San Francisco); (30) George W. Henderson (c. 1915, Nashville, Tennessee); (31) Zylpha Gray Mapp (1916, Boston); (32) Annie K. Lewis (New York, 1917); (33) Alain Locke, PhD (1918,

Washington, DC); (34) Georgia M. DeBaptiste Faulkner (1918, Chicago); (35) Roy Williams (1918, New York); (36) Amy Williams (1918, New York); (37) Felice LeRoy Sadgwar (c. 1918, Wilmington, North Carolina); (38) Dorothy Champ (1919, New York); (39) John Shaw (1919, San Francisco); (40) Caroline W. Harris (c. 1920, Harper's Ferry, West Virginia).[101]

Doubtless there were more. But these names are what have so far been uncovered.

HISTORICAL CONTEXT FOR THE TABLETS IN THE BAHÁ'Í FAITH: BAHÁ'U'LLÁH ON EMANCIPATION AND ABOLITION

The pupil of the eye racial metaphor should be seen within the wider historical context of Bahá'í teachings on ideal race relations. Thus, it is important to analyze Bahá'u'lláh's position on slavery. In the nineteenth century, slavery was widespread in the world. Ideal race relations must begin with eradicating the most egregious form of racism and oppression: slavery. Metaphor was previously discussed in this chapter. Symmetry and synergy between word and deed were part and parcel of Bahá'u'lláh's vision for race relations. Metaphor, if used well, adds rhetorical force to persuasive discourse. Bahá'u'lláh's pupil of the eye racial metaphor may be further appreciated in light of his position on slavery. He decisively forbade slavery in 1873:

> It is forbidden you to trade in slaves, be they men or women. It is not for him who is himself a servant to buy another of God's servants, and this hath been prohibited in His Holy Tablet. Thus, by His mercy, hath the commandment been recorded by the Pen of justice. Let no man exalt himself above another; all are but bondslaves before the Lord, and all exemplify the truth that there is none other God but Him. He, verily, is the All-Wise, Whose wisdom encompasseth all things.[102]

Bahá'u'lláh clearly forbade trading in slaves. Much like many northern states in America stopped people from selling slaves but allowed them to continue owning them for a particular period of time, it may be that Bahá'u'lláh favored a gradual emancipation plan where the trade in slaves would stop immediately but the institution itself be gradually eliminated over the course of a generation. However, Shoghi Effendi, for Bahá'ís an authoritative interpreter of Bahá'u'lláh's writings, categorically states that Bahá'u'lláh "prohibits slavery,"[103] which would be in its totality and not simply in terms of trade. Bahá'u'lláh's abrogation of slavery, as a moral imperative in the form of a religious decree, is perfectly consistent with the positive pupil of the eye metaphor that 'Abdu'l-Baha ascribed to his father.

Some historical context regarding slavery will add to our understanding. Slavery in nineteenth-century Persia (Iran) was of a much different character than the kind that African Americans experienced in the New World. These two systems of labor management and property relations were quite distinct from one another, as Behnaz A. Mirzai notes, integrating Terence Walz and Kenneth Cuno's analysis:

> [U]ntil recently slavery was not a major area of study for historians of the modern Middle East for various reasons. One reason was the absence of anything resembling the traumatic American experience of slavery: indeed, that more than one tenth of the US population descends from enslaved Africans helps explain how slavery divided the nation and led to civil war. Postemancipation racial oppression and segregation has further driven scholarly research on the subject. By comparison, . . . although slavery was integral to Middle Eastern societies, its history and notions of race were constructed differently. Moreover, minority and marginal populations have largely been ignored because of absent or inaccessible historical materials and archives.[104]

Long before 1873, Bahá'u'lláh demonstrated his moral opposition to slavery in actions that he personally undertook. Upon the death of his father, Mírzá 'Abbás-i Núrí (better known as Mírzá Buzurg, the Vizier), Bahá'u'lláh freed his father's household slaves. The former Vizier died sometime between March 17 and May 29, 1839 (1255 AH).[105] This is 'Abdu'l-Baha's account of this significant episode:

> My grandfather [Bahá'u'lláh's father] had many colored maids and servants. When the Blessed Perfection [Bahá'u'lláh] became the head of the family he liberated all of them, and gave them permission to leave or stay, but if they desired to remain it would, of course, be in a different manner. However, all of them, reveling in their newfound freedom preferred to leave, except Esfandayar [Isfandiyar], who remained in the household and continued to serve us with proverbial faithfulness and chastity.[106]

This narrative offers historical evidence of Bahá'u'lláh's perspective on slavery as a twenty-one-year-old young man. Although an anecdotal report, it adds important context to the pupil of the eye account given above and is consistent with the 1873 decree abrogating slavery as a matter of religious principle, thereby "sacralizing," as it were, contemporary secular and Christian abolitionist anti-slavery positions that were taking place across the Atlantic in the United States (as well as in Britain, and elsewhere). This is significant because a number of Protestant churches, in fact, split into separate factions over slavery and its moral and theological implications, as it related to their very own congregations; and radical (violent) antislavery activists, from Nat Turner to John Brown, were driven by deep Christian convictions. In historical perspective then, the Bahá'í Faith is part of a continuation of antislavery religious thought and not its inventor. That said, Bahá'u'lláh's express abolition of slavery, as a religious as well as a moral and social imperative, is historically significant in its own context.

As further historical warrant of Bahá'u'lláh's long-standing antislavery stance, the following prayer, possibly written on the occasion of the manumission of one of those slaves, reveals a certain dignified humility on the part of Bahá'u'lláh toward an unnamed, former slave, when setting that slave free:

> Glorified art Thou, O Lord my God! Behold how one slave hath stood at the door of another, seeking from him his freedom, and this despite the fact that his owner is himself but Thy thrall and Thy servant, and is evanescent before the revelations of Thy supreme Lordship. I testify at this moment, as I stand before Thee, to that which Thou didst testify to Thyself by Thyself, that verily Thou art God and there is none other God but Thee. From everlasting Thou hast inhabited the loftiest heights of power, might and majesty, and wilt, to everlasting, continue to abide in the sublimity of Thy glory, awe and beauty.
>
> All kings are as vassals before the gate of Thy grace, the rich are but destitute at the shore of Thy sacred dominion, and all great ones are but feeble creatures within the court of Thy glorious bounty. How, then, can this thrall claim for himself ownership of any other human being? Nay, his very existence before the court of Thy might is a sin with which no other sin in Thy kingdom can compare. Glorified, immeasurably glorified, art Thou beyond every description and praise.
>
> O my God! Since he hath asked this servant for his freedom, I call Thee to witness at this moment, that I verily have set him free in Thy path, liberated him in Thy name, and lifted from his neck the shackles of servitude, that he may serve Thee in the daytime and in the night-season, whilst I pray that Thou mayest never free mine own neck from the chain of Thy servitude. This verily is my highest hope and supreme aspiration, and to this Thou Thyself art a mighty witness.[107]

Liberation from slavery (manumission) was only the beginning of racial emancipation. In the United States, the badges of bondage and the stigmas of racial prejudice, the pernicious legacy and historical aftermath of slavery, persisted long after emancipation and, indeed, persists in its subtle, and sometimes gross forms, to this day. 'Abdu'l-Bahá continued advancing Bahá'u'lláh's radical stance.

'ABDU'L-BAHÁ'S PUBLIC STATEMENTS ON RACE

This survey of the seven pupil of the eye tablets should also be seen within the wider historical context of 'Abdu'l-Bahá's public discourse on race. He was most vocal on the race issue during his 1912 speaking tour in America and Canada. On May 11, 1912, in New York, one month after his arriving in the United States, the following observation documents how "horrified" 'Abdu'l-Bahá was on witnessing racism in America firsthand:

> He had been horrified in Washington by the prejudice against the Negroes. "What does it matter," He asked, "if the skin of a man is black, white, yellow, pink, or green? In this respect the animals show more intelligence than man. Black sheep and white sheep, white doves and blue do not quarrel because of difference of colour."[108]

Prior to that, however, it appears that 'Abdu'l-Bahá's first public statement on race relations was on the occasion of the historic First Universal Races Congress held in July 26–29, 1911, at the University of London. This Congress represented a cosmopolitan turning point in discussions on race among intellectual elites, as well as representatives from across the world. Although it attracted scant notice in the white press, this event was a brief, global moment in the history of race relations. That Major Wellesley Tudor Pole, a prominent British Bahá'í at the time, read parts (in rough translation) of 'Abdu'l-Bahá's address to the Congress must have lent some Western credibility, as it were, to the "Bahá'í Movement," as it was known then.

The original Persian of this Tablet, which 'Abdu'l-Bahá had sent to the Congress, and was read during the Third Session, was later published in its proceedings that same year. It has been provisionally translated by the scholar, Sen McGlinn,[109] who relied on the published Persian text.[110] 'Abdu'l-Bahá wrote, in part:

> The Light of the Word is now shining on all horizons. Races and nations, with their different creeds, are coming under the influence of the Word of Unity in love and in peace.[111]
>
> The Blessed One, Baha'u'llah, likens the existing world to a tree, and the people to its fruits, blossoms and leaves. All should be fresh and vigorous, the attainment of their beauty and proportion depending on the love and unity with which they sustain each other and seek the Life eternal.[112]
>
> The friends of God should become the manifestors in this world of this mercy and love. They should not dwell on the shortcomings of others. Ceaselessly should they be thinking how they may benefit others and show service

and co-operation. Thus should they regard every stranger, putting aside such prejudices and superstitions as might prevent friendly relations.[113]

To-day the noblest person is he who bestows upon his enemy the pearl of generosity, and is a beacon-light to the misguided and the oppressed. This is the command of Baha'u'llah.[114]

O dear friends! The world is in a warlike condition, and its races are hostile one to the other. The darkness of difference surrounds them, and the light of kindness grows dim. The foundations of society are destroyed and the banners of life and joy are overthrown. The leaders of the people seem to glory in the shedding of blood—Friendship, straightness, and truthfulness are despised . . . .[115]

The call to arbitration, to peace, to love, and to loyalty is the call of Baha'u'llah. His standard floats since fifty years, summoning all of whatever race and creed.[116]

As this speech relates to race, what the audience heard, and readers later read, is that the teachings of Baha'u'llah had the power to transform race hatred into interracial harmony. The problem of racial strife was thereby placed within the wider context of social ferment and war across the world. In this respect, the speech represented 'Abdu'l-Bahá's internationalization of the race problem, using the same basic analysis to characterize both problems and solutions.[117] Significantly, leaders of the Black intelligentsia, such as W. E. B. Du Bois and Alain Locke, were in attendance, and they may have first become acquainted with the "Bahá'í Movement" (as it was then known), at this Congress.[118]

Nearly a year later, on April 23, 1912, 'Abdu'l-Bahá spoke in Rankin Chapel on the campus of Howard University. Before a standing room only audience, black and white, 'Abdu'l-Bahá recounted the Civil War experience where predominantly white Northerners sacrificed their time, treasure, and even lives on the battlefields to free African Americans from the shackles of slavery. For this massive undertaking to free the American nation of slavery once and for all, 'Abdu'l-Bahá told the African Americans in the audience that they should be grateful. Of course, the Civil War involved other issues as well, but the rhetorical point was accepted and well received. In a message to the whites in the audience, 'Abdu'l-Bahá urged them to dedicate their efforts to the amelioration and advancement of their fellow American citizens, the African Americans. The overall message was that the races should embrace each other in fraternity and common humanity. A close analysis of 'Abdu'l-Bahá's Howard University speech, was published in 2013. Although the pupil of the eye metaphor was not used in this particular speech, similar metaphors were employed, with much the same rhetorical purpose and effect.[119]

CONCLUSION

> Strive (*bi-kūshīd*) with heart and soul (lit. "soul and heart," *jān va dil*) in order to bring about union and harmony (*'ulfat*) among the white and the black (*sīyāh va sifīd*) and prove thereby the unity (*vaḥdat*) of the Bahá'í world wherein distinction of colour findeth no place, but where hearts only are considered. Praise be to God, the hearts (*qulūb*) of the friends are united and linked together, whether they be from the east or the west, . . . and whether they pertain to the white, the black, the red, the yellow or the brown race. Variations of colour, of land and of race are of no importance in the Bahá'í Faith. . . .[120]

This tablet was translated in 1919 by Oxford-educated "Shoghi Rabbani," that is, Shoghi Effendi, presumably shortly after it was written and addressed: "To his honor, Mr. Louis Gregory" in Washington, DC.[121] Although addressed to Louis Gregory individually, the message was meant for the American Bahá'ís collectively.[122]

'Abdu'l-Baha was as clear as he was emphatic on the issues of race: "And among the teachings of Bahá'u'lláh is that religious, racial, political, economic and patriotic prejudices destroy the edifice of humanity."[123] "Therefore," 'Abdu'l-Baha concludes, " . . . the world of humanity cannot be saved from the darkness of nature and cannot attain illumination except through the abandonment of prejudices. . . ."[124] He was optimistic about the future of race relations:

> Hence the unity of all mankind can in this day be achieved. Verily this is none other but one of the wonders of this wondrous age, this glorious century. Of this past ages have been deprived, for this century—the century of light—hath been endowed with unique and unprecedented glory, power and illumination. Hence the miraculous unfolding of a fresh marvel every day. Eventually it will be seen how bright its candles will burn in the assemblage of man.
>
> Behold how its light is now dawning upon the world's darkened horizon. The first candle is unity in the political realm, the early glimmerings of which can now be discerned. The second candle is unity of thought in world undertakings, the consummation of which will erelong be witnessed. The third candle is unity in freedom which will surely come to pass. The fourth candle is unity in religion which is the corner-stone of the foundation itself, and which, by the power of God, will be revealed in all its splendour. The fifth candle is the unity of nations—a unity which in this century will be securely established, causing all the peoples of the world to regard themselves as citizens of one common fatherland. *The sixth candle is unity of races, making of all that dwell on earth peoples and kindreds of one race.* The seventh candle is unity of language, i.e., the choice of a universal tongue in which all peoples will be instructed and converse. Each and every one of these will inevitably come to pass, inasmuch as the power of the Kingdom of God will aid and assist in their realization.[125]

This passage has been quoted more fully in order to place the Bahá'í principle of ideal race relations within the broader, or at least coextensive, context of productive international relations, along with the abandoning of religious prejudice, which is a continuing source of sectarian conflict (including civil war and terrorism). Prejudice, whether racial, religious, or otherwise, has great sway in the present day and vast, ghastly destructive power. The Bahá'í social discourse of interracial harmony, including the ennobling and socially uplifting pupil of the eye racial metaphor, makes sacred, and therefore religiously important and more intersubjectively available by way of public discourse, what philosophy can only promote by persuasion among the intellectual elite. Efforts by early American Bahá'ís to promote "race amity" was a social phenomenon notable in that it ran directly counter to the prevailing currents of Jim Crow America.[126]

In public discourse (i.e., speech acts), metaphors can serve important roles in human language and thought, including the influencing of social attitudes, such as toward race relations, as in Jim Crow America, which had its own universe of discourse. Positive racial rhetoric was one effective strategy by 'Abdu'l-Bahá to counter the prevailing negative stereotypes of Jim Crow America. The pupil of the eye metaphor, although physical in description, was essentially a spiritual image. It was a way to spiritualize, and therefore humanize, through harmony, the issue of race. Today, 'Abdu'l-Bahá's pupil of the eye metaphor is still part and parcel of Bahá'í public discourse on ideal race relations, and even in terms of Bahá'í self-identity itself, in a continuing effort to promote racial healing and ideal race relations and thereby help bridge the racial divide.

NOTES

1. *Encyclopedia of African American History*, s.v. "Plessy v. Ferguson," http://christopherbuck.com/pdf/Buck_2010_Plessy_Ferguson.pdf.

2. For instance, on November 23, 1912, in New York, the Great Northern Hotel turned away black Bahá'ís who arrived to attend a banquet. The very next night, "'Abdu'l-Bahá held a separate banquet for them at the Kinney residence, where the whites served them." Robert Stockman, *'Abdu'l-Bahá in America* (Wilmette, IL: Bahá'í Publishing, 2012), 341. The fact that whites served blacks was highly symbolic of the importance that 'Abdu'l-Bahá placed on fostering ideal race relations in the United States and abroad.

3. Shoghi Effendi, *The Advent of Divine Justice* (Wilmette, IL: Bahá'í Publishing Trust, 1938; repr., Wilmette, IL: Bahá'í Publishing Trust, 1990), 37. Here, Bahá'u'lláh's comparison is explicit, thereby rendering the "pupil of the eye" image technically a simile (i.e., a literal comparison), by way of a direct analogy. Yet, when compressed so as to exclude the typical "like" and "as" prepositions that so clearly

mark similes, a metaphor is what remains. (This clarification addresses a long-standing controversy as to whether a simile is literal or metaphorical in nature.)

4. Christopher Buck, "The Bahá'í 'Race Amity' Movement and the Black Intelligentsia in Jim Crow America: Alain Locke and Robert S. Abbott," *Bahá'í Studies Review* 17 (2011): 3–46, https://bahai-library.com/pdf/b/buck_race_amity_movemen t.pdf.; and Christopher Buck, "The Interracial 'Bahá'í Movement' and the Black Intelligentsia: The Case of W. E. B. Du Bois," in "Bahá'í History," ed. Todd Lawson, special issue, *Journal of Religious History* 36, no. 4 (December 2012): 542–62, https ://bahai-library.com/pdf/b/buck_interracial_bahai_du-bois.pdf.

5. Richard W. Thomas, "The 'Pupil of the Eye': African-Americans and the Making of the American Bahá'í Community," in *Lights of the Spirit: Historical Portraits of Black Bahá'ís in North America, 1898–2000*, eds. Gwendolyn Etter-Lewis and Richard W. Thomas (Wilmette, IL: Bahá'í Publishing, 2006), 19–48, Kindle.

6. Richard W. Thomas, "The 'Pupil of the Eye': African-Americans and the Making of the American Bahá'í Community, 1898–2003," in *The Black Urban Community: From Dusk Till Dawn*, eds. Gayle Tate and Lewis Randolph (New York: Palgrave Macmillan, 2006), 167–92.

7. Thomas, "The 'Pupil of the Eye': African-Americans and the Making of the American Bahá'í Community," in *Lights of the Spirit*, 46, Kindle.

8. There may be more such tablets, of course. The seven included in the present study are based on an intensive archival search (over a period of forty-nine weeks) by Lewis V. Walker, Assistant Archivist, National Bahá'í Archives, United States. Personal communication, October 7, 2016. It is possible that other documents exist in local archives. A "tablet" is what Bahá'ís call a letter written by Bahá'u'lláh or 'Abdu'l-Bahá.

9. Shoghi Effendi, *The Advent of Divine Justice*, 37.

10. Christina Alm-Arvius, *Figures of Speech* (Lund, Sweden: Studentlitteratur, 2003), 21 (emphasis in original).

11. Alm-Arvius, *Figures of Speech*, 20–21.

12. Alm-Arvius, *Figures of Speech*, 22 (emphasis in original).

13. Alm-Arvius, *Figures of Speech*, 22 (emphasis in original).

14. Alm-Arvius, *Figures of Speech*, 23.

15. Alm-Arvius, *Figures of Speech*, 23.

16. 'Abdu'l-Bahá, "Notes of a conversation with 'Abdu'l-Bahá," *'Abdu'l-Bahá in London* (London: Bahá'í Publishing Trust, 1982), 68.

17. Shoghi Effendi, "African Intercontinental Conference (Kampala, Uganda, February 12–18, 1953)," in *Messages to the Bahá'í World: 1950–1957* (Wilmette, IL: Bahá'í Publishing Trust, 1971), 136.

18. Abdu'l-Bahá, *'Abdu'l-Bahá in London*, 68.

19. Ibid.

20. The Green Acre Bahá'í School is a retreat and conference center currently overseen by the National Spiritual Assembly of the Bahá'ís of the United States. It played an integral role in the American Bahá'í experience during the period being studied.

21. *The Bahá'í World: A Biennial International Record* 4, 1930–1932 (New York: Bahá'í Publishing Committee, 1933; repr., Wilmette, IL: Bahá'í Publishing

Trust, 1980), 118–19. Sarah Farmer was an abolitionist and Transcendentalist. Her family home was a stop for the Underground Railroad. She founded Green Acre after attending the Parliament of Religions at the 1893 World's Columbian Exposition in Chicago. She met 'Abdu'l-Bahá in 1900 in Palestine, where he was a prisoner of the Ottoman Empire, and converted to the Bahá'í Faith.

22. 'Abdu'l-Bahá, tablet to Sarah Farmer (1902). Full text published in Kathryn Jewett Hogenson, *Lighting the Western Sky: The Hearst Pilgrimage and the Establishment of the Bahá'í Faith in the West* (Oxford: George Ronald, 2010), 271–72. The author thanks Bijan Masumian for the reference, personal communication, December 9, 2016.

23. 'Abdu'l-Baha, tablet to Sarah Farmer, published in *Tablets of Abdul-Baha Abbas* (Bahá'í Publishing Committee, 1909) 2, 292. This tablet was translated by Ali-Kuli Khan on September 13, 1902, according to notes Albert Windust made in his set of books. Windust was the editor and typesetter for the three volumes of *Tablets of Abdul-Baha Abbas*. The author thanks Robert Stockman, personal communication, December 5, 2016, for this information.

24. 'Abdu'l-Bahá, tablet to Sarah Farmer (1902). The pupil of the eye section of this tablet was previously published in *The Power of Unity: Beyond Prejudice and Racism*, 69 (no. 31). It was republished in *The Pupil of the Eye: African Americans in the World Order of Bahá'u'lláh*, 2nd ed., compiled by Bonnie J. Taylor (Rivera Beach, FL: Palabra Publications, 1998), 189 (no. 1).

25. 'Abdu'l-Bahá, tablet to Sarah Farmer (translated by Ali-Kuli Khan, September 13, 1902). Translations of Tablets of 'Abdu'l-Bahá Collection, National Bahá'í Archives, United States (tablet to Sarah Farmer, extract). See also Hannen-Knobloch Family Papers, Box 28. Courtesy of Lewis V. Walker, Assistant Archivist, National Bahá'í Archives.

26. Albert Vail, "National Teaching Committee: News of the Cause," *Bahá'í News Letter* no. 9 (December 1925–January 1926): 8.

27. 'Abdu'l-Bahá, tablet to Alma Knobloch (translated by Rouhi M. Afnan, Haifa, Palestine, August 3, 1921). Translations of Tablets of 'Abdu'l-Bahá Collection, National Bahá'í Archives, Wilmette, IL. See also Albert Windust Papers, Box 18, National Bahá'í Archives, United States (same tablet, but without a date). Courtesy of Lewis V. Walker, Assistant Archivist, National Bahá'í Archives, Wilmette, IL. Omid Ghaemmaghami (Binghamton University, SUNY) identified the pupil of the eye tablet in question after seeing digital scans of the documents sent to him, making it possible to study the terminology used in the original text.

28. 'Abdu'l-Bahá, *Tablets of Abdul-Baha Abbas*, 310; tablet to Marie L. Botay, translated on June 10, 1902 by Anton Haddad. Reference courtesy of Richard Hollinger, personal communication, September 4, 2017.

29. 'Abdu'l-Bahá, tablet to Sarah Farmer, published in *Tablets of Abdul-Baha Abbas* (Bahá'í Publishing Committee, 1909), 2, 303. This tablet was translated by Ahmad Sohrab in February 1906, according to notes Albert Windust made in his set of books.

30. Moojan Momen, "Esslemont's Survey of the Bahá'í World, 1919–1920," in *Bahá'ís in the West*, ed. Peter Smith, *Studies in the Bábí and Bahá'í Religions* 14 (Los Angeles: Kalimát, 2004), 88.

31. Ibid.

32. Digital scans of four archival documents with the original translation were consulted: (1) 'Abdu'l-Bahá, tablet to Alma S. Knobloch (translated in Akko, Palestine, December 12, 1906). Source: Translations of tablets of 'Abdu'l-Bahá Collection, National Bahá'í Archives, Wilmette, IL; (2) Hannen-Knobloch Family Papers, Box 15; (3) Louis G. Gregory Papers, Box 4; (4) Ahmad Sohrab Papers, Box 14. Courtesy of Lewis V. Walker, Assistant Archivist, National Bahá'í Archives.

33. Paul Bidwell, compiler, "Pocahontis Pope" (sic), https://www.pinterest.com/paulabidwell/pocahontis-pope.

34. See Newspapers.com, https://www.newspapers.com/papers. Search for "Pocahontas Pope" (thirty-six matching results).

35. Elizabeth W. Wilborn, Boyd Cathey, and Jerry L. Cross, *The Roanoke Valley: A Report for the Historic Halifax State Historic Site*, https://ia600500.us.archive.org/7/items/roanokevalleyrep00wilb/roanokevalleyrep00wilb.pdf.

36. *FamilySearch*, https://www.familysearch.org/search/record/results?count=20&query=%2Bgivenname%3APocahontas~%20%2Bsurname%3APope~.

37. Wilborn, Cathey, and Cross, *The Roanoke Valley*.

38. Wilborn, Cathey, and Cross, *The Roanoke Valley*.

39. Wilborn, Cathey, and Cross, *The Roanoke Valley*.

40. "John W. Pope Promoted," *The Patron and Gleaner*, September 1, 1898, 3, clipped by Paula Bidwell, https://www.newspapers.com/clip/1191995/jw_in_washington_since_spring_the.

41. "Our Schools," *The Banner-Enterprise* (Raleigh, North Carolina), September 6, 1883, 2, clipped by Paula Bidwell, https://www.newspapers.com/clip/1083771/first_mention_of_j_w_popes_work_at; "Banner–Waves," *The Banner-Enterprise* (Raleigh, North Carolina), January 26, 1884, 3, clipped by Paula Bidwell, https://www.newspapers.com/clip/1083164/bannerenterprise_raliegh_nc_26; "Our Halifax Letters. Scotland Neck and Schools—Address by Hon. James E. O'Hara—The Improved Condition of the Colored People," *The Raleigh Signal* (Raleigh, NC), August 11, 1887, 2, clipped by Steven Kolins, https://www.newspapers.com/clip/12606265/john_w_pope_scotland_neck_normal.

42. "A Grand Concert," *The Patron and Gleaner*, December 31, 1896, 2, clipped by Paula Bidwell, https://www.newspapers.com/clip/1192071/jw_pope_manager_ame_sunday_school.

43. "Halifax County," *The Raleigh Signal*, June 23, 1887, clipped by Steven Kolins, https://www.newspapers.com/clip/6348244/mrs_john_w_pocahontas_pope_later_a.

44. "The Colored People," *The Patron and Gleaner*, August 12, 1897, 3, clipped by Steven Kolins, https://www.newspapers.com/clip/12617998/jw_pope_husband_of_later_bahai.

45. "City Paragraphs," *The Colored American* (Washington, DC), February 9, 1901, 11, clipped by Steven Kolins, https://www.newspapers.com/clip/6323527/john_w_pope_husband_of_soon_bahai.

46. "Officers and Delegates," *Evening Star*, June 9, 1902, 10, clipped by Steven Kolins, https://www.newspapers.com/clip/6326523/note_of_j_w_and_later_bahai_mrs.

47. "City Paragraphs," *The Colored American*, March 21, 1903, 16, https://www.newspapers.com/clip/1191944/the_colored_american.

48. "Widow Sole Beneficiary," *The Washington Herald*, June 6, 1918, 6, clipped by Steven Kolins, https://www.newspapers.com/clip/1095504/bahai_pocahontas_pope_inherits.

49. United States Census, 1920, https://www.familysearch.org/ark:/61903/3:1:33S7-9R63-NCG?cc=1488411.

50. United States Census, 1930, https://www.familysearch.org/search/record/results?count=20&query=%2Bgivenname%3APocahontas~%20%2Bsurname%3APope~.

51. Pocahontas Kay Pope," https://www.findagrave.com/cgi-bin/fg.cgi?page=cr&CRid=81286 (search "Pocahontas" as "First Name).

52. Pauline Knobloch Hannen (d. 1939) was a white Southerner who grew up in Wilmington, NC. In 1902, she became a Bahá'í in Washington, DC. She and her husband, Joseph Hannen, were early American Bahá'ís who were instrumental in introducing the Bahá'í teachings of ideal race relations and world unity to African Americans in Washington, DC. See Robert Stockman, *The Bahá'í Faith in America*, vol. 2, *Early Expansion 1900–1912* (Oxford: George Ronald, 1985).

53. Bahá'u'lláh, Arabic Hidden Word no. 68, *The Hidden Words of Bahá'u'lláh* (Wilmette, IL: Bahá'í Publishing Trust, 1985), 20. The translation of this book that Hannen would have read is not easily available.

54. Buck, *Alain Locke: Faith and Philosophy*, 37–38. Based on Robert Stockman, chapter sixteen, "New England and Washington DC," in *The Bahá'í Faith in America: Early Expansion 1900*–1912, vol. 2 (Oxford: George Ronald, 1985), 225–26.

55. Pauline Hannen, quoted in Buck, *Alain Locke: Faith and Philosophy*, 38, citing Pauline Hannen to Mirza Ahmad Sohrab, (handwritten), May 1909, Ahmad Sohrab Papers, NBA. Courtesy of Roger M. Dahl, Archivist, National Bahá'í Archives, Bahá'í National Center, Wilmette, IL, enclosure sent 2 July 2002. Lua Getsinger, Howard MacNutt, and Hooper Harris were all well-known Bahá'ís in this era.

56. "City Paragraphs," *The Colored American*, March 21, 1903, 16, 2017, https://www.newspapers.com/clip/1191944/the_colored_american.

57. "City Paragraphs," *The Colored American*, July 21, 1900, Saturday, First Edition, 16, clipped by Steven Kolins, https://www.newspapers.com/clip/6326508/later_bahai_mrs_j_w_pocahontas_pope.

58. 'Abdu'l-Bahá, tablet to Pocahontas Pope (Washington, DC), in *A Compilation on Women*, 6 (no. 10), http://www.bahai.org/library/authoritative-texts/compilations/women. For an earlier translation, see 'Abdu'l-Bahá, tablet to Pocahontas Pope, Translations of Tablets of 'Abdu'l-Bahá Collection, National Bahá'í Archives, Wilmette, IL. See also Hannen-Knobloch Family Papers, Box 27 (Pocahontas Pope). Courtesy of Lewis V. Walker, Assistant Archivist, National Bahá'í Archives.

59. Christopher Buck and Nahzy Abadi Buck, "The Black Pupil: Where the Light of the Spirit Shines," September 9, 2016, http://bahaiteachings.org/black-pupil-eye-source-light.

60. Hogenson, *Lighting the Western Sky*, 49. The author thanks Bijan Masumian for this reference, personal communication, December 9, 2016.

61. Thomas, "The 'Pupil of the Eye,'" *Lights of the Spirit*, 23–24.

62. 'Abdu'l-Bahá, tablet to Robert Turner, *Selections from the Writings of 'Abdu'l-Bahá* (Haifa: Bahá'í World Centre, 1982), 114 (Section 78). Original Arabic text: 'Abdu'l-Bahā, *Muntakhabātī az makātīb-i Ḥaḍrat-i 'Abdu'l-Bahā*, vol. 1 (Wilmette, IL: Bahá'í Publishing Trust, 1979), 111 (Section 78).

63. Nahzy Abadi Buck, in Christopher Buck and Nahzy Abadi Buck, "Pupil of the Eye: An Ennobling Racial Metaphor," presented May 23, 2015, "Memorials of the Faithful" weekend, Desert Rose Bahá'í Institute, Eloi, AZ (May 23–24, 2015).

64. Omid Ghaemmaghami reminded the author of this, personal communication, December 8, 2016.

65. Hogenson, *Lighting the Western Sky*, 143–44.

66. May Maxwell, *An Early Pilgrimage* (1917; reprint: Oxford: George Ronald, 1953), 20–21. See also Hogenson, *Lighting the Western Sky*, 144.

67. Selena M. Crosson, *Searching for May Maxwell: Bahá'í Millennial Feminism, Transformative Identity and Globalism in the New World Order Shaping Women's Role in Early Bahá'i Culture 1898–1940* (PhD diss., University of Saskatchewan, 2013), 136–37, https://harvest.usask.ca/bitstream/handle/10388/ETD-2013-10-1145/CROSSON-DISSERTATION.pdf?sequence=4&isAllowed=y.

68. 'Abdu'l-Bahá, tablet to Robert Turner (translated by Mirza Ahmad Sohrab, August 17, 1909, Chicago). ("Ayn Ayn" are Arabic initials; in English "A. A." stands for the writer's name, 'Abdu'l-Bahá Abbás.) Source: Translations of Tablets of 'Abdu'l-Bahá Collection, National Bahá'í Archives, Wilmette, IL. Arabic original: Original Tablets of 'Abdu'l-Bahá Collection, National Bahá'í Archives, Wilmette, IL. Courtesy of Lewis V. Walker, Assistant Archivist, National Bahá'í Archives.

69. Christopher Buck and Nahzy Abadi Buck, "The Black Pupil: Where the Light of the Spirit Shines."

70. Hogenson, *Lighting the Western Sky*, 258.

71. Wendy Heller, "Gail, Marzieh," *Encyclopaedia Iranica*, http://www.iranicaonline.org/articles/gail-marzieh.

72. Marzieh Gail, *Arches of the Years* (Oxford: George Ronald, 1991), 54.

73. 'Abdu'l-Bahá, tablet to Ali-Kuli Khan, translation by Ali-Kuli Khan, quoted in Gail, *Arches of the Years*, 54.

74. This is a Bahá'í invocation which means God is All-Glorious.

75. 'Abdu'l-Bahá, tablet to Ali-Kuli Khan (translated by Ali-Kuli Khan, Carmel, California, summer 1909), quoted in Gail, *Arches of the Years*, 55.

76. Ibid. *The Bahá'í World: A Biennial International Record* 4, 118–19.

77. *The New York Age* (New York, Saturday, December 24, 1938), 5. Found by Richard Hollinger, and posted online, accessed December 10, 2016, https://www.newspapers.com/clip/1484096/louise_washington_bahai_marriage_to.

78. *New York Age* (New York, Thursday, October 10, 1912), 8. Found by Steven Kolins, and posted online, https://www.newspapers.com/clip/286449/ the_new_york_age.

79. 'Abdu'l-Bahá, tablet to Louise Washington (1910). Text from the following two archival, digital scans: (1) "To Louise Washington." "Translated by Mirza Ahmad Sohrab, Washington, DC, October 31, 1910." Translations of Tablets of

'Abdu'l-Bahá Collection, National Bahá'í Archives, Wilmette, IL. See also Thornton Chase Papers, Box 8. Courtesy of Lewis V. Walker, Archivist, National Bahá'í Archives; (2) "To Louise Washington." "Translated by Mirza Ahmad Sohrab, Washington, D.C., October 31, 1910." "Dup" [Duplicate]. Translations of Tablets of 'Abdu'l-Bahá Collection, National Bahá'í Archives, Wilmette, IL. Courtesy of Lewis V. Walker, Archivist, National Bahá'í Archives.

80. 'Abdu'l-Bahá, quoted in *The Power of Unity: Beyond Prejudice and Racism*, 6 (#17); republished in *The Pupil of the Eye: African Americans in the World Order of Bahá'u'lláh*, 26 (#10).

81. The four archival copies consulted are: (1) 'Abdu'l-Bahá, tablet to Louise Washington (translated by Mirza Ahmad Sohrab, Washington, DC, October 31, 1910). Source: Translations of Tablets of 'Abdu'l-Bahá Collection, National Bahá'í Archives, Wilmette, IL; (2) Albert Windust Papers, Box 19 (Louise Washington); (3) Hannen-Knobloch Family Papers, Box 28 (Louise Washington); (4) Thornton Chase Papers, Box 8 (Louise Washington). Courtesy of Lewis V. Walker, Assistant Archivist, National Bahá'í Archives.

82. 'Abdu'l-Bahá, quoted in *The Power of Unity: Beyond Prejudice and Racism*, 6 (#17); republished in *The Pupil of the Eye: African Americans in the World Order of Bahá'u'lláh*, 26 (#10).

83. Tablet by 'Abdu'l-Bahá to the Bahá'ís of Washington, DC, quoted in Louis Gregory, *A Heavenly Vista: The Pilgrimage of Louis G. Gregory*. Reprinted as *A Heavenly Vista*, 1997 ed. (Ferndale, MI: Alpha Services, 1997), http://bahai-library.com/gregory_heavenly_vista.

84. *Bahá'í World Faith: Selected Writings of Bahá'u'lláh and 'Abdu'l-Bahá* (Wilmette, IL: Bahá'í Publishing Trust, 1971), 359.

85. Manuscripts' typescripts consulted: (1) 'Abdu'l-Bahá, tablet to George A. Anderson (translated by Mirza Ahmad Sohrab, House of 'Abdu'l-Bahá, July 16, 1914). Source: Translations of Tablets of 'Abdu'l-Bahá Collection, National Bahá'í Archives, Wilmette, IL; (2) See also: Leone Barnitz Papers, Box 18 (George A. Anderson, 5th tablet); and (3) Hannen-Knobloch Family Papers, Box 27 (George A. Anderson). Courtesy of Lewis V. Walker, Assistant Archivist, National Bahá'í Archives.

86. Donnie Radcliffe, "Washington Ways," *Washington Post* (July 5, 1983), C4, ProQuest. (Courtesy of Lex Musta and Steven Kolins for digital scans of this story.)

87. Buck, *Alain Locke: Faith and Philosophy*, 41.

88. Christopher Buck and Nahzy Abadi Buck, "The Black Pupil: Where the Light of the Spirit Shines."

89. "In Memoriam," *Bahá'í News*, U.S. Supplement, no. 22 (December 1959), 2, http://www.h-net.org/~bahai/diglib/Periodicals/US_Supplement/022.pdf.

90. 'Abdu'l-Bahá, tablet to George A. Anderson, *Selections from the Writings of 'Abdu'l-Bahá*, 113 (Section 76). Original Persian text: 'Abdu'l-Bahā, *Muntakhabātī az makātīb-i Ḥaḍrat-i 'Abdu'l-Bahā*, vol. 1, 110 (Section 76). Transliteration of key Persian terms provided by the present writer.

91. 'Abdu'l-Bahá, tablet to George A. Anderson (Persian original, July 16, 1914). Source: Original Tablets of 'Abdu'l-Bahá Collection, National Bahá'í

Archives, Wilmette, IL. See also: Hannen-Knobloch Family Papers, Box 27 (George A. Anderson). Courtesy of Lewis V. Walker, Assistant Archivist, National Bahá'í Archives.

92. Christopher Buck and Nahzy Abadi Buck, "The Black Pupil: Where the Light of the Spirit Shines."

93. Louis G. Gregory, "Some Recollections of the Early Days of the Bahá'í Faith in Washington, D.C.," handwritten manuscript, dated December 7, 1937, 16 pages, TS, Louis G. Gregory Papers, U.S. National Bahá'í Archives, Wilmette, IL, 1–4.

94. Christopher Buck, "Fifty Bahá'í Principles of Unity: A Paradigm of Social Salvation," *Bahá'í Studies Review* 18 (2012): 3–44 (published June 23, 2015 and presented at Princeton University (February 21, 2014), https://bahai-library.com/buck_unity_social_salvation.

95. 'Abdu'l-Bahá, tablet to Louis Gregory, translated Nov. 17, 1909, Translations of Original Tablets of 'Abdu'l-Bahá Collection, National Bahá'í Archives, Wilmette, IL, quoted by Gayle Morrison, "Gregory, Louis George (1874–1951)," *The Bahá'í Encyclopedia Project*, http://www.bahai-encyclopedia-project.org/index.php?view=article&catid=56%3Aa-selection-of-articles&id=63%3Agregory-louis-george&option=com_content&Itemid=74.

96. 'Abdu'l-Bahá, tablet to Louis G. Gregory, in *The Power of Unity: Beyond Prejudice and Racism*, 66 (entry no. 25).

97. In early 1911, 'Abdu'l-Bahá invited Louis Gregory to Ramleh (in Alexandria), Egypt, where he was staying. Gregory arrived on April 10, 1911. In a section titled "The Race Question," "'Abdu'l-Bahá asked, 'What of the conflict between the white and colored races?'" Gregory commented, "This question made me smile, for I at once felt that my Inquirer, although He had never in person visited America, yet knew more of conditions than I could ever know." Louis Gregory also asked, "What is the Will of 'Abdu'l-Bahá concerning this unworthy servant?" 'Abdu'l-Bahá replied, "Work for unity and harmony between the races." Gregory, *A Heavenly Vista: The Pilgrimage of Louis G. Gregory*, 10. Reprinted as *A Heavenly Vista*, 1997 ed. (Ferndale, MI: Alpha Services, 1997). Without a supporting text in the original Persian, this statement cannot be authenticated verbatim. Yet the gist of it may be considered historically reliable. At the very least, this is the impression that Louis Gregory himself was given. 'Abdu'l-Bahá's mandate, as recalled here and as understood, gave Gregory a clear sense of mission, which was to promote ideal race relations, to the extent possible, in Jim Crow America.

98. Shoghi Effendi, *The Advent of Divine Justice*, 33–34 (emphasis added).

99. Reported statements by 'Abdu'l-Bahá, quoted in Gregory, *A Heavenly Vista*, 17.

100. Coralie Cook was Chair of Oratory at Howard University, and her husband, George William Cook, was Secretary and Business Manager, later Finance Professor of Commercial and International Law and Dean of the School of Commerce and Finance. According to Gwendolyn Etter-Lewis, "Coralie and her husband George became Bahá'ís in 1913." See Etter-Lewis, *Lights of the Spirit*, 71 (citing archivist Roger Dahl, Correspondence, National Bahá'í Archives, Wilmette, IL). However, there is some doubt as to whether George Cook formally identified himself as a

Bahá'í. See Buck, *Alain Locke: Faith and Philosophy*, 78, in which Louis Gregory and Alain Locke state otherwise.

101. This information is culled, for the most part, from a combination of the following sources: Gayle Morrison, *To Move the World: Louis G. Gregory and the Advancement of Racial Unity in America* (Wilmette, IL: Bahá'í Publishing Trust, 1982), passim; Etter-Lewis, *Lights of the Spirit*, passim; Louis Venters, *No Jim Crow Church: The Origins of South Carolina's Bahá'í Community* (Gainesville, FL: University Press of Florida, 2015), 33–40; correspondence with the National Bahá'í Archives, Wilmette, IL; and correspondence with Steven Kolins. At this time, there were about one to two thousand American Bahá'ís.

102. Bahá'u'lláh, *The Kitáb-i-Aqdas* (Haifa: Bahá'í World Centre, 1992), 45 (Par. 72).

103. Shoghi Effendi, *God Passes By* (Wilmette, IL: Bahá'í Publishing Trust, 1979), 214.

104. Behnaz A. Mirzai, *A History of Slavery and Emancipation in Iran, 1800–1929* (Austin: University of Texas Press, 2017), 3.

105. Muhammad-Alí Malik-Khusraví Núrí, *Iqlím-i Núr* (Tehran: Mu'assisiy-i-Millíy-i-Matbú'át-i-Amrí, 1962), 115–16. See also P. P. Soucek, "'Abbas b. Reza-Qoli Khan Nuri," *Encyclopaedia Iranica*, I, fasc. 1, 84, http://www.iranicaonline.org/articles/abbas-b-reza-qoli-khan-nuri . (References courtesy of Omid Ghaemmaghami, December 14, 2016.) See also Hasan M. Balyuzi, *Eminent Bahá'ís in the Time of Bahá'u'lláh* (Oxford: George Ronald, 1985), 339–41.

106. 'Abdu'l-Bahá, "The Sterling Faithfulness of Esfandayar," *Star of the West* 9, no. 3 (April 28, 1918), 38–39 [38], https://bahai.works Star_of_the_West/Volume_9/Issue_3#pg38.

107. See Christopher Buck, "The Slave's Prayer of Freedom" (September 22, 2014), http://bahaiteachings.org/the-slaves-prayer-of-freedom. This translation has not been published elsewhere.

108. Juliet Thompson, *The Diary of Juliet Thompson* (Los Angeles: Kalimat Press, 1983), 284. Reference courtesy of Anthony Lee, PhD, personal communication, September 2, 2017.

109. Sen McGlinn, "Speech for the Universal Races Congress," https://abdulbahatalks.wordpress.com/1911/07/26/speech-for-the-universal-races-congress.

110. 'Abdu'l-Bahá, *Majmū'ih-yi Khiṭābāt Ḥaḍrat-i 'Abdu'l-Bahā fī Ūrūpā va Āmrīkā*: al-juz' al-awwal fī safarah al-awwal ilá Ūrubā (Addresses Delivered during the first journey to Europe), compiled by Mahmud Zarqani (Cairo: Faraj Allāh Zakī al-Kurdi, 1921), 35 ff., in which Volume 1, which was personally reviewed by 'Abdu'l-Bahá and approved by him for publication, is prefaced by this note of the compiler, Maḥmúd Zarqání: "Praised be God, the Glory of Glories! Through the grace and loving-kindness of the Center of the Covenant, this lowly servant has succeeded in collecting the talks delivered by 'Abdu'l-Bahá during the course of His first trip to Europe in 1320AH/1912CE. All of the talks have been approved by 'Abdu'l-Bahá' and are published at His request. His lowly servant, Maḥmúd Zarqání." Translated by Omid Ghaemmaghami, personal communication, December 26, 2011.

111. 'Abdu'l-Bahá, "Letter from Abdu'l-Baha to the First Universal Races Congress," *Papers on Inter-Racial Problems: Communicated to the First Universal Races Congress, Held at the University of London, July 26–29, 1911*, 155–57, ed. Gustav Spiller (London: P. S. King and Son; Boston: World's Peace Foundation, 1911), https://ia902605.us.archive.org/18/items/papersoninterrac00univiala/papersoninterrac00univiala.pdf. This passage corresponds with Paragraph no. 10 in McGlinn's provisional translation of the original Persian of 'Abdu'l-Bahá's speech presented at the First Universal Races Congress.

112. Ibid. This passage corresponds with Paragraph no. 12 in McGlinn's provisional translation of the original Persian of 'Abdu'l-Bahá's speech presented at the First Universal Races Congress.

113. Ibid. This passage corresponds with Paragraph no. 13 in McGlinn's provisional translation of the original Persian of 'Abdu'l-Bahá's speech presented at the First Universal Races Congress.

114. Ibid. This passage corresponds with Paragraph no. 14 in McGlinn's provisional translation of the original Persian of 'Abdu'l-Bahá's speech presented at the First Universal Races Congress.

115. Ibid. This passage corresponds with Paragraph no. 15 in McGlinn's provisional translation of the original Persian of 'Abdu'l-Bahá's speech presented at the First Universal Races Congress.

116. Ibid. This passage corresponds with Paragraph no. 17 in McGlinn's provisional translation of the original Persian of 'Abdu'l-Bahá's speech presented at the First Universal Races Congress.

117. In the first chapter of her dissertation, Leah Victoria Khaghani has written an extended account and analysis of 'Abdu'l-Bahá's contribution to the Congress. "To 'proceed in a new direction': The 1911 First Universal Races Congress in London," in *"One World or None": Transnational Struggles against Imperialism in the American Century* (PhD diss., Yale University, 2011), 14–75, ProQuest Dissertations Publishing.

118. See Elliott M. Rudwick, "W. E. B. DuBois and the Universal Races Congress of 1911," *The Phylon Quarterly* 20, no. 4 (1959): 372–78, JSTOR; and Buck, *Alain Locke: Faith and Philosophy*, 43–44.

119. Christopher Buck, "'Abdu'l-Baha's 1912 Howard University Speech: A Civil War Myth for Interracial Emancipation," in *'Abdu'l-Baha's Journey West: The Course of Human Solidarity*, ed. Negar Mottahedeh, 111–44 (New York: Palgrave Macmillan, 2013), http://christopherbuck.com/pdf/Buck_2013_Howard_Speech.pdf.

120. 'Abdu'l-Bahá, tablet to Louis G. Gregory (translated by Shoghi Rabbani [Shoghi Effendi]), July 24, 1919, Bahji, near Akka), *Selections from the Writings of 'Abdu'l-Bahá*, 112–113 (Section 75). Original Persian text, 'Abdu'l-Bahā, *Muntakhabātī az makātīb-i Ḥaḍrat-i 'Abdu'l-Bahā*, vol. 1 (Wilmette, IL: Bahá'í Publishing Trust, 1979), 109–10 (Section 75). Transliteration of key terms added by the present writer.

121. 'Abdu'l-Bahá, tablet to Louis G. Gregory, translated by Shoghi Rabbani [Shoghi Effendi], Acca [Acre, Akko, Akka], Palestine [now Israel]), July 24, 1919, in *Star of the West* 11, no. 5 (June 1920), 92, https://bahai.works/Star_of_the_West/Vol

ume_11/Issue_5 (e-text) and https://bahai.works/File:SW_v11no5pg12.png (scan of publication).) Reference courtesy of Omid Ghaemmaghami, December 14, 2016. Old translations (from the years when letters were received from 'Abdu'l-Bahá Abbas, or those published in *Star of the West*) are not considered to be contemporary, authorized translations, except those identified as translated by Shoghi Effendi, in his capacity as Guardian of the Bahá'í Faith. The original translation is used for its historical pertinence.

122. As a general rule, tablets by 'Abdu'l-Baha were published for the benefit of all Bahá'ís collectively, as instanced in the two previous footnotes, citing the original publication of 'Abdu'l-Bahá's tablet to Louis G. Gregory in *Star of the West* 11, no. 5 (June 1920), 92.

123. 'Abdu'l-Bahá, *Selections from the Writings of 'Abdu'l-Bahá*, 299 (Section 227).

124. Ibid.

125. 'Abdu'l-Bahá, *Selections from the Writings of 'Abdu'l-Bahá*, 32 (emphasis added).

126. See Morrison, "The Era of Racial Amity," in *To Move the World: Louis G. Gregory and the Advancement of Racial Unity in America*, 129–214. See also Buck, "The Bahá'í 'Race Amity' Movement and the Black Intelligentsia in Jim Crow America: Alain Locke and Robert S. Abbott."

BIBLIOGRAPHY

'Abdu'l-Bahá. *'Abdu'l-Bahá in London.* London: Bahá'í Publishing Trust, 1982. Also available at http://reference.bahai.org/en/t/ab/ABL/abl-31.html.

'Abdu'l-Bahá. "Letter from Abdu'l-Baha to the First Universal Races Congress." In *Papers on Inter-Racial Problems: Communicated to the First Universal Races Congress, Held at the University of London, July 26–29, 1911*, edited by Gustav Spiller, 155–57. London: P. S. King and Son; Boston: World's Peace Foundation, 1911. https://ia902605.us.archive.org/18/items/papersoninterrac00univiala/papersoninterrac00univiala.pdf.

'Abdu'l-Bahá, *Muntakhabāt-ī az makātīb-i Ḥaḍrat-i 'Abdu'l-Bahā.* Vol. 1. Wilmette, IL: Bahá'í Publishing Trust, 1979. (Persian and Arabic.) Also available at http://reference.bahai.org/fa/t/ab/SWA1.

'Abdu'l-Bahá. *Selections from the Writings of 'Abdu'l-Bahá.* Compiled by the Research Department of the Universal House of Justice. Translated by a Committee at the Bahá'í World Centre and by Marzieh Gail. Haifa: Bahá'í World Centre, 1982. Also available at http://www.bahai.org/library/authoritative-texts/abdul-baha/selections-writings-abdul-baha/#r=swa_en-title.

'Abdu'l-Bahá. *Tablets of Abdul-Baha Abbas.* New York: Bahá'í Publishing Committee, 1909. Also available at http://reference.bahai.org/en/t/ab/TAB.

'Abdu'l-Bahá. Tablet to Louis G. Gregory. Translated by Shoghi Rabbani [Shoghi Effendi]. July 24, 1919. *Star of the West* 11, no. 5 (June 1920), 92. https://bahai.works/Star_of_the_West/Volume_11/Issue_5.

'Abdu'l-Bahá. "The Sterling Faithfulness of Esfandayar." *Star of the West* 9, no. 3 (April 28, 1918), 38–39, https://bahai.works/ Star_of_the_West/Volume_9/ Issue_3#pg38.

Albert Vail. "National Teaching Committee: News of the Cause." *Bahá'í News Letter* no. 9 (December 1925–January 1926), 8. Also available at https://bahai.works/ Baha%27i_News.

Alm-Arvius, Christina. *Figures of Speech*. Lund, Sweden: Studentlitteratur, 2003.

Bahá'í World: A Biennial International Record, 1930–1932. Vol. 4. New York: Bahá'í Publishing Committee, 1933. Reprint, Wilmette, IL: Bahá'í Publishing Trust, 1980. Also available at http://bahai-library.com/pdf/bw/bahai_world_v olume_4.pdf.

Bahá'í World Faith: Selected Writings of Bahá'u'lláh and 'Abdu'l-Bahá. Wilmette, IL: Bahá'í Publishing Trust, 1971. The section with 'Abdu'l-Bahá's writings is also available at http://reference.bahai.org/en/t/c/BWF.

Bahá'u'lláh. *The Hidden Words of Bahá'u'lláh*. Translated by Shoghi Effendi. Wilmette, IL: Bahá'í Publishing Trust, 1985. Also available at http://www.bahai.org/ library/authoritative-texts/bahaullah/hidden-words.

Bahá'u'lláh. *The Kitáb-i-Aqdas: The Most Holy Book*. Haifa: Bahá'í World Centre, 1992. Translated by Shoghi Effendi, in part, and by The Universal House of Justice. Also available at http://www.bahai.org/library/authoritative-texts/bahaul lah/kitab-i-aqdas.

Balyuzi, Hasan M. *Eminent Bahá'ís in the Time of Bahá'u'lláh*. Oxford: George Ronald, 1985.

"Banner–Waves." *The Banner-Enterprise* (Raleigh, North Carolina), January 26, 1884, 3, clipped by Paula Bidwell. https://www.newspapers.com/clip/1083164/ bannerenterprise_raliegh_nc_26.

Bidwell, Paula, compiler. "Pocahontis Pope" [*sic*]. https://www.pinterest.com/paul abidwell/pocahontis-pope.

Buck Christopher. "'Abdu'l-Bahá's 1912 Howard University Speech: A Civil War Myth for Interracial Emancipation." In *'Abdu'l-Baha's Journey West: The Course of Human Solidarity*, edited by Negar Mottahedeh, 111–44. New York: Palgrave Macmillan, 2013. http://christopherbuck.com/pdf/Buck_2013_Howard_Sp eech.pdf.

Buck, Christopher. *Alain Locke: Faith and Philosophy*. Los Angeles: Kalimat Press, 2005. Also available at https://bahai-library.com/pdf/b/buck_locke_faith_philos ophy.pdf.

Buck, Christopher. "The Bahá'í 'Race Amity' Movement and the Black Intelligentsia in Jim Crow America: Alain Locke and Robert S. Abbott." *Bahá'í Studies Review* 17 (2011): 3–46. https://bahai-library.com/pdf/b/buck_race_amity_movement.pdf.

Buck, Christopher. "Fifty Bahá'í Principles of Unity: A Paradigm of Social Salvation." *Bahá'í Studies Review* 18 (2012): 3–44. https://bahai-library.com/buck _unity_social_salvation.

Buck, Christopher. "The Interracial 'Bahá'í Movement' and the Black Intelligentsia: The Case of W. E. B. Du Bois." In "Bahá'í History," edited by Todd Lawson. Special Issue, *Journal of Religious History* 36, no. 4 (December 2012): 542–62. https ://bahai-library.com/pdf/b/buck_interracial_bahai_du-bois.pdf.

Buck, Christopher. "The Slave's Prayer of Freedom." *BahaiTeachings.org*. September 22, 2014. http://bahaiteachings.org/the-slaves-prayer-of-freedom.

Buck, Christopher, and Nahzy Abadi Buck. "The Black Pupil: Where the Light of the Spirit Shines." *BahaiTeachings.org*. September 9, 2016. http://bahaiteachings.org/black-pupil-where-light-spirit-shines.

Buck, Christopher, and Nahzy Abadi Buck. "Pupil of the Eye: An Ennobling Racial Metaphor." *BahaiTeachings.org*. August 20, 2015. http://bahaiteachings.org/pupil-of-the-eye-an-ennobling-racial-metaphor.

"City Paragraphs." *The Colored American*, July 21, 1900, Saturday, First Edition, 16, clipped by Steven Kolins. https://www.newspapers.com/clip/6326508/later_bahai_mrs_j_w_pocahontas_pope.

"City Paragraphs." *The Colored American* (Washington, DC), February 9, 1901, 11, clipped by Steven Kolins. https://www.newspapers.com/clip/6323527/john_w_pope_husband_of_soon_bahai.

"City Paragraphs." *The Colored American*, March 21, 1903, 16, https://www.newspapers.com/clip/1191944/the_colored_american.

"Colored People." *The Patron and Gleaner*, August 12, 1897, 3, clipped by Steven Kolins. https://www.newspapers.com/clip/12617998/jw_pope_husband_of_later_bahai.

Compilation on Women. Compiled by the Research Department of the Universal House of Justice. Haifa: Bahá'í World Centre, 1986. http://www.bahai.org/library/authoritative-texts/compilations/women.

Crosson, Selena M. "Searching for May Maxwell: Bahá'í Millennial Feminism, Transformative Identity and Globalism in the New World Order Shaping Women's Role in Early Bahá'i Culture 1898–1940." PhD diss., University of Saskatchewan, 2013. https://harvest.usask.ca/bitstream/handle/10388/ETD-2013-10-1145/CROSSON-DISSERTATION.pdf?sequence=4&isAllowed=y.

Etter-Lewis, Gwendolyn, and Richard W. Thomas, eds. *Lights of the Spirit: Historical Portraits of Black Bahá'ís in North America, 1898–2000*. Wilmette, IL: Bahá'í Publishing, 2006.

FamilySearch. https://www.familysearch.org.

Find a Grave. findagrave.com.

Gail, Marzieh. *Arches of the Years*. Oxford: George Ronald, 1991.

"Grand Concert." *The Patron and Gleaner*, December 31, 1896, 2, clipped by Paula Bidwell. https://www.newspapers.com/clip/1192071/jw_pope_manager_ame_sunday_school.

Gregory, Louis G. *A Heavenly Vista: The Pilgrimage of Louis G. Gregory*. Washington: R. L. Pendleton, 1911. Reprint, Ferndale, MI: Alpha Services, 1997. Also available at http://bahai-library.com/pilgrims/louis.html.

"Halifax County." *The Raleigh Signal*, June 23, 1887, clipped by Steven Kolins. https://www.newspapers.com/clip/6348244/mrs_john_w_pocahontas_pope_later_a.

Heller, Wendy. "Gail, Marzieh." *Encyclopaedia Iranica*. http://www.iranicaonline.org/articles/gail-marzieh

Hogenson Kathryn Jewett. *Lighting the Western Sky: The Hearst Pilgrimage and the Establishment of the Bahá'í Faith in the West*. Oxford: George Ronald, 2010.

"In Memoriam." *Bahá'í News*, U.S. Supplement, no. 22 (December 1959), 2. http://www.h-net.org/~bahai/diglib/Periodicals/US_Supplement/022.pdf.

"John W. Pope Promoted." *The Patron and Gleaner*, September 1, 1898, 3, clipped by Paula Bidwell. https://www.newspapers.com/clip/1191995/jw_in_washington_since_spring_the.

Khaghani, Leah Victoria. *"One World or None": Transnational Struggles against Imperialism in the American Century*. PhD diss., Yale University, 2011. ProQuest Dissertations Publishing.

Maxwell, May. *An Early Pilgrimage*. 1917. Reprint, Oxford: George Ronald, 1953. Also available at http://bahai-library.com/maxwell_early_pilgrimage.

McGlinn, Sen, trans. "Speech for the Universal Races Congress." https://abdulbahatalks.wordpress.com/1911/07/26/speech-for-the-universal-races-congress.

Mirzai, Behnaz A. *A History of Slavery and Emancipation in Iran, 1800–1929*. Austin: University of Texas Press, 2017.

Momen, Moojan. "Esslemont's Survey of the Bahá'í World, 1919–1920." In *Bahá'ís in the West*, edited by Peter Smith, 88–92. *Studies in the Bábí and Bahá'í Religions* 14. Los Angeles: Kalimát, 2004.

Morrison, Gayle. "Gregory, Louis George (1874–1951)." *The Bahá'í Encyclopedia Project*. http://www.bahai-encyclopedia-project.org/index.php?view=article&catid=56%3Aa-selection-of-articles&id=63%3Agregory-louis-george&option=com_content&Itemid=74.

Morrison, Gayle. *To Move the World: Louis G. Gregory and the Advancement of Racial Unity in America*. Wilmette, IL: Bahá'í Publishing Trust, 1982.

National Bahá'í Archives, United States. Ahmad Sohrab Papers. Wilmette, IL: U.S. Bahá'í National Center.

National Bahá'í Archives, United States. Albert Windust Papers. Wilmette, IL: U.S. Bahá'í National Center.

National Bahá'í Archives, United States. Hannen-Knobloch Family Papers. Wilmette, IL: U.S. Bahá'í National Center.

National Bahá'í Archives, United States. Leone Barnitz Papers. Wilmette, IL: U.S. Bahá'í National Center.

National Bahá'í Archives, United States. Louis G. Gregory Papers. Wilmette, IL: U.S. Bahá'í National Center.

National Bahá'í Archives, United States. Original Tablets of 'Abdu'l-Bahá Collection. Wilmette, IL: U.S. Bahá'í National Center.

National Bahá'í Archives, United States. Thornton Chase Papers. Wilmette, IL: U.S. Bahá'í National Center.

National Bahá'í Archives, United States. Translations of Tablets of 'Abdu'l-Bahá Collection. Wilmette, IL: U.S. Bahá'í National Center.

New York Age, Thursday, October 10, 1912, 8. https://www.newspapers.com/clip/286449/ the_new_york_age.

Núrí, Muhammad-Alí Malik-Khusraví. *Iqlím-i Núr*. Tehran: Mu'assisiy-i-Millíy-i-Matbú'át-i-Amrí, 1962.

"Officers and Delegates." *Evening Star*, June 9, 1902, 10, clipped by Steven Kolins. https://www.newspapers.com/clip/6326523/note_of_j_w_and_later_bahai_mrs.

"Our Halifax Letters. Scotland Neck and Schools—Address by Hon. James E. O'Hara—The Improved Condition of the Colored People." *The Raleigh Signal*

(Raleigh, NC), August 11, 1887, 2, clipped by Steven Kolins. https://www.newspapers.com/clip/12606265/john_w_pope_scotland_neck_normal.

"Our Schools." *The Banner-Enterprise* (Raleigh, North Carolina), September 6, 1883, 2, clipped by Paula Bidwell. https://www.newspapers.com/clip/1083771/first_mention_of_j_w_popes_work_at.

Power of Unity: Beyond Prejudice and Racism. Compiled by Bonnie J. Taylor and the National Race Unity Committee. Wilmette, IL: Bahá'í Publishing Trust, 1986. Also available at https://bahai-library.com/taylor_power_unity.

Pupil of the Eye: African Americans in the World Order of Bahá'u'lláh. 2nd ed. Compiled by Bonnie J. Taylor. Rivera Beach, FL: Palabra Publications, 1998. Also available at https://bahai-library.com/taylor_pupil_eye.

Radcliffe, Donnie. "Washington Ways." *Washington Post*, July 5, 1983, C4. ProQuest Central.

Rudwick, Elliott. "W. E. B. DuBois and the Universal Races Congress of 1911." *The Phylon Quarterly* 20, no. 4 (1959): 372–78. Jstor.

Shoghi, Effendi. *Advent of Divine Justice.* Wilmette, IL: Bahá'í Publishing Trust, 1990. Also available at http://www.bahai.org/library/authoritative-texts/shoghi-effendi/advent-divine-justice.

Shoghi, Effendi. *God Passes By.* Wilmette, IL: Bahá'í Publishing Trust, 1979. Also available at http://www.bahai.org/library/authoritative-texts/shoghi-effendi/god-passes-by.

Shoghi, Effendi. *Messages to the Bahá'í World: 1950–1957.* Wilmette, IL: Bahá'í Publishing Trust, 1971. Also available at http://reference.bahai.org/en/t/se/MBW.

Soucek, P. P. "'Abbas b. Reza-Qoli Khan Nuri." *Encyclopaedia Iranica.* Vol. I, fasc. 1 (December 15, 1982), 84. http://www.iranicaonline.org/articles/abbas-b-reza-qoli-khan-nuri.

Stockman, Robert. *'Abdu'l-Bahá in America.* Wilmette, IL: Bahá'í Publishing, 2012.

Stockman, Robert. *The Bahá'í Faith in America.* Vol. 2. *Early Expansion 1900–1912.* Oxford: George Ronald, 1985.

Thomas, Richard W. "The 'Pupil of the Eye': African-Americans and the Making of the American Bahá'í Community, 1898–2003." In *The Black Urban Community: From Dusk Till Dawn*, edited by Gayle Tate, and Lewis Randolph, 167–92. New York: Palgrave Macmillan, 2006.

Thompson, Juliet. *The Diary of Juliet Thompson.* Los Angeles: Kalimát Press, 1995. Also available at http://bahai-library.com/books/thompson/4.html.

Venters, Louis. *No Jim Crow Church: The Origins of South Carolina's Bahá'í Community.* Gainesville, FL: University Press of Florida, 2015.

"Widow Sole Beneficiary." *The Washington Herald*, June 6, 1918, 6, clipped by Steven Kolins. https://www.newspapers.com/clip/1095504/bahai_pocahontas_pope_inherits.

Wilborn, Elizabeth W., Boyd Cathey, and Jerry L. Cross. *The Roanoke Valley: A Report for the Historic Halifax State Historic Site.* https://ia600500.us.archive.org/7/items/roanokevalleyrep00wilb/roanokevalleyrep00wilb.pdf.

Chapter 2

"The Most Vital and Challenging Issue"

The Bahá'í Faith's Efforts to Improve Race Relations, 1922–1936

Loni Bramson

The most outstanding example of how the Bahá'í Faith in the United States, during the 1920s and the first half of the 1930s, changed the lives and outlook of its members was in the realm of race relations. Further, the small American Bahá'í community of this era (1,500 to 3,000 members) engaged in interracial work that affected the lives of African Americans and their organizations. The black and white Bahá'ís must be given full credit for attempting to transform their own prejudices, even if they sometimes failed, and their courage must be recognized for trying to overcome societal impasses in the field of race relations. Although occasionally individual white churches refused to bow to societal pressures to oppress African Americans, the only religious organizations with a majority of white members that officially strove for better race relations were the Society of Friends (the Quakers) and the Bahá'í Faith. The Bahá'í Faith's race amity efforts in the 1920s and the first half of the 1930s had a lasting impact in two distinct ways.

One important effect was on Alain Locke, who converted to the Bahá'í Faith in 1918.[1] His prominence in African American and United States history is uncontested. How he was influential is debated. Locke has been analyzed as a polemicist for black identity and culture, a cosmopolitan, a promoter of difference in African American culture, an early cultural pluralist or a co-founder of this philosophy with Horace Kallen, and a founder of multiculturalism.[2] How Locke was influenced to develop his theories represents a deep historiographical gap.[3] The purpose of this chapter is not to analyze Locke's philosophy, history, influence on African American studies, or to focus on the historiography of the development of cultural pluralism and multiculturalism. Rather, it will detail elements that influenced Locke that are not yet appreciated by scholars of early twentieth-century African American history. Specifically, this refers to the Bahá'í Faith and its race relations efforts in the 1920s and first half of the 1930s. Locke kept himself up-to-date with these activities both through his connections with people such as Louis Gregory (see figure 2.1), a particularly important person for Locke's religious development through their longstanding friendship, and through Locke's active service in Bahá'í race amity efforts, including being a member of the National Race Amity Committee (with Louis Gregory) between 1924 and 1932.[4] Locke was influenced by Bahá'í race amity efforts, and he helped develop them through his membership on the national committee. By examining this historical background and context to Alain Locke's religious life while he was developing his philosophical theories, scholars will better understand these theories and how they evolved. This thread will be picked up again in the conclusion.

Figure 2.1 Louis Gregory Around 1930. *Source*: Photograph courtesy of U.S. National Bahá'í Archives.

The second important lasting effect of the role that Bahá'í race relations work during the period being studied in this chapter had relates to the internal development of the American Bahá'í community. The race amity work changed the outlook of American Bahá'ís toward race relations. When the American Bahá'í community became a leading partner in the international effort to propagate the Bahá'í Faith around the world, the multicultural outlook that the Bahá'ís had arduously developed helped to diversify the Bahá'í population in terms of ethnicities and racial groupings. This chapter provides the historical context and background to this work, but, again, does not directly study it.[5]

The key to American Bahá'í efforts to create racial amity and improve race relations was primarily a series of race amity conferences uniting blacks and whites to work together to organize them and discuss controversial topics. Over the years, about thirty-five major conferences were held in almost every major city. In addition to these conferences, or conventions as they were often called, many less formal meetings and activities were organized, including interracial dinners. All these meetings embraced the presence of people who were not Bahá'ís (often called non-Bahá'ís). The Bahá'í National Race Amity Committee,[6] which worked directly under the aegis of the National Spiritual Assembly of the Bahá'ís of the United States and Canada (the national Bahá'í coordinating body), also wrote articles for the press, but its most important task was to help the Bahá'ís realize the prejudices they had so they could try and overcome them. The National Race Amity Committee also collaborated with local Bahá'í institutions, the local spiritual assemblies, in multiple ways.

These activities not only developed a cadre of individuals capable of engaging in social discourse on one of the most difficult topics in American society, but they also advanced the development and maturation of national and local Bahá'í institutions and taught the Bahá'ís multicultural competence. In order to examine the points raised throughout this introduction, the focus of this chapter will be a survey of American Bahá'í race relation efforts from 1922, shortly after Shoghi Effendi became Guardian of the Bahá'í Faith following the death of his grandfather, 'Abdu'l-Bahá, to 1936, when Shoghi Effendi considered the Bahá'í community and its administrative order sufficiently mature to embark on the first of a series of systematic plans of development and propagation in the Western hemisphere. This treatment provides scholars of African American studies more insight into one of the important influences for Alain Locke's contributions to philosophy and African American history.

RACE AMITY WORK: 1920–1923

It needs to be stated at the outset that around 1920, improving race relations was not a desired goal for all the Bahá'ís in America, and conflicting information about this elemental aspect of the Bahá'í Faith was widespread. An example of this is one set of notes written by Edward C. Getsinger from talks with 'Abdu'l-Bahá while Getsinger was in Haifa.[7] between January 26 and February 5, 1915. He had explained to 'Abdu'l-Bahá the work being done to improve race amity in Washington, DC, which was certainly a challenging area for this effort. The notes state that 'Abdu'l-Bahá commented: "Very good! Have one meeting for colored people where such do not wish to attend mixed meetings. . . . No obstacle should be placed before any soul which might prevent it, (the soul), from finding the truth. Baha'o'llah revealed His directions, teachings, and laws, so that souls might know God, and not that any utterance might become an obstacle in their way."[8]

The first race amity event during Shoghi Effendi's administration, but which was the second Race Amity Convention, took place in Springfield, Massachusetts, from December 5 to 6, 1921.[9] This convention included, as many of the others did, musical interludes of African American spiritual and gospel music, with the purpose of helping white people better understand and appreciate black culture. The speakers were both non-Bahá'í and Bahá'í and included three African American reverends; a rabbi; a white reverend; a prominent African American, Colonel Charles L. Young (his wife, Ada, was a Bahá'í);[10] the mayor of Springfield; and four Bahá'ís. Approximately 1200 people attended, about equally black and white. The black reverends and the mayor of Springfield did not skirt around the issue at hand. They forcefully spoke of the need for economic equality and the end of white terrorist lawlessness (the Ku Klux Klan and others), and the mistreatment of blacks, including physical abuse. They strongly condemned the murder and lynching of African Americans in the South. The Bahá'ís spoke about the Bahá'í Faith, presenting it as the solution to society's problems.[11] Other regions where Bahá'ís lived were starting to think about organizing a similar conference. For example, around the same time, the Western States Regional Teaching Committee, chaired by Ella G. Cooper, wrote in its second letter to the Bahá'ís and Bahá'í assemblies in the West:

> Ever since the remarkable success of the "mother" convention in Washington, D. C., we have longed to hold one on the Pacific Coast whenever the righte [*sic*] time should arrive. Shortly before the ascension of Abdul Baha he wrote in a tablet to Mrs. Parsons that an amity convention should be held in New York this year and, if the majority of the friends wished, also one in San Francisco. As its success would undoubtedly depend upon holding it at the psychological moment it needs very careful consideration. Therefore it should be a matter for earnest consultation among all the Western friends.[12]

A couple of months later, Louis Gregory, one of the most important members of the National Race Amity Committee, and at times a member of the

National Spiritual Assembly, came to the West Coast to promote the race amity work there. He wrote letters to many people and traveled up and down the coast to foster race relations within and without the Bahá'í community. In a letter dated February 17, 1922, Gregory thanked the Portland, Oregon, Bahá'ís for the events they successfully organized for him during his visit there. He noted that the San Francisco Bahá'ís were keeping him busy, and that between February 24 and March 5, he would be engaged in Bahá'í work in Los Angeles.[13] Gregory had been in Portland from February 4 to 12, having previously spent time in Vancouver, Washington. Gregory, it should be noted, was paid by the National Spiritual Assembly to engage in this work until his retirement. There is no clergy in the Bahá'í Faith, but from its earliest days, and continuing to the present, sometimes individuals are financially supported (usually a stipend is sufficient to cover basic expenses) to carry out specific functions.[14]

Gregory's program during his time in the Portland Metro area, summarized below, allowed the Bahá'ís to strengthen their organizational and administrative skills by arranging a series of meetings for "brother Louis." The local Bahá'ís also enhanced their multicultural skills by inviting African Americans to attend the meetings and to have Gregory speak to their groups. At this time, as noted, the Ku Klux Klan was visibly active in Oregon. To stay safe, Gregory regularly changed the place where he slept, especially because he was in the homes of white families.

Gregory initially stayed with Mr. and Mrs. Tom May (white). He lectured at the First Divine Science Church during their Sunday morning service and ate at the home of the Weed family (white),[15] who that same evening hosted a social evening for him with the local Bahá'ís. At this meeting, they also discussed and planned the activities for the week to come. On Monday (February 6), he spoke to the Psychology Club at the public library, and in the evening, Beatrice Morrow Cannady, the editor of the weekly African American newspaper, *The Advocate*, and a civil rights activist, organized an evening in her home for Gregory to meet her friends.

On Tuesday, Gregory spoke on racial amity at the Theosophical Society. On Wednesday, he addressed the weekly luncheon of the Oregon Social Workers on interracial harmony. Thursday evening, the Bahá'ís organized a unity feast, that is, a social evening with Gregory, at the home of Mr. and Mrs. Nash (white), where Gregory spoke about national Bahá'í needs. On Friday, he gave a talk to the African American Old Rose Club at the YWCA on another Bahá'í principle, the equality between women and men. That evening, he discoursed generally about the Bahá'í Faith at the regular weekly public meeting organized by the Portland Bahá'ís. Saturday evening, he stayed at the home of another family. Sunday evening, he spoke twice at the Bethel African Methodist Episcopal (AME) Church, first to the Epworth

League, and then, on peace, to the entire congregation. The next day he was the primary speaker at the Lincoln-Douglas memorial meeting for the Portland NAACP, held in the First AME Zion Church.[16] His theme was the necessity to eliminate prejudice.[17]

As we can see, this was an extensive and intense program organized by the Portland local spiritual assembly, of which only a summary is noted. The effort expended to plan and organize Gregory's tour helped its members to advance their ability to contact African American leaders in Portland, organize publicity, and carry out a complex, tightly packed series of events. Equally important, Portland Bahá'ís improved their understanding of the realities of life for African Americans.

Gregory, as can be seen, did not shirk from an effort that could possibly be dangerous, nor did the Bahá'ís. Another example is from September 1921. Gregory was in Chicago speaking for a public campaign organized by the Chicago Bahá'ís at a time when the Ku Klux Klan had raised its hooded head in that city.[18] Alain Locke was aware of all Louis Gregory's activities through the Bahá'í newsletters and letters he received from Gregory.

In its February 1923 issue, *Star of the West*, the Bahá'í newsletter, published an article by Louis Gregory on America's race problem, entitled "Inter-Racial Amity: Spirit of the New Age Enters the South. Constructive Efforts and Marked Progress." The article was but one of many that he wrote for national Bahá'í institutions and agencies throughout the years. In this essay, he explains that, although the moral decay of the South, as shown by its mob violence and ignorance, was evident, yet enlightened people could be found in the South who applied the ideals found in the Sermon on the Mount to both blacks and whites. Certain individuals were taking the lead, such as James H. Dillard, former president of Tulane University in New Orleans, who had called together a conference of universities in the South to discuss race relations and how to solve the race problem.[19] The sessions for this meeting had to be held in secret, but the movement to eliminate race problems was alive. Sometimes conferences were even held between students of white and black institutions. Gregory explained that the attitudes of whites were definitely improving, but they were in no hurry to pursue the necessary changes. They were satisfied with a gradual evolution toward change that would take several generations. African Americans, though, were asking for specific goals:

Justice in the administration of law.
Prevention of lynching under all circumstances.
Improvement in sanitary living.
Better schools, lights, pavements, and sewerage.
Economic justice.
Discouragement of vice.

Improvement in traveling facilities on street cars and railroads.
Better recreational facilities, such as parks and play grounds.
Advancement of moral standards.
The elevation of practical religion.[20]

Gregory informed the Bahá'ís that the people in the South who were working toward racial unity were a fertile field in which the Bahá'ís could propagate their teachings.[21]

Between 1920 and 1923, the Baha'is were just beginning to understand what their religion's policy was on race relations and to learn about the reality of life for African Americans. They were discussing the issues and establishing relationships with the African American community, primarily through its leaders. The idea to hold race amity conferences spread to other regions of the United States as a result of the success of the first two. Louis Gregory traveled to different parts of the country, thus causing some local Bahá'í institutions to start developing the capacity to find and meet with African Americans and organize intimate gatherings and public events. The Bahá'ís forayed into learning about multiculturalism.[22] The National Spiritual Assembly furthered the understanding of race issues by having Gregory write articles and essays describing what he had witnessed during his travels. These were published in newsletters sent to all Bahá'ís, including Locke. In addition, Gregory wrote many letters to a wide variety of people informing them how his work was going and helping many to better understand the challenges of race relations; Locke, his friend and race amity co-worker was one of the recipients.[23]

RACE AMITY WORK: 1924–1928

The period between 1924 and 1928 witnessed the rise of public meetings organized by the Bahá'ís that were dedicated to the purpose of fostering interracial amity. The initial race amity conferences had broken the ice in the Bahá'í communities in regard to discussing race matters. In these interracial meetings, the race problem was seriously discussed, with no subject being considered taboo. The goal of the meetings was to direct the participants toward taking action to solve the racial problems. Meetings were held across the United States, except in the Deep South: Washington, DC; Philadelphia; Dayton, Ohio; Eliot, Maine; Brooklyn; Boston; Chicago; New York City; Seattle; and Portland, Oregon.[24] Many Bahá'í communities appointed biracial local race amity committees that worked toward establishing racial harmony in their towns and cities.[25] In the West, race amity work included Asians, American Indians, and Mexican Americans, in addition to African Americans.

The third interracial amity conference was in spring 1924 in New York City. The major speakers and organizers were Dr. John Herman Randall of Community Church;[26] the eminent anthropologist Dr. Franz Boaz of Columbia University; James Weldon Johnson, the NAACP secretary; the internationally renowned Jane Addams of Hull House in Chicago; and three Bahá'ís in addition to Randall, Roy C. Wilhelm, Horace Holley, and Mountford Mills.[27] The purpose of this conference was to show that there was no scientific or spiritual basis for considering that one race is superior to another. Other participants, helpers, and speakers at this conference were the National Urban League, the committee on International Cooperation of the League of Women Voters, America's Making, Alain Locke, Rabbi Stephen S. Wise, and Taraknath Das.[28]

Race amity issues became a part of other Bahá'í public activities. In the series of World Unity conferences organized by the Bahá'ís, there were sessions on interracial unity. Clergy, rabbis, deans of universities, and university professors participated in these conferences, which were often held in churches. Again, the speakers were candid. For example, in a 1925 World Unity meeting, Reverend W. J. J. Byers, from the AME Church, spoke on the attitudes and situation in American society that oppressed the black people and prevented them from taking their full responsibility in helping to advance civilization.[29] In the 1927 series of World Unity conferences, the Bahá'ís were able to obtain some distinguished speakers, such as Dr. Samuel C. Mitchell of Richmond University (history professor); Dr. Pezavia O'Connell, an African American well known for championing the African American cause regardless of personal consequences, at the time a dean at Morgan College in Baltimore; Rabbi Abram Simon, who was chair of the Synagogue Council of America; Professor Leslie Pinckney Hill (a Bahá'í) of the Institute for Colored Youth in Cheyney, Pennsylvania (now Cheyney University of Pennsylvania); and Dr. Mordecai W. Johnson, the first African American president of Howard University. Other Bahá'ís who spoke were Horace Holley, Louis Gregory, Albert Vail, Mountford Mills, and Siegfried Schopflocher.[30]

From 1924 to 1928, the National Race Amity Committee organized its annual season of conference work with a Race Amity Conference at the Green Acre Bahá'í summer school in Eliot, Maine. These conferences, and in fact the general efforts of the Bahá'ís in race relations, were well known in certain circles; they progressively became better known and were especially appreciated by African Americans. As a result of this work, Bahá'ís were often welcome, even invited, to send speakers on the Bahá'í Faith to various African American groups, institutions, and organizations.

The conferences also helped individuals who were crisscrossing the United States to talk to whoever would listen about racial amity work by giving them a venue. They were appointed to do this work, and the sponsoring Bahá'í institution generally financially supported them with a stipend. The people helping these traveling teachers increased their efforts to learn how to engage in outreaching to African Americans and other minorities. This was important "practice" for later international Bahá'í propagation work. Successfully organizing such tours required progressively enhanced administration and organizational skills, and an increased capacity to enter into dialog with people quite different from them. Louis Gregory was, again, at the heart of this work. A typical Gregory teaching trip began right after the 1924 Green Acre session. This particular one lasted eight months and stretched from Michigan through South Carolina. He spoke in schools, churches, holiday venues, movie theaters, businessmen clubs, YMCAs, and prison camps.[31]

Another prominent Bahá'í teacher who engaged in race amity work was Fadil Mazandarani (known as Jinab-i-Fadil), sent to the United States to propagate the Bahá'í Faith by Shoghi Effendi. In January 1925, the Portland, Oregon, Bahá'ís, in collaboration with the Portland NAACP, organized an evening public meeting on race relations, followed by a reception for everyone who came. Jinab-i-Fadil spoke on the "Conquest of Prejudice." In addition, the president of the NAACP educated the public on what that organization does. Other elements of the meeting were an invocation, poetry, and music.[32]

Louis Gregory and others involved in race reconciliation efforts also wrote many letters encouraging the Bahá'ís (including Locke) to become active in this work. For example, while at rest at the Green Acre school in Eliot, Maine, Gregory wrote to Helen Bishop, with whom he carried on regular correspondence, and included a copy of the Green Acre race amity convention.[33] A month later, he again wrote to Bishop about working toward race relations:

> It is significant of any sincere service in the Cause of Baha'u'llah and may have a bearing upon the effort to conciliate the races in America, for which there is a great and increasing demand as well as a capacity on the part of interested people. It has been conveyed to us that inter-racial work would be the means of drawing people of capacity among the races into a knowledge of the Divine Cause. This assurance should prompt all who can to know and value the importance of the work.[34]

Other Bahá'ís also worked for better race relations in the South, such as Howard MacNutt, Alain Locke, and Louise Boyle.[35] Boyle, when she travelled to the South, especially concentrated on encouraging isolated Bahá'ís and informally organized Bahá'í groups to collaborate, an important step in developing administrative capacity.[36] In the 1925–1926 winter, a special effort was made to establish the Bahá'í Faith in Florida. Two Bahá'ís, Dr.

Walter and Frances Guy, resided in St. Augustine. They had experienced "severe opposition and criticism for many years"[37] as they tried to spread the Bahá'í Faith with its teachings of racial harmony. By fall 1925, the Bahá'ís believed that this opposition was almost over, and from that autumn to spring, an intensive campaign for race amity was organized with talks in churches, schools, clubs, and private homes.[38] Many Bahá'ís, including Alain Locke, temporarily resided in Florida in order to participate in this effort. Special emphasis was given to working with interracial groups and encouraging isolated Bahá'ís to take on a more active role.[39] Louis Gregory helped in Florida, but spent part of his time traveling in New Jersey, Pennsylvania, and the District of Columbia.[40]

Christopher Buck writes briefly about the Gregory-Locke teaching trip to the South. He emphasizes the importance of the Bahá'í race amity teachers mentioned above for the creation of the Bahá'í administrative system in Miami.[41] Although not much information is yet available on the history of this local spiritual assembly, it is on a list of local Bahá'í assemblies in the *Bahá'í Year Book* (1926).[42] Howard and Mary MacNutt moved to Miami to support the nascent spiritual assembly and to continue working for race amity. Howard MacNutt is an example of how this focus on race relations changed Bahá'ís because previously he had expressed views that today we consider racist and were not acceptable according to Bahá'í doctrine.[43]

In 1927, the National Spiritual Assembly took a step further in its work toward race amity, which included fostering greater collaboration between national and local Bahá'í institutions; this, in turn, developed enhanced administrative proficiency. The National Spiritual Assembly informed all local spiritual assemblies of the importance of the race amity work and said that they were to fully cooperate with the National Race Amity Committee. The committee received a mandate to formulate a program to stimulate racial harmony in the local Bahá'í communities, as the National Spiritual Assembly fully realized that cleansing one's heart of racial prejudice was not an easy goal to accomplish. The National Race Amity Committee was given the charge of arranging for Bahá'í speakers for integrated youth groups, especially in schools and colleges, and bringing together groups from both races to consult on the issue of race relations. The Committee was also to prepare a compilation of the Bahá'í Writings on racial amity for public distribution and to help the Bahá'ís eliminate their own prejudice.[44]

Until this time, in Bahá'í public meetings, the contact between the two races had been on a formal level. This was also true within the Bahá'í community, except for a few cases. Although already a significant step, greater than the vast majority of the American population had taken, it still did not approach the Bahá'í standard, and Shoghi Effendi called the Bahá'ís to this higher standard. He explained that the racial problem in the United States would become progressively more serious and complex. The number of Bahá'ís of different races was going to increase, and the growth and prestige of the Bahá'í Faith would, to a large extent, depend on how the Bahá'ís carried out among themselves and with others the Bahá'í Faith's "high standards of inter-racial amity."[45] Shoghi Effendi challenged the Bahá'ís:

> I direct my appeal with all the earnestness and urgency that this pressing problem calls for to every conscientious upholder of the universal principles of Bahá'u'lláh to face this extremely delicate situation with the boldness, the decisiveness and wisdom it demands. I cannot believe that those whose hearts have been touched by the regenerating influence of God's creative Faith in His day will find it difficult to cleanse their souls from every lingering trace of racial animosity so subversive of the Faith they profess. How can hearts that throb with the love of God fail to respond to all the implications of this supreme injunction of Bahá'u'lláh, the unreserved acceptance of which, under the circumstances now prevailing in America, constitutes the hall-mark of a true Bahá'í character?
>
> Let every believer, desirous to witness the swift and healthy progress of the Cause of God, realize the twofold nature of his task. Let him first turn his eyes inwardly and search his own heart and satisfy himself that in his relations with his fellow believers, irrespective of color and class, he is proving himself increasingly loyal to the spirit of his beloved Faith. Assured and content that he is exerting his utmost in a conscious effort to approach nearer every day the lofty station to which his gracious Master[46] summons him, let him turn to his second task, and with befitting confidence and vigor, assail the devastating power of those forces which in his own heart he has already succeeded in subduing. Fully alive to the unfailing efficacy of the power of Bahá'u'lláh, and armed with the essential weapons of wise restraint and inflexible resolve, let him wage a constant fight against the inherited tendencies, the corruptive instincts, the fluctuating fashions, the false pretenses of the society in which he lives and moves.
>
> In their relations amongst themselves as fellow-believers, let them not be content with the mere exchange of cold and empty formalities often connected with the organizing of banquets, receptions, consultative assemblies, and lecture-halls. Let them rather, as equal co-sharers in the spiritual benefits conferred upon them by Bahá'u'lláh, arise and, with the aid and counsel of their local and national representatives, supplement these official functions with those opportunities which only a close and intimate social intercourse can adequately provide. In their homes, in their hours of relaxation and leisure, in the daily contact of business transactions, in the association of their children, whether in their study-classes, their playgrounds, and clubrooms, in short under all possible circumstances, however insignificant they appear, the community of the followers of Bahá'u'lláh should satisfy themselves that in the eyes of the world at large and in the sight of their vigilant Master they are the living witnesses of those truths which He fondly cherished and tirelessly championed to the very end of His days. If we relax in our purpose, if we falter in our faith, if we neglect the varied

> opportunities given us from time to time by an all-wise and gracious Master we are not merely failing in what is our most vital and conspicuous obligation, but are thereby insensibly retarding the flow of those quickening energies which can alone insure the vigorous and speedy development of God's struggling Faith.[47]

The National Race Amity Committee planned a new series of race amity conferences in cooperation with various local spiritual assemblies: Boston, the District of Columbia, New York City, Chicago, and Philadelphia.[48] The model for these conferences was the annual Green Acre Race Amity Conference; the core subject was the Bahá'í Faith, with Bahá'í speakers, but also including non-Bahá'í speakers. The advice to have non-Bahá'í speakers was heeded, and several prominent people spoke at these conferences.[49]

Local spiritual assemblies, such as those for the District of Columbia and New York City, also became more active in organizing less formal local meetings. Henry B. Duncan of Liberia inaugurated the New York City meetings with a lecture. The Local Spiritual Assembly of Seattle went the furthest by attracting, in conjunction with their international evenings, leading citizens to attend to give brief talks on race amity and cooperation, combining these with occasional interracial suppers.[50]

Before Shoghi Effendi's letter, the National Race Amity Committee had sent out a circular letter to all local spiritual assemblies stressing the importance of racial harmony and the holding of race amity conventions. Only six communities had responded.[51] After Shoghi Effendi's letter was distributed, many more local spiritual assemblies rose to the challenge, and on December 12, the National Race Amity Committee sent out another letter giving suggestions on how to advance the race amity work, and also informing the assemblies what other communities were doing to work toward racial amity. The Chicago community, for instance, distributed a regular local bulletin on the subject of race relations. In this second letter, the National Race Amity Committee reminded the local spiritual assemblies how it thought the race amity conferences should be conducted, that is, distinguished public men should speak, but the conference should absolutely be under Bahá'í auspices; and the ultimate goal of these conferences was to find new Bahá'ís.[52] We can see in this chapter's brief survey so far that Bahá'í institutions were gaining administrative capacity at the local and national level and were improving their institutional effectiveness. In addition, they had significantly raised the bar in their multicultural efforts by starting to socialize with people of different races.

In 1928, race amity conferences were held in Green Acre, (Eliot) Maine; New York City; Rochester, New York; Geneva, New York; Buffalo, New York; Portsmouth, New Hampshire; Columbus, Ohio; and Dayton, Ohio.[53] Most of the work during the year was done on the level of smaller public meetings rather than conferences, and there were meetings in about fifty cities and towns. Interracial outreach was starting in universities, especially in Urbana, Illinois, the seat of the University of Illinois.[54] Seattle, Washington, and Portland, Oregon were the two Bahá'í communities that were working the most in the direction desired by Shoghi Effendi. They were now holding a regular series of interracial dinners, with the theme of each one being related to a different race. Meetings were also held, but their concept of race amity meetings had evolved toward showing hospitality as well as having a meeting. This was a novel enough idea to receive press coverage.[55] Louis Gregory was still traveling extensively and at an even more exhausting pace.[56]

The rising number of race amity conferences demonstrated both enhanced organizational skills for the administrative institutions and the ability of these same institutions to connect with African American leaders. One way the administrative capacity increased was by establishing a system for providing speakers to support a variety of meetings. Although Louis Gregory remained the main teacher and speaker on race amity issues around the country, the national administration was able to organize and fund more such teachers (mostly white, but also some African Americans). The travels of these race amity teachers helped the local Bahá'í administrative institutions in the development of their administrative capacity to organize local activities and events. As can be seen in Louis Gregory's travels, increasing emphasis was being placed on reaching out to a wide diversity of people.

In December 1929, the National Race Amity Committee reported to the National Spiritual Assembly and all local spiritual assemblies. The summary of the report demonstrates its increased administrative and organizational capacity. The committee had learned that race amity workers needed six to ten weeks of preparation. Writing a general circular letter to clergy and social workers did not achieve results. It was important to send a letter with the program to the above groups and other organizations far enough ahead of time as some of them only met monthly. Further, life should be made easier for journalists by giving them pre-written articles and copies of the speaker's talk; this would reduce errors. Local Bahá'ís needed to develop the capacity to personally contact the people to invite and the religious organizations, schools, clubs, and all other groups to have five minutes of their meeting times to explain the conference. In addition, public relations skills were needed to circulate the program widely, in hotels, apartment buildings, stores, club houses, chambers of commerce, youth organizations, Americanization groups, peace leagues, Jewish groups, the NAACP, and esoteric centers.[57]

The letter-writing campaign that was established was most likely organized by the National Race Amity Committee. The National Spiritual Assembly fostered greater collaboration between this national committee and local spiritual assemblies, which allowed a more complex administrative capacity to develop as race amity efforts moved to a larger number of local communities whose administrative bodies were ultimately responsible for organizing these activities with the support of the National Race Amity Committee. Whereas this committee continued to organize the large race amity conventions, the local spiritual assemblies undertook the planning of more informal events. This allowed the Bahá'ís to further advance their multicultural skills. Alain Locke was a member of the National Race Amity Committee in 1924 (about half the year), 1925, 1926, 1927, 1928, 1929, 1930, 1931, and part of 1932.[58] More research is needed in currently unavailable archives to determine how active he was and the extent of his influence on the direction that Bahá'í race relations went.

RACE AMITY WORK: FINANCIAL STRESS INCREASES LOCAL AND INDIVIDUAL WORK

By 1930, the financial crunch of the U.S. Bahá'í community, following the project to construct the Chicago House of Worship (sometimes called Temple)[59] and the Great Depression, hit the National Race Amity Committee in full. The National Teaching Committee and the National Race Amity Committee were instructed by the National Spiritual Assembly to merge their propagation programs, and where possible, a series of interracial, interreligious public meetings was held, specifically in Geneva, Rochester, Buffalo, and New York City, New York; Cleveland, Columbus, and Dayton, Ohio; Detroit; Portsmouth, Maine; and Chicago.[60] For example, according to the 1930 program brochure for the New York City meeting, the organizers were the National Teaching Committee, the Urban League, and the New York Local Spiritual Assembly.[61]

In 1931, only two independent race amity conventions were held. There was, of course, one in early November at the Green Acre school with some sessions being held there, and others at the Unitarian Church in Portsmouth. The speakers included Louis Gregory, Eleanor Sawtell, the secretary of the YWCA, Philip Marangella, and the Ensign of the Salvation Army. Members of the Congregational Church, the Unitarian Church, the Universalist Church, the Baptist Church, and the Bahá'í Faith collaborated to organize it.[62] The first race amity conference organized by the National Race Amity Committee in 1931 was in Atlantic City, New Jersey. Co-organizers were the YMCA, YWCA, Unity Truth Center, and the Jews, Episcopalians, and AME church members.[63] This was yet another sign of the Bahá'í administrative institutions gaining in capacity, especially in collaborating with other religious groups. The second race amity convention was held on January 19 in Philadelphia in which the speakers were Louis Gregory and Albert Vail.[64]

Most of the race amity work was carried out at the local level. Regular public meetings were held all over the United States demonstrating a significant growth in local institutional capability.[65] In addition, on the national level, whenever a large public conference was organized, for example the public meeting that accompanied the Annual Convention to elect the National Spiritual Assembly, a session was dedicated to the race issue and how to overcome the problem.[66]

The National Race Amity Committee undertook several tasks for the National Spiritual Assembly during the year 1929–1930.[67] One was to respond to a series of questions sent by the Kenosha, Wisconsin, Local Spiritual Assembly about the origin of races. That the Baḥá'ís of Kenosha were unsure about the equality of the races is the least one can say. That individuals in this era would be skeptical with regard to the equality of the races is to be expected.[68] More and more people were converting to the Bahá'í Faith, and it was necessary for them to understand and accept the essential Bahá'í doctrine of the oneness of humanity. With the help of certain individuals, such as Louis Gregory, many local spiritual assemblies, and the National Race Amity Committee, the transition in the process to adhere to Bahá'í principles was more smoothly and easily made.

The National Race Amity Committee was also asked to draft a letter that the National Spiritual Assembly sent to Mrs. Herbert Hoover. She had invited the wife and daughter of Oscar De Priest, the only black member of the House of Representatives, to a White House social function. For this she was generally censured, and the National Spiritual Assembly sent her a letter congratulating her on her stand, and to inform her of the Bahá'í teachings on race relations. It also sent her a copy of *The Bahá'í World*.[69]

The more the work was carried out on the local level because of financial limitations of the national committee, with social activities becoming the rule,[70] the more people made individual sacrifices and undertook individual propagation efforts within communities of color, thus enhancing multicultural understanding and appreciation. In addition, there was, of course, Louis Gregory, whose itinerary was planned by the National Race Amity Committee. Between April 1929 and April 1930, he went to about twenty different cities, going as far west as Kansas City, Missouri.[71] The highlight of his year's work was in Milwaukee, when for the first time blacks came to a white person's private home to attend an informational meeting on the Bahá'í Faith. Also, an interracial dinner was held in a private home.[72]

From April 1930 to April 1932, more than fifty local Bahá'í communities held interracial amity activities of some sort; this was slightly more than 50 percent of the local spiritual assemblies and groups.[73] Of these activities, two of the most important ones were in New York City. One was an interracial banquet held on February 27, 1932, that was organized by the National Race

Amity Committee and the New York Spiritual Assembly, with the driving force behind it being Loulie Mathews.[74] The banquet was held in honor of the NAACP and the New York Urban League. The speakers were W. E. B. Du Bois, then editor of *The Crisis*; William J. Schieffelin, president of the Citizens Union and chair of Tuskegee Institute's Board of Trustees; John Franklin Hope, then president of Atlanta University; Arthur C. Holden, president of the New York Urban League; Walter White, secretary of the NAACP; James H. Hubert, secretary of the New York Urban League; and several Bahá'í speakers, including Loulie Mathews, Louis Gregory, Mary Hanford Ford, Hooper Harris, and Horace Holley. With such prominent speakers, and with many other prominent people in the race relations movement present among the approximately 125–150 attendees, the Bahá'í Faith received good publicity, especially in African American newspapers across the United States.[75]

The second important event was a Christmas dinner and party for several hundred white and black children, mostly arranged by the New York City Bahá'í youth. Welfare workers and the New York Urban League brought all the children, three-fourths of whom were black. It was a large party with "goodies and gifts" and a Santa Claus, convincingly played by a Bahá'í of Jewish origin. The party lasted three hours, during which the organizers also showed movies. The goal of the youth was to provide a small ray of joy for some children in the midst of the Depression and to show them that it was easy to play and have fun with someone of a different race. While the children enjoyed the party, the parents were in the Urban League auditorium in Harlem listening to talks about the Bahá'í Faith.[76]

An interesting example of the kinds of frank discussions held during race amity meetings across America took place in Portland, Oregon, on July 10, 1931, during the regular weekly public meeting organized by the Bahá'ís. The guest speaker for the evening was the Reverend Walter Raleigh Lovell of the First AME Zion Church in Portland. His topic was "The American Negro's Changing Attitude toward the Christian Church." He discussed how the slaves had been Christianized and that the Church justified slavery by the Bible. This caused slaves to be loyal to their masters during the Civil War, and afterwards the Church embarked on educating the former slaves. African Americans began to reason that if Christianity had been able to free them, then it should also be able to establish equality between the races. Its inability to do so caused African Americans to doubt the capacity of the Church to practice what it preached. Reverend Lovell further explained that African American mothers wanted their sons to enter the ministry, but the youth refused. Youth were becoming alienated from the Church. African American intellectuals, such as W. E. B. Du Bois criticized the Church, even though Du Bois had never attended an African American church. Lovell further spoke about African American criticism of Christianity originating in the

Church not promoting "the brotherhood of man." These African American critics asked why, if there was equality, there were separate black and white churches. Even worse, at national meetings, such as that of the Board of Methodist Bishops in Washington, DC, African American bishops were not allowed to attend. Lovell also discussed the disenfranchisement of African Americans in the South and how the Church, rather than fighting it, permitted peonage to continue. Because of all this, the Christian Church was losing African American support, and this was a mistake on the part of African Americans. Lovell ended by praising the Bahá'ís for practicing what they preached about "the brotherhood of man."[77]

With the financial stress deepening, the National Teaching Committee and the National Race Amity Committee were fully merged by the National Spiritual Assembly.[78] This probably means that only their budgets were merged because there continued to be a National Race Amity Committee. However, racial amity activities had taken hold in the U.S. Bahá'í community, and they continued, albeit on a much smaller scale. Bahá'ís converted their activities to a race amity theme, such as the two-day annual Blossom Picnic on a farm in Geneva, New York. About 130 people generally took part in this event, and in 1930, James Hubert, executive secretary of the New York Urban League attended.[79] The Bahá'ís, at least on the East Coast, had gained the full confidence of the two leading and most influential national African American organizations, the National Urban League and the NAACP. Further, the events at Green Acre, besides the annual Race Amity Conference, had become occasions for blacks and whites to live together in harmony for a short period of time.[80]

Most of the other activities around the country were on a much smaller scale: a discussion group in the District of Columbia under Bahá'í auspices; talks, classes, and dinners in the Midwest; meetings in the Northeast; dinners in the Northwest; and dinners and small, informal meetings in the West. This demonstrates yet another level of administrative development as organizing more intimate gatherings can be more challenging. Periodically there were larger meetings, but these could not compare in size or scope with the previous race amity conventions. Further, these smaller, more intimate meetings that included socializing were a significant and important step forward in developing multicultural capacity. Seattle held an annual peace and race amity conference. New York City continued to have race amity conferences with the National Urban League and the NAACP.[81]

The New York City meetings were the only ones that could compare with those held in the past, and they received excellent publicity in *The Chicago Defender*, the largest of the African American newspapers with a national circulation of about 250,000.[82] The New York activities resulted from an informal consultation in June 1930 between the National Teaching Committee and representatives from the New York Urban League on race relation problems. An exchange was set up between the Bahá'ís and the Urban League, with Urban League speakers attending the residential Green Acre Amity Conferences and the Bahá'ís lodging in homes in Harlem during the New York City Amity Conventions.[83] Some other cities and towns where race amity conventions were held were Boston; St. Augustine, Florida; Pittsfield and Portsmouth, New Hampshire; Eliot, Maine; Cleveland, Ohio; New Haven, Connecticut; Portland, Oregon; Atlantic City, New Jersey; and Pittsburgh, Pennsylvania. The Pittsburgh Bahá'ís coordinated their conventions with the Pittsburgh Urban League.[84]

The Bahá'ís also began to seriously discuss how interracial propagation work should be carried out. This was an important development in the evolution of the Bahá'í administrative institutions for the future plans to be given to them by Shoghi Effendi.[85] It was considered especially important to reach out to black people by joining race amity-oriented organizations, and to invite African Americans to the homes of Bahá'ís, the goal being to instill confidence in them as to the Bahá'ís' intentions. The Urban League was suggested as an ideal group with which to make contact and inviting African Americans to one's home for dinner was considered an excellent way to show sincere and friendly intentions.[86]

With all these activities involving a great deal of contact with the more prominent African Americans, it is not surprising that some converted to the Bahá'í Faith. When this happened, it was often a stimulus for the Bahá'ís to more closely examine their own prejudices, unconscious as they might have been, because the African American Bahá'ís prominent in the field of race relations caused the Bahá'ís to become aware of the attitudes that they considered to be racist. One such person was Samuel Allen, industrial secretary of the New York Urban League, who called on the Bahá'ís to stop using "colored" for African Americans as this was a derogatory term. Therefore, part of the purpose of the race relations effort made by the Bahá'ís was to spread their religion and increase the number of their converts. However, the more successful they became, the more they were stimulated to alter their opinions and attitudes toward racial minorities; and thus, they were motivated to become less prejudiced. This effect was counterbalanced by the increasing number of whites who became Bahá'ís, some of whom found it difficult to practice the Bahá'í doctrine of racial equality. Nevertheless, the Bahá'í community as a whole was considerably stronger and more willing to fully accept the doctrine of racial amity in its community life.[87]

This theme was echoed in one of Shoghi Effendi's letters written on his behalf by his secretary, Ruhi Afnan, to an American on December 18, 1930:

> As to the racial aspects of your work Shoghi Effendi believes that no chances should be lost, for the Master stressed constantly the importance of reconciling

> the Negro and white people of North America. This field of service, not only attracts the attention of innumerable persons to the Cause, but also furthers one of the ideals of the Faith, namely the abolition of racial prejudice. [88]

Samuel Allen was present at the race amity session at Green Acre, Maine, in August 1931. He recommended that lectures go beyond race amity. Further, race amity was more than just the black-white divide. He wanted Japanese, Chinese, and Jews to be present at these conferences. He suggested having courses about literature written by blacks. Annie Lewis (a black Bahá'í) noted that no African American delegate had been elected to attend the national convention in 1930. If Bahá'ís, she stated, did not integrate the entire administration, there was little difference between them and Christians who had separate churches. Bahá'ís needed to practice what they preached. Louise Thompson related her notes from her recent trip to visit Shoghi Effendi. According to her, Shoghi Effendi wanted the white Bahá'ís to invite African Americans into their homes "and not be afraid of criticism."[89] At the same conference, E. B. M. Dewing also spoke of what Shoghi Effendi told him when he had visited Haifa. Shoghi Effendi wanted children to play with those of other races in sports.[90]

One of the ultimate, most important goals of the Bahá'í Faith is to create a society "in which the flame of racial animosity will have been finally extinguished."[91] In order to accomplish this, more and more Bahá'ís were concentrating their propagation efforts in the South, especially Orcella Rexford, Elizabeth Greenleaf, Alma and Fanny Knobloch, Rowena Powell, Dr. Walter Guy, and, of course, Louis Gregory.[92] For several years, Shoghi Effendi had expressed the desire for biracial teams to propagate the Bahá'í Faith in the South. By 1931, the Bahá'ís and the Bahá'í communities were mature enough to accept this radical step in the development of their community life, even though interracial meetings were still generally not possible in the South. One such mixed team comprised Philip Marangella (white) and Chauncey Northern (black), who spent two weeks in the District of Columbia; Baltimore; Richmond, Virginia; Columbia and Orangeburg, South Carolina; and Enfield, North Carolina. They spoke mostly at universities and colleges, both black and white, although at some white universities, only Marangella could speak.[93]

A second biracial team consisted of Willard McKay (white) and Louis Gregory (black), who toured for eighteen days in early December. They traveled "by motor busses, eating together and most of the time sharing the same room, in their social relations thus running counter to all the traditions of their environment, yet without a single unpleasant incident to mar the harmony and usefulness of their trip. . . ."[94] Before McKay joined Gregory, Gregory had already spoken to the students and faculty of Randolph-Macon College for white women in Lynchburg, Virginia, as well as at Bennett College, a school for black women in Greensboro, North Carolina. He had also given talks at the Atlanta School of Social Services, and addressed the interracial committee of the City of Atlanta, the students of three black colleges, and some clergymen at an interracial meeting at the First Congregational Church.[95]

McKay and Gregory left from Atlanta for their trip. The first stop was three days at the Tuskegee Institute in Alabama, where they held seven meetings, including one with about 1800 attendees. The next location was Montgomery, Alabama, and then Normal, Alabama. McKay and Gregory spoke at the State Institute for Colored Youth at Normal shortly after the school had suffered a brutal case of racial violence. Two of the Institute's teachers had been severely beaten by some whites: "One was knocked senseless for a day or two and the other died in a few hours as a result of his injuries."[96] They continued on to Fisk University in Nashville, Tennessee. Although there had been many interracial meetings there, it was still so unusual for a black man and a white man to be together that at one of the meetings a child asked her mother why a "colored and white man" were traveling together.[97] While in Nashville, McKay and Gregory also spoke at a high school and a state normal school. The next city on the trip was Louisville, Kentucky, where two meetings were held in a black church. Then came Cincinnati, Ohio, for a public meeting, and where McKay and Gregory spoke to a sociology class at the University of Cincinnati. Finally, they left for Columbus, Ohio, which was the end of their trip.[98]

It is true that there were no unfortunate incidents as a result of these biracial teams traveling to propagate the Bahá'í Faith, but it should be noted that none of them entered Mississippi. They also scrupulously avoided breaking any of the many segregation laws that were formally enforced; at times an accommodation could be made. Nevertheless, one just needs to remember what happened to the integrated teams sent on the Freedom Rides in the 1960s to understand what the Bahá'ís were risking. In the 1930s, violence against African Americans and those who supported full equality remained a serious problem in the United States.

The Great Depression forced the Bahá'í assemblies to think creatively about how to foster the Bahá'í principle of racial unity. The first method was to move responsibility for organizing the work to the local level. This was an important way for local Bahá'í institutions to develop further multicultural, administrative, and organizational skills in order to plan and implement local activities. Second, local communities focused on systematically reaching out to their local African American leaders. These were smaller activities than the race amity conferences, and they were sometimes quite audacious and considerably more effective in working toward the ultimate aim for the Bahá'ís, which was the eradication of racial prejudice. This work also helped the Bahá'ís to better understand the principle of race amity and strive to embrace it, which attracted African Americans to convert to the Bahá'í Faith. In the West, this work was advancing with the Asian population as well. Both administrative and multicultural capacity were rapidly developing through the race amity efforts.

RACE AMITY: NATIONAL EFFORTS FROM 1932–1936

In April 1932, an independent National Race Amity Committee (in terms of the budget) was once again appointed but with minimal funding due to the Depression. They had one hundred dollars to work with.[99] This meant that the committee could not hold any public events and needed to be creative in engaging in the necessary work. The most effective way to do this was working with the local spiritual assemblies. On October 31, 1932, the National Spiritual Assembly explained that the committee needed to offer the local spiritual assemblies concrete suggestions for successfully engaging in race amity work.[100] Although Alain Locke was no longer on the committee, he continued supporting its work. For example, he spoke at the New York City December 1932 race amity conference planned with the Urban League, which was advertised as being solely organized by the Urban League.[101]

By the year 1933–1934, the National Race Amity Committee was deeply involved in promoting race amity both outside and inside the Bahá'í community. The committee also offered suggestions to the National Spiritual Assembly. In 1933, it recommended that race amity matters be prominent (as opposed to incidental) in the National Spiritual Assembly's agenda, in the annual meeting to elect the National Spiritual Assembly, and in the annual meetings to choose the membership of local spiritual assemblies. Local spiritual assemblies should help their communities see that race amity was not a distant ideal, but something to be implemented in everyone's daily lives. Local communities should hold at least one annual race amity conference to be followed by multiple smaller activities in which more intimate relations could be established.[102]

On March 17, 1934, Shoghi Effendi wrote:

> The question of prejudice is a very important one. We should not expect a new believer to be free from every prejudice. It would be asking too much from him. For even a believer cannot claim to have such a station. The main thing on which much stress must be laid when accepting a new member into the community is sincerity and a willingness to discard as much as possible all forms of prejudice and bigotry. More than that we cannot do.[103]

With this quotation in mind, the National Race Amity Committee gave the Bahá'ís five ideas for their work. One was to continue holding local race amity conferences, as this method was suggested by 'Abdu'l-Bahá and was the best known one at that time to advance racial harmony. The second was to use different formats for these conferences, such as roundtable discussions during which people could share their experiences and interact socially. The third suggestion emphasized the implementation of the principle of the oneness of humanity in all Bahá'í activities. The fourth recommended following the practice of other liberal groups and arrange for blacks to stay in the same hotels as the whites, whenever hotels were necessary for meetings. The final one was to include the youth on local Race Amity Committees and inform liberal-minded groups of meetings that were organized by the Bahá'í youth. The National Race Amity Committee ended its proposal with the following advice:

> The matter of racial adjustment in all seriousness appears to be the outstanding problem of American life. For this the Religion of Bahá'u'lláh furnishes the program, methods and means which will make such an adjustment possible. It cultivates the ideals of justice, wisdom, love, patience, guidance, service and joyousness, which make such a realization practicable, as a menace to no one, as favor for all. To this end the teachings on racial amity should be tactfully and wisely, but never tediously or with the force of insistence, held both before friends and the outer world, and at the same time demonstrated in action. Thus may the circle of harmony be complete and that unity which is near to God and the reality of man become an accomplished fact.[104]

The National Race Amity committee decided that a special, intense effort should now be made since economic conditions were aggravating the social situation. After its consultation via correspondence with the National Spiritual Assembly, it suggested that Bahá'í communities make a special effort to attract African American leaders, and if there were no local black Bahá'ís, then the communities should consult with non-Bahá'í African Americans in their work for racial amity. The committee wanted the Bahá'í communities to arrange for blacks to speak to non-Bahá'í white audiences, as this would advance race amity work. The National Race Amity Committee expressed that it would also be productive to discuss other Bahá'í principles at these meetings, and the local spiritual assemblies should study how non-Bahá'í African Americans in the city or town could best be served, because it is when society is under stress that oppressed minorities feel the most pressure. Last, the National Race Amity Committee hoped that there would be frank discussion during the Nineteen Day Feast on race relations.[105] The Committee ended with the following plea:

> Strengthening the bond of mutual appreciation and good will between the races is our goal. As an aid to this may it not be reasonable to hope that each racial group will strive to remove within its own ranks whatever prejudices exist. Prejudices are both interracial and intraracial. Distinctions based upon unrealities have no standing either in modern science or in pure religion. The difficulties involved in our own advancements should make us patient over the slow yet certain progress toward universal results. While it is clear that rank based upon merit is essential to the order of the world, yet divisions that signify less than worth are symptoms of a sick world. A consistent attitude on the basis of faith, of freedom from bias, brings joy to the individual, efficiency to the group and harmony to mankind. Blindness to praiseworthy effort with concentration upon mere shortcomings tends to deepen veils and delay relief. The approach of the amity worker should be that of the kind physician rather than the crusader. He becomes a channel for the pure health which the Spirit of Truth brings to all. Those who harbor prejudices and other attitudes inimical to unity and progress, owe it to their own better natures as well as to humanity to forsake them. On the other hand those victimized by such reactions of pride or tradition will find much solace in cultivating mental and spiritual gifts which draw even the opposer.
>
> When we contemplate the tragic injustices of the world, let us recall with reverent gratitude the fact that in the blessed Cause of Bahá'u'lláh all prejudice and discrimination does not exist. Our highest contribution, then is to extend the ranks of believers, adding new souls of all races as confirmed believers, that the power of Bahá'í example may be multiplied throughout America.[106]

On January 27, 1935, Shoghi Effendi again raised his expectations for the American Bahá'í community:

> In regard to your question concerning the nature and character of Bahá'í marriage . . . your statement to the effect that the principle of the oneness of mankind prevents any true Bahá'í from regarding race itself as a bar to union is in complete accord with the Teachings of the Faith on this point. For both Bahá'u'lláh and 'Abdu'l-Baha never disapproved of the idea of inter-racial marriage, nor discouraged it. The Bahá'í Teachings, indeed, by their very nature transcend all limitations imposed by race, and as such can and should never be identified with any particular school of racial philosophy.[107]

The American Bahá'í community was now called upon to come to grips with the fullest implication of race unity: interracial marriage. The Bahá'ís seemed ready to accept the challenge. The 1934 annual National Convention had called for the National Spiritual Assembly to appeal "for greater and more effective action to improve race relations."[108] This task was given to the National Race Amity Committee, which composed a long letter to the Bahá'ís early in 1935.

This letter from the National Race Amity Committee began by re-establishing that the purpose of the Bahá'í Faith was to unite humanity. 'Abdu'l-Bahá was given as the example all Bahá'ís should follow; he served and taught both races in public and private meetings. Shoghi Effendi, through his letters and pilgrims to the Bahá'í World Centre, also encouraged the Bahá'ís to work toward racial harmony. The National Race Amity Committee noted that scientists taught the oneness of humanity, such as Professor A. E. Steinard of Grinnell University in his book *Against the Current.* A Bahá'í's basis for belief in race amity needed to be solidly grounded in science, especially a field that had been "lighted by the Hand of God,"[109] and efforts were needed to ensure that it became the basis of great spiritual strength because Americans were looking for guidance.

The National Race Amity Committee concluded that what needed to be done was quite clear. Each local spiritual assembly could have a local Race Amity Committee responsible for organizing local race amity conferences, with the help of the national committee, if necessary. The committee recommended that conferences follow the general plan of the National Teaching Committee for organizing conferences, since these had proven so successful, with the subject being, instead, race amity. The National Race Amity Committee published pamphlets for distribution at these local conferences. Each conference needed to be followed by smaller meetings with the goal of cultivating conversations on the Bahá'í Faith. The local conferences could include a question-answer period, refreshments, and even a dinner. The National Race Amity Committee noted that it expected to reprint literature on race amity, but new authors were needed. In larger communities, local amity conferences could also be followed up by courses on race relations, similar to those offered at universities and by certain progressive organizations. This was being considered for the Green Acre Race Amity Conference. Further, Bahá'ís were asked to keep themselves well informed by reading scientific books on the race question that illuminated the Bahá'í perspective, for example those by Franz Boas, H. G. Wells, and W. E. B. Du Bois. The Bahá'í Writings would, of course, remain the basis of all study, but other works could be studied to complement the Bahá'í texts. All the Bahá'ís should, in a sense, become human welfare workers and take a firm and courageous stand to teach, by theory and practice, better race relations.

The National Race Amity committee continued in its letter to local spiritual assemblies that non-Bahá'í speakers could be invited to give talks at the local conferences, but that the spiritual assemblies must be cautious because any statement made during the conference would logically be imputed to the Bahá'í Faith. Therefore, in meetings with non-Bahá'í speakers, there should be a Bahá'í chair and a Bahá'í speaker to follow non-Bahá'í ones. In the conferences, no set rules should be given as to how African Americans and other minorities could attain equal status with whites, except for the Golden Rule as restated by Bahá'u'lláh, "If thou lookest toward justice, choose for others what thou choosest for thyself."[110] The Bahá'ís needed to realize that color differences were an accident of birth; God only meant them as ornamentation, not as a division. The image in Bahá'í Scripture is a garden with multihued and shaped flowers. Above all, the Bahá'ís were to avoid all issues that could create disunity, for example discussing the negative aspects of the race issue and "the real or supposed shortcomings of races."[111] Rather, a positive presentation would "[c]orrectly appraise and value the virtues and services of other races, thus inspiring a similar attitude on the part of those so regarded."[112] Another approach was to "use every means upon the basis of education, business, sociology and religion to overcome the superstitions, fancies, prejudices and pride which create those divisions which always go with artificial standards."[113] Most of all, the Bahá'ís needed, "[t]o rest assured that faith and sincerity and effort must inevitably bring success."[114]

The National Race Amity Committee suggested that those who were interested in actively working toward race amity should join community organizations, such as the NAACP, the Urban League, and the black YWCA or YMCA, and attend the meetings that they sponsored, for it was there that the Bahá'ís would meet African Americans and learn to appreciate them, their culture, their problems, and their accomplishments. The Bahá'ís could then invite the people they met to their homes for receptions, teas, conferences, or anything else that was organized, the goal being not only to propagate the Bahá'í Faith, but also to overcome prejudice. Bahá'ís could attend dinners where other races were present. Sitting together, the National Race Amity Committee stated, eating together, and talking with each other all help to create friendships. Further, in smaller communities, showing kindness to African Americans would greatly advance race amity efforts. In summary, the National Race Amity Committee counseled service toward those of other races with a prayerful and joyful attitude, and above all, a spirit of happiness and a sense of humor.[115]

The advice, suggestions, and encouragement on the part of the National Race Amity Committee were successful. For example, in 1935, a public meeting was held in Nashville for race amity. It was the first time that an integrated audience had been allowed in the large ballroom of the city's leading hotel.[116] Also in 1935, the San Francisco Local Spiritual Assembly became the first one in the United States to have among its nine members, men, women, blacks, whites, and Americans of Asian descent.[117]

In September 1935, the National Race Amity Committee, at the request of the National Spiritual Assembly, organized a survey of all Bahá'ís to determine their views on race amity. It distributed a questionnaire to each local spiritual assembly asking if race adjustment was easy or difficult for Bahá'ís in their community. If it was not, why? Was it because of individuals or everyone? How did the Bahá'ís feel about "alien races"? What did the local race amity committee do? Did it function properly? Did it cooperate with the local spiritual assembly? Did it want race amity literature or a teacher or speaker?[118]

Between 1932 and 1936, the National Race Amity Committee's primary role was one of support and guidance for the local Bahá'í communities. Based on what it had learned over the last decades, it strongly encouraged the Bahá'ís to increase their race amity efforts and to consult about topics that were uncomfortable for the average American. In a move that separated Bahá'ís from every other religious group, Shoghi Effendi clearly stated that if Bahá'ís were going to be true to their religion, they must support interracial marriage. The National Race Amity Committee also promoted interracial social activities. The American Bahá'ís were far advanced in instilling a multicultural ethos in their communities. From this period on, Alain Locke was no longer a member of the National Race Amity Committee. Louis Gregory was and he continued to correspond with Locke. Locke did, albeit at a much lighter pace, continue with his Bahá'í activities.[119]

RACE AMITY: LOCAL MEANS TO IMPLEMENT NATIONAL ADMINISTRATIVE POLICY

All the local spiritual assemblies responded to the National Race Amity Committee's questionnaire, which demonstrates how much these local institutions had developed, including in their commitment to improving race relations. Most spiritual assemblies reported that they did the work and not a local race amity committee, and that there were generally good race relations in their city or town, and problems were rare. This demonstrates a certain naivety in local Bahá'í communities. Lynchings continued. Discrimination in employment and housing was a problem during the Depression. African Americans were somewhat optimistic about New Deal policies, but quite realistic. For example, they understood the discrimination behind the 1935 National Labor Relations Act.

The National Race Amity Committee's questionnaire showed that every local spiritual assembly held a race unity meeting of some kind. The National Race Amity Committee had sent pamphlets to each local assembly. The main race amity teacher for these meetings remained Louis Gregory. Perhaps most important was that the Bahá'ís reported that they were meeting with less opposition to their race amity efforts.[120] According to the responses to the questionnaire, the means used by the local spiritual assemblies to implement the policies and suggestions of Shoghi Effendi, the National Spiritual Assembly, and the National Race Amity Committee varied.

The banquet in New York City in honor of the NAACP and the Urban League became an annual event. Gregory reported that Locke continued to promote race amity work. In 1932, at least in the major cities, race amity conferences and meetings were regular activities, and often took place on a large scale. Further, the meetings demonstrated a more social tone; for example, there were an increasing number of interracial dinners. In New York City, a musical with African music was organized at the Harlem branch of the New York City Public Library.[121] In 1933, the Bahá'í community of Chicago, at least, attended meetings of other groups working toward race amity and held their own meetings. As a result, the other groups invited Bahá'í speakers to their meetings, and good newspaper publicity was received.[122]

The answers also revealed that race amity work in universities continued, especially in Urbana, at the University of Illinois.[123] By 1934, the race amity work had spread to many towns, and the southern Bahá'ís were also trying their best to engage in this work.[124] The Bahá'ís were, again, at the forefront in treating even the most controversial of the race issues, for example, the problem of apartheid in South Africa, which was discussed at the 1934 Green Acre Amity Conference.[125] As a result, the Bahá'ís received excellent newspaper coverage in the three best known African American weeklies, *the Chicago Defender, the Pittsburgh Courier,* and *the Amsterdam News.*[126] In 1934, Robert Abbott, the editor of *the Chicago Defender*, converted to the Bahá'í Faith, and this helped the Bahá'ís obtain better newspaper publicity. Eventually there was a weekly column on the Bahá'í Faith in his newspaper.[127]

Some people continued to devote themselves to propagating the Bahá'í Faith in the South, notably Elizabeth Greenleaf, Louis Gregory, Dr. Walter Guy, one of the Knobloch sisters, and Dr. Stanwood Cobb.[128] Loulie Mathews, in 1932, traveled extensively in the West promoting race amity. Gregory, from April 1932 to April 1933, traveled to the South with a white Bahá'í, C. A. Wragg,[129] from Australia. They visited eleven cities in Virginia.[130] Due to the trips by white and black teams, and to the Bahá'ís who had moved to the South to settle, with the express purpose of propagating the Bahá'í Faith there, numerous professors in black colleges became Bahá'ís, and these new recruits further advanced the spread of the Bahá'í Faith among African Americans in academic circles.[131]

CONCLUSION

The Bahá'í Faith played a part, albeit small, in the progressive change toward racial equality, as the Bahá'ís and Bahá'í institutions were quite public and highly vocal in their stand for racial harmony, especially to the leaders of the African American community. The Bahá'í population was also small; in

1926, it had about 1700 adherents; in 1936, about 3000.[132] If nothing else, African American leaders received constant, badly needed encouragement from a majority white Bahá'í community in their ongoing struggle to be recognized as equal. There were problems in integrating African American Bahá'ís into Bahá'í community life, especially in the South, due to the Jim Crow laws that enforced the segregation of whites and blacks.[133] In the South, it was also difficult for whites to teach blacks the Bahá'í Faith for personal as well as social reasons, but these were problems that the National Spiritual Assembly helped the Bahá'ís overcome, based on guidance from Shoghi Effendi and with the aid of the National Race Amity Committee, of which Alain Locke was a member for most of the time period under consideration. The Bahá'í community was slowly becoming able to manifest its beliefs, no matter how different they were from those of the rest of American society, and no matter how much it was different from that society. As the Bahá'í community continued to work for race amity, its efforts were increasingly opposed by elements of American society.[134]

The American Bahá'í community and its institutions employed numerous strategies to achieve the race amity goals during the period being examined. To date, the ones that have attracted the most attention among academic researchers are the race amity conferences or conventions. This chapter briefly explored some of the other strategies that were used: interracial dinners; newspaper articles in the white and black press; itinerate teachers talking about racial amity; articles in the Bahá'í media to help the Bahá'ís understand the principle of racial amity; appointing a biracial membership to national and local committees; engaging in outreach in colleges, black churches and to the NAACP, the Urban League, and to integrated youth groups; letter writing; personal transformation; local activities for race amity; promoting interracial meetings; forming interracial teams to proclaim racial amity in the South; and promoting interracial marriage.

The American Bahá'í institutions developed and evolved in the multitude of efforts engaged in to achieve race amity. The race amity conferences, as they spread across the country, required significant organizational capacity. The Bahá'ís around the United States needed to become expert not only at event planning and management, but also in public relations and in outreach to the academic world, church leaders, and prominent African Americans. Improved public relations skills were leveraged to establish working relations with the white and black press. As their experience developed, the Bahá'í institutions learned how to foster relationships with academics and to reach out to college students. Planning the travel itineraries and logistics for the large number of individuals who crisscrossed the country promoting racial amity required increased fundraising skills, and the ability to plan and organize the events for the visits. The more experienced ones, such as Louis

Gregory, sometimes visited African American churches and organizations and organized their own meetings, but often the local Bahá'ís did all or most of the organizational work for these traveling teachers. This included hosting the traveler, publicity, and outreach to local African American leaders. Experience was garnered in appointing and supervising racial amity committees at the national and local levels. The institutions learned to work with individuals to nurture personal transformation. Local spiritual assemblies gained administrative experience in planning and organizing a wide variety of race amity events and projects. At the national level, Bahá'ís learned about publishing pamphlets, position papers, and articles by writing about race amity. Finally, the concerted effort to promote the Bahá'í principle of race amity required developing increased collaboration between national and local institutions.

The focus on race amity also helped the American Bahá'í community develop a cultural ethos that today we call multiculturalism. Alain Locke named it cultural pluralism. It can reasonably be argued that Locke's intellectual work was influenced by his Bahá'í belief. This chapter has described the Bahá'í context for Locke's philosophy. Yet, a great deal more research is needed to determine how much that context influenced Locke. The full correspondence between Louis Gregory and Locke remains to be located. An examination of the role of Locke in the Bahá'í race amity work, including his active participation in Bahá'í administration, his other Bahá'í activities, and his relationships with Bahá'ís, are all important areas for future research.

The process of the American Bahá'í community achieving an understanding of multiculturalism in theory and in deed started with 'Abdu'l-Bahá and Shoghi Effendi. They progressively educated the Bahá'ís on the teachings of their religion related to race amity. The race amity conferences liberally included African American music and other cultural elements; topics of serious concern to African Americans were treated and discussed. In attempts to engage in this work, numerous forays were made into African American society to meet people, especially in churches, the Urban League and the NAACP. Religious meetings for the purposes of fostering unity were held that evolved into interracial social meetings so that whites and blacks could learn more about each other and become friends. Blacks and whites slept in each other's homes. Interracial marriage was encouraged. To a certain extent, in the western United States, the effort included Asian Americans. The full impact of this work on African American history is a study that has yet to be written. Rich local archives have not yet been touched, including those of the Urban League and NAACP.

In 1936, the Bahá'í community of the United States was now ready to embark, with Canada, on the first international Bahá'í propagation plan, the Seven Year Plan (1937–1944), in which the Bahá'ís had been assigned by Shoghi Effendi, among other goals, to establish the Bahá'í Faith throughout the Americas. As the Bahá'ís launched this new stage of their work, Shoghi Effendi did not leave them in doubt as to the importance of race amity:

> The unity of the human race, as envisaged by Bahá'u'lláh, implies the establishment of a world commonwealth in which all nations, races, creeds and classes are closely and permanently united. . . .[135]
>
> The recrudescence of religious intolerance, of racial animosity, and of patriotic arrogance. . . . [T]hese appear as the outstanding characteristics of a decadent society, a society that must either be reborn or perish.[136]

The race amity work over the years had been excellent training for the multicultural and racial awareness needed to succeed in propagating the Bahá'í Faith in Latin America. Further, the organizational and administrative skills developed to successfully engage in the race amity work were crucial in achieving the goals of the Seven Year Plan. Although building the Bahá'í temple on the shores of Lake Michigan was primarily responsible for the development of administrative skills and capacity,[137] the race amity work was also, secondarily, responsible. Therefore, in training the Bahá'ís to be multiculturally and racially aware and in enhancing their administrative skills, the race unity work had a lasting impact. The task falls on future scholars to examine local Bahá'í and African American archives to develop a more comprehensive picture of how planning and organizing race unity activities and events aided in the maturation of Bahá'í administrative institutions, helped African American activists, and shaped Alain Locke.

NOTES

1. Christopher Buck, *Alain Locke: Faith and Philosophy* (Los Angeles: Kalimát Press, 2005), 22.

2. For a discussion on Locke's pivotal role in the development of cultural pluralism, see David Weinfeld, "What Difference Does Difference Make? Horace Kallen, Alain Locke, and the Birth of Cultural Pluralism," in *Philosophic Values and World Citizenship*, eds. Jacoby Adeshei Carter and Leonard Harris (Lanham, MD: Lexington, 2010), 165–187.

3. Christopher Buck's *Alain Locke: Faith and Philosophy* is the best analysis to date in understanding the influence of the Bahá'í Faith on Alain Locke. Future scholars will be able to build on it. Three other works also attempt to include the Bahá'í Faith in their analysis of Locke, but do not see his religion as integral to the development of his philosophy: Two of them are Leonard Harris and Charles Molesworth, *Alain L. Locke: Biography of a Philosopher* (Chicago: University of Chicago Press, 2008) and Johnny Washington, *A Journey into the Philosophy of Alain Locke* (Westport, CT: Greenwood Press, 1994). The third, Jeffrey Stewart's *The New Negro: The*

Life of Alain Locke (New York: Oxford University Press, 2018) goes the furthest in integrating Locke's adherence to the Bahá'í Faith into his analysis, but it remains only as paragraphs in a nine-hundred-page book.

4. Buck, *Alain Locke: Faith and Philosophy*, 73–74. For more on the debate over Locke's role and importance in African American history, see, for example, Michelle Smith, "Alain Locke: Culture and the Plurality of Black Life," PhD diss. Cornell University, 2009, https://ecommons.cornell.edu/bitstream/handle/1813/14009/Smith,%20Michelle.pdf?sequence=1, David Weinfeld, "What Difference Does the Difference Make? Horace Kallen, Alain Locke, and the Development of Cultural Pluralism in America," PhD diss. New York University, 2014, http://pqdtopen.proquest.com/doc/1615089470.html?FMT=ABS, and Daniele Fiorentino, "Multiculturalism and the Legacy of Cultural Pluralism," *RSA Journal* 20 (2009), http://www.aisna.net/sites/default/files/rsa/rsa20/20fiorentino.pdf. Louis Gregory (1874–1951) was quite unusual for the era. His wife (Louisa) was an English white woman, so they could not be seen together in several states, unless he wished to be imprisoned, if not killed. He was one of the "talented tenth," having graduated from Fisk University and Howard University's law school. For more information on Louis Gregory, see Gayle Morrison, *To Move the World: Louis G. Gregory and the Advancement of Racial Unity in America* (Wilmette, IL: Bahá'í Publishing Trust, 1982).

5. It is clear, and I have argued, that the building of the Chicago House of Worship (Temple) was the most important factor in developing the American Bahá'í community and its administrative order. In addition, many other events, efforts, and activities helped in this development, but this does not detract from underscoring the importance of the race amity efforts in this evolution. For more on how building the Temple was crucial in the evolution of the American Bahá'í community, see Loni Bramson-Lerche, "Some Aspects of the Development of the Bahá'í Administrative Order in America, 1922–1936," in *Studies in Bábí and Bahá'í History*, vol. 1, ed. Moojan Momen (Los Angeles: Kalimát Press, 1982), 255–300, 321–324. The United States Bahá'í community engaged in its first systematic international propagation from 1937 to 1944 in Latin America. After World War II, these efforts spread to Europe. In 1953, the entire Bahá'í community embarked on a "World Crusade." Academic analyses of these efforts are still lacking but are starting to be published. For example, see Ali Nakhjavani, "The Ten Year Crusade," *The Journal of Bahá'í Studies* 14, nos. 3–4 (2004), http://bahai-studies.ca/wp-content/uploads/2014/03/14.3-4.Nakhjavani1.pdf.

6. This committee was called by several names over the years: Interracial Amity Committee, National Interracial Amity Committee, Inter-Racial Amity Committee, National Interracial Committee, Interracial National Committee, and National Race Amity Committee. In this essay, to avoid confusion, it will uniformly be called the National Race Amity Committee, which is how it was called toward the end of the period being studied.

7. Haifa, Israel, is the location of the Bahá'í World Centre.

8. Notes by Edward C. Getsinger, Archives of the Spiritual Assembly of the Bahá'ís of Portland, Oregon (hereafter cited as Portland Archives). At this time, the term actually used for anything related to African Americans was "colored." Edward

C. Getsinger (1866–1935) was a prominent early American Bahá'í. He was a homeopath and earned his living giving lectures. Willard P. Hatch, "Edward Christopher Getsinger," in "In Memoriam," 493–496, *The Bahá'í World* 6 (1937; repr., Wilmette, IL: Bahá'í Publishing Trust, 1980). No analysis is made as to the accuracy of these notes. Their importance lies in how widely they were distributed. For more on the situation in Washington, DC, and a more accurate rendering of 'Abdu'l-Bahá's position on race relations, see Gayle Morrison, *To Move the World: Louis G. Gregory and the Advancement of Racial Unity in America* (Wilmette, IL: Bahá'í Publishing Trust, 1982) and Louis Venters, *No Jim Crow Church: The Origins of South Carolina's Bahá'í Community* (Gainsville, FL: University of Florida Press, 2015). Some might argue that the misunderstanding was not about the elemental Bahá'í principle of the oneness of humanity, but, rather, how it should be implemented. How the Bahá'í administrative bodies dealt with clear misunderstandings about the equality of the races will be discussed later in the chapter. To help Western Bahá'ís better understand the Bahá'í position on race, 'Abdu'l-Bahá sent the Persian Bahá'í teacher Mirza Assadu'llah Fadil Mazandarani (Jenabe Fazel; also transliterated as Jinab-i-Fazel depending on the era; both will be used) to the United States to help educate the Bahá'ís in this basic doctrine and other aspects of the Bahá'í Faith. Jinab-i-Fazel (d. 1957) was a leading scholar of the Bahá'í Faith, and entrusted by 'Abdu'l-Bahá to complete numerous sensitive missions. Fazel traveled across the continent. As part of his program, he spoke on the foundational Bahá'í principle that there should be no prejudices. During his trip, he spent a week in Portland, Oregon, in February 1921, and while there lectured to the Oregon Social Workers' Association on "Racial Antagonisms and International Justice." Public flyer of Jenabe Fazel's series of lectures, Portland Archives. Oregon, in the 1920s, was a hotbed of the Ku Klux Klan. See, for instance, Eckard Toy, "Ku Klux Klan," *The Oregon Encyclopedia*, https://oregonencyclopedia.org/articles/ku_klux_klan/#.WXugR62ZNBw.

9. The first race amity conference was held in May 1921 in Washington, DC. Louis G. Gregory, "Teaching Activity Serving Race Unity," in *The Bahá'í Centenary, 1844–1944*, compiled by the National Spiritual Assembly of the Bahá'ís of the United States and Canada (Wilmette, IL: Bahá'í Publishing Trust, 1944), 202–203. For analysis of this conference, see Christopher Buck, "The Baha'i 'Race Amity' Movement and the Black Intelligentsia in Jim Crow America: Alain Locke and Robert S. Abbott," *Baha'i Studies Review* 17 (2011): 3–46, https://bahai-library.com/pdf/b/buck_race_amity_movement.pdf.

10. Charles L. Young (1864–1922) was the third African American to graduate from West Point, achieving the rank of Colonel. He was friends with W. E. B. Du Bois. Barbara Bair, "Though Justice Sleeps," in *To Make Our World Anew: A History of African Americans from 1880*, eds. Robin D. G. Kelley and Earl Lewis (Oxford: Oxford University Press, 2005), 52. For more information, see Brian G. Shellum, *Black Cadet in a White Bastion: Charles Young at West Point* (Lincoln: University of Nebraska Press, 2006), or David Kilroy, *For Race and Country: The Life and Career of Colonel Charles Young* (Westport, CT: Praeger, 2003). The National Bahá'í Archives does not yet have a system for detailing when people converted to the Bahá'í Faith before 1932. It is known that Ada Young was a Bahá'í before 1932,

but that is all. Currently, the first known reference to her as a Bahá'í is her activity in the Dayton, Ohio, race amity efforts. "Annual Committee Reports," *Bahá'í News* no. 100 (May 1936), 10 and from the National Bahá'í Archives, United States (herein cited as National Bahá'í Archives), Roger M. Dahl, email message, August 14, 2017.

11. Roy Wilhelm, "Convention for Amity between the White and Colored Races," in *Star of the West* 13, no. 3 (April 1922): 51–55, 60–61 (repr. Oxford: George Ronald, 1978).

12. Letter No. 2 of the Western States Regional Teaching Committee, E. G. Cooper, Chairman, the Spiritual Assemblies and Beloved Friends in the Western Region, Portland Archives. Ella Goodall Cooper (1870–1951) became a Bahá'í in 1898 and was among the first group of Westerners to visit 'Abdu'l-Bahá in what is now Israel. She was one of the founding members of the San Francisco-Oakland Bahá'í communities. For more on Cooper, see "Ella Goodall Cooper," in "In Memoriam," 681–684, *The Bahá'í World* 12 (1956; repr., Willmette, IL: Bahá'í Publishing Trust, 1981). Agnes Parsons (d. 1934) became a Bahá'í while on a visit to 'Abdu'l-Bahá. With guidance from 'Abdu'l-Bahá, she initiated the official race amity work and was a long-time member of the Washington, DC, local Bahá'í administration. Parsons was an active Bahá'í teacher and generously supported various Bahá'í projects financially. For more on Parsons, see her diary, Richard Hollinger, ed., *Agnes Parson's Diary* (Los Angeles: Kalimát Press, 1996).

13. Louis Gregory, letter to the Spiritual Assembly, Portland, Oregon, February 17, 1922, Portland Archives.

14. For more on this, see Morrison, *To Move the World,* 92–95, 217–230.

15. It is not easy to find accurate information about the May or Weed families. What is important to know is that they were white. Of interest is the fact that Howard and Margaret Weed lived in Beaverton, which at the time was a small town about ten miles outside of Portland surrounded by many farms. This further demonstrates the organizational skill required to transport Gregory around the region. National Bahá'í Archives, Roger M. Dahl, email message, September 8, 2016.

16. Again, it is not easy to find information about the Nash family other than that they were white. From the National Bahá'í Archives, Roger M. Dahl, email message, September 8, 2016. The Epworth League is a Methodist organization for youth. The Lincoln-Douglas memorial meeting was probably the annual Lincoln-Douglas banquet meeting or celebration program commemorating the historic debates that helped Lincoln win the presidency.

17. Letter from George Latimer, secretary of the Portland Local Spiritual Assembly to Mariam Haney, secretary of the National Teaching Committee, February 19, 1922, Portland Archives.

18. In this chapter, Louis Gregory's activities will be detailed as an example of the extensive tours that individuals made to promote race amity. This is just one example of all the efforts made. In a letter about purchasing books, Mary Lesch wrote to George Latimer that Louis Gregory was in Chicago and there was significant tension in the African American community due to the creation of a Ku Klux Klan group in Chicago. Mary Lesch, secretary of the Bahá'í Publishing Society to George Latimer, September 8, 1921, Portland Archives.

19. For more information on James Hardy Dillard, see Teri L. Castelow, "James Hardy Dillard," *Dictionary of Virginia Biography*, http://www.lva.virginia.gov/public/dvb/bio.asp?b=Dillard_James_Hardy.

20. Louis Gregory, "The Spirit of the Century: Inter-Racial Amity," *Star of the West* 13, no. 11 (February 1923): 305 (repr., Oxford: George Ronald, 1978).

21. Ibid., 304–305.

22. The explanation of what multiculturalism is varies in time and space. The goal of the Bahá'í Faith is to establish "unity in diversity," all the while respecting the inherent cultural differences of the groups in a society. During the period being studied, whereas the Bahá'ís spoke of unity in diversity as a principle, they were coping with accepting differences. Therefore, multiculturalism is an appropriate term to use.

23. Some of the letters between Locke and Gregory have been located. Buck uses what he could find in his book, *Alain Locke: Faith and Philosophy*. One avenue for future researchers is to locate and analyze more of these letters.

24. One was also held in Montreal.

25. Horace Holley, "Survey of Current Bahá'í Activities in the East and West," *The Bahá'í World* 2 (1928; repr., Wilmette, IL: Bahá'í Publishing Trust, 1980), 21–22.

26. Dr. Randall was a Bahá'í. At this point, Bahá'ís were not yet required to relinquish church membership.

27. In 1931, Jane Addams won the Nobel Peace Prize. Roy Wilhelm (1875–1951) was a long-time member of the National Spiritual Assembly and one of the early East Coast Bahá'ís. He had a successful import business in New York City. For more information, see Horace Holley, "Roy C. Wilhelm," in "In Memoriam," 662–664, *The Bahá'í World* 12. Horace Holley (1887–1960) became a Bahá'í in Paris around 1910. Besides having a keenly analytical mind, he was also a poet and the author of several books and many articles on the Bahá'í Faith. In 1925, he went to work full-time for the National Spiritual Assembly, serving as its elected secretary for many years. Holley was also a member of the New York Local Spiritual Assembly and several national committees. For more information, see Rúhíyyih Rabbani, "Horace Hotchkiss Holley," in "In Memoriam," 849–858, *The Bahá'í World* 13 (Haifa, Israel: The Universal House of Justice, 1970). Mountford Mills (d. 1949) was a lawyer and the primary author of the Declaration of Trust and By-Laws of the National Spiritual Assembly, of which he was a long-time member. He served Shoghi Effendi in resolving legal and diplomatic problems, such as trying to reverse the confiscation of Bahá'u'lláh's house in Baghdad by the government. For more information, see Horace Holley, "Mountfort Mills," in "In Memoriam," 509–511, *The Bahá'í World* 11 (repr., Wilmette, IL: Bahá'í Publishing Trust, 1981).

28. Gregory, "Inter-Racial Amity," 282–283 in *The Bahá'í World* 2. Bahá'ís believe in the harmony of science and religion. During the period under consideration for this chapter, the National Race Amity Committee looked for and shared with the Bahá'ís academic research arguing for the physical and mental equality of the races. This is discussed later in the chapter. See, for example, Keven Brown, ed., *Evolution and Bahá'í Belief: 'Abdu'l-Bahá's Response to Nineteenth-Century Darwinism* (Los Angeles: Kalimát Press, 2001). America's Making, Inc. was an organization that

produced exhibits to highlight the contributions of the nations whose people made up the United States. However, Germany and Asian countries were excluded. Dr. Wise was a prominent rabbi. For more information on him, see, for instance, Robert Donald Shapiro, *A Reform Rabbi in the Progressive Era: The Early Career of Stephen S. Wise* (New York: Garland, 1988). Dr. Das was a Bengali revolutionary political scientist who taught at Columbia University. See Tapan K. Mukherjee, *Taraknath Das: Life and Letters of a Revolutionary in Exile* (Calcutta: National Council of Education, Bengal, Jadavpur University, 1988).

29. The series of World Unity Conferences was another attempt by the National Spiritual Assembly to engage in dialog on important topics of the day with the Bahá'í perspective. They were organized in a similar manner to the Race Amity conferences. J. V. Breitwieser, "A Conference for World Unity at San Francisco, March 20–22, 1925," 97 in *Bahá'í Year Book* 1 (1926; repr. Wilmette, IL: Bahá'í Publishing Trust, 1980). The *Bahá'í Year Book* became *The Bahá'í World.*

30. For information on Hill, see "Leslie Pinckney Hill" by Patsy B. Perry, 200–201, in Joseph M. Flora and Amber Vogel, eds., *Southern Literary Studies: Southern Writers, A New Biographical Dictionary* (Baton Rouge: Louisiana State University Press, 2006). Interestingly, Hill was a student at Harvard at the same time as Horace Kallen. David Weinfeld, "What Difference Does the Difference Make? Horace Kallen, Alain Locke, and the Development of Cultural Pluralism in America" (PhD diss., New York University, 2014), 64, http://pqdtopen.proquest.com/doc/1615089470.html?FMT=ABS. Albert Vail (1880–1966) was a relatively early Chicago Bahá'í. Until his withdrawal from the Bahá'í Faith over differences with the National Spiritual Assembly about who should receive a stipend to teach the Bahá'í Faith, he had been active in Bahá'í propagation efforts as an author and member of the National Teaching Committee, which was responsible for the propagation of the Bahá'í Faith. Siegfried (Fred) Schopflocher (d. 1953) was a wealthy Canadian Bahá'í. For more information, see "Siegfried Schopflocher" in "In Memoriam," 664–666, *The Bahá'í World* 12.

31. The report of his activities ended with him at Fisk University in Nashville, Tennessee. "Work of National Committees," *Bahá'í News Letter*, no. 4 (April 1925), 4. Further research is needed to determine how these activities were planned and who assisted in the planning. This is important information in order to further analyze how the race amity efforts helped develop Bahá'í administrative institutions and multicultural capacity. Access to local archives is important and many of them are not yet available.

32. Program of Meeting at the First AME Zion Church, Portland, Oregon, January 12, 1925. Portland Archives.

33. Letter dated August 5, 1927, from Louis Gregory to Mrs. Charles Reed Bishop. Portland Archives. Further research is needed to determine if the letter-writing campaign was administratively sponsored, who else was involved, and its extent.

34. Letter dated September 9, 1927, from Louis Gregory to Helen (Bishop), Portland Archives.

35. Howard MacNutt (d. 1926) was one of the first New York City Bahá'ís. He was designated "a disciple" of 'Abdu'l-Bahá for his many services. For more on

MacNutt and his wife, Mary, see Robert Stockman, *MacNutt, Howard,* https://bahai-library.com/stockman_macnutt. Louise Boyle was one of the early Washington, DC, Bahá'ís.

36. "News of the Cause," *Bahá'í News Letter*, no. 9 (December 1925 to January 1926), 5–6, and "News of the Cause," *Bahá'í News Letter*, no. 10 (February 1926), 6.

37. "News of the Cause," *Bahá'í News Letter*, no. 9 (December 1925 to January 1926), 6. Walter Guy (d. 1940) immigrated to the United States from England. He practiced medicine in Boston until he moved to St. Augustine, Florida. For more on Walter and Frances (d. 1952) Guy, see Kathryn Vernon, *Baha'u'llah's Garden, Jacksonville, Fla. 1919–1969*. The author thanks Larry Marquardt for sending her a pdf copy of the book, and Don Calkins for providing the year of Frances Guy's death. Further research is required to analyze the intersection of administrative support and the efforts of these race amity workers. Until access is granted to spiritual assembly administrative minutes, detailed analysis is not possible.

38. "News of the Cause," *Bahá'í News Letter*, no. 9 (December 1925 to January 1926), 6 and "News of the Cause," *Bahá'í News Letter*, no. 13 (September 1926), 6. At this point it is not clear who organized and planned this campaign.

39. "Eighteenth Annual Convention of the Baha'is of the United States and Canada," *Bahá'í News Letter*, no. 12 (June to July 1926), 4.

40. "News of the Cause," *Bahá'í News Letter*, no. 9 (December 1925 to January 1926), 6.

41. Buck, *Alain Locke: Faith and Philosophy*, 126.

42. *Bahá'í Year Book*, 102.

43. Stockman, *Macnutt.*

44. "National Committee on Racial Amity Appointed," *Bahá'í News Letter*, no. 16 (March 1927), 5.

45. Shoghi Effendi, *Bahá'í Administration* (Wilmette, IL: Bahá'í Publishing Trust, 1968), 129.

46. This refers to 'Abdu'l-Bahá.

47. Shoghi Effendi, *Bahá'í Administration*, 129–131.

48. "Inter-Racial Amity Conferences," *Bahá'í News Letter*, no. 22 (March 1928), 5; "Inter-Racial Amity Committee Holds Convention in Washington, D. C.," *Bahá'í News Letter,* no. 19 (1927), 2. A conference was also planned in Montreal.

49. "Inter-Racial Amity Conferences," *Bahá'í News Letter*, no. 22 (March 1928), 5.

50. "New Bahá'i Publications," *Bahá'í News Letter*, no. 21 (January 1928), 5. Duncan eventually became a high-ranking member of the Liberian government.

51. "Report of the National Inter-Racial Amity Committee," *Bahá'í News Letter*, no. 17 (April 1927), 12.

52. "Inter-Racial Amity Conferences," *Bahá'í News Letter*, no. 22 (March 1928), 5–6.

53. "Report of the Twenty-First Annual Convention," *Bahá'í News Letter*, no. 32 (May 1929), 3.

54. "Inter-Racial Amity Meetings," *Bahá'í News Letter*, no. 25 (July 1928), 3.

55. "Western Assemblies Combine Material with Spiritual Hospitality," *Bahá'í News Letter*, no. 23 (April 1928), 3.

56. Ibid. "Mr. Louis Gregory's Teaching Activities," *Bahá'í News Letter*, no. 30 (March 1929), 8. While Gregory was concentrating on race amity in America, Shoghi Effendi had asked Gregory's white wife to work to advance the Bahá'í Faith in Eastern Europe. This meant that they rarely saw each other, which was difficult for both of them. Shoghi Effendi never required them to remain separated for such long periods, and he would tell Louisa Gregory that she should return to the United States to see her husband if she truly felt she should, but he always encouraged her to remain in Europe to continue her work there. Why he did this remains a subject for speculation; however, it is a fact that Gregory could not have worked for race amity in many states as he did, especially in the South, if he had been with his wife. It would not have legally been possible. Louisa Mathew (Gregory) was born into a wealthy English family. She attended Cambridge University, and afterwards worked in social services. They married in 1912, upon the encouragement of 'Abdu'l-Bahá. She returned to the United States from her Eastern and Central European propagation work in 1932. For details on Louis and Louisa Gregory's marriage, see Morrison, *To Move the World.*

57. National Interracial Amity Committee to National and local Spiritual Assemblies of the United States and Canada, December 28, 1929. From the National Bahá'í Archives, Roger M. Dahl, email message, August 9, 2017.

58. See Buck, *Alain Locke: Faith and Philosophy*, 73–74. Locke was a member for about eight years in total.

59. For more information on the Bahá'í House of Worship, see Bruce W. Whitmore, *The Dawning Place*, 2nd ed. (Wilmette, IL: Bahá'í Publishing Trust, 2015) and Loni Bramson-Lerche, "Some Aspects of the Development of the Bahá'í Administrative Order in America, 1922–1936."

60. "Report of National Teaching Committee," *Bahá'í News Letter*, no. 34 (October 1929), 6.

61. Program for the Conference for Interracial Amity, November 2, 8, and 9, 1930. From the National Bahá'í Archives, Roger M. Dahl, email message, August 9, 2017.

62. "Racial Amity Forum," *Bahá'í News Letter*, no. 37 (January 1930), 6–7, and Program, Convention for Interracial Amity. From the National Bahá'í Archives, August 1931, Roger M. Dahl, email message, August 9, 2017. Philip Marangella (1874–1974) actively propagated the Bahá'í Faith and supported the race amity work. In 1937, he began Bahá'í international missionary service in Cuba. For more on Marangella, see Ayned Louise McComb, "Philip A. Marangella," in "In Memoriam," 525–527, *The Bahá'í World* 16 (Haifa, Israel: Bahá'í World Centre, 1978).

63. Program, From the National Bahá'í Archives, Roger M. Dahl, email message, August 9, 2017.

64. "Teaching Work of Mr. Gregory," *Bahá'í News Letter*, no. 38 (February 1930), 7.

65. Ibid., "Inter-Racial Work," *Bahá'í News Letter,* no. 35 (November 1929), 7; "Report of Progress From Urbana, Illinois," *Bahá'í News Letter,* no. 38 (February

1930), 3–4; "Interracial Amity Committee," *Bahá'í News Letter,* no. 40 (April 1930), 11; *The Bahá'í World* 3 (1930; repr., Wilmette, IL: Bahá'í Publishing Trust, 1980), 59–60.

66. "Interracial Amity," *Bahá'í News*, no. 41 (May 1930), 3. *Bahá'í News Letter* became *Bahá'í News* in 1930.

67. The Bahá'í administrative year extends from April to April.

68. "Interracial Amity Committee," *Bahá'í News Letter*, no. 40 (1930), 12.

69. Ibid.

70. Ibid., "Letter From Los Angeles Assembly," *Bahá'í News Letter,* no. 38 (1930), 6.

71. Ibid., "Teaching Committee," *Bahá'í News Letter*, no. 40 (1930), 13.

72. Ibid., no. 38 (1930), 7.

73. *The Bahá'í World*, 4, 60. A Baha'i group is when there are fewer than nine adults in a Bahá'í community. Nine adult Bahá'ís are required to form a local spiritual assembly.

74. Loulie Mathews (1869?–1966) became a Bahá'í around 1914. She is best known for her Bahá'í missionary work in Latin America. For more on Mathews, see Marion Little, "Loulie Albee Mathews," in "In Memoriam," 360–362, *The Bahá'í World* 14 (Haifa, Israel: The Universal House of Justice, 1974).

75. "Annual Reports of the National Committee of the National Spiritual Assembly of the Bahá'ís of the United States and Canada, 1931–1932: Report of Racial Amity Committee," *Bahá'í News* no. 62 (May 1932), 8–9; *The Bahá'í World* 4, 60–62. The Citizens Union in this period was a non-partisan watchdog organization for public interests and good government in New York City and State. Mary Hanford Ford (1856–1937) was the wife of the owner and editor of the Kansas City, Missouri, *Evening Mail.* She was an authority on art, literature, and music, and worked as an art critic for the Kansas City *Star.* She became a Bahá'í in the early 1900s. Ford helped propagate the Bahá'í Faith in the United States, Italy, Switzerland, France, and England. For more on Ford, see Rúháníyyih Khánum (Madame 'Alí-Kuli), "Mary Hanford Ford," in "In Memoriam," 541–542, *Bahá'í World* 7 (1939; repr., Wilmette, IL: Bahá'í Publishing Trust, 1980). Hooper Harris (1866–1934) was a lawyer and court reporter. He became a Bahá'í in New York City around 1899. In 1906–1907, he went on a seven-month trip to India to propagate the Bahá'í Faith. He served on the National Teaching Committee and the New York Spiritual Assembly. For more on Harris, see Marie B. Moore, "Hooper Harris," in "In Memoriam," 486–488, *Bahá'í World* 6 (1937; repr., Wilmette, IL: Bahá'í Publishing Trust, 1980).

76. *The Bahá'í World* 4, 60–62; "Feast for White and Colored Children," *Bahá'í News*, no. 48 (February 1931), 5–6.

77. Notes taken of the talk given at the regular weekly meeting, by G. O. Latimer, chairman, July 10, 1931, Portland Archives. No analysis is being made here about the accuracy of Reverend Lovell's remarks or that of the notes of the talk made by George Latimer. These notes were widely distributed among the Bahá'ís. Even with some errors, the frankness of the discussion in 1931 is noteworthy in an interracial meeting. George O. Latimer (d. 1948) was one of the first Bahá'ís in the Pacific Northwest. He served for many years on the National Spiritual Assembly and the

Portland, Oregon, Spiritual Assembly and spent as much time as he could propagating the Bahá'í Faith in the Pacific Northwest and Canada. He also made several trips abroad to spread the Bahá'í Faith. For more on Latimer, see Horace Holley, "George Orr Latimer," in "In Memoriam," 511–512, *The Bahá'í World* 11 (1950; repr., Wilmette, IL: Bahá'í Publishing Trust, 1981).

78. "Committees of the National Spiritual Assembly, 1930–1931," *Bahá'í News*, no. 42 (1930), 2.

79. Ibid., 3; "Bahá'i Contacts in Harlem, New York City," *Bahá'í News* 48 (February 1931), 3.

80. *The Bahá'í World* 4, 66; "Bahá'i Contacts in Harlem, New York City," *Bahá'í News* 48 (February 1931), 4.

81. "New York Amity Conference Reported in Leading Negro Paper," *Bahá'í News*, no. 48 (February 1931), 10.

82. "Bahá'i Contacts in Harlem, New York City," *Bahá'í News*, 48 (February 1931), 4.

83. Ibid.

84. "Annual Reports of the National Committee of the National Spiritual Assembly of the Bahá'ís of the United States and Canada, 1931–1931: Report of Racial Amity Committee," *Bahá'í News*, no. 62 (May 1932), 7–8.

85. In 1937, Shoghi Effendi gave the Bahá'ís of the United States and Canada a seven-year plan to establish the Bahá'í Faith throughout Latin America and the Caribbean, and a local spiritual assembly in every state and province. This was the springboard for the second Seven-Year Plan (1946 to 1953) to spread the Bahá'í Faith in Europe, support the teaching work in Africa, and further the development of the administrative order throughout the Americas.

86. "Reports from Teaching Committee," *Bahá'í News*, no. 49 (March 1931), 6.

87. Determining the success rate the Bahá'ís had with the non-elite African Americans, in terms of conversion, is not yet possible because of the way in which the early Bahá'í communities kept statistics. However, an analysis of photographs of different Bahá'í activities during the period under consideration show a steady increase in the percentage of African Americans in the Bahá'í community until it was proportionate to the number of African Americans in American society at large. A more detailed analysis of these photographs would be an interesting future research project.

88. *The Power of Unity: Beyond Prejudice and Racism*, compiled by Bonnie J. Taylor and National Race Unity Committee (Wilmette, IL: Bahá'í Publishing Trust, 1986), 106–107.

89. E. B. M. Dewing, "Report of Conference Sessions of the Interracial Amity Convention, Green Acre Me. August 21–31, 1931." From the National Bahá'í Archives, Roger M. Dahl, email message, August 9, 2017.

90. Ibid.

91. Shoghi Effendi, *The World Order of Bahá'u'lláh*, 2nd ed. (Wilmette, IL: Bahá'í Publishing Trust, 1974), 41.

92. Orcella Rexford (1887–1946) became a Bahá'í shortly after World War I. She earned her living lecturing across the United States, at the same time propagating the

Bahá'í Faith. Her original name was Louise Cutts-Powell. For more on Rexford, see National Spiritual Assembly of the Bahá'ís of Iraq, "Orcella Rexford" in "In Memoriam," 495–498, *The Bahá'í World* 11 (1950; repr., Wilmette, IL: Bahá'í Publishing Trust, 1981). Elizabeth Greenleaf (d. 1942) became a Bahá'í during the earliest years of the Bahá'í Faith in Chicago. For more on Greenleaf, see Albert R. Windust, "Elizabeth R. Greenleaf" in "In Memoriam," 608, *The Bahá'í World* 9 (1945; repr., Wilmette, IL: Bahá'í Publishing Trust, 1981). Alma (d. 1943) and Fanny Knobloch (d. 1950) became Bahá'ís in 1902 and devoted their lives to propagating the Bahá'í Faith, especially in Germany and Austria for the former, and South Africa for the latter. For more on A. Knobloch, see Rosa Schwartz "Alma Knobloch" in "In Memoriam," 641–643, *The Bahá'í World* 9 (1945; repr., Wilmette, IL: Bahá'í Publishing Trust, 1981). For more on F. Knobloch, see Viola Ioas Tuttle, "Fanny A. Knobloch" in "In Memoriam," 473–476, *The Bahá'í World* 11 (1950; repr., Wilmette, IL: Bahá'í Publishing Trust, 1981). Rowena Powell was a Los Angeles Bahá'í and concentrated most of her many teaching activities in the West. She was an especially effective lecturer.

93. "The Heart of Dixie Teaching Amity in the South," *Bahá'í News*, no. 58 (January 1932), 2–3. Chauncey Northern was a professional singer from Harlem. As with other exceptional African American singers and artists, he had to go to Europe to sing in opera. When he returned to the United States, he became a voice teacher.

94. "The Heart of Dixie Teaching Amity in the South," *Bahá'í News*, no. 58 (January 1932), 3. Willard McKay died in 1966. His wife, Doris, wrote a book about their experiences and lives. Doris McKay and Paul Vreeland, *Fires in Many Hearts* (Manotick, ON: Nine Pines, 1993).

95. Ibid.

96. "The Heart of Dixie Teaching Amity in the South," *Bahá'í News*, no. 58 (January 1932), 3.

97. Ibid.

98. Ibid.

99. Letter dated June 21, 1932 from National Spiritual Assembly to National Committee on Inter-racial Amity. From the National Bahá'í Archives, Roger M. Dahl, email message, August 9, 2017.

100. Letter dated October 31, 1932 from National Spiritual Assembly to Louis Gregory. From the National Bahá'í Archives, Roger M. Dahl, email message, August 9, 2017.

101. Invitation to The Third Annual Inter-Racial Conference of the Industrial Department of the New York Urban League, December 1932. From the National Bahá'í Archives, Roger M. Dahl, email message, August 9, 2017.

102. Letter dated 30 November 1933 from National Baha'i Committee for Racial Amity to National Spiritual Assembly. From the National Bahá'í Archives, Roger M. Dahl, email message, August 9, 2017.

103. "Annual Committee Reports, 1933–1934: Race Amity," *Bahá'í News*, no. 88 (November 1934), 10.

104. Ibid. Emphasis was on African Americans, however, in the West, outreach was made to other ethnic and racial groups. For example, in 1932, members of the Matsura (Japanese Americans) family converted to the Bahá'í Faith in Portland, Oregon. Notes by George O. Latimer, June 15, 1932, Portland Archives.

105. The Nineteen Day Feast is a regular gathering (once every nineteen days) for Bahá'ís to meet together in prayer, discuss community affairs, and share refreshments.

106. "Letter From Inter-Racial Amity Committee," *Bahá'í News*, no. 80 (January 1934), 7.

107. "Instructions and Explanations from Shoghi Effendi," *Bahá'í News*, no. 90 (March 1935), 1.

108. "Divine Call to Race Amity," *Bahá'í News*, no. 90 (March 1935), 4. There are currently no statistics or reports as to whether the number of interracial marriages increased because of this communication. For Bahá'ís, an interracial marriage would also have been between a Persian and a non-Persian. At this time in history, Mexicans and Persians held an ambiguous racial status. Significant immigration on the part of Persians did not start until the 1940s.

109. Ibid., 5–6.

110. Ibid., 7.

111. Ibid.

112. Ibid.

113. Ibid.

114. Ibid.

115. Ibid., 4–7.

116. National Spiritual Assembly, comp., *Bahá'í Centenary*, 170. This chapter does not go to 1937. The Bahá'ís organized another meeting that year in Nashville that was criticized by W. E. B. Du Bois. Chris Buck analyzes this incident. See Christopher Buck, "The Interracial 'Baha'i Movement' and the Black Intelligentsia: The Case of W. E. B. Du Bois."

117. *The Bahá'í World* 6, 669 (photograph). The Portland, Oregon minutes of the Local Spiritual Assembly report a meeting held at the home of the new Japanese Bahá'í, Mrs. Matsura. Portland Archives.

118. National Spiritual Assembly to Race Amity Committee, August 7, 1935. From the National Bahá'í Archives, email Roger Dahl, August 9, 2017. "Annual Committee Reports, 1935–1936: Race Amity," *Bahá'í News*, no. 100 (May 1936), 9–10. It is not clear what they meant by an "alien" race. It probably meant foreign.

119. See Buck, *Alain Locke: Faith and Philosophy*.

120. "Annual Committee Reports, 1935–1936: Race Amity," *Bahá'í News*, no. 100 (May 1936), 10. The questionnaire did not bring out why local spiritual assemblies thought they were experiencing less resistance to their race relations efforts. An example of the challenges facing local communities can be seen in the April 22, 1936 minutes of the Spiritual Assembly of the Bahá'ís of Portland, Oregon. The Assembly theoretically had a Race Amity Committee but did not appoint anyone as members. The reason for this was not stated. Portland, Oregon Archives.

121. "Teaching Report for Western States July, 1932," *Bahá'í News*, no. 67 (October 1932), 3; "Inter-Racial Amity Activities," *Bahá'í News*, no. 72 (1933), 6; "Committee Reports: Committee on Inter-Racial Amity," *Bahá'í News*, no. 74 (April 1933), 13.

122. Ibid., "Annual Committee Reports, 1933–1934: Race Amity," *Bahá'í News*, no. 88 (November 1934), 10.

123. *The Bahá'í World* 5, 112.

124. *The Bahá'í World* 6, 118–119.

125. "Annual Committee Reports, 1934–1935: Race Amity," *Bahá'í News*, no. 91 (April 1935), 11.

126. "Spirit of the Convention: Race Amity Report," *Bahá'í News*, no. 84 (June 1934), 5, and *The Bahá'í World* 6, 118–119.

127. Little is yet available on Robert Abbott's membership in the Bahá'í Faith. See, for example, Bruce Whitmore, *The Inspirational Life of Robert Sengstacke Abbott*, 8–9, http://www.theabbottinstitute.org/assets/abbott_brucewhitmore_thelifeofrobertsengstackeabbott.pdf. For more on Abbott and his relationship to the Bahá'í Faith, see Christopher Buck, "The Baha'i 'Race Amity' Movement and the Black Intelligentsia in Jim Crow America: Alain Locke and Robert S. Abbott."

128. "Mr. Louis Gregory at Nashville, Tennessee," *Bahá'í News*, no. 89 (January 1935), 10 and *The Bahá'í World* 5, 85. Dr. Stanwood Cobb (1881–1982) was a well-known Bahá'í and educator in the Washington, DC area.

129. Charles Wragg lived in Canada and Europe before settling in the United States. During this period, he was active in promoting interracial harmony. Wragg earned his living as a lecturer. He also might have had income from patents from his airplane inventions. Bernard Duckworth, "Charles Wragg and the Victoria Aero Club Biplane Glider," *Australian Gliding Museum Newsletter* 24 (August 2010), 2–4. The author thanks Don Calkins for providing her with the pdf copy of this newsletter.

130. "Letter from the Inter-Racial Amity Committee," *Bahá'í News*, no. 69 (December 1932), 2; "Committee Reports: Committee on Inter-Racial Amity," *Bahá'í News*, no. 74 (May 1933), 14.

131. *The Bahá'í World* 5, 112.

132. Robert Stockman, "The Bahá'í Faith in the United States, 1921 to the Present," 6, http://hurqalya.ucmerced.edu/sites/hurqalya.ucmerced.edu/files/page/documents/rs-bahai_1921.pdf.

133. See Morrison, *To Move the World* and Venters, *No Jim Crow Church*.

134. Letter dated March 21, 1937 from Zia Bagdadi to Louis Gregory, National Bahá'í Archives.

135. Shoghi Effendi, *The World Order of Baha'u'llah*, 203.

136. Ibid., 187–188.

137. Loni Bramson-Lerche, "Some Aspects of the Development of the Bahá'í Administrative Order in America, 1922–1936."

BIBLIOGRAPHY

"Annual Committee Reports." *Bahá'í News* no. 100 (May 1936), 9–11. Also available at http://bahai-news.info.

"Annual Committee Reports, 1933–1934: Race Amity." *Bahá'í News*, no. 88 (November 1934), 9–10. Also available at http://bahai-news.info.

"Annual Committee Reports, 1934–1935: Race Amity." *Bahá'í News*, no. 91 (April 1935), 10–11. Also available at http://bahai-news.info.

"Annual Committee Reports, 1935–1936: Race Amity." *Bahá'í News*, no. 100 (May 1936), 9–10. Also available at http://bahai-news.info.

"Annual Reports of the National Committee of the National Spiritual Assembly of the Bahá'ís of the United States and Canada, 1931–1932: Report of Racial Amity Committee." *Bahá'í News* no. 62 (May 1932), 7–9. Also available at http://bahai-news.info.

"Bahá'i Contacts in Harlem, New York City." *Bahá'í News* 48 (February 1931), 3–4. Also available at http://bahai-news.info.

Bahá'í World. Volumes 2–6 available at http://www.bahai.org/library/other-literature/periodicals-supplementary-materials/bahai-world/; volumes 7–24 available at https://bahai-library.com/tags/Bahai%20World%20volumes.

Bahá'í Year Book. Available as Volume 1 of *The Bahá'í World* at http://www.bahai.org/library/other-literature/periodicals-supplementary-materials/bahai-world.

Bramson-Lerche, Loni. "Some Aspects of the Development of the Bahá'í Administrative Order in America, 1922–1936." In *Studies in Bábí and Bahá'í History*. Vol. 1. Edited by Moojan Momen, 255–300, 321–324. Los Angeles: Kalimát Press, 1982.

Brown, Keven, ed. *Evolution and Bahá'í Belief: 'Abdu'l-Bahá's Response to Nineteenth-Century Darwinism*. Los Angeles: Kalimát, 1982.

Buck, Christopher. *Alain Locke: Faith and Philosophy*. Los Angeles: Kalimát Press, 2005. Also available at https://www.academia.edu/4333260/Alain_Locke_Faith_and_Philosophy.

Buck, Christopher. "The Baha'i 'Race Amity' Movement and the Black Intelligentsia in Jim Crow America: Alain Locke and Robert S. Abbott." *Baha'i Studies Review* 17 (2011), 3–46. Also available at https://bahai-library.com/pdf/b/buck_race_amity_movement.pdf.

Buck, Christopher. "The Interracial 'Baha'i Movement' and the Black Intelligentsia: The Case of W. E. B. Du Bois." *Journal of Religious History* 36, no. 4 (December 2012), 542–562. Also available at http://christopherbuck.com/pdf/Buck_2012_DuBois.pdf.

Castelow, Teri L. "James Hardy Dillard." *Dictionary of Virginia Biography*. http://www.lva.virginia.gov/public/dvb/bio.asp?b=Dillard_James_Hardy.

"Committee Reports: Committee on Inter-Racial Amity." *Bahá'í News*, no. 74 (April 1933), 13–14. Also available at http://bahai-news.info.

"Committees of the National Spiritual Assembly, 1930–1931." *Bahá'í News*, no. 42 (1930), 2. Also available at http://bahai-news.info.

Dahl, Roger M. Archivist, National Bahá'í Archives, United States. Wilmette, IL: U.S. Bahá'í National Center. Email message to the author. August 9, 2017.

Dahl, Roger M. Archivist, National Bahá'í Archives, United States. Wilmette, IL: U.S. Bahá'í National Center. Email message to the author. August 14, 2017.

Dahl, Roger M. Archivist, National Bahá'í Archives, United States. Wilmette, IL: U.S. Bahá'í National Center. Email message to the author. September 8, 2016.

"Divine Call to Race Amity." *Bahá'í News*, no. 90 (March 1935), 4–6. Also available at http://bahai-news.info.

Duckworth, Bernard. "Charles Wragg and the Victoria Aero Club Biplane Glider." *Australian Gliding Museum Newsletter* 24 (August 2010), 2–4.

"Eighteenth Annual Convention of the Baha'is of the United States and Canada." *Bahá'í News Letter*, no. 12 (June-July 1926), 4, 2–6. Also available at http://bahai-news.info.

"Feast for White and Colored Children." *Bahá'í News*, no. 48 (February 1931), 5–6. Also available at http://bahai-news.info.

Fiorentino, Daniele. "Multiculturalism and the Legacy of Cultural Pluralism." *RSA Journal* 20 (2009). http://www.aisna.net/sites/default/files/rsa/rsa20/20fiorentino.pdf.

Flora, Joseph M., and Amber Vogel, eds. *Southern Literary Studies: Southern Writers, A New Biographical Dictionary*. Baton Rouge: Louisiana State University Press, 2006.

Gregory, Louis G. "Inter-Racial Amity: Spirit of the New Age Enters the South. Constructive Efforts and Marked Progress." *Star of the West* 13, no. 11 (February 1923), 304–306. Reprint, Oxford: George Ronald, 1978). Also available at https://bahai.works/Star_of_the_West.

Harris, Leonard, and Charles Molesworth. *Alain L. Locke: Biography of a Philosopher*. Chicago: University of Chicago Press, 2008.

"Heart of Dixie Teaching Amity in the South." *Bahá'í News*, no. 58 (January 1932), 2–4. Also available at http://bahai-news.info.

Hollinger, Richard, ed. *Agnes Parsons' Diary*. Los Angeles: Kalimát, 1996.

"Instructions and Explanations from Shoghi Effendi." *Bahá'í News*, no. 90 (March 1935), 1. Also available at http://bahai-news.info.

"Interracial Amity." *Bahá'í News*, no. 41 (May 1930), 3. Also available at http://bahai-news.info.

"Inter-Racial Amity Activities." *Bahá'í News*, no. 72 (1933), 6; no. 74 (April 1933), 13. Also available at http://bahai-news.info.

"Interracial Amity Committee." *Bahá'í News Letter*, no. 40 (April 1930), 10–12. Also available at http://bahai-news.info.

"Inter-Racial Amity Committee Holds Convention in Washington, D. C." *Bahá'í News Letter*, no. 19 (1927), 2. Also available at http://bahai-news.info.

"Inter-Racial Amity Conferences." *Bahá'í News Letter*, no. 22 (March 1928), 5–6. Also available at http://bahai-news.info.

"Inter-Racial Amity Meetings." *Bahá'í News Letter*, no. 25 (July 1928), 3. Also available at http://bahai-news.info.

"Inter-Racial Work." *Bahá'í News Letter*, no. 35 (November 1929), 7. Also available at http://bahai-news.info.

Kelley, Robin D. G., and Earl Lewis, eds. *To Make Our World Anew: A History of African Americans from 1880*. Oxford: Oxford University Press, 2005.

Kilroy, David. *For Race and Country: The Life and Career of Colonel Charles Young*. Westport, CT: Praeger, 2003.

McKay, Doris, and Paul Vreeland. *Fires in Many Hearts*. Manotick, ON: Nine Pines, 1993.

"Letter from the Inter-Racial Amity Committee." *Bahá'í News*, no. 69 (December 1932), 2–3. Also available at http://bahai-news.info.

"Letter from Inter-Racial Amity Committee." *Bahá'í News*, no. 80 (January 1934), 7–8. Also available at http://bahai-news.info.

"Letter from Los Angeles Assembly." *Bahá'í News Letter,* no. 38 (1930), 6–7. Also available at http://bahai-news.info.

Morrison, Gayle. *To Move the World: Louis G. Gregory and the Advancement of Racial Unity in America*. Wilmette, IL: Bahá'í Publishing Trust, 1982.

"Mr. Louis Gregory at Nashville, Tennessee." *Bahá'í News*, no. 89 (January 1935), 10. Also available at http://bahai-news.info.

"Mr. Louis Gregory's Teaching Activities." *Bahá'í News Letter*, no. 30 (March 1929), 8. Also available at http://bahai-news.info.

Mukherjee, Tapan K. *Taraknath Das: Life and Letters of a Revolutionary in Exile*. Calcutta: National Council of Education, Bengal, Jadavpur University, 1988.

Nakhjavani, Ali. "The Ten Year Crusade." *The Journal of Bahá'í Studies* 14, nos. 3–4 (2004), 1–33. http://bahai-studies.ca/wp-content/uploads/2014/03/14.3-4.Nakhjavani1.pdf.

National Bahá'í Archives, United States. Wilmette, IL: U.S. Bahá'í National Center.

"National Committee on Racial Amity Appointed." *Bahá'í News Letter*, no. 16 (March 1927), 5. Also available at http://bahai-news.info.

National Spiritual Assembly, comp. *The Bahá'í Centenary*. Wilmette, IL: Bahá'í Publishing Committee, 1944. Also available at https://bahai.works/Bahá'%C3%AD_Centenary_1844-1944.

"New Bahá'i Publications." *Bahá'í News Letter*, no. 21 (January 1928), 5. Also available at http://bahai-news.info.

"News of the Cause." *Bahá'í News Letter*, no. 4 (April 1925), 3–4. Also available at http://bahai-news.info.

"News of the Cause." *Bahá'í News Letter*, no. 9 (December 1925 to January 1926), 4–8. Also available at http://bahai-news.info.

"News of the Cause." *Bahá'í News Letter*, no. 10 (February 1926), 5–8. Also available at http://bahai-news.info.

"New York Amity Conference Reported in Leading Negro Paper." *Bahá'í News*, no. 48 (February 1931), 10. Also available at http://bahai-news.info.

Perry, Patsy B. "Leslie Pinckney Hill." In *Southern Literary Studies: Southern Writers, A New Biographical Dictionary*, edited by Joseph M. Flora and Amber Vogel, 200–201. Baton Rouge: Louisiana State University Press, 2006.

Portland, Oregon, Bahá'í Archives. Portland, OR: Portland Bahá'í Center.

Power of Unity: Beyond Prejudice and Racism. Compiled by Bonnie J. Taylor and National Race Unity Committee. Wilmette, IL: Bahá'í Publishing Trust, 1986. Available at https://bahai-library.com/taylor_power_unity.

"Racial Amity Forum." *Bahá'í News Letter*, no. 37 (January 1930), 6–7. Also available at http://bahai-news.info.

"Report of the National Inter-Racial Amity Committee." *Bahá'í News Letter*, no. 17 (April 1927), 12. Also available at http://bahai-news.info.

"Report of National Teaching Committee." *Bahá'í News Letter*, no. 34 (October 1929), 6. Also available at http://bahai-news.info.

"Report of Progress from Urbana, Illinois." *Bahá'í News Letter,* no. 38 (February 1930), 3–4. Also available at http://bahai-news.info.

"Report of the Twenty-First Annual Convention." *Bahá'í News Letter*, no. 32 (May 1929), 1–5. Also available at http://bahai-news.info.

"Reports from Teaching Committee." *Bahá'í News*, no. 49 (March 1931), 5–7. Also available at http://bahai-news.info.

Shapiro, Robert Donald. *A Reform Rabbi in the Progressive Era: The Early Career of Stephen S. Wise*. New York: Garland, 1988.

Shellum, Brian G. *Black Cadet in a White Bastion: Charles Young at West Point*. Lincoln: University of Nebraska Press, 2006.

Shoghi, Effendi. *Bahá'í Administration*. Wilmette, IL: Bahá'í Publishing Trust, 1968. Also available at http://www.bahai.org/library/authoritative-texts/shoghi-effendi/bahai-administration.

Shoghi, Effendi. *The World Order of Bahá'u'lláh*. 2nd rev. ed. Wilmette, IL: Bahá'í Publishing Trust, 1968. Also available at http://www.bahai.org/library/authoritative-texts/shoghi-effendi/world-order-bahaullah.

Smith, Michelle. "Alain Locke: Culture and the Plurality of Black Life." PhD diss. Cornell University, 2009. https://ecommons.cornell.edu/bitstream/handle/1813/14009/Smith,%20Michelle.pdf?sequence=1.

"Spirit of the Convention: Race Amity Report." *Bahá'í News*, no. 84 (June 1934), 5. Also available at http://bahai-news.info.

Stewart, Jeffrey C. *The New Negro: The Life of Alain Locke*. New York: Oxford University Press, 2018.

Stockman, Robert. "The Bahá'í Faith in the United States, 1921 to the Present." http://hurqalya.ucmerced.edu/sites/hurqalya.ucmerced.edu/files/page/documents/rs-bahai_1921.pdf.

Stockman, Robert. Macnutt, Howard. https://bahai-library.com/stockman_macnutt.

"Teaching Committee." *Bahá'í News Letter*, no. 40 (1930), 12–15. Also available at http://bahai-news.info.

"Teaching Report for Western States July, 1932." *Bahá'í News*, no. 67 (October 1932), 2–4. Also available at http://bahai-news.info.

"Teaching Work of Mr. Gregory." *Bahá'í News Letter*, no. 38 (February 1930), 7–8. Also available at http://bahai-news.info.

Toy, Eckard. "Ku Klux Klan." *The Oregon Encyclopedia*. https://oregonencyclopedia.org/articles/ku_klux_klan/#.WXugR62ZNBw.

Venters, Louis. *No Jim Crow Church: The Origins of South Carolina's Bahá'í Community*. Gainesville, FL: University Press of Florida, 2015.

Vernon, Kathryn L. *Baha'u'llah's Garden, Jacksonville, Fla. 1919–1969*. October 3, 2009.

Washington, Johnny. *A Journey into the Philosophy of Alain Locke*. Westport, CT: Greenwood Press, 1994.

Weinfeld, David. "What Difference Does Difference Make? Horace Kallen, Alain Locke, and the Birth of Cultural Pluralism." In *Philosophic Values and World Citizenship: Locke to Obama and Beyond*, edited by Jacoby Adeshei Carter and Leonard Harris, 165–187. Lanham, MD: Lexington, 2010.

Weinfeld, David. "What Difference Does the Difference Make? Horace Kallen, Alain Locke, and the Development of Cultural Pluralism in America." PhD diss. New

York University, 2014. http://pqdtopen.proquest.com/doc/1615089470.html?FMT=ABS.

"Western Assemblies Combine Material with Spiritual Hospitality," *Bahá'í News Letter*, no. 23 (April 1928), 3. Also available at http://bahai-news.info.

Wilhelm, Roy. "Convention for Amity between the White and Colored Races." *Star of the West* 13, no. 3 (April 1922): 51–55, 60–61. Reprint, Oxford: George Ronald, 1978. Also available at https://bahai.works/Star_of_the_West.

Whitmore, Bruce W. *The Dawning* Place. 2nd ed. Wilmette, IL: Bahá'í Publishing Trust, 2015.

Whitmore, Bruce W. *The Inspirational Life of Robert Sengstacke Abbott*. http://www.theabbottinstitute.org/assets/abbott_brucewhitmore_thelifeofrobertsengstackeabbott.pdf.

Chapter 3

Alain Locke on Race, Religion, and the Bahá'í Faith

Christopher Buck

We must not look for material things.
There are other treasures.

– Alain Locke.[1]

Race relations in America is a benchmark of social progress. Many factors affect race relations. One of the most significant of these is religion. It is the great intensifier. For good or ill, religion sacralizes all that it holds dear. Cherished beliefs, whatever they may be, are strengthened by their status as "sacred" values. Therefore, religion can, and does, operate as a driving impulse within the realm of will and volition. It is an engine of motivation, then, which can have significant impact on the state of race relations. The Bahá'í Faith in America is a case in point. In terms of race relations, this has not escaped the notice of contemporary scholars and other public intellectuals. One historian notes that the Bahá'í Faith "was not only the first religion to initiate racial amity activities in America but the first to elicit interfaith support."[2] Among contemporary black intellectuals, Cornel West has expressed his admiration for the Bahá'í "race amity" efforts:

> When you talk about race and the legacy of white supremacy, there's no doubt that when the history is written, the true history is written, the history of this country, the Bahá'í Faith will be one of the leaven in the American loaf that allowed the democratic loaf to expand because of the anti-racist witness of those of Bahá'í faith. So that there is a real sense in which a Christian like myself is profoundly humbled before Bahá'í brothers and sisters and the Dizzy Gillespie's and the Alain Locke's and so forth.[3]

Cornel West mentions Dizzy Gillespie and Alain Locke, two recognized figures in African American history and culture who are well known as Bahá'ís. The present study focuses on Alain Locke (1885–1954), who embraced the Bahá'í Faith in 1918, the very same year that he was awarded his doctorate in philosophy from Harvard University. He remained a Bahá'í until his death in 1954. Cornel West's mention of Alain Locke invites a closer look at Locke's role in promoting ideal race relations, both within the American historical context in general, and in the Bahá'í context in particular.

The present study will show that Alain Locke was somewhat cynical about the prospect of any real progress in race relations within Christianity itself (which, after all, historically played a role in legitimizing, and at the same time, elsewhere opposing, the practice of slavery). However, Locke saw great potential in Bahá'í efforts to promote "race amity," that is, interracial harmony, for the advancement of African Americans in particular, and with a sense of common cause with oppressed minorities in general. In addition to making America more truly "American" in terms of its founding values, Locke sought to make democracy more egalitarian in terms of the rights and status of minorities who have been denied their share of the American dream. As a public spokesman for African Americans, and more broadly as an advocate for living up to the ideals of American democracy as a benchmark of social progress, the figure of Alain Locke deserves, if not commands, attention. The present study focuses on Locke's perspective on race and religion, with special emphasis on his evaluation as a Bahá'í.

ALAIN LOCKE ON RACE AND RELIGION

Alain Locke was a philosopher within the American pragmatist tradition who used his prestige and vocation as a public intellectual in order to promote ideal race relations, which, in his era, was often referred to in Bahá'í sources as "race amity." "Amity," of course, means friendship. This term was occasionally noted by the press the few times that Bahá'í-sponsored race amity events attracted media attention. For instance, the following notice was in the December 1924 issue of *The Crisis*, published under the auspices of the National Association for the Advancement of Colored People (NAACP): "Under the auspices of the Bahai (sic) movement a convention of amity between white and colored races in America was held in Philadelphia. Among the speakers were Leslie P. Hill and Louis G. Gregory."[4] Alain Locke was a speaker at this event.[5] Such brief news notices, in and of themselves, were noticeably silent as to the significance of these interracial Bahá'í events, the purpose of which was to promote ideal race relations. Had the NAACP, or *The Crisis* editor, W. E. B. Du Bois himself, seen greater social significance in these interracial initiatives, surely there would have been more press coverage and public discourse about the importance of these interracial solutions to America's racial crisis.

During the Jim Crow era, when African Americans had virtually no political recourse, Alain Locke turned his attention to the arts. His goal was to serve as a cultural ambassador to break racial stereotypes by showcasing the artistic genius, be it visual, literary, dramatic or musical, of African Americans. Although his first claim to fame was as the first African American Rhodes scholar in 1907, Alain Locke is far more widely known as the prime mover of the Harlem Renaissance, a highly successful artistic movement that flourished from the mid-1920s through the mid-1930s.

Alain Locke was a public intellectual who advocated for the civil and human rights of African Americans, and who is credited with having internationalized the problem of racism. Although he published a number of articles, along with several books, during his lifetime, he was not as prolific as he had the potential to be, probably because he was in such great demand as a speaker. A study of the "Alain Locke Papers" at Howard University reveals a very busy schedule as he tried to balance his responsibilities as a professor with his public role as a "race man." To illustrate Alain Locke's national prominence and historic importance as a spokesman for African Americans, one anecdote may suffice. The Rev. Dr. Martin Luther King, Jr., who held Locke in high esteem, mentioned Locke in an unpublished speech at the Poor People's Campaign Rally in Clarksdale, Mississippi, on March 19, 1968. Dr. King declared: "We're going to let our children know that the only philosophers that lived were not Plato and Aristotle, but W. E. B. Du Bois and Alain Locke came through the universe."[6]

Arguably, Dr. King has overrated Alain Locke as a philosopher with respect to his contributions to the discipline of philosophy. Nevertheless, Dr. King's remarks ring true and resound in the annals of history considering the role that Alain Locke had to play in promoting ideal race relations, while at the same time publicly advocating on behalf of the advancement of his fellow African Americans by taking advantage of his reputation as a philosopher. Locke used his prestige as a philosopher to advocate for social change and for the amelioration of the very real circumstances of oppression that African Americans and other minorities suffered and chafed under, knowing full well, and painfully so, the irony of America's professed ideals, which were sadly lacking in their practical application, in terms of both public policy and prevailing social attitudes (i.e. prejudices). As "the most influential African American intellectual born between W. E. B. Du Bois and Martin Luther King, Jr.,"[7] Locke is a natural choice for exploring the relationship between race and religion in the American historical context.

As a public intellectual, Locke chose not to publicly identify himself as a Bahá'í, yet he allowed himself to be publicly identified as a member by others. This distinction may be overstated but is generally useful in noting a pattern in Locke's public life. When invited, he did speak at Bahá'í-sponsored events. In the same way, Locke contributed to Bahá'í publications when invited to do so. The result is that Alain Locke was a public Bahá'í in a selective sense. In other words, if one knew where to look, or was socially interactive in Bahá'í circles, or had read the occasional newspaper article on the Bahá'í Faith that happened to mention Alain Locke as an adherent, then, in that sense, Locke was indeed a public Bahá'í figure, in a nuanced historical context. Posthumously, however, Alain Locke has emerged as one of the most public Bahá'í figures in the American context, down to this day.

Locke was actively involved in the Bahá'í community at local, national, and international levels. At the national level, he was a member of several successive "Race Amity" committees.[8] At the international level, Alain Locke contributed several essays to the *Bahá'í World* volumes, which were the public face of the Bahá'í Faith. These publications were often presented to civic leaders and religious leaders. They chronicle and richly document the growth and burgeoning recognition of the Bahá'í Faith as an emerging world religion.[9]

Alain Locke has not left posterity an autobiography, although he had hoped to write one.[10] Therefore, any and all claims to his "influences," cumulative or convergent, are inferential at best, and require further nuancing. The following may be said: Locke's worldview was enriched—infused, one might say—by the Bahá'í ideals of unity (interracial, interreligious, and international) that clearly synergize with his prior cosmopolitan outlook and philosophical interests. Rather than arguing influence, it is perhaps more sound to speak of a certain "confluence" in which synergy, that is, intensive interaction of the sum total of Locke's influences, may be the best way to describe the role that Locke's Bahá'í ideals and principles played in his thinking and public performances, whether as a speaker, writer, philosopher, art critic, or public advocate of minority rights in the name of a more truly "democratic" and more idealistically authentic "American" expression of democracy.

Alain Locke was raised an Episcopalian and continued to represent himself as one in short biographical notices.[11] Locke's dual identity as an Episcopalian by heritage and a Bahá'í by conviction is an apparent contradiction that can be easily resolved. In his day, the Bahá'í Faith did not strictly require its adherents to formally disaffiliate themselves from their former religious affiliations. Rather, it was possible and, indeed, a common practice to maintain a dual religious identity.[12] Therefore, it could be said of Alain Locke that not only had he an Episcopal heritage that carried over into his public religious affiliation, but that he actually maintained a dual religious identity. It must be remembered that the Bahá'í Faith was still an obscure religion, and so Alain Locke probably found it more expedient, in certain contexts, simply to identify himself as Episcopalian. That said, there is no strong evidence that he was an active, much less a committed, Episcopalian. In fact, in an autobiographical statement, Locke qualified his Christian identity:

> I am really a Xtian (Christian) without believing any of its dogma, because I am incapable of feeling hatred, revenge or jealously—though filled all the time with Righteous indignation . . . I have always hoped to be big enough to have to justify myself not to my contemporaries but to posterity. Small men apologize to their neighbors, big men to posterity.[13]

Locke's Bahá'í biography was published in 2005;[14] his long association with Bahá'í circles has been noted by such historians as Leonard Harris, Charles Molesworth, and Jeffrey Stewart.[15] Locke's contributions to the Bahá'í "Race Amity" movement were further chronicled in 2012.[16] These studies demonstrate how Locke's Bahá'í perspective enriched and reinforced his innate cosmopolitanism, which expressed itself most eloquently and resolutely in his advocacy of ideal race relations. The following historical anecdotes and selected statements by Alain Locke himself are consistent with his dual religious identity as an ostensible Episcopalian by heritage and a quasi-public Bahá'í by conviction.

RACE AND RELIGION: THE NATIONAL INTERRACIAL CONFERENCE, 1928

Alain Locke was a social barometer of the state of race relations in America. His year-by-year published statements on race relations chronicled efforts as well as progress, retrospectively and contemporaneously, in promoting and advancing race relations. In addressing the state of race relations in America, as he was occasionally invited to do, Alain Locke included religion within the scope of his social analysis. For instance, in 1928, Locke largely authored an official report on the state of race relations in America, in which he made a few cogent comments about the social role of Christianity within the context of race relations in the United States. The report was presented at the National Interracial Conference held in December 16–19, 1928, in Washington, DC,[17] an ambitious public event organized by the National Urban League. Founded in 1910 as the "National League on Urban Conditions among Negroes" following the merger of three predecessor organizations (Committee on Urban Conditions among Negroes, the Committee for the Improvement of Industrial Conditions among Negroes in New York, and the National League for the Protection of Colored Women), the National Urban League proclaimed its stated mission as being "to enable African Americans to secure economic self-reliance, parity, power and civil rights."[18] Two retrospective reports were written, one private (archived and now made public by the Library of Congress), the other public (published in 1928; see below). The latter one was penned by Locke himself.

The first private report is thirty-seven pages long, submitted by the "Committee on Findings." Under the heading, "Problems of Race Relations," questions are posed as to the role of religion in promoting ideal (or, more pragmatically, ameliorated) race relations: "Suggested basic questions as to the conditions of improved race relations," included, *inter alia*: "B. To what extent is the improvement of race relations conditional upon the acceptance of inter-marriage between the races?" The specifically religious dimension is introduced under the subheading, "C. The Christian implications of the problem." "1. At what points do the teachings of Christ and social expediency conflict?" and "2. What immediate commitments for the improvement of racial relationships are practicable for Christian men and women?"[19] These appear to be proposed questions for discussion at the National Interracial Conference itself.

Locke's report on the National Interracial Conference was noted in the press: "Dr. Locke states that never before has there been such a large number of sponsoring organizations connected with any one conference; that in addition to the many organized groups invited to send delegates, many other organizations and activities were represented through delegates at large."[20] In the public report, Alain Locke uses religious imagery:

> And it was at that point that the meeting became, as I said at the beginning, pentecostal. For what the workers in this field most needed was that realization which the conference achieved of the essential unity of their cause, and the "gift of tongues" to hear in one another's programs and policies the practical evangelization in each province of the same great principles of social democracy. The conference opened the way for an abiding realization that the Negro problem is not sectional but national; that it differs only in degree and emphasis between North and South; that it cannot be either exclusively the white man's burden or the black man's burden, but is fundamentally interracial, both in its negative handicaps, its joint responsibilities and its possible positive benefits. That, further, it is neither exclusively educational, economic nor political, but a composite; and that religious and secular, philanthropic and public agencies must conjoin in resolving it.[21]

This rhetoric ("pentecostal," "gift of tongues," and "practical evangelization") not only invokes religion as a trope, it also specifically points to the role that religion must play in improving race relations. Locke is making an important statement, something of a manifesto as it were, with wide-ranging and far-reaching implications. The most significant point is that the problem of racism, and how best to solve it, "is fundamentally interracial" in nature. In other words, it is neither "exclusively the white man's burden" nor "the black man's burden." Since the problem is interracial in nature (even though the primary problem stems from racial prejudice on the part of whites toward blacks), the solution must be interracial in nature as well. Locke is careful to point out that America's racial crisis is multidimensional; it is "a composite" of "educational," "economic," "political," "religious," aspects, and "religious and secular, philanthropic and public agencies must conjoin in resolving it." The most effective way for this to happen is when religious influence is brought to bear in the religiously leavened civil sphere ("religious and secular"), whereby spiritual principles can contribute to the public discourse.

RACE AND RELIGION: RELEVANCE OF RELIGIOUS VALUES

As previously pointed out, Alain Locke, by education and vocation, was a philosopher. However, his contributions to formal philosophy, that is, American pragmatism, was not his primary focus. He had more pressing issues on his agenda. Similarly, Locke has also been referred to as a "Bahá'í philosopher."[22] A formal "Bahá'í philosophy" has yet to emerge. Alain Locke's exposure to the Bahá'í principles of unity, and his later affiliation as a declared Bahá'í, can be seen as part of his intellectual as well as spiritual and social development. To the extent that his public statements and publications can loosely be described as his "social philosophy" (without formal reference to the philosophical school of American pragmatism itself), Alain Locke is still aptly described as a philosopher, whether as an American pragmatist, a "Bahá'í philosopher," a "social philosopher," or as a combination of all philosophical endeavors.

Locke's views on race and religion received their greatest inspiration from the Bahá'í principles. Their finest expression was when he, whether explicitly or implicitly, mirrored those principles. During the time that he was writing his Harvard dissertation, Locke had been personally investigating the Bahá'í Faith. This extracurricular personal interest was concurrent and convergent with the writing of his doctoral dissertation, which is of intrinsic interest. A brief look at Alain Locke's study of philosophy may contribute to a better understanding of his views on religion, in relation to race.

Locke specialized in the philosophy of values. The dimension of the spiritual, or sacred, figures prominently in Locke's typology of values. In his Harvard doctoral dissertation, "The Problem of Classification in the Theory of Value: Or an Outline of a Genetic System of Values" (1917), Locke recognized the pivotal place that religion has in human society, that is, in these six value dimensions that inform his taxonomy of values: (1) Hedonic; (2) Economic; (3) Artistic; (4) Logical; (5) Ethical; (6) Religious.[23] In his 1935 essay, "Values and Imperatives," however, Locke reduces his values paradigm to four "Value Types": (1) Religious; (2) Ethical or Moral; (3) Aesthetic or Artistic; (4) Logical or Scientific.[24] Of course, Locke's typology of values is more complex than this. In his "Values and Imperatives" essay (his first formal publication in philosophy at age fifty), Locke correlates each "Value Type" with: (1) "Modal Quality"; (2) "Value Predicates"; and (3) "Value Polarity."[25] For the "Religious" Value Type, the associated characteristics are as follows: (1) "Modal Quality" (Exaltation and Awe-Worship: Inner Ecstasy, Religious Zeal); (2) "Value Predicates" (Holy and Unholy; Good and Evil); and (3) "Value Polarity" (Holiness and Sin; Salvation and Damnation).[26] These values underpin the outcome-oriented moral and social imperatives that Locke proposes.

This inclusion of a specifically religious dimension informed not only Alain Locke's philosophy of values per se, but his social philosophy as well. It also included attention to religion as a social force and as a wellspring, for good or ill, and as a source of America's prevailing social attitudes and values, which were often, if not characteristically, contradictory and therefore compromised. Given the importance of the religious dimension in Locke's philosophy and worldview, this chapter will now focus on Locke's views on race and religion, particularly on the role of religion both as a contribution to the problem and as a potential solution to the issue of racial prejudice and economic disparity.

RACE AND RELIGION: ORIGINAL SINS

Locke's general outlook on race and religion provides a more immediate context for his specifically Bahá'í outlook, which may be characterized as a contrast between his critique of Christianity and his positive regard for Bahá'í principles as applied to race relations, both pragmatically and ideally. Framing the problems that religion presents, for Locke, is a prerequisite to proposing possible solutions. The social problematic, in the context of religion, is the failure of adherents to faithfully live up to their professed religious values. This is often referred to in one word: "hypocrisy."

In "Whither Race Relations? A Critical Commentary" (1944), Locke points to the hypocrisy of spiritual ideals as measured against social reality: "In the field of organized religion the discrepancies between democratic professions and democratic practise on race are not only most glaring but most ironically self-contradictory."[27]

However, he explains that there were positive developments in American Christianity with respect to ameliorating (instead of exacerbating) race relations:

> Yet out of the present-day exposures of such self-contradictions has come a marked demand for reform. In different degrees but all with some accelerated pace the various Protestant Churches and the Catholic Church have responded, it would seem. The Catholic Church, in addition to having instituted a new interracial council movement, has recently opened up many of its schools to Negro students. As to the democratic practise of human equality, however, the Christian church is still far from activating its own basic formula of the "brotherhood of man," and accordingly cannot claim either moral or actual leadership in the sphere of race relations.[28]

In "Peace between Black and White in the United States" (a manuscript posthumously published in 2005), Locke wrote:

> We used to say that Christianity and democracy were both at stake in the equitable solution of the race question. They were; but they were abstract ideals that did not bleed when injured. Now we think with more realistic logic, perhaps, that economic justice cannot stand on one foot; and economic reconstruction is the dominant demand of the present-day American scene.[29]

In this reference to Christianity and democracy, Alain Locke is specifically referring to what generally may be described as the "religious and secular" dimensions of America's racial crisis. Their respective "abstract ideals" promised, in theory, an "equitable solution of the race question." In practice, however, these same "abstract ideals" remained abstract, that is, inert and thereby useless, rather than pragmatically applied as they should have been. This is why Locke makes the polite, but rather damning statement: "We used to say that Christianity and democracy were both at stake in the equitable solution of the race question. They were; but they were abstract ideals that did not bleed when injured." In this poignant way, Locke succinctly framed the fundamental problem as to religion and race. But in spite of this brief social critique of institutional Christianity, Alain Locke proposed some spiritual solutions.

RACE AND RELIGION: SALVIFIC SOLUTIONS

On November 16, 1924, Locke spoke at the jubilee celebration of the Salem A. M. E. Church in Harlem on the topic of "Social Salvation."[30] The article is short on details about the substance of Locke's talk. The term, "Social Salvation," notwithstanding, finds its illumination in another speech, unearthed by the present writer in August 2001 as an unpublished manuscript. It has since been published as "The Gospel for the Twentieth Century"[31] after its opening phrase. This essay may be Locke's most definitive statement on race and religion. It begins as follows:

> The gospel for the Twentieth Century rises out of the heart of its greatest problems, and few who are spiritually enlightened doubt the nature of that problem. The clashing ominous [n?]est of issues of the practical world of today, the issues of race, sect, class and nationality, all have one basic spiritual origin, and for that reason, we hope and believe one basic cure.[32]

In this opening paragraph, the word "gospel" obviously is religious, Christian, in fact. It is a deliberate choice of words on Locke's part. "Gospel" is no mere "message." As a religious mandate, "gospel" typically demands a higher level of commitment since the message is considered to be a moral imperative of a decidedly sacred nature. By contrast, the term "Twentieth Century" is secular. "Race" is only one of a complex of social problems that confront American society. Such social problems are inextricably intertwined and interrelated. Locke demonstrates that he is acutely aware of the social fact that this aggravates and accentuates the problem of racism within the spectrum of other social issues, which typically includes "race, class, and gender" in everyday parlance, even today. Locke elsewhere put this complex of social issues another way: "No more progressive step can be made in our present civilization than the breaking down of the barriers which separate races, sexes and nations."[33] For Locke, this is a moral imperative, not only for America itself, but for the world at large.

In the essay, Locke frames "race, sect, class and nationality" as a constellation of social ills, which are fundamentally "spiritual" (or unspiritual) in nature. "Sect" refers to the ongoing challenge of sectarianism or intercommunal religious strife, whether within a particular religion or between religions. "Class" implicates economic disparity. "Nationality" probably refers to nationalism (more than national origin), especially since nationalism stands in tension with internationalism. Locke was a cosmopolitan and a staunch internationalist in his outlook.

In speaking of "one basic cure," Locke rhetorically uses disease as a metaphor. He continues with his description of America's social problem of race:

> Too long have we tried to patch these issues up and balm them over; instead of going to the heart and seat of the trouble in the limited and limiting conceptions of humanity which are alone, like a poisonous virus circulating through

> our whole social system, responsible for them. A change of condition will not remedy or more than temporarily ameliorate our chronic social antagonisms; only a widespread almost universal change of social heart, a new spirit of human attitudes, can achieve the social redemption that must eventually come.[34]

This discourse is suffused with diagnostic and prognostic pronouncements where "our whole social system" stands for the body politic, afflicted with a "poisonous virus" that is "chronic" and in dire need of a true remedy for the cause and not just a superficial balm for the symptoms. The cure, or "social redemption," is spiritual in nature, which can only come about when the "social heart" of humanity is infused with a "new spirit" that will difuse over time "social antagonisms."

Locke continues:

> The finest and most practical idea of Christianity, the idea of the millenium [*sic*], of peace on earth, has been allowed to lapse as an illusion of the primitive Christian mind, as a mystic's mirage of another world. And as a consequence the Brotherhood of Man, taken as a negligible corollary of the fatherhood of God, has if anything in practical effect put the truth of its own basic proposition to doubtful uncertainty. The redemption of society, social salvation, should have been sought after first, the pragmatic test and proof of the fatherhood of God is afterall [*sic*] whether belief in it can realize the unity of mankind; and so the brotherhood of man, as it has been inspirationally expressed, the "oneness of humanity," must be in our day realized or religion die out gradually into ever-increasing materiality. The salvation we have sought after as individuals in an after-life and another sphere must be striven for as the practical peace and unity of the human family here in this [world]. In some very vital respects God will be rediscovered to our age if we succeed in discovering the common denominator of humanity and living in terms of it and valuing all things in accordance with it.[35]

In this passage, Alain Locke adds a distinctively social dimension to the religious goal of "salvation," which he terms "social salvation." Evangelical and even conservative Christianity have typically emphasized personal and individual "salvation." "Social salvation" is the term that Locke invokes, if not coins, here. It implies that religion has a social mandate as well.[36] The salvation of individuals, standing alone, is not sufficient to effect a sea-change in society. Individual salvation (whatever that means or entails) is not enough to cure the ills of society, including the problem of racism. Locke was keenly aware of this problem, and very much alive to possible solutions. A collective problem requires a collective solution. It can even be said that individual salvation is bound up with social salvation. In any case, Locke's assertion that, "the Brotherhood of Man, taken as a negligible corollary of the fatherhood of God, has if anything in practical effect put the truth of its own basic proposition to doubtful certainty," is a powerful critique of the social failings of institutional Christianity, which, according to Locke, had become alien to its original spirit. He uses the term "social salvation" as synonymous with "social redemption."

Locke now endows a secular term with spiritual significance:

> The world has not yet sounded the depths and realized the profundities of its most moving contemporary ideal, or sensed the challenge of its most popular slogan. Much has been accomplished in the name of Democracy, but Spiritual Democracy, its largest and most inner meaning, is so below our common horizons. Only a few from the elevation of some jutting human problem see it, and they too often as through a tragic rift through which it appears more the solution of their particular issue, the light for their particular valley than as the sun of a new universal day for humanity at large.[37]

If Alain Locke himself espoused a secular "Gospel," then that would be the idea of the "Spiritual Democracy." In fact, Locke's greatest contribution to philosophy is his philosophy of democracy, which has been systematically described in previous publications.[38] Locke's philosophy of democracy may be characterized as a grand theory (in the positive, not pejorative, sense of the term): (1) Local Democracy; (2) Moral Democracy; (3) Political Democracy; (4) Economic Democracy; (5) Cultural Democracy; (6) Racial Democracy; (7) Social Democracy; (8) Spiritual Democracy; (9) World Democracy, with adjunct notions of natural, practical, progressive, creative, intellectual, equalitarian democracy.[39] One of these nine dimensions is "spiritual democracy." According to Locke, "Spiritual Democracy" is democracy's "largest and most inner meaning."[40]

For civilization to advance, a universal perspective is needed. For American society to evolve, a coherent, multifaceted approach must be adopted. The following passage connects the problem of racism with that of the economy:

> America, that has in an economic and material way labored through to the most promising material elements of democracy, is spiritually very far from the realization of her own organic [i]deal. One would despair except for the knowledge from history that the solutions come out of the crater pots of the deepest and most seething problems. The fundamental problems of current America are materiality and prejudice. They seem to rise out of separate positions, but their common base is selfishness. They rest primarily not upon the economic and historical conditions in terms of which they are so often explained and discussed, but upon false human values, a blind ness [*sic*] of heart, an obstruction of social vision. And so we must say with the acute actualities of America's race problem and the acute potentialities of her economic problem, the land that is nearest to

material democracy is furthest away from spiritual democracy, unless, as we have said, the heart of the solution is to come out of the crux of the problem.[41]

The "crux" of America's overarching social "problems" are racial and economic, that is, "materiality and prejudice." The two problems, of course, are interrelated. Racism and poverty are intimately related in terms of cause and effect. Together, they exacerbate each other in a vicious cycle, with no end in sight. Therefore, it makes sense that Alain Locke, in a manner of speaking, is basically saying that money (i.e., avarice) is the proverbial root of all evil. Locke reduces the "fundamental problems of current America" to naked "materiality and prejudice," which share a "common base" of "selfishness." Intractable problems attract new solutions, especially when the former approaches simply have not worked.

Locke develops his analysis of America's social problematic yet further. Bleak as these problems may seem, there still is hope, as Locke notes:

> Perhaps this is so. Practical philanthropy is welling up in rapidly increasing volume out of the heart of the capitalist system; and even before the class issues have begun perceptably [*sic*] to ameliorate, we witness at last a favorable trend to the most crucial of all the American issues, the strained relations of the race question. New and promising efforts of race cooperation and help have sprung up within the last decade from the very section where the issues are most acute; of course the Old South still lingers both as an unfortunate social condition and state of mind. But essentially a New South is breaking through; and it is interesting to note not in terms of the old notion of help but of the new discovery of common interests, in other words in terms of cooperation.[42]

At the time that Locke was writing, just how "new and promising" these positive developments actually were is uncertain. Progress was possible, but not inevitable. The main point here is that the "Old South" (i.e., a backward, low-wage regional market economy) must be replaced by the "New South" (i.e., a reformed and revitalized economy, such as integration into the national labor market, leading to some measure of prosperity).[43] Both in Alain Locke's day and today, the term "New South" refers to post-Civil War economic and social progress in general.

Locke extends this paradigm of the new replacing the old social order:

> The inter-racial commissions spreading their work of common council through the better and more representative elements of the two races in the South, the new movement for the equalisation [*sic*] of public school expenditures, health and public welfare measures and activities that has significantly but only recently begun, the challenge of the great industrial migration of the Negro away from the South, which has led to ameliorative measures to retain this economically

> valuable but hitherto socially mis-valued group, and the increasing self-esteem and direction of the New Negro himself which though it has, like the assertive rise of suppressed minorities the world over today, the potentialities of clash and rivalry and increasing sectarianism, holds nevertheless with the right social attitude toward it the possibilities of finer mutual respect and reciprocity; all these are hopeful signs out of a spiritually dark and threatening situation.[44]

The term "reciprocity" is a key concept found throughout Locke's essays and speeches. "Reciprocity" is Locke's racial golden rule. Locke continues, contrasting "unity" and "uniformity," which ultimately are antithetical to each other:

> I have often thought that one of the great obstacles that has prevented the world from realizing unity was the notion, especially characteristic of the West, that to be one effectively we must all be alike, and that to be at peace we must all have the same interests. But the increasing breaking-up of Western society may not be the debacle of civilization which the Occidental materialistic uniformitarians have imagined it to be, but rather the preparatory step that will force us to abandon this false idea and adopt the true one, not of uniformity, but reciprocity, not of an outward union of bodies and cultures, but of social heart and feeling. Once we rid ourselves of the proprietary notion of civilization, we enter upon an era of spiritual reciprocity.[45]

One can say that Locke's thesis is "reciprocity, not uniformity." "Reciprocity" is the golden rule condensed into a single watchword. That very word is often met throughout Alain Locke's writings. It has profound philosophical, spiritual, and social import. Locke states that a major obstacle to world "unity" has been the "Western" emphasis on "uniformity." Although the two words, "uniformity" and "unity" sound similar, they are polar opposites and are functionally antithetical. To favorably compare or erroneously equate these two values is social folly of world-historical proportions. The same is true if one confuses, confounds, or otherwise conflates these two concepts. In Locke's view, uniformity is a formidable barrier to unity. Reciprocity, then, is a moral imperative, collectively as well as individually. Indeed, the well-being of society depends upon it. "Reciprocity" implicates "universal values":

> This, I take it, is from the intellectual point of view the one great new idea and ideal to be added in our day to our science and wrought into our practice of education. Segments of it come from many quarters; none more promising, to mention one significant light, it seems than the philosophy of the Austrian Holzapfel, with its professed basic principle of the "Pan-Ideal", where universal values, the point of view of all mankind is to be substituted for the narrowing

and hopelessly conflicting scales of value that race, class, nation and sect have made almost chronic defects in our thinking.[46]

Rudolf Maria Holzapfel (1874–1930) was an Austrian philosopher, social psychologist, and theorist of art whose *magnum opus*, *Panideal, das Seelenleben und seine soziale Neugestaltung* ("Pan-idealism: The Life of the Soul and Its Social Reform"), was published in 1923. He advocated "a new kind of conscience" transcending "individual or collective egoism, whether of a national or a racist character," with the goal of advancing civilization by means of an overarching, world ideal.[47] Locke eschewed absolutisms, but embraced universals. He called for "universal values" that transcend the narrow scope of "race, class, nation and sect."

Locke now adopts a visionary, utopian tone:

> We must begin working out the new era courageously, but it must be a revolution within the soul. How many external wars and revolutions it will make unnecessary, if it is only possible! And we must begin heroically with the great apparent irreconcilables; the East and the West, the black man and the self-arrogating Anglo-Saxon, for unless these are reconciled, the salvation of society in this world cannot be. If the world had believingly understood the full significance of Him [Jesus Christ] who taught it to pray and hope "Thy Kingdom come on earth as it is in Heaven" who also said "In my Father's house are many mansions," already we should be further toward the realization of this great millenial [*sic*] vision.[48]

According to Locke, a "revolution within the soul" is needed. The "salvation of society" depends, in large part, on resolving "the great apparent irreconcilables," whether nationalism or racism. Locke concludes his essay as follows:

> The word of God is still insistent, and more emphatic as the human redemption delays and becomes more crucial, and we have what Dr. Elsemont [Esslemont] rightly calls Bahá'u'lláh's "one great trumpet-call to humanity": "That all nations shall become one in faith, and all men as brothers; that the bonds of affection and unity between the sons of men should be strengthened; that diversity of religion should cease, and differences of race be annulled. . . . These strifes and this bloodshed and discord must cease, and all men be as one kindred and family."[49]

Locke is quoting the words of Bahá'u'lláh delivered when Cambridge Orientalist, Edward Granville Browne was granted an audience with him on Wednesday, April 16, 1890.[50] It is quite clear that this well-known statement by Bahá'u'lláh resonated profoundly with Locke and resounds conceptually throughout his writings.

Religion most typically concerns the affairs of the heart and spirit. The "spiritual" dimension is a pivotal concept in Locke's public discourse. For instance, in the Oxford anthology, *The Works of Alain Locke*,[51] which excludes his Bahá'í publications, one encounters the terms "spiritual" and "spiritually" in a wide array of examples.[52] According to Locke, racial prejudice and religious prejudice arise from the very "psychology of prejudice" (i.e., the attitudinal orientation and mental dynamics of racial prejudice) itself:

> It seems to me, as I study it, that the psychology of prejudice—that the habit of social group discrimination—is a very infectious and vicious thing which, if allowed to grow, spreads from one group to another; and *I also feel that in talking against American racial prejudice we are at the same time talking against religious prejudice*, cultural prejudice of all kinds, and even social class prejudice to a certain extent. The same psychology seems to feed them all.[53]

As for a religious solution to the problem of racial prejudice and discrimination, Alain Locke declared in 1925:

> America's democracy must begin at home with a spiritual fusion of all her constituent peoples in brotherhood, and in an actual mutuality of life. Until democracy is worked out in the vital small scale of practical human relations, it can never, except as an empty formula, prevail on the national or international basis. Until it establishes itself in human hearts, it can never institutionally flourish. Moreover, America's reputation and moral influence in the world depends on the successful achievement of this vital spiritual democracy within the lifetime of the present generation. (Material civilization alone does not safeguard the progress of a nation.) Bahá'í Principles and the leavening of our national life with their power, is to be regarded as the salvation of democracy. In this way only can the fine professions of American ideals be realized.[54]

His conclusion, that "Bahá'í Principles and the leavening of our national life with their power, is to be regarded as the salvation of democracy," may be regarded as Alain Locke's most distinct and definitive statement as to the relevance and importance of Bahá'í social principles as applied to racism and related social ills afflicting American society. This was a bold and courageous statement on Locke's part. Although, at sundry times, Locke may have been somewhat skeptical, even cynical, about the practical application of these principles (both within Bahá'í communities themselves and in American society at large), he remained committed to these Baha'i principles throughout his personal and professional life.[55]

RACE AND RELIGION: RETROSPECT AND PROSPECT

This study focused on Alain Locke's perspectives on race and religion in general, and on race and the Bahá'í Faith in particular. As social phenomena, race and religion, whether characterized by self-segregation or integration, by prejudice or camaraderie, are as dynamically interrelated as they are intercommunal. For better or worse, their reciprocal interactions have been and continue to be historically at play. A lesson that can be drawn from this brief historical retrospective is that religion can be a motivating and effective sociomoral force for the "social salvation" of the body politic. Although religion, ideally and ideologically, can foster fraternity and equality and thereby contribute to racial harmony, it takes a concerted effort to overcome the legacy of prejudice that continues to bedevil American society, albeit more covertly than overtly. The leadership of such influential protagonists for social progress as Dr. Martin Luther King, Jr., and, before him, Dr. Alain Leroy Locke, are worthy of study for better understanding the past, negotiating the present, and priming the prospect of a better future. Not only is this an ongoing interracial project, but it has an interreligious dimension as well.

Throughout his professional career as a public intellectual, Alain Locke was a champion of "race amity." His advocacy for ideal race relations expressed itself as a recurring theme throughout his writings and public discourse. "On the one hand there is the possibility," Locke wrote to the *New York Times* in 1931, "of a fine collaboration spiritually between these two groups [black and white] with their complementary traits and qualities. They have great spiritual need, the one of the other, if they will so see it.'[56] Locke stated quite the same in *The Negro in America* (1933):

> If they will but see it, because of their complementary qualities, the two racial groups have great spiritual need, one of the other. It would truly be significant in the history of human culture, if two races so diverse should so happily collaborate, and the one return for the gift of a great civilization the reciprocal gift of the spiritual cross-fertilization of a great and distinctive national culture.[57]

This latter statement has been quoted in a Bahá'í compilation on race, which is interesting and significant in that during the era being studied such compilations, by and large, primarily quote from the scriptural texts, and rarely from individuals.[58] "No more progressive step can be made in our present civilization," Locke elsewhere wrote, "than the breaking down of the barriers which separate races, sexes and nations."[59] This grand imperative, so eloquently yet succinctly stated, synchronizes, synergizes, and intensifies in concert with Alain Locke's Bahá'í ideals.

Race and religion are dynamically interlinked. Depending on how it is interpreted and applied, religion can be a source of good or evil, a blessing or a curse, the cause of amity or enmity, the reason for harmony or hatred, and the cradle of benediction or malediction. Locke's views on race and religion naturally depended on context. Steeped in the philosophy of values, he was very much alive to the potential of religious values as they variously impacted on race relations. "Race, nationality, language and religion can all be sharp and serious issues of difference and hostility. Yet none of them need be."[60] He viewed the Bahá'í Faith, as a new world religion born in the fullness of modernity, especially suited for promoting ideal race relations. This great potential was only partly realized in practice during this era. Much more is needed to be done in order to more fully democratize democracy and "Americanize Americans," as Locke wrote.[61] The present study has shown that Alain Locke, while skeptical and somewhat cynical about the prospect of any real progress in race relations within Christianity itself, saw great potential in Bahá'í efforts to promote "race amity," and believed that they were a radical departure from prevailing social (and religious) racial norms in Jim Crow America.[62]

NOTES

1. Alain Locke, "Negro Art and Culture," quoted in Louis G. Gregory, "A Convention for Amity," *The Bahá'í Magazine* (*Star of the West*) 15, no. 9: 273.

2. Gayle Morrison, "To Move the World: Promoting Racial Amity, 1921–1927," *World Order* 14, no. 2 (Winter 1980): 19.

3. In the same video, Cornel West added: "I have come to have a profound admiration for brothers and sisters of the Bahá'í Faith. I've actually met Dizzy Gillespie and he, of course, one of the great artists of the twentieth century, was of Bahá'í Faith, and talked over and over again about what it meant to him. Alain Locke, of course, probably one of the greatest philosophic minds of the middle part of the twentieth century, was also of Bahá'í Faith, the first Black Rhodes scholar and chairman of the philosophy department at Howard University, for over forty-two years. What I've always been taken by is the very genuine universalism of the Bahá'í Faith, one of the first religious groups to really hit racism and white supremacy head on, decades ago. By decades, I mean many decades ago and remain consistent about it." See Cornel West, "Towards Oneness—Cornel West," https://www.youtube.com/watch?v=SbEDC8wAWiI.

4. *The Crisis* 29, no. 2 (December 1924): 77. More notices appeared in other issues, for example, *The Crisis* 40, no. 10 (October 1931): 345–346.

5. Christopher Buck, *Alain Locke: Faith and Philosophy* (Los Angeles: Kalimát Press, 2005), 111–113.

6. Rev. Martin Luther King, Jr., "Rally Speech, Mississippi Tour, Clarksdale, Mississippi, Pre-Washington Campaign," St. Paul Methodist Church, March 19,

1968. Manuscript Collection, No. 1083, Subseries 11.2, Martin Luther King Speaks program files, 1967–1985, Box 612, Folder 22, Manuscript 68#40C, page 7. Manuscript, Archives, and Rare Book Library (MARBL), Emory University.

7. Leonard Harris and Charles Molesworth, *Alain L. Locke: The Biography of a Philosopher* (Chicago: University of Chicago Press, 2008), 1.

8. Buck, *Alain Locke: Faith and Philosophy*, 73–74 and passim.

9. The present writer has published a monograph and a number of articles documenting Alain Locke's life and contributions as a Bahá'í. See, *inter alia*, Christopher Buck, *Alain Locke: Faith and Philosophy* (Los Angeles: Kalimát Press, 2005); Buck, "Alain Locke's Philosophy of Democracy," *Studies in Bahá'í Philosophy* 4 (2015): 24–45; Buck, "Alain Locke," *The African American Experience: The American Mosaic*, eds. Marian Perales, Spencer R. Crew, and Joe E. Watkins (Santa Barbara, CA: ABC-CLIO, 2013); Buck, "The Bahá'í 'Race Amity' Movement and the Black Intelligentsia in Jim Crow America: Alain Locke and Robert S. Abbott," *Bahá'í Studies Review* 17 (2011): 3–46; Buck, "Alain Locke: Four Talks Redefining Democracy, Education, and World Citizenship," edited and introduced by Christopher Buck and Betty J. Fisher, *World Order* 38, no. 3 (2006–2007): 21–41; Buck, "Alain Locke: Race Leader, Social Philosopher, Bahá'í Pluralist," in "Alain Locke: Dean of the Harlem Renaissance and Bahá'í Race-Amity Leader," special issue, *World Order* 36, no. 3 (2005): 7–36; Buck, "Alain Locke in His Own Words: Three Essays," edited and annotated by Christopher Buck and Betty J. Fisher, *World Order* 36, no. 3 (2005): 37–48; Buck, "Alain Locke," *American Writers: A Collection of Literary Biographies*, ed. Jay Parini (Farmington Hills, MI: Scribner's Reference, The Gale Group, 2004), 195–219; Buck, "Alain Locke and Cultural Pluralism," *Search for Values: Ethics in Bahá'í Thought*, eds. Seena Fazel and John Danesh (Los Angeles: Kalimát Press, 2004), 94–158; Buck, "Alain Locke: Bahá'í Philosopher," *Bahá'í Studies Review* 10 (2001–2002): 7–49.

10. Buck, *Alain Locke: Faith and Philosophy*, 195.

11. Buck, *Alain Locke: Faith and Philosophy*, 279.

12. See, for example, Mehrdad Amanat, *Jewish Identities in Iran: Resistance and Conversion to Islam and the Bahá'í Faith* (London: I. B. Tauris, 2013), 92.

13. Locke, quoted in Buck, *Alain Locke: Faith and Philosophy*, 279.

14. Buck, *Alain Locke: Faith and Philosophy*.

15. Leonard Harris and Charles Molesworth, *Alain L. Locke: The Biography of a Philosopher* (Chicago: University of Chicago Press, 2008); Jeffrey C. Stewart, *The New Negro: The Life of Alain Locke* (Oxford: Oxford University Press, 2017).

16. Buck, "The Bahá'í 'Race Amity' Movement and the Black Intelligentsia in Jim Crow America: Alain Locke and Robert S. Abbott."

17. Library of Congress, "National Urban League Papers. National Interracial Conference, 1928," https://memory.loc.gov/cgi-bin/query/r?ammem/cool:@field(DOCID+@lit(mu03T000)):.

18. National Urban League, "Mission and History," http://nul.iamempowered.com/who-we-are/mission-and-history.

19. Library of Congress, "The Revised Draft of Findings Committee Report," https://memory.loc.gov/cgi-bin/query/r?ammem/cool:@field(DOCID+@lit(mu0313)).

20. "Dr. Alain Locke Reviews Interracial Conference," *The Interstate Tattler* (New York, January 4, 1929), 3, personal communication by Steven Kolins, November 20, 2017.

21. See National Urban League Papers. National Interracial Conference, 1928 (Library of Congress), https://memory.loc.gov/cgi-bin/query/r?ammem/cool:@field(DOCID+@lit(mu032))#mu03010. See also Alain Locke, "The Boxed Compass of Our Race Relations," *The Survey* 51 (January 1929): 469–472; reprint, "The Boxed Compass of Our Race Relations. North and South: The Washington Conference on the American Negro," *Southern Workman* 58 (February 1929): 51–56.

22. Buck, "Alain Locke: Baha'i Philosopher."

23. Buck, *Alain Locke: Faith and Philosophy*, 20–21 and 270. See also Alain Locke, *The Problem of Classification in the Theory of Values* (PhD diss., Harvard University, 1917).

24. Buck, *Alain Locke: Faith and Philosophy*, 20–21. See also Alain Locke, "Values and Imperatives," in *American Philosophy, Today and Tomorrow*, eds. Sidney Hook and Horace M. Kallen (New York: Lee Furman, 1935), 313–33; reprint, Freeport, NY: Books for Libraries Press, 1968.

25. Buck, *Alain Locke: Faith and Philosophy*, 20–21.

26. Buck, *Alain Locke: Faith and Philosophy*, 20–21.

27. Alain Locke, "Whither Race Relations? A Critical Commentary," *Journal of Negro Education* 13, no. 3, Yearbook: Education for Racial Understanding (Summer, 1944): 401.

28. Locke, "Whither Race Relations?" 401.

29. Alain Locke, "Peace Between Black and White in the United States," in Alain Locke, "Alain Locke in His Own Words: Three Essays," *World Order* 36, no. 3 (2005): 45. Alain Locke Papers, MSRC, Box 164–123: Folder 19 ("Peace Between Black and White in the United States").

30. "Drs. E. P. Roberts and Alain Leroy Locke Address Salem M. E. Church Lyceum Sun," *The New York Age* (November 22, 1924), 5, https://www.newspapers.com/clip/358274/alain_locke_at_opening_of_new_church.

31. Alain Locke, "The Gospel for the Twentieth Century," in Alain Locke, "Alain Locke in His Own Words: Three Essays," edited and annotated by Christopher Buck and Betty J. Fisher. *World Order* 36, no. 3 (2005): 39–42. Published by permission from the Alain Locke Papers, Moorland-Spingarn Research Center (MSRC), Howard University, Washington, D.C. See Alain Locke, "The Gospel for the Twentieth Century" [untitled essay], Alain Locke Papers, MSRC, Box 164–143, Folder 3 (Writings by Locke—Notes. Christianity, spirituality, religion).

32. Locke, "The Gospel for the Twentieth Century," 39–40.

33. Locke, quoted in "Locke Holds Smashing of Humanity's Barriers Civilization's Present Need: Howard University Professor Views Elimination of Bars Between Races, Sexes and Nations as Necessity for Progress," *The New York Amsterdam News* (26 March 1930), 11.

34. Locke, "The Gospel for the Twentieth Century," 40.

35. Locke, "The Gospel for the Twentieth Century," 40.

36. Liberal, progressive, and socially conscious Christian reformers, such as Washington Gladden, Josiah Strong, Walter Rauschenbusch, and Harry F. Ward,

were leading advocates of what has come to be known as the "Social Gospel." In Locke's day and age, the Niebuhr brothers and their Neo-Orthodoxy were tinged with Christian Socialism and were a contemporary parallel of Locke's social salvation. See, for example, H. Richard Niebuhr's *Social Sources of Denominationalism.*

37. Locke, "The Gospel for the Twentieth Century," 40.

38. Buck, "Philosophy of Democracy: America, Race, and World Peace," *Alain Locke: Faith and Philosophy*, 241–65; Buck, "Alain Locke's Philosophy of Democracy," 30–31 and passim.

39. Buck, "Alain Locke's Philosophy of Democracy," 30–31 and passim.

40. Buck, "Alain Locke's Philosophy of Democracy," 40.

41. Locke, "The Gospel for the Twentieth Century," 40.

42. Locke, "The Gospel for the Twentieth Century," 41.

43. See, for example, Gavin Wright, *Old South, New South: Revolutions in the Southern Economy since the Civil War* (Baton Rouge, LA: LSU Press, 1997).

44. Locke, "The Gospel for the Twentieth Century," 41. "The New Negro" is an iconoclastic term that is used to dispel prevailing negative stereotypes of the "Negro." It became the watchword of the "New Negro" movement, of which Locke was a leading proponent. See Christopher Buck, "New Negro Movement," *Encyclopedia of African American History*, vol. 3, eds. Leslie Alexander and Walter Rucker (Santa Barbara, CA: ABC-CLIO, 2010), 925–927.

45. Locke, "The Gospel for the Twentieth Century," 41.

46. Locke, "The Gospel for the Twentieth Century," 41.

47. Hans Thomas Hakl, *Eranos: An Alternative Intellectual History of the Twentieth Century*, trans. Christopher McIntosh (Montreal: McGill–Queens University Press, 2014), 26. Holzapfel's influence on Locke's philosophy of values, in evidence here, awaits further research and study.

48. Locke, "The Gospel for the Twentieth Century," 41.

49. Locke, "The Gospel for the Twentieth Century," 42.

50. Locke quotes from John E. Esslemont, *Bahá'u'lláh and the New Era: An Introduction to the Bahá'í Faith* (New York: Brentano's, 1923), 46. Esslemont, in turn, cites Cambridge Orientalist, Edward Granville Browne from 'Abdu'l-Baha, *A Traveller's Narrative written to illustrate the Episode of the Bāb (Maqālah-*'i shakhṣī-i sayyāḥ kih dar qaẕīyah-'*i Bāb nivishtah ast).* Edited by Edward G. Browne, vol. 1. Persian Text, vol. 2, English Translation and notes (Cambridge: Cambridge University Press, 1891), Vol 2, xxxix–xl. See Christopher Buck and Youli A. Ioannesyan, "Scholar Meets Prophet: Edward Granville Browne and Bahá'u'lláh (Acre, 1890)," *Bahá'í Studies Review* 20 (2018): 21–38.

51. See Alain Locke, *The Works of Alain Locke*, ed. Charles Molesworth (Oxford: Oxford University Press, 2012).

52. See Locke, *The Works of Alain Locke*: "spiritual kinship" (110); "spiritually refined" (111); "spiritual selfhood" (114); "spiritual quickening" (125); "spiritual release" (125); "spiritual freedom" (125); "spiritual interpretation" (159); "spiritual values" (159); "spiritually inside" (160); "spiritual view of life" (165); "spiritual advantage"(183); "spiritual endowment" (183); "spiritually compensating for the present lacks of America" (187); "spiritualizing reaction" (187); "the proud stigmata of spiritual immunity and moral victory" (187); "spiritually free" (187); "spiritual

discipline and a cultural blessing" (199); "colorful and distinctive spiritual things in American life" (199); "cornerstone spiritually in the making of a distinctive American culture" (199); "national spiritual life" (200); "spiritual declaration of independence" (200); "spiritual emancipation" (200); "deep spirituality" (202); "spiritual gain" (206); "deeper spiritual identification" (206); "deeper spiritual identification" (206); "spiritual discipline and intensification of mood" (208); "spiritual espousal" (209); "spiritual loyalty" (210); "spiritual bloom" (212); "precious spiritual gifts" (218); "our spiritual growth" (219); "borrowed spiritual clothes" (222); "spiritually unmoored" (224); "spiritual portrait" (224); "spiritual truancy" (224); "spiritual bread" (227); "spiritual maturity" (228); "spiritual progress" (229); "spiritual ghetto" (241); "moral and spiritual superiority" (286); "the race's spiritual creativeness" (290); "this great spiritual curse" (294); "spiritual solidarity of minorities" (294); "cultural and spiritual advance" (307); "becomes an American spiritually" (429); "Spiritual capital must be accumulated" (438); "spiritual development" (450); "spiritual Coming of Age" (451); "religious beliefs as expressions of spiritual needs" (469); "new spiritual stature" (487); "man's carnal and spiritual selves" (500); "a spiritual imperative not to be denied" (534); "a spiritual, or at least an intellectual virtue" (545); "a spiritual corporate idea" (555); "moral and spiritual brotherhood" (556); "ancient spiritual lineage" (562); "intellectual and spiritual disarmament" (567).

53. Alain Locke, "The Negro Group," in *Group Relations and Group Antagonisms: A Series of Addresses and Discussions*, ed. Robert M. MacIver (New York: Institute for Religious Studies, 1944), 49. (Emphasis added.)

54. Locke, "America's Part in World Peace," quoted in Harlan Ober, "The Bahá'í Congress at Green Acre," *The Bahá'í Magazine* (*Star of the West*) 16, no. 5 (August 1925): 525.

55. Buck, *Alain Locke: Faith and Philosophy*, 161–162.

56. Alain Locke, quoted in "Says Art Raises Status of Negroes: Dr. Alain Locke Declares Nation is Re-evaluating Race for Its Contributions," *New York Times* (8 September 1931), 17. Locke, who was in Germany at the time, sent to the *New York Times* the text of his paper entitled "The Negro in Art," which had been read in absentia on September 7, 1931, at the Conference of International Student Service, held at Mount Holyoke College in South Hadley, Massachusetts. *The New York Times* excerpted the paper in its article.

57. Alain Locke, *The Negro in America* (Chicago: American Library Association, 1933), 50.

58. 'Abdu'l-Bahá and Shoghi Effendi, *Race and Man: A Compilation*, compiled by Maye Harvey Gift (Wilmette, IL: Bahá'í Publishing Committee, 1943), 36.

59. Alain Locke, quoted in "Locke Holds Smashing of Humanity's Barriers Civilization's Present Need: Howard University Professor Views Elimination of Bars Between Races, Sexes and Nations as Necessity for Progress," *The New York Amsterdam News* (26 March 1930), 11.

60. Locke, *The Works of Alain Locke*, 390.

61. Buck, *Alain Locke: Faith and Philosophy*, 239.

62. This chapter is dedicated to Sandra Kay (Thompson) Buck (September 4, 1928–April 24, 1991) and George Hugh Buck (March 10, 1926–May 10, 2010), the

present writer's parents, in perpetual honor: "Gratitude urges us to repay kindness; justice disposes us to do what is right; kindness moves us to act graciously; humanity constrains us to show mercy." John Page Hopps, *First Principles of Religion and Morality* (1874), 22.

BIBLIOGRAPHY

'Abdu'l-Bahá, and Shoghi Effendi. *Race and Man: A Compilation*, comp. Maye Harvey Gift. Wilmette, IL: Bahá'í Publishing Committee, 1943.

"Alain Locke Reviews Interracial Conference." *The Interstate Tattler*. New York, January 4, 1929, 3.

"Along the Color Line." *The Crisis* 40, no. 10 (October 1931): 344–348.

Amanat, Mehrdad. *Jewish Identities in Iran: Resistance and Conversion to Islam and the Bahá'í Faith*. London: I. B. Tauris, 2013.

Browne, Edward Granville, ed. and trans. *A Traveller's Narrative written to illustrate the Episode of the Bāb (Maqālah-'i shakhṣī-i sayyāḥ kih dar qaẓīyah-'i Bāb nivishtah ast)*. By 'Abdu'l-Baha, edited in the original Persian, and translated into English, with an Introduction and Explanatory Notes. Vol. 1. Persian Text. Vol. 2. English Translation and notes. Cambridge: Cambridge University Press, 1891.

Buck, Christopher. "Alain Locke." *American Writers: A Collection of Literary Biographies*. Supplement 14. Edited by Jay Parini. Farmington Hills, MI: Scribner's Reference, 2004, 195–219. Also available at https://psu-us.academia.edu/ChristopherBuck.

Buck, Christopher. "Alain Locke." *The African American Experience: The American Mosaic*. Edited by Marian Perales, Spencer R. Crew, and Joe E. Watkins. Santa Barbara, CA: ABC-CLIO, 2013. Also available at https://psu-us.academia.edu/ChristopherBuck.

Buck, Christopher. "Alain Locke and Cultural Pluralism." *Search for Values: Ethics in Baha'i Thought*. Edited by Seena Fazel and John Danesh. Los Angeles: Kalimát Press, 94–158. Also available at https://psu-us.academia.edu/ChristopherBuck.

Buck, Christopher. "Alain Locke: Baha'i Philosopher." *Baha'i Studies Review* 10 (2001–2002): 7–49. Also available at https://psu-us.academia.edu/ChristopherBuck.

Buck, Christopher. *Alain Locke: Faith and Philosophy*. Los Angeles: Kalimát Press, 2005. Also available at https://psu-us.academia.edu/ChristopherBuck.

Buck, Christopher. "Alain Locke: Four Talks Redefining Democracy, Education, and World Citizenship." Edited and introduced by Christopher Buck and Betty J. Fisher. *World Order* 38, no. 3 (2006–2007): 21–41. Also available at https://psu-us.academia.edu/ChristopherBuck.

Buck, Christopher. "Alain Locke in His Own Words: Three Essays." Edited and annotated by Christopher Buck and Betty J. Fisher. *World Order* 36, no. 3 (2005): 37–48. Also available at https://psu-us.academia.edu/ChristopherBuck.

Buck, Christopher. "Alain Locke's Philosophy of Democracy." *Studies in Baha'i Philosophy* 4 (2015): 24–45. Also available at https://psu-us.academia.edu/ChristopherBuck.

Buck, Christopher. "Alain Locke: Race Leader, Social Philosopher, Baha'i Pluralist." Special Issue, Alain Locke: Dean of the Harlem Renaissance and Baha'i Race-Amity Leader. *World Order* 36, no. 3 (2005): 7–36. Also available at https://psu-us.academia.edu/ChristopherBuck.

Buck, Christopher. "The Bahá'í 'Race Amity' Movement and the Black Intelligentsia in Jim Crow America: Alain Locke and Robert S. Abbott." *Bahá'í Studies Review* 17 (2011): 3–46. Also available at https://psu-us.academia.edu/ChristopherBuck.

Buck, Christopher. "New Negro Movement." *Encyclopedia of African American History*. Vol 3. Edited by Leslie Alexander and Walter Rucker. Santa Barbara, CA: ABC-CLIO, 2010, 925–927. Also available at https://psu-us.academia.edu/ChristopherBuck.

Buck, Christopher, and Youli A. Ioannesyan, "Scholar Meets Prophet: Edward Granville Browne and Bahá'u'lláh (Acre, 1890)." *Bahá'í Studies Review* 20 (2018). Also available at https://www.academia.edu/36015012/_Scholar_Meets_Prophet_Edward_Granville_Browne_and_Baha_u_llah_Acre_1890_2018_.

"Drs. E. P. Roberts and Alain Leroy Locke Address Salem M. E. Church Lyceum Sun." *The New York Age* (November 22, 1924). https://www.newspapers.com/clip/358274/alain_locke_at_opening_of_new_church.

Esslemont, John E. *Bahá'u'lláh and the New Era: An Introduction to the Bahá'í Faith*. New York: Brentano's, 1923.

Hakl, Hans Thomas. *Eranos: An Alternative Intellectual History of the Twentieth Century*. Translated by Christopher McIntosh. Montreal: McGill-Queens University Press, 2014.

Harris, Leonard, and Charles Molesworth. *Alain L. Locke: The Biography of a Philosopher*. Chicago: University of Chicago Press, 2008.

Hopps, John Page. *First Principles of Religion and Morality*. London: Trübner, 1874.

"Horizon." *The Crisis* 29, no. 2 (December 1924): 72–77.

Library of Congress. "National Urban League Papers. National Interracial Conference, 1928." https://memory.loc.gov/cgi-bin/query/r?ammem/cool:@field(DOCID+@lit(mu03T000)).

Library of Congress. "Prosperity and Thrift: The Coolidge Era and the Consumer Economy, 1921–1929." https://www.loc.gov/teachers/classroommaterials/connections/prosperity-thrift.

Library of Congress. "The Revised Draft of Findings Committee Report." Accessed September 3, 2016. https://memory.loc.gov/cgi-bin/query/r?ammem/cool:@field(DOCID+@lit(mu0313)).

Locke, Alain. "America's Part in World Peace." In Harlan Ober, "The Bahá'í Congress at Green Acre." *The Bahá'í Magazine* (*Star of the West*). 16, no. 5 (August 1925): 525. Also available at http://starofthewest.info.

Locke, Alain. Quoted in "Locke Holds Smashing of Humanity's Barriers Civilization's Present Need: Howard University Professor Views Elimination of Bars Between Races, Sexes and Nations as Necessity for Progress." *The New York Amsterdam News*, 26 March 1930, 11.

Locke, Alain. "Negro Art and Culture." Quoted in Louis G. Gregory, "A Convention for Amity." *The Bahá'í Magazine* (*Star of the West*). 15, no. 9: 273. Also available at http://starofthewest.info.

Locke, Alain. Quoted in "Says Art Raises Status of Negroes: Dr. Alain Locke Declares Nation is Re-evaluating Race for Its Contributions." *The New York Times.* 8 September 1931, 17.

Locke, Alain. "Peace Between Black and White in the United States." In Alain Locke, "Alain Locke in His Own Words: Three Essays." *World Order* 36, no. 3 (2005): 45. Alain Locke Papers, MSRC, Box 164–123: Folder 19 ("Peace Between Black and White in the United States").

Locke, Alain. "The Boxed Compass of Our Race Relations." *The Survey* 51 (January 1929): 469–472. Reprint, "The Boxed Compass of Our Race Relations. North and South: The Washington Conference on the American Negro." *Southern Workman* 58 (February 1929): 51–56.

Locke, Alain. "The Gospel for the Twentieth Century." In Alain Locke, "Alain Locke in His Own Words: Three Essays." Edited and annotated by Christopher Buck and Betty J. Fisher. *World Order* 36, no. 3 (2005): 39–42. Also available at https://www.academia.edu/29901524/_Alain_Locke_in_His_Own_Words_Three_Essays_2005_. Published by permission from the Alain Locke Papers, Moorland-Spingarn Research Center (MSRC), Howard University, Washington, D.C. See Alain Locke, "The Gospel for the Twentieth Century" [untitled essay], Alain Locke Papers, MSRC, Box 164–143, Folder 3 (Writings by Locke—Notes. Christianity, spirituality, religion).

Locke, Alain. "The Negro Group." In *Group Relations and Group Antagonisms: A Series of Addresses and Discussions*. Edited by Robert M. MacIver. New York: Institute for Religious Studies, 1944.

Locke, Alain. *The Negro in America*. Chicago: American Library Association, 1933.

Locke, Alain. *The Problem of Classification in the Theory of Values*. PhD dissertation, Harvard University, 1917.

Locke, Alain. *The Works of Alain Locke*. Edited by Charles Molesworth. Oxford: Oxford University Press, 2012.

Locke, Alain. "Values and Imperatives." In *American Philosophy, Today and Tomorrow*. Edited by Sidney Hook and Horace M. Kallen. New York: Lee Furman, 1935, 313–33. Reprint, Freeport, NY: Books for Libraries Press, 1968.

Locke, Alain. "Whither Race Relations? A Critical Commentary." *Journal of Negro Education* 13, no. 3 (Summer, 1944): 401.

King, Rev. Martin Luther, Jr. "Rally Speech, Mississippi Tour, Clarksdale, Mississippi, Pre-Washington Campaign." St. Paul Methodist Church, March 19, 1968. Manuscript Collection, No. 1083, Subseries 11.2, Martin Luther King Speaks program files, 1967–1985, Box 612, Folder 22, Manuscript 68#40C, page 7. Manuscript, Archives, and Rare Book Library (MARBL), Emory University.

Morrison, Gayle. "To Move the World: Promoting Racial Amity, 1921–1927." *World Order* 14, no. 2 (Winter 1980): 9–31. Also available at https://bahai.works/World_Order.

National Urban League. "Mission and History." Accessed September 3, 2016. http://nul.iamempowered.com/who-we-are/mission-and-history.

National Urban League Papers. "National Interracial Conference, 1928." Washington, DC: Library of Congress. Accessed November 19, 2017. https://memory.loc.gov/cgi-bin/query/r?ammem/cool:@field(DOCID+@lit(mu032))#mu03010.

Niebuhr, Richard. *The Social Sources of Denominationalism*. New York: Meridian Books, 1922.

Stewart, Jeffrey C. *The New Negro: The Life of Alain Locke*. Oxford: Oxford University Press, 2017.

West, Cornel. "Towards Oneness—Cornel West," https://www.youtube.com/watch?v=SbEDC8wAWiI.

Wright, Gavin. *Old South, New South: Revolutions in the Southern Economy since the Civil War*. Baton Rouge, LA: LSU Press, 1997.

Chapter 4

The Most Challenging Issue Revisited

African American Bahá'í Women and the Advancement of Race and Gender Equality, 1899–1943

Gwendolyn Etter-Lewis

> As to racial prejudice, the corrosion of which, for well nigh a century, has bitten into the fibre, and attacked the whole social structure of American society, it should be regarded as constituting the most vital and challenging issue confronting the Bahá'í community at the present stage of its evolution.[1]

The Bahá'í Faith was introduced to the United States in 1892 by two Lebanese immigrants who initially settled in New York City.[2] In California in 1898, Robert Turner, a butler employed by heiress Phoebe Hearst, became the first African American to enroll in the Bahá'i Faith.[3] Approximately a year later in 1899, New York City dressmaker Olive Jackson became the first African American woman to embrace the Bahá'í Faith.[4] Thus began a small, but steady flow of African Americans into the Bahá'í Faith, a relatively new religion based on the principle of unity across all differences. However, unity did not appear to be a remote possibility at that time. Blatant racial discrimination and gender disenfranchisement was the American norm. As a result, the early generations of black women who enrolled in the Bahá'í Faith (in the years between 1899 and 1943) found themselves in the midst of radical social change. Rather than stand mute on the sidelines, African American Bahá'í women became advocates on their own behalf as well as activists seeking to transform human relations. The following examination of *strategic* moments in the lives of selected early black women Bahá'ís exposes their resistance to the status quo, a strong sense of purpose, and unfailing resilience.

"KNOWLEDGE OF RESISTANCE": OVERVIEW

Reconstructing black women's past experiences is more than simply adding to information that might already exist. It involves a process of contextualizing their lives and making visible that which has been hidden in plain sight. The impact of black women on race and gender relations in the United States is significant. Yet, their contributions to the advancement of humanity continues to be overlooked, or at best, minimized. The book *Hidden Figures: The Story of the African-American Women Who Helped Win the Space Race* (2016) by Margot Lee Shetterly, and later a movie by the same name, is a prime example of the enduring historical invisibility of black women no matter how great their accomplishments. Why were such brilliant women, Katherine Johnson, Dorothy Vaughn, and Mary Jackson, unnoticed for so long? How could their successful negotiation of uncharted territory (i.e., male, white domains) *not* have become a training manual of sorts, for others trapped within the prescribed confines of race and gender? Whether unintentional or deliberate, this ongoing pattern of omission effectively generates more ignorance. As Darlene Clark Hine observes: "We cannot accurately comprehend either our hidden potential or the full range of problems that besiege us until we know about the successful struggles that generations of foremothers waged against virtually insurmountable odds."[5] Given the wisdom of these words, knowledge is but a first step toward disrupting the prevailing order. Any progress toward social justice must be facilitated by the *will* to create change as well as *action* to implement that change: "The attainment of any object is conditioned upon knowledge, volition and action. Unless these three conditions are forthcoming there is no execution or accomplishment."[6] As the activist foremothers demonstrated, the simple equation of *knowledge* plus *will*, plus *action* yielded powerful outcomes.

The reclamation of black women's past cannot be fully achieved without acknowledging theoretical constructs that underpin scholarly research on women in general, and black women in particular. Theorizing about black women's lives is not a clear-cut proposition free of controversy. Rather, it is a complex task mediated by several race and gender related variables. Patricia Hill Collins notes that, "Despite long-standing claims by elites that Blacks, women, Latinos, and other similarly derogated groups in the United States remain incapable of producing the type of interpretive, analytical thought that is labeled theory in the West, powerful knowledges of resistance that toppled former structures of social inequality repudiate this view. Members of these groups do in fact theorize, and our critical social theory has been central to our political empowerment and search for justice."[7]

Activism in the service of social justice generates theory that has the power to transform dominant ways of thinking. Anna Julia Cooper discharged a theory of liberation when she wrote, "Only the black woman can say 'when and where I enter . . . then and there the whole race enters with me";[8] Ida B. Wells Barnett created a theory of social action when she stood against the routine lynching of black people and said, "The very frequent inquiry made after my lectures by interested friends is, 'What can I do to help the cause?' The answer always is, 'Tell the world the facts.'"[9] Coralie Franklin Cook promoted a theory of equal rights witnessed by her passionate words, "Disfranchisement because of sex is curiously like disfranchisement because of color. It cripples the individual, it handicaps progress, it sets a limitation upon mental and spiritual development."[10] These are but a few examples of black women producing critical social theories *and* actions of resistance. Even though Cooper, Barnett, and Cook did not label themselves as feminists, their commitment to the advancement of women, in conjunction with the progress of the race, was a strong expression of *black feminism*, a contemporary term that captures "the emancipatory vision and acts of resistance among a diverse group of African American women who . . . articulate their understanding of the complex nature of black womanhood, the interlocking nature of the oppressions black women suffer, and the necessity of sustained struggle in their quest for self-definition, the liberation of black people, and gender equality."[11] While an extensive discussion of black feminism (e.g., womanism, stiwanism, black feminist thought, etc.) is beyond the scope of this paper, suffice it to say that black feminism is a way of being and thinking as well as a theoretical construct that places black women at the center of analysis in order that their words and deeds may be understood and valued. As black feminist scholars note, black women continue to be about the business of *doing*. Janet Mock best summarized this idea: "My grandmother and my two aunts were an exhibition in resilience and resourcefulness and black womanhood. They rarely talked about the unfairness of the world with the words that I use now with my social justice friends, words like 'intersectionality' and 'equality', 'oppression', and 'discrimination'. They didn't discuss those things because they were too busy living it, navigating it, surviving it."[12]

The state of being different in a sometimes-hostile world is challenging, especially if a person embodies more than one difference simultaneously. For black women, race is intricately connected to gender. One cannot be isolated from the other without distorting black women's unique perspectives and life experiences. Kimberlé Crenshaw and others[13] before her described black women's unique dilemma: "The concept of political intersectionality highlights the fact that women of color are situated within at least two subordinated groups. . . . Because women of color experience racism in ways not always the same as those experienced by men of color, and sexism in ways not always parallel to experiences of white women, dominant conceptions of antiracism and feminism are limited, even on their own terms."[14]

As a member of the Bahá'í Faith, another layer of complexity is added to black women's intersectionality given the fact that the Bahá'í Faith was a relatively young and not widely known religion in the late nineteenth and early twentieth centuries. Being at the crossroads of gender, race, class, *and* religion meant that black Bahá'í women were vulnerable to additional risks: "one of the dangers of standing at an intersection . . . is the likelihood of being run over by oncoming traffic."[15] As previously discussed, the aftermath of being "run over" entails injuries such as invisibility, namelessness, obscurity, anonymity, and so on. Black Bahá'í women, then, were the ultimate *other*. They did not fit neatly into any familiar category of identity or religious affiliation. Lacking such pre-defined credentials, early black women in the Bahá'í Faith were conspicuously absent from historical accounts of black life in the late nineteenth and early twentieth centuries.

One way to restore the historical presence of black women and prevent more casualties from being "run over" is to search for and listen to their stories, in their own words and without the expectation that one account will be the same for all of the women. The first generation of African American women Bahá'ís was a diverse group. Some were working class (e.g. dressmakers, housekeepers, etc.); others were well educated, middle class (e.g., educators, nurses, lawyers, etc.); and a few were in-between the lowest and highest social classes. Thus, it is impossible for one story to capture the variety of their experiences and personal points of view. Nigerian writer Chimamanda Ngozi Adichie effectively cautioned listeners about the limitations of a single story in a 2009 TED Talk entitled "The Danger of a Single Story." In a poetic and sometimes humorous presentation, Adichie warned against representing the experiences of any person or group as a *single* story. She explained that "the single story creates stereotypes and the problem with stereotypes is not that they are untrue but that they are incomplete, they make one story become the only story."[16] If we pay close attention to outside perceptions of black women, we find that such is the case—only a single story represents the whole of black womanhood. Most Americans, for example, are acquainted with antislavery heroes Harriet Tubman and Sojourner Truth even though the two are frequently confused with one another.[17] Often their distinctive stories are merged into one, representing a limited perspective of black womanhood during the slavery era and ignoring other outstanding women of that time. Another prime example of the risk involved with knowing only *one* story is found in the narrative of Rosa Parks who refused to give up her seat for a white passenger on a city bus. This is probably the *one* fact that stands out about Parks' civil rights involvement. However, she had a life outside of the movement and participated in other civil rights activities as well. Parks's contribution to the civil rights movement is undeniably significant, but she was not the only black woman to fight against segregation on public transportation. There were several women before Rosa Parks (1955): Frances Watkins Harper (1858), Elizabeth Jennings Graham (1864), Sojourner Truth (1865), Ida B. Wells Barnett (1884), Irene Morgan (1944), Sarah Keys (1952), Aurelia Browder, Susie McDonald, Claudette Colvin, and Mary Louise Smith (1955).[18] This list does not include women who were not permitted access to a bus or train such as Sarah Mayrant Fossett. In 1860, Fossett was physically blocked from boarding a Cincinnati street car and was dragged for several blocks. Her story does not end here. Later, she sued the company and won.[19] The point of these examples is that these historical figures were different from one another: some were young, others were older; some were employed, others were not; some were married, but some were single; some were committed to the civil rights movement while others simply were tired. They shared a single goal—desegregation of public transportation, but their lives were not identical. Therefore, it is important to keep in mind that a *single* story is inadequate to account for the myriad varieties of African American women's lives. Not all black foremothers were enlisted under the banner of Christianity—we need to know their stories as well.

A LEGACY OF ACTIVISM

Many of the early generation of black women Bahá'ís were predisposed to activism by virtue of parental role models. Attorney Alexander Martin and Mary Brown Martin, a schoolteacher, became Bahá'ís in 1913.[20] Mary was born in Raleigh, North Carolina, in 1877 to Scott and Jane Brown, former slaves. In spite of a humble beginning, she graduated from Central High School in 1900, and then attended Cleveland Normal Training School, graduating in 1903. She married Alexander Martin, a successful African American attorney, in 1905, and subsequently gave birth to four children: Lydia, Alexander, Jr., Stuart, and Sarah.[21] Mary was a popular educator, who became the first African American elected to the Cleveland, Ohio, board of education in 1929, and served two terms. She was so respected by colleagues that in 1963, a school built on the East Side of Cleveland at 8200 Brookline Avenue was named after her.[22] Mary's involvement with the Suffragist movement seemed like a natural fit. After all, she herself fulfilled many concurrent roles: wife, mother, educator, community activist, and so on, and understood first-hand the difficulties of living in a male dominant world.

Sarah Martin Pereira (1909–1995), the youngest child, credited her parents with her accomplishments in later life (see figure 4.1). In 1942, Pereira earned a PhD in Romance Languages from the Ohio State University in Columbus, Ohio. She held several academic positions, including Department Chair of Romance Languages at West Virginia State College and Academic Dean of

Figure 4.1 Sarah Martin Pereria Speaking at a Bahá'í Conference. *Source*: Photo Courtesy of U.S. National Bahá'í Archives.

the District of Columbia College of Education. Raised as a Bahá'í, Pereira served many Bahá'í institutions, such as the National Spiritual Assembly of the Bahá'ís of the United States, the Auxiliary Board (an advisory Bahá'í institution), and the Continental Board of Counselors for the Americas (another advisory Bahá'í institution).[23] She recalled in detail her mother's activism:

> And then my mother, as you know, became a suffragette who was an activist to get out the vote in 1918. She would even march in parades, carried banners and posters that said, "If a woman is good enough to be the mother of a president, she's good enough to vote." So that became my mother's type of life. And not at all in line with the dignity and the gentility that her mother had given as an example.[24]

Mary Martin's activism contrasted sharply with her mother's desire for her daughter to live up to the genteel southern woman image so important to black women in this early generation newly freed from slavery. According to Patton, "A proper lady of the period was expected to remain in the home,"[25] and emulate the attributes of true womanhood, "piety, purity, submissiveness, and domesticity."[26] Of course, these qualities were denied to black women who struggled to restore the damaged reputation conferred upon them by the institution of slavery. As Willis and Williams pointed out: "they [black women] had no class status; even after the abolition of slavery, the black female was the perpetual 'working girl,' in that she could never possess a status in European culture that was unrelated to her labor, whether forced or paid."[27] Mary unapologetically rejected the prescribed subordinate roles expected of black women. Her unconventional way of thinking led her to a lifestyle unencumbered by tradition. A generation later, Sarah recalled that her mother's dedication to service was inspirational, but costly. After serving two terms on the school board, Mary took a few years off, but that respite was short lived:

> After being freed from that service . . . we had said to mother, "Now don't run again because it's really too severe a trial and you become so emotionally upset when things are unjust." But while we were away at college, she let some of these people [school board committee] persuade her to let them run her name again. And she was elected a third term [1939]. But shortly after the election, she had a heart attack and passed away. She was only 62. . . . Her creed: to love humanity and to try to serve it.[28]

Undoubtedly, Mary Brown Martin was a woman with extraordinary drive. In fact, some would be tempted to label her as a strong black woman, relentless in her commitment to take care of everyone and everything. Nevertheless, to be marked as a strong black woman is not necessarily a compliment. As bell hooks argues: "Racist stereotypes of the strong, superhuman black woman are operative myths." that disguise "the extent to which black women are likely to be victimized in this society."[29] In other words, this kind of labeling has the potential to camouflage the pain and anguish black women may experience in trying to accomplish sometimes competing or conflicting goals of their own choice, or imposed from outside. This issue does not in any way diminish the significance of Mary Brown Martin's contributions, but it casts a sober perspective on the covert ramifications of black women's activism.

Attorney H. Elsie Austin (1908–2004) was another black Bahá'í influenced by her parents' activism (see figure 4.2). Born in Tuskegee, Alabama, she grew up in Cincinnati, Ohio. After finishing Walnut Hills High school, Austin became the first African American woman to graduate from the University of Cincinnati College of Law in 1930, and the first African American woman to serve as Assistant Attorney-General of the State of Ohio.[30] At twenty-six, she became a member of the Bahá'í Faith. Thereafter, Austin spent nearly a decade in Africa as a Foreign Service officer with the U.S. Information Agency. In addition to working on cultural and educational programs, she created the agency's first women's activities program in Africa.[31]

Figure 4.2 Elsie Austin. *Source*: Photo courtesy of U.S. National Bahá'í Archives.

Elsie Austin's mother, Mary, taught Household Science at Tuskegee University and later at the Stowe School in Cincinnati, Ohio. Her father, George, served as Commandant of Men at Tuskegee.[32] Both parents left indelible memories of activism that shaped Elsie's view of her purpose in life. She also maintained a life-long commitment to education and learned hard lessons from her mother's struggle to earn a baccalaureate degree:

> My mother was the youngest of thirteen children. Her mother sent her to Tuskegee. . . . And she was fiercely independent. She did not want her mother, who was in her late years in life, to put her through Tuskegee. So she marched into Booker T. Washington's office and asked if she could have a job. And he gave her a job at the school. And she worked her way through.[33]

This was not Mary's only experience in higher education. After her children became adults, she went back to school at the University of Cincinnati. As Austin's family history suggests, the quest for education was a priority for many black families at that time. Paula Giddings wrote, "The great desire for education combined with the status of teaching, provided an escape from the limitations that society imposed on women."[34] With a baccalaureate in hand, black women could move away from the low paid domestic work that followed them out of slavery and shepherd the next generation into a new kind of civic life and productivity. Darlene Clark Hine best described the significance of black women's contributions to every key aspect of life, "We now know that black women played essential roles in ensuring survival and progress of families, institutions, and communities."[35]

Both George and Mary Austin were committed to educating their children beyond the norm. Having lived through times of unrelenting prejudice, the Austins wanted to increase their children's chances of survival in an environment hostile to African Americans. Linda Perkins's research confirms that notion, "Because education had been denied both African American men and women, it was perceived as being important for the entire race rather than a particular sex."[36] However, schooling was only one way to convey education and life skills. Believing in the power of multiple sources of knowledge, George reveled in exposing his children to different experiences in order to educate them beyond the classroom:

> My father was in the military service most of his life and when he came back from the First World War, he went into what they used to call unity service and then into insurance. My father was always interested in taking us to see people and to see things. I remember visiting and meeting Marcus Garvey with him.[37]

Regardless of education, black people were not accorded the same treatment as whites in almost all professions. "Throughout the late nineteenth century and well into the twentieth, blacks as a group were barred from machine work within the industrial sector, and from white-collar clerical and service work."[38] Even though George served the country in at least two wars, he was not exempt from discrimination. According to Elsie:

> He [father] died a major and met a lot of discrimination, had a lot of overcoming to do, but he was never bitter. . . . I have a letter from President Harding. Although my father had all the qualifications for Major ten years before he was granted it, the president wrote and said it was the policy of the United States Army not to commission any more Negro officers. And he [father] kept fighting. . . . He came from that period and my mother also faced it [discrimination] in early Illinois which was not a very liberal state even though it was a free state.

> And I remember as a child hearing about lynchings and discriminations and I grew up incidentally quite bitter.[39]

Joining the Bahá'í Faith helped Elsie Austin overcome her bitterness, but life lessons acquired from childhood shaped her activism in specific ways. She was tireless as well as fearless in her pursuit of justice. "More than seven decades after she stood up for the truth in her classroom, Dr. Austin delivered a lecture in which she said that there are times when it is necessary to protest, not violently but with the courage to reject the false and the unjust . . . 'After all, the battle we face is essentially a spiritual battle to transform the souls and spirits of human beings, to empower them to express love and justice, and to develop a unity of conscience.'"[40]

MULTIPLE OVERLAPPING IDENTITIES

> The world of humanity has two wings—one is women and the other men. Not until both wings are equally developed can the bird fly.[41]

Black Bahá'í women played key roles in the Suffragist movement and civil rights movement. While it seems practical to separate these movements, at least chronologically, in reality, black women's civic engagement was not necessarily divided into separate spheres. Instead, there was significant overlap. Paula Giddings argues that "for Black women it was the issue of race that sparked their feminism."[42] Fighting one battle went hand in hand with fighting the other. As previously discussed, intersectionality illuminates the multiple ways that women of color experience oppression. Therefore, the discussion that follows arbitrarily places discussion of one movement before the other for the sake of convenience rather than as an indication of their compartmentalization in black women's lives.

The question of gender in black women's lives raises complex issues not easily disentangled. A woman cannot live one day as black *only* and the next day as female *only*. Historically, there has been much debate about the priority of race and gender in black women's experiences. bell hooks observed that, "Whether she has called herself a feminist or not, there is no radical black woman subject who has not been forced to confront and challenge sexism."[43] Black women Bahá'ís, strengthened by the Bahá'í principle of the equality of women and men, regularly faced sexism in their personal and professional lives.

Attorney H. Elsie Austin, who shattered the glass ceiling in law and related fields, found that coping with sexism was a constant occurrence. She described one of her first professional experiences as part of her role in breaking down barriers in a heretofore man's domain.

> It wasn't as difficult in law school as it was when I came out, took the bar, and started to practice. Because I had to overcome the tradition of a male, this being a male field. And I would go down to the courts and take my seat in the section, which is reserved for lawyers. And the bailiff would come over and say, "Young lady this is reserved for lawyers. You have to sit back there." And I was continually having to prove myself but I took all that in stride because you know you're in a pioneer field and you have to go with the flow of it, you know.[44]

Austin was neither surprised nor defeated by her reception at the court. She went on to overcome more barriers to women in the professions. However, H. Elsie Austin was not content with her success at overcoming obstacles imposed by race and gender in the United States. She traveled the world expressing her distinctive activism and lived in several different countries, specifically Morocco, Nigeria, Kenya, and the Bahamas.[45]

From a different perspective, pianist, composer, and music educator, Zenobia Powell Perry (1908–2004) experienced sexism when out of necessity she stepped into a man's world—housing construction. The historical record is not clear, but it appears that Zenobia became a Bahá'í in the mid-to-late seventies. Even though she was not among the earlier generations of black women Bahá'ís, her story is particularly relevant to this discussion. Zenobia Powell Perry was born in Boley, Oklahoma, to a middle-class family. Her father, Calvin Bethel Powell, was a black physician, and her mother, Birdie Lee Thompson, was Creek Indian and black.[46] When Zenobia accepted a position as faculty member and composer-in-residence at Central State University, she found herself at odds with the community. As a divorced woman with a child and new to Wilberforce, Ohio, she discovered that navigating the hidden constraints of class, race, and gender was extremely troublesome and difficult:

> I wanted to build a house because nobody wanted to rent to me [because] I wasn't in the AME church. I got Mr. Turner to take my money which he would not take until I had Dr. Wessley [department chair] OK it, even though I had the money to buy the lot. I designed the house. The contractor said, "We don't build a house like this." I think he would have taken it had I been a man. He did not want to take my design. So then I tried to find another one [contractor] that would take it [design]. I couldn't find another one. So I paid a contractor for cement . . . to put my basement in. And when he put sleepers on it, I paid him off . . . and a retired carpenter put this house together. It took me three years to build it.[47]

Perry successfully completed the project and lived in that house for the rest of her life. Like other black women in her generation, she faced an intimidating number of obstacles in almost every facet of life. However, she refused to be ignored. Zenobia Powell Perry's prolific career is testimony to her unwavering determination. She wrote songs, piano pieces, chamber works, an opera, and music for orchestra and symphonic wind band. Perry received many honors and awards related to her teaching, composing, and volunteer community work. But the most significant tribute is the continuing performances of her works by a devoted group of musicians, many of them former students, and by those who have only recently discovered her works.[48]

Lecile Webster (b. 1926) became a Bahá'í in 1946 in Cleveland, Ohio, where she was a student at Cleveland College. Within a span of ten years, Webster found herself living and working in Japan. The story of her employment with the U.S. Foreign Service is one of sheer resoluteness and patience. When Webster finally was given an assignment, she was sent to Japan for approximately a year and a half, and then transferred to Korea in 1956.[49] To no surprise, she also discovered that *sexism* was unavoidable in professional life:

> We were invited to the University of Gwangju[50] 'cause Bill [another Bahá'i] was teaching there. The chancellor of the university said he was giving a luncheon for us. Food was very scarce. We must have been about twelve people and they had this, I imagine it was one chicken. They cut it in little pieces. We all sat on the floor oriental style and the chancellor gave us a wonderful welcoming speech. He said, "We are very honored to have an American lady for the first time visiting our university." He [chancellor] said, "In honor of the lady, we're going to give you the choice piece of chicken," which was the chicken head with the eyes still in it. They put this on my plate. Bill then nudged me in the side and said [whispered], "OK, you women's libber [liberation], what are you going to do about this?" So I made all of the polite overtures toward the chancellor and I said, "Well, I'm in your country. I honor your traditions [e.g., men eat first]. . . . I would like to continue some of those traditions in our social afternoon—and I give my chicken to Bill Smidt." So I put it on his plate. And the professors applauded. They thought that it was the greatest thing.[51]

Webster solved the dilemma by appropriating a male tradition and using it to her advantage. After her time in Korea, Lecile was posted to several other countries including Mexico, Bolivia, Brazil, Norway, and France.[52] She continued to practice bridging cultural differences with grace and keen insight.

BLACK WOMEN, RACE, AND RESISTANCE

> There are no whites and blacks before God. All colors are one, and that is the color of servitude to God.[53]

Black Bahá'í women in this early generation possessed an acute perception of the racial inequality that touched almost every aspect of their lives. Each one had a different way of contesting racial injustice, and some were on the very forefront of the movement for civil rights while others assumed a more subtle approach. Both kinds of actions are important. Based on her study of black foremothers such as Maria Stewart, Giddings wrote that "all Black women abolitionists . . . were feminists, but when it came to the question of priorities, race, for most of them, came first."[54] Furthermore, it is not reasonable to measure black women's feminism by their traditional allegiance to race instead of gender. The intersectional nature of their lives means that one state of being (i.e., black, female) cannot be separated from the other.

Such is the case of black women Bahá'ís. Belonging to a religion based on unity did not shield them from the lingering effects of slavery and its aftermath. bell hooks's words are most appropriate here: "people who are truly oppressed know it even though they may not be engaged in organized resistance."[55] Black Bahá'í women articulated their experiences, clearly and unembellished. Zenobia Powell Perry, a musical prodigy who did not receive the recognition that she deserved early on in her career, remembered that,

> Now racism, it's one of those things you know is going to be there . . . one other experience I had that was very poignant was the fact that something I had done was selected for a national award. And they didn't know . . . that I was black. When they found out, then the award was no longer available.[56]

Looking back on the experience, Perry was philosophical. However, such ill treatment did not occur without leaving a mark. She continued to create award winning music in spite of the odds against her. One of her works in particular is fitting testimony to Zenobia's articulation of the African American experience through music. The opera entitled *Tawawa House* is the story of a group of escaped slaves who came to Tawawa House as one of the important safe houses in Ohio's Underground Railroad network. The opera premiered on May 2, 2014, at the Townsend Opera of Modesto California.[57]

Lecile Webster desperately wanted to serve the Bahá'í Faith as a pioneer,[58] and decided to join the U.S. foreign service in order to accomplish that goal. This was a noble endeavor, but not without difficulties. She remembered,

> I did a lot of research for jobs overseas and I sent applications to almost every place that had any kind of job opening. And I knew some of the rejection was because you know, I'm black and they weren't hiring me. Oil companies, fruit companies . . . many of the big corporations had offices overseas. They just were not hiring black women.[59]

Aware that the odds were not in her favor, Webster continued the search for an international job. The applications that she submitted included one to the

U.S. State Department. She was delighted to receive notification of a job opening, finally:

> So I received a notice from the State Department saying that they had an opening . . . So when I got the appointment here [Washington, DC] at the State Department, I came up and took an examination in a separate room. I was the only black in recruitment in 1954. And I don't really think today that they knew I was black until I got there. . . . I was kept for about six months before I was given an assignment. And I was then assigned to Tokyo.[60]

Differential treatment due to race seemed to be the norm. Even when she arrived at her post in Japan, she found her colleagues to be *hands off*: "On weekends you were left to your own so had it not been for the Japanese friends [Bahá'ís], I would have been a very unhappy, lonely person."[61] Webster remained in Japan, and then Korea for several years before going on to other parts of the world including Hong Kong, Macau, Rangoon, Thailand, New Delhi, Malaysia, Mexico, Bolivia, Brazil, Norway, and France. Webster mentioned that local people in the Asian countries where she worked tended to make comments about her height rather than her race or gender. Such response is not surprising as confirmed by Chelcee Johns in a more current experience abroad, "the fortunate side of this is that the ignorance regarding Black women abroad is typically not steeped in negativity and racism. Instead, it is a true lack of knowledge and experience."[62]

Other women in this early generation took different approaches to racial injustice and became heavily invested in the civil rights movement as *race women.* Evelyn Higginbotham noted, "For African Americans, race signified a cultural identity that defined and connected them as a people, even as a nation. To be called a 'race leader,' 'race man,' or 'race woman' by the black community"[63] was an honorable designation bestowed upon those "who devoted their lives to the advancement of their people."[64] Among the lesser-known race women is Coralie Franklin Cook (1861–1942). She and her husband, George, were faculty members at Howard University. They became Bahá'ís in 1913. George and Coralie's life stories are inspirational. Both were born in slavery and Coralie, "Brown Colbert's great-granddaughter, became the first descendant of a Monticello slave known to have graduated from college."[65] Even with these humble beginnings, Mrs. Cook was a staunch activist, especially committed to the education of young black girls. She is considered to be one of the founders of the National Association of Colored Women (NACW)[66] as well as a suffragist. In 1915, Coralie published an essay in the NAACP magazine *The Crisis* entitled "Votes for Mothers." She wrote, "I wonder if anybody in all this great world ever thought to consider *man's* rights as an individual, by his status as a father? Yet, you ask me to say something about

'Votes for Mothers,' as if mothers were a separate and peculiar people."[67] Even though Coralie agreed that mothers were special; she wanted her words to raise awareness of the uneven standards set for women and men.

Coralie Cook was the only African American woman invited to make an official statement at the eightieth birthday celebration of Susan B. Anthony. Given the tensions between white and black suffragists, she was diplomatic in her "greetings from colored women" and remarked:

> And so Miss Anthony, in behalf of the hundreds of colored women who wait and hope with you for the day when the ballot shall be in the hands of every intelligent woman; and also in behalf of the thousands who sit in darkness and whose condition we shall expect those ballots to better, whether they be in the hands of white women or Black, I offer you my warmest gratitude and congratulations.[68]

Her comments reflected an indirect challenge to the popular suffrage idea that only educated (i.e., white) women deserved the right to vote after white men's vote was securely established. Following the 1893 NAWSA convention, white suffragists promoted the idea that "educational requirements would ensure permanent supremacy for the native-born White portion of the population."[69] Many black suffragists considered this strategy of *expediency* to be a setback, but they continued to be active in the suffrage movement while simultaneously fighting against racist tactics within. In spite of her commitment to the suffrage cause, Cook felt that tensions between white and black women were a serious detriment to progress. Ultimately, she became disillusioned and in 1921 wrote to Mary White Ovington, "I regret also to have to say that I am not an 'active' suffragist. The old Nat'l W.S.A. of which I was once an ardent supporter and member, turned its back on the woman of color because they felt her presence a menace to southern affiliation."[70]

Coralie Cook's loss of faith in suffragists' ability to bring about change did not dampen her activist spirit. She was deeply concerned about issues of race, especially within the Bahá'í Faith. Encouraged by fellow Bahá'ís, she wrote a letter to 'Abdu'l-Bahá dated March 2, 1914, offering a candid assessment of race relations in the United States, and by extension, the Bahá'í Faith. She prefaced this five-page, single-spaced document by writing: "However that may be, you will know that I shall write no thoughtless word and shall try to be just and honest in every statement."[71] She described racist attitudes and blatant incidents of discrimination throughout the country including a special attention to interracial marriages:

> No phase of the color question excites so much rancor and misrepresentation as the one of mixed marriage. It is constantly made use of by all classes of whites

> from the statesman to the boot-black and now includes some so-called Bahá'ís to arouse passion and strife and to flatter Saxon vanity.[72]

Given the racial tensions at that time, the question of interracial marriage was an especially delicate topic. In stark contrast, the Bahá'í Faith considered interracial marriage as an important strategy for achieving race unity: "Thou must endeavor that they intermarry. There is no greater means to bring about affection between the white and the black than the influence of the Word of God. Likewise marriage between these two races will wholly destroy and eradicate the root of enmity."[73] Cook wisely used this complex social dilemma as a barometer for progress or lack thereof.

No one escaped Coralie Cook's scrutiny. She utilized the Bahá'í concept of the importance of deeds, to point out alarming weaknesses within the Bahá'í community, "Let deeds not words be your adorning."[74] She took Bahá'ís to task for their slow response to race problems and reluctance to be involved in solutions:

> To any one of the Bahá'í Faith to whom the tempter says "temporize" or let the matter work itself out I say beware! When was ever a mighty principle championed by temporizing or delay. I know some must suffer both white and black, but who better able to wear the mantle of suffering than the real Bahá'í?[75]

From Coralie Cook's perspective, the *real* Bahá'í, empowered by the teachings of the Faith, should play a key role in the establishment of race unity as instructed in the Bahá'í teachings, "Ye are the fruits of one tree, and the leaves of one branch. Deal ye with one another with the utmost love and harmony, with friendliness and fellowship."[76] For Cook, these words were an unambiguous call to action.

Erma Morris Hayden (1911–1997), a music teacher and concert pianist, became a Bahá'í in 1942, and her husband, poet laureate Robert Hayden joined the Bahá'í Faith in 1943.[77] In the 1960s, Erma volunteered to travel the southern states to help establish the Bahá'í Faith in the South. Her journey was marked by a difficult racial incident that she could never forget.

> I was on my way to Mississippi again and I had to change buses. I never liked Alabama and I had to change buses in Alabama. And it meant I had to wait about an hour. At that time, they had said that if people were doing interstate travel, they could sit anywhere. And whenever there was a law, even though I was scared to death, I believed if the law is here, we must begin to use it or it will fade into oblivion. So when I got off the bus I asked one of the Red Caps carrying the bags, I said, "Where is the interstate waiting room?" Because I wanted to be sure, I was going [to the right place]. He said, "You can sit anywhere in there [main waiting room]." So I went in and somehow I didn't feel

altogether certain about this so I sat in the last row. That was the easiest one to get out the door if I needed to get out. And I had a book with me and of course, I read the same page over and over again.[78]

Erma was referring to the 1961 order by the Interstate Commerce Commission (ICC) which struck down discriminatory seating practices on interstate bus travel.[79] The ruling covered a range of public facilities such as bus stations and restaurants, and also outlawed "whites only" signs in interstate bus terminals. Red Caps,[80] black men who served as porters in bus and train stations, played a key role in Hayden's experience.

And while I was looking at this book, first it was the bus driver came to me and said, "I think you have the wrong waiting room." I said, "Oh, I'm an interstate passenger," as though I didn't know anything. He said, "Let me see your ticket." And so I did and he said, "You're alright." So I thought I'll sit here comfortably. But I still didn't feel right about it 'cause it was Alabama. I had been down to Alabama many times, but never this late at night. Then here comes this old sort of redneck who's pretending to be drunk. He said, "We made this waiting room over there for you [black people]." I said, "I'm an interstate passenger." But he was too ignorant to understand any of that. He stood around trying to talk to me and I was trying to talk to him in some intelligent way, but was getting nowhere fast. So I just stopped. He eventually went over further into the waiting room and got a real red neck with a thick accent. He came over with this man and said, "Alright, come on. We don't want you in here." I said, "But I'm an interstate passenger," knowing full well he wasn't listening. He said, "We don't care what you are. We don't want you in here." And he started to pick up my things. At that point, I got mad. I said, "Don't you touch my things!" He stepped back. But I was only angry. It wasn't because I was brave. I said, "Now don't you touch my things. I'm leaving here because I don't want to cause trouble for the rest of these people. Because all of the porters, you see, had gathered together over the baggage.[81]

Hayden's self-conscious description of her fear was extraordinary. She anticipated trouble ahead, but exercised her right to *act* anyway. The situation was dangerous and could have spun out of control at any point.

The thoughts that go through your mind are like turning on electricity. They're [thoughts] kind of immediate and fast. I said, "Now see these men have families and there's no sense in their families being disrupted for my pride or anything like that. It will be better if I just go on and do what I have to do—go on out the door and let these men keep their jobs and don't have any problems." And so I did just that. I took my things and the redneck and his friend followed me to the door then they pitched me out the door. Yes they did. And of course, you're so embarrassed . . . So at any rate, I got my stuff together and I first went to

> the black waiting room. And you know there's a silence that gathers, that lets you know that in the split second of time that things have been happening. That everybody in there knows what has been happening. . . . If I had not been going on a mission for the Faith, I wouldn't have done it.[82]

In spite of the imminent danger to herself, Hayden was most concerned about the porters who had begun to show interest in her dilemma. Clearly, she did not want them to be penalized because of her actions. The situation appeared to have deescalated after Hayden was thrown out of the white waiting room. Eventually she arrived in Mississippi safely.

Approximately thirty years later, Erma Hayden's experience at the Alabama bus station remained fresh in her memory. She did not reimagine herself as a hero, instead Hayden connected her activism to commitment to the Bahá'í Faith. Her determination to facilitate the Bahá'í principle of the oneness of humanity fueled her civil rights efforts in spite of the possible danger. She said with unflinching certainty, "If I had not been going on a mission for the Faith, I wouldn't have done it."

CONCLUSION

In reflecting on her monumental research on black women's history, Darlene Clark Hine observed, "Through the study of Black women it becomes increasingly obvious how historians shape, make, or construct history, and why we omit, ignore, and sometimes distort the lives of people on the margins."[83] Inarguably early African American Bahá'í women can be counted among those on the margins because of their complex intersectionality. Not only are they African American *and* women belonging to various social classes, they are also members of a "non-mainstream" religion. Coralie Franklin Cook and H. Elsie Austin, for example, were prominent figures during their lifetimes, but many historical accounts mention their membership in the Bahá'í Faith only briefly, if at all. This is a serious oversight given the influence of this religion on these very dynamic women as well as their contributions to advancing the principles of the Bahá'í Faith in both local and international contexts. Thus, one of the major benefits of knowing about and studying black women in the Bahá'í Faith is to expand the historical record, especially for the purpose of broadening our knowledge of black women's *diverse* experiences. Echoing Chimamanda Ngozi Adichie's idea—a single story does not fit all.

The stories uncovered by close examination of strategic moments in the lives of earlier generations of black Bahá'í women suggest that they used their grounding in the Bahá'í Faith to fuel their activism on behalf of all women and people of color. They did not shrink from the challenges of being black women in a white man's world. Instead, they persisted, making new inroads in the struggle for civil rights and equal rights. Their lives were fitting testimonies to the power of resistance, purposefulness, and resilience.

NOTES

1. Shoghi Effendi, *The Advent of Divine Justice* (Wilmette, IL: Bahá'í Publishing Trust, 1984), 33–34. In order to narrow the time frame and contextualize historical events, the period 1899–1943 is used to indicate the date of enrollment in the Bahá'í Faith with the understanding that most women continued to be active well beyond this initial period. Zenobia Powell Perry is the one exception in that she joined the Faith in the 1970s.

2. Robert Stockman, "United States of America: History of the Bahá'í Faith," https://bahai-library.com/stockman_encyclopedia_usa.

3. Richard Thomas, "'The Pupil of the Eye': African-Americans and the Making of the American Bahá'í Community," in *Lights of the Spirit: Historical Portraits of Black Bahá'ís in North America, 1898–2000*, ed. Gwendolyn Etter-Lewis and Richard W. Thomas, 19–48 (Wilmette, IL: Bahá'í Publishing Trust, 2006), 23.

4. Gwendolyn Etter-Lewis, "Radiant Lights," in *Lights of the Spirit*, 49.

5. Darlene Clarke Hine, ed., *Black Women in America: An Historical Encyclopedia*, vol. 1, 2nd ed. (Brooklyn, New York: Carlson Publishing Inc., 1993), xix.

6. 'Abdu'l-Bahá, *Foundations of World Unity* (Wilmette, IL: Bahá'i Publishing Trust, 1945), 101.

7. Patricia Hill Collins, *Fighting Words: Black Women and the Search for Justice* (Minneapolis, MN: University of Minnesota Press, 1998), xvi.

8. Anna Julia Cooper, *A Voice from the South* (New York: Oxford University Press, 1988), 31.

9. Ida B. Wells-Barnet, excerpt from *A Red Record*, in *The Norton Anthology of African American Literature*, edited by Henry Louis Gates Jr. and Nellie Y. Mckay (New York: Norton, 1997), 605.

10. Coralie Franklin Cook, "Votes for Mothers," *The Crisis* 10, no. 4 (August 1915): 184.

11. Beverly Guy-Sheftall, ed., *Words of Fire: An Anthology of African-American Feminist Thought* (New York: New Press, 1995), xiv.

12. Janet Mock, *Redefining Realness: My Path to Womanhood, Identity, Love and So Much More* (New York: Atria, 2014), 64–65.

13. For example, the Combahee River Collective, 1977. See "A Black Feminist Statement," in Guy-Sheftall, 232.

14. Kimberlé Crenshaw, "Mapping the Margins: Intersectionality, Identity Politics, and Violence against Women of Color," *Stanford Law Review* 43, no. 6 (July 1991): 1251–1252.

15. Ann DuCille, "The Occult of True Black Womanhood: Critical Demeanor and Black Feminist Studies," *Signs* (spring 1994): 593.

16. Chimamanda Ngozi Adichie, "The Danger of a Single Story," *TED: Ideas Worth Spreading*, https://www.ted.com/talks/chimamanda_adichie_the_danger_of_a_single_story.

17. Nell Irvin Painter explained that, "Many people confuse the two because both lived in an era shadowed by human bondage, but Truth and Tubman were contrasting figures." Nell Irvin Painter, "Sojourner Truth: A Life, A Symbol." *Washington Post*, http://www.washingtonpost.com/wp-srv/style/longterm/books/chap1/sojournertruth.htm.

18. See Paula Giddings, *When and Where I Enter: The Impact of Black Women on Race and Sex in America* (New York: Bantam Books, 1984), 262–263.

19. Sarah M. Fossett, *Ohio History Central*, http://www.ohiohistorycentral.org/w/Sarah_M._Fossett.

20. Alexander and Mary Martin were attracted to the Bahá'í Faith by a talk given by Louis Gregory in Cleveland in 1913. Louis George Gregory (1874–1951) was an African American attorney and prominent Bahá'í who paved the way for the enrollment of other prominent African Americans. He was instrumental in facilitating the success of 'Abdu'l-Bahá's (son of founder Bahá'u'lláh) 1912 visit to the United States. See Gayle Morrison's, *To Move the World* (Wilmette, IL: Bahá'í Publishing Trust, 1982), 55, 254.

21. "Martin, Mary Brown," *The Encyclopedia of Cleveland History*, https://case.edu/ech/articles/m/martin-mary-brown.

22. Tonya, Sams, "Mary B. Martin, Was First Black Woman on School Board: Black History Month," *Cleveland.com*, February 16, 2011, http://blog.cleveland.com/metro/2011/02/mary_b_martin_was_first_black.html.

23. Richard Thomas, compiler, *Exploring the Historical and Spiritual Significance of Being a Person of African Descent in the Bahá'í Faith* (Wilmette, IL: National Bahá'í Spiritual Assembly, 1998), 54.

24. Sarah Martin Pereira, oral history interview conducted by Gwendolyn Etter-Lewis, August 18, 1986, Charlotte, North Carolina, transcript no. 3, 60, personal collection.

25. Venetria Patton, *Women in Chains: The Legacy of Slavery in Black Women's Fiction.* (Albany, NY: SUNY Press, 1999), 30.

26. Barbara Welter, "The Cult of True Womanhood: 1820–1860," *American Quarterly* 18, no. 2 (summer 1966): 152, http://www.jstor.org/stable/2711179.

27. Deborah Willis and Carla Williams, *The Black Female Body: A Photographic History* (Philadelphia, PA: Temple University Press, 2002), 3.

28. Sarah Martin Pereira, oral history interview by Gwendolyn Etter-Lewis, August 8, 1986, Charlotte, North Carolina, transcript no. 3, 3, personal collection.

29. bell hooks, *Feminist Theory: From Margin to Center*, 2nd ed. (Boston: South End Press, 2000), 15.

30. "Elsie Austin," *Ohio History Central,* http://www.ohiohistorycentral.org/w/Elsie_Austin. See also, "H. Elsie Austin," *Bahá'í Chronicles: A Journey to the Past and Present*," http://bahaichronicles.org/h-elsie-austin/Eternality3.

31. "Elsie Austin," *Ohio History Central,* http://www.ohiohistorycentral.org/w/Elsie_Austin.

32. "Elsie Austin," *Ohio History Central*, http://www.ohiohistorycentral.org/w/Elsie_Austin.

33. Gwendolyn Etter-Lewis, "Race, Gender and Difference: African American Women and the Struggle for Equality," in *Lights of the Spirit*, 90.

34. Giddings, *When and Where I Enter*, 101.

35. Darlene Clark Hine, *Hinesight: Black Women and the Re-Construction of American History* (New York: Carlson Publishing, 1994), 242.

36. Linda Perkins, "Education," in *Black Women in America*, ed. Darlene Clark Hine, vol. I, 380.

37. Gwendolyn Etter-Lewis, "Race, Gender and Difference," in *Lights of the Spirit*, 90.

38. Jacqueline Jones, "Black Workers Remember," *The American Prospect* (November 30, 2000), http://prospect.org/article/black-workers-remember.

39. Gwendolyn Etter-Lewis,"Race, Gender and Difference," in *Lights of the Spirit,* 91.

40. *Bahá'í World News Service*, December 5, 2004, http://news.bahai.org/story/338.

41. 'Abdu'l-Bahá, *Promulgation of Universal Peace*, 2nd ed. (Wilmette, IL: Bahá'í Publishing Trust, 1982), 175, http://www.bahai.org/library/authoritative-texts/abdul-baha/promulgation-universal-peace.

42. Giddings, *When and Where I Enter*, 55.

43. bell hooks, *Black Looks: Race and Representation* (Boston: South End Press, 1992), 57.

44. Elsie Austin quoted in Gwendolyn Etter-Lewis, *My Soul is My Own: Oral Narratives of African American Women in the Professions* (New York: Routledge, 1993), 29.

45. "Elsie Austin," *Ohio History Central,* http://www.ohiohistorycentral.org/w/Elsie_Austin.

46. Zenobia Powell Perry, http://www.zenobiapowellperry.org/biography.html.

47. Zenobia Powell Perry, oral history interview by Gwendolyn Etter-Lewis, July 6, 1987, Wilberforce, Ohio, transcript no. 27, 57–58, personal collection.

48. Zenobia Powell Perry, http://www.zenobiapowellperry.org/biography.html.

49. Barbara R. Sims, *Raising the Banner in Korea: An Early Bahá'í History*, https://bahai-library.com/sims_raising_banner_korea&chapter=7, 19.

50. Sometimes spelled as Kwangju.

51. Cited in Gwendolyn Etter-Lewis and Richard Thomas, *Lights of the Spirit,* 138–141.

52. Gwendolyn Etter-Lewis, "Unrestrained as the Wind: African American Women Answer the Call," in *Lights of the Spirit*, 141.

53. 'Abdu'l-Bahá, *The Promulgation of Universal* Peace, 44.

54. Giddings, *When and Where I Enter,* 55.

55. bell hooks, *Feminist Theory*, 11.

56. Zenobia Powell Perry, oral history interview by Gwendolyn Etter-Lewis, July 6, 1987, Wilberforce, Ohio, transcript no. 27, 56, personal collection.

57. Africlassical, May 8, 2014, http://africlassical.blogspot.com/2014/05/world-premiere-zenobia-powell-perrys.html.

58. "'Pioneer' (in English) and *mohājer* (in Persian: migrant, pl. *mohājerin*) are terms used in Bahá'i literature to designate those who leave their homes to settle in another locality with the intention of spreading the Bahá'í Faith or supporting existing Bahá'í communities." Moojan Momen, "Bahá'í Pioneers," *Bahá'í Library Online*, https://bahai-library.com/momen_bahai_pioneers_iranica.

59. Cited in Gwendolyn Etter-Lewis and Richard Thomas, *Lights of the Spirit*, 138–141.

60. Ibid.

61. Ibid.

62. Chelcee Johns, "What I've Learned from Being Black, Abroad, and a Woman," *Ebony*, http://www.ebony.com/life/black-abroad-women#axzz4yWbc4p9m.

63. Evelyn Brooks Higginbotham, "African-American Women's History and the Metalanguage of Race," in *"We Specialize in the Wholly Impossible:" A Reader in Black Women's History*, eds. Darlene Clark Hine, Wilma King, and Linda Reed (New York: NYU Press, 1995), 13.

64. Higginbotham, in *"We Specialize in the Wholly Impossible,"* ed. Hine, 14.

65. *Getting Word: African American Families of Monticello*, https://www.monticello.org/getting-word/people/coralie-franklin-cook.

66. The black women's club movement was a powerful response to social and political ills of the time. In the late 1890s, the NACW was formed and "through its regional, state, and city federations, developed institutions to serve" the social welfare needs of the black community. Dorothy Salem, "National Association of Colored Women" in *Black Women in America: An Historical Encyclopedia,* ed. Darlene Clark Hine, Vol. II (New York: Carlson Publishing, 1993), 842.

67. Cook, "Votes for Mothers," 184.

68. Roselyn Terborg-Penn, *African American Women in the Struggle for the Vote, 1850–1920* (Bloomington, IN: Indiana University Press, 1998), 69.

69. Giddings, *When and Where I Enter*, 124.

70. Coralie Franklin Cook, letter to Mary White Ovington, January 21, 1921, NAACP Administrative Files, Box C 407, Folder: Suffrage-Noman's, January 11–February 7, 1921, Library of Congress.

71. Hannen-Knobloch Papers, M-192, Box 3, Folder 12. National Bahá'i Archives.

72. Hannen-Knobloch Papers, M-192, Box 3, Folder 12. National Bahá'i Archives.

73. 'Abdu'l-Bahá, quoted in Bonnie Taylor, *The Power of Unity: Beyond Prejudice and Racism* (Wilmette, IL: Bahá'i Publishing Trust, 1986), 55.

74. Bahá'u'lláh, *The Hidden Words of Bahá'u'lláh* (Wilmette, IL: Bahá'í Publishing Trust, 1963), 23–24.

75. Hannen-Knobloch Papers, M-192, Box 3, Folder 12, National Bahá'í Archives.

76. Bahá'u'lláh, *Gleanings from the Writings of Bahá'ulláh* (Wilmette, IL: Bahá'í Publishing Trust, 1952), 288.

77. Christopher Buck, "Robert Hayden," in *Oxford Encyclopedia of American Literature,* ed. Jay Parini, vol. 2 (New York: Oxford University Press, 2004), 171–181.

78. Erma Hayden, oral history interview by Gwendolyn Etter-Lewis, June 26, 1986, Ann Arbor, MI, transcript no. 5 (side 2), 5–7.

79. "ICC Bans Segregation in Interstate Travel Facilities," *Today in Civil Liberties History*, http://todayinclh.com/?event=icc-bans-segregation-in-interstate-travel-facilities.

80. Eric Arnesen, *Brotherhoods of Color: Black Railroad Workers and the Struggle for Equality* (Cambridge, MA: Harvard University Press, 2002), 161.

81. Erma Hayden, interview by author, Ann Arbor, MI, June 26, 1986, transcript no. 5 (side 2), 5–7.

82. Erma Hayden, Oral history interview by Gwendolyn Etter-Lewis, June 26, 1986, Ann Arbor, MI, Transcript No. 5 (side 2), 5–7.

83. Hine, *Hinesight*, xxi.

BIBLIOGRAPHY

'Abdu'l-Bahá. *Foundations of World Unity.* Wilmette, IL: Bahá'í Publishing Trust, 1945. Also available at http://reference.bahai.org/en/t/c/FWU.

'Abdu'l-Bahá. *Promulgation of Universal Peace*. 2nd ed. Wilmette, IL: Bahá'í Publishing Trust, 1982. Also available at http://www.bahai.org/library/authoritative-texts/abdul-baha/promulgation-universal-peace.

Adichie, Chimamanda Ngozi. "The Danger of a Single Story." *TED: Ideas Worth Spreading*. Accessed January 31, 2018. https://www.ted.com/talks/chimamanda_adichie_the_danger_of_a_single_story.

Africlassical. Accessed May 8, 2014. http://africlassical.blogspot.com.

Arnesen, Eric. *Brotherhoods of Color: Black Railroad Workers and the Struggle for Equality*. Cambridge, MA: Harvard University Press, 2002.

Bahá'u'lláh. *Gleanings from the Writings of Bahá'u'lláh*. Wilmette, IL: Bahá'í Publishing Trust, 1952. Also available at http://www.bahai.org/library/authoritative-texts/bahaullah/gleanings-writings-bahaullah.

Bahá'u'lláh. *The Hidden Words of Bahá'u'lláh*. Wilmette, IL: Bahá'í Publishing Trust, 1963. Also available at http://www.bahai.org/library/authoritative-texts/bahaullah/hidden-words.

Bahá'í Chronicles: A Journey to the Past and Present. Accessed November 18, 2017. http://bahaichronicles.org.

Bahá'í World News Service. December 5, 2004. http://news.bahai.org/story/338.

Buck, Christopher. "Robert Hayden." In *Oxford Encyclopedia of American Literature*. Edited by Jay Parini. Vol. 2. New York: Oxford University Press, 2004.

Chelcee, Johns. "What I've Learned from Being Black, Abroad, and a Woman." *Ebony*. http://www.ebony.com/life/black-abroad-women#axzz4yWbc4p9m.

Collins, Patricia Hill. *Fighting Words: Black Women and the Search for Justice*. Minneapolis, MN: University of Minnesota Press, 1998.

Cook, Coralie Franklin. Letter to Mary White Ovington, January 21, 1921, NAACP Administrative Files, Box C 407, Folder: Suffrage-Noman's, January 11–February 7, 1921. Library of Congress.

Cook, Coralie Franklin. "Votes for Mothers." *The Crisis* 10, no. 4 (August 1915): 184.

Cooper, Anna Julia. *A Voice from the South.* New York: Oxford University Press, 1988.

Crenshaw, Kimberlé. "Mapping the Margins: Intersectionality, Identity Politics, and Violence against Women of Color." *Stanford Law Review* 43, no. 6 (July 1991): 1241–1299.

DuCille, Ann. "The Occult of True Black Womanhood: Critical Demeanor and Black Feminist Studies." *Signs* (Spring 1994): 591–629.

"Elsie Austin." *Ohio History Central.* http://www.ohiohistorycentral.org/w/Elsie_Austin.

Etter-Lewis, Gwendolyn. *My Soul is My Own: Oral Narratives of African American Women in the Professions.* New York: Routledge, 1993.

Etter-Lewis, Gwendolyn, and Richard Thomas, eds. *Lights of the Spirit: Historical Portraits of Black Bahá'ís in North America, 1898–2000.* Wilmette, IL: Bahá'i Publishing Trust, 2006.

Getting Word: African American Families of Monticello. Accessed February 2, 2018. https://www.monticello.org/getting-word.

Giddings, Paula. *When and Where I Enter: The Impact of Black Women on Race and Sex in America.* New York: Bantam Books, 1984.

Guy-Sheftall, Beverly, ed. *Words of Fire: An Anthology of African-American Feminist Thought.* New York: The New Press, 1995.

Hine, Darlene Clark, ed. *Black Women in America: An Historical Encyclopedia.* Vols. 1 and 2. New York: Carlson Publishing, 1993.

Hine, Darlene Clark. *Hinesight: Black Women and the Re-Construction of American History.* New York: Carlson Publishing, 1994.

Hine, Darlene, Wilma King, and Linda Reed, eds. *We Specialize in the Wholly Impossible: A Reader in Black Women's History.* New York: NYU Press, 1995.

hooks, bell. *Black Looks: Race and Representation.* Boston: South End Press, 1992.

hooks, bell. *Feminist Theory: From Margin to Center.* 2nd ed. Boston: South End Press, 2000.

"ICC Bans Segregation in Interstate Travel Facilities," *Today in Civil Liberties History,* http://todayinclh.com/?event=icc-bans-segregation-in-interstate-travel-facilities.

Jones, Jacqueline. "Black Workers Remember." *The American Prospect.* November 30, 2000. http://prospect.org/article/black-workers-remember.

"Martin, Mary Brown." *The Encyclopedia of Cleveland History.* https://case.edu/ech/articles/m/martin-mary-brown.

Mock, Janet. *Redefining Realness: My Path to Womanhood, Identity, Love and So Much More.* New York: Atria, 2014.

Momen, Moojan. "Bahá'i Pioneers." *Bahá'i Library Online.* https://bahai-library.com/momen_bahai_pioneers_iranica.

Morrison, Gayle. *To Move the World: Louis Gregory and the Advancement of Racial Unity in America.* Wilmette, IL: Bahá'í Publishing Trust, 1982.

National Bahá'i Archives. Wilmette, IL.

Painter, Nell Irvin. "Sojourner Truth: A Life, A Symbol." *Washington Post,* http://www.washingtonpost.com/wp-srv/style/longterm/books/chap1/sojournertruth.htm.

Patton, Venetria. *Women in Chains: The Legacy in Black Women's Fiction.* Albany, NY: SUNY Press, 1999.

Perry, Zenobia Powell. http://www.zenobiapowellperry.org.

Sams, Tonya. "Mary B. Martin, Was First Black Woman on School Board: Black History Month." *Cleveland.com*, February 16, 2011, http://blog.cleveland.com/metro/2011/02/mary_b_martin_was_first_black.html.

"Sarah M. Fossett." *Ohio History Central.* http://www.ohiohistorycentral.org/w/Sarah_M._Fossett.

Shoghi Effendi. *The Advent of Divine Justice.* Wilmette, IL: Bahá'i Publishing Trust, 1984. Also available at http://www.bahai.org/library/authoritative-texts/shoghi-effendi/advent-divine-justice.

Sims, Barbara. "Raising the Banner in Korea: An Early Bahá'i History." *Bahá'i Library Online.* https://bahai-library.com/sims_raising_banner_korea.

Stockman, Robert. "United States of America: History of the Bahá'í Faith." *Bahá'i Library Online.* https://bahai-library.com/stockman_encyclopedia_usa.

Taylor, Bonnie, compiler. *The Power of Unity: Beyond Prejudice and Racism.* Wilmette, IL: Bahá'í Publishing Trust, 1986. Also available at https://bahai-library.com/taylor_power_unity.

Terborg-Penn, Roselyn. *African American Women in the Struggle for the Vote, 1850–1920.* Bloomington, IN: Indiana University Press, 1998.

Thomas, Richard, compiler. *Exploring the Historical and Spiritual Significance of Being a Person of African Descent in the Bahá'í Faith.* Wilmette, IL: National Bahá'í Spiritual Assembly, 1998.

Wells-Barnett, Ida B. *A Red Record* (excerpt). In *The Norton Anthology of African American Literature.* Edited by Henry Louis Gates Jr. and Nellie Y. McKay. New York: Norton, 1997.

Welter, Barbara. "The Cult of True Womanhood: 1820–1860." *American Quarterly* 18, no. 2 (summer 1966): 151–174. https://www.jstor.org/stable/2711179?seq=1#page_scan_tab_contents.

Willis, Deborah, and Carla Williams. *The Black Female Body: A Photographic History.* Philadelphia, PA: Temple University Press, 2002.

Chapter 5

Hand in Hand

Race, Identity, and Community Development among South Carolina's Bahá'ís, 1973–1979

Louis Venters

In the early twenty-first century, the Bahá'í Faith received a great deal of attention in social media and the traditional press as the second-largest religion after Christianity in South Carolina, the only state in the country where this was the case. South Carolina is home to one of the strongest and most successful state-level Bahá'í communities[1] in the United States, with a relatively large number of local administrative institutions, a few of which own modest properties; a regional training facility and community-service radio station; and a solid reputation among public officials and leaders of thought in the areas of race relations and interfaith dialogue. Since 2003, in Charleston, the local Bahá'í community has even operated the childhood home of Louis G. Gregory, the native son who first brought the Bahá'í Faith's teachings to South Carolina from Washington, DC, in the early twentieth century, as a museum. While this religion's presence in the state dates at least to Gregory's visit in 1910, the current status of the Bahá'í Faith in South Carolina is due in no small part to what one scholar of religion has aptly dubbed the "Carolinian Pentecost," a series of growth campaigns in the 1970s and 1980s during which some 20,000 people, the majority of them African Americans in rural areas, identified with the Bahá'í Faith. Almost overnight, an egalitarian new religious movement that had struggled for decades to establish and maintain interracial local branches across the Jim Crow South could count members in every county of South Carolina, one of the most conservative states in the region. By 1973, South Carolina was home to approximately a quarter of all the Bahá'ís in the country.[2]

The rapid expansion in South Carolina, the first such burst of growth for the young faith in an industrialized country, was a seminal moment for the

Bahá'í movement in the United States, indelibly shaping its identity, structures, and aspirations for decades to come. Yet, the phenomenon remains poorly understood, both among scholars of race and religion in the United States and among contemporary American Bahá'ís themselves. Despite the American Bahá'í community's long track record of breaching the color line around the country, at the end of the 1960s, the Bahá'í Faith's membership in the United States was still overwhelmingly white, urban, middle-class, and non-southern. Beginning in winter 1970, the South Carolina phenomenon not only challenged the American Bahá'í community to learn to initiate and sustain such large-scale growth in other parts of the country and among other demographic groups, but perhaps more importantly, to embrace new forms of diversity within its ranks. The Bahá'í Faith in the United States had been committed to interracialism since the early twentieth century and already counted an unusually diverse membership in the Deep South and across the country. However, during an era when national politics and culture were dominated by the conservative turn, the decline of the integrationist ideal that had animated the civil rights movement of the 1950s and 1960s, the proliferation of group identities, and an increasingly chaotic international scene, the unprecedented membership growth in South Carolina required that the American Bahá'í community as a whole devote renewed attention to cultivating the kinds of attitudes, structures, and collective practices appropriate for a movement that held pursuit of unity, justice, equality, and collaborative social transformation as its core values. In this context, what the Bahá'ís of South Carolina, many of them quite new converts, undertook in dozens of towns and hamlets across the state during the 1970s and 1980s was little short of revolutionary in the story of American race relations. To be sure, it was a quieter revolution than the one waged by civil rights activists, but the relative lack of publicity it received (then and now) should not mask the significance of a process, however localized in scope, however halting and chaotic at times, in which thousands of black, white, and indigenous people, of all ages and from a variety of geographic, cultural, and educational backgrounds, attempted to build a new, shared religious identity and the institutions and patterns of community life that went along with it. While a number of religious organizations in the state and region promoted interracial cooperation and a progressive social agenda during the 1970s, for example, South Carolina's Christian Action Council, which involved both black and white Protestant denominations, and the better-known Delta Ministry in Mississippi, a project of the National Council of Churches, the commitment of the Bahá'í Faith to building racially integrated religious bodies at the local, state, and national levels made it unusual among American faith communities.[3]

This chapter provides an initial examination of these themes from 1973 to 1979, a brief period which the Universal House of Justice, the religion's international governing body, designated as a Five Year Plan, plus a transitional year (1973) between it and the previous plan. All were part of a series of global plans, initiated during Shoghi Effendi's period of leadership and continued by the House of Justice, for the religion's diffusion and growth in all parts of the world. The first new plan to take place after the initial burst of growth in South Carolina, the Five Year Plan, was outlined by the Universal House of Justice but implemented in highly decentralized fashion at the national and local levels around the world. It provided specific objectives and operational guidelines in a critical period of the South Carolina community's development. The plan represented the framework in which a statewide movement that had grown rapidly in size attempted to make good on the admonition of the Universal House of Justice that expansion and consolidation, the two principal aspects of large-scale growth, were "twin processes that must go hand in hand." During the Five Year Plan, a new large burst of enrollments like those of earlier in the decade failed to materialize, but numerical growth, measured both in increased membership and in the opening of new localities to the Bahá'í Faith, continued in more modest fashion, usually as a result of local initiative. In terms of the consolidation of this expansion, a goal of mobilizing a majority of new Bahá'ís as confident protagonists in the community's development remained elusive, however by the end of the plan, the number of such workers across the state had reached to hundreds. At the same time, a number of elements, for example, a high degree of racial and sexual equality; extensive use of the arts, particularly singing; widespread participation by children and youth; a pronounced rurality; the centrality of the Louis Gregory Institute, a new training facility established in Georgetown County; attention to the community's history, to learning about the processes of growth, and to cultivating an ethic of global citizenship; and a tradition of effective statewide planning, coordination, and collaboration emerged and coalesced into a South Carolina Bahá'í culture that was vibrant, distinctive, and, to an extent, unmatched among Bahá'ís anywhere else in the country, largely shaped by the expectations, priorities, and talents of rural African Americans.[4]

A "COMPLETELY NEW PHASE"

In order to appreciate the importance of the Five Year Plan in South Carolina, a brief review of developments over the previous few years is necessary. At the outset of the Nine Year Plan (1964–1973), the first global plan undertaken at the direction of the newly established Universal House of Justice, the body began to set out a broad vision for the next stage of the Bahá'í Faith's growth. With its worldwide administrative structure essentially complete and the religion successfully established in virtually every country during the preceding decade, the Universal House of Justice called for a "huge expansion of the Cause of God." While most of this religion's previous growth outside of Iran had been limited to a relative trickle of individual inquirers and new believers in urban areas, now the House of Justice said that National Spiritual Assemblies (the national Bahá'í governing bodies) should increasingly turn their attention to reaching "all strata of society," including what it termed the "masses of mankind" residing primarily in rural areas. Recalling the world-historical effects of mass conversions to Christianity and Islam in centuries past, the vision introduced by the Universal House of Justice focused on the movement of entire populations toward the Bahá'í Faith, a process that would enable the emerging global community to more fully draw on the cultural richness of the human race and more thoroughly penetrate the life of society.[5]

In the United States, where the urban centers of the North and the West Coast had long dominated the Bahá'í community, this new approach implied a substantial revision of the way human and financial resources were deployed and indeed of the religion's very definition of itself. Even in South Carolina, a state whose population was still mostly rural, the emergence of new local Bahá'í groups in small towns and rural areas such as Florence, Lake City, and St. Helena Island during the late 1950s and early 1960s had been the exception, not the rule. During the early years of the Nine Year Plan (1964–1973), the American Bahá'í community sent out the lion's share of international pioneers (individuals who aid in the geographic diffusion of the Bahá'í Faith by taking up residence in a new area), while a series of ambitious domestic goals, including doubling the number of local spiritual assemblies (to 600) and specific teaching efforts aimed at minority groups advanced more slowly. Even so, between 1963 and 1968, the Bahá'í population of the United States grew by more than one-third, from 11,000 to nearly 18,000. Significantly, most of the new believers were teenagers and young adults, with college campuses increasingly becoming centers of Bahá'í activity, a development that would soon have important bearing on growth of this religion in the South. After 1968, amid increasing social and political upheaval, and spurred by additional guidance from the Universal House of Justice about the urgency of teaching the Bahá'í Faith to ever-increasing numbers of people, a growing cadre of believers in the South, mostly young people, and many of them relatively new Bahá'ís themselves, engaged in new attempts to bring their new faith to rural areas. The National Spiritual Assembly responded positively, appointing a Deep South Committee in 1969 to help coordinate the effort. By summer 1970, membership growth measured in dozens or hundreds of individuals in a few localities had even found its way into the national press, with a wire service story noting the "startling success" of the Bahá'ís in "attracting black people of the South" in recent months.[6]

Buoyed by such initial results, in fall 1970, the Deep South Committee planned a regional teaching campaign, that is a series of locally managed projects for specific geographic areas in each state, to take place over the winter holidays. While unprecedented growth, measured in the hundreds, or in a few cases thousands, took place everywhere there was a project, by far the most startling success of the winter campaign came in South Carolina, where at least eight thousand people, centered on the county-seat town of Dillon in the northeastern corner of the state, became Bahá'ís. During one day of the Dillon project alone, more than one thousand people signed Bahá'í membership cards, a completely unheard-of development in the American Bahá'í experience that was greeted with a great deal of enthusiasm by the National Spiritual Assembly and the Universal House of Justice. A second major burst of new believers came in the first half of 1972, with a project dubbed the "Army of Light," that started at the opposite side of the state in North Augusta and moved eastward. By the end of the Nine Year Plan in early 1973, the U.S. Bahá'í population had more than tripled to some 60,000, with approximately one-quarter, at least 15,000, residing in South Carolina alone. Since 1968, the Bahá'í Faith in South Carolina had gone from about 200 believers in a handful of localities to a budding mass movement with members in every county.[7]

Not only had the South Carolina Bahá'í community experienced membership growth that was unprecedented for this religion in the United States, but the social and racial identity of the statewide movement had undergone a transformation. During the decades of Jim Crow, when a variety of formal and informal strictures severely hampered interracial organizing, Bahá'ís in the state had struggled to build and maintain local communities characterized by a high degree of interracial fellowship and cooperation, primarily in the Augusta-North Augusta area on the Georgia border, Charleston, Columbia, and Greenville. By the late 1960s, Bahá'í membership closely mirrored the racial demography of the state, with slightly more whites than blacks. Moreover, the Bahá'ís represented a virtual cross section of the population in terms of gender and socioeconomic background. In short, compared to the state's Protestant, Catholic, and Jewish communities, the small Bahá'í community stood out for its integration at the local and state levels. In the wake of the teaching campaigns of the early 1970s, however, the statewide community had quickly become a black-majority movement—not because of "white flight," but because by far the largest number of new believers were African Americans. In addition, most of the new Bahá'ís resided not in the state's cities but in small towns and rural hamlets, and many faced limited educational and economic opportunities. Almost overnight, the statewide movement, and the national Bahá'í community of which it now formed such a substantial portion, found itself faced with a new set of challenges, social and cultural as much as practical and logistical, that proved both thrilling and daunting.

Very quickly, the experience in South Carolina and other Deep South states came to define a new set of expectations and a new collective identity for Bahá'ís in the United States. The surge of growth led some confident proponents to predict that South Carolina would eventually become "the first all-Bahá'í state in the country." Whether or not that was to be the case, the road ahead would be infinitely more complex and difficult than anyone imagined at the outset of the southern campaign. The swelling membership in South Carolina and elsewhere severely tested the capacity of the national administration to maintain unity of vision in an increasingly diverse community and to marshal the necessary resources, human and financial, to support continued growth. As early as spring 1971, the National Spiritual Assembly admitted that the recent upsurge would "tax to the utmost" the community's means for "absorbing huge numbers of new believers and ensuring the transformation of their lives in conformity with Bahá'í principles." The National Assembly anticipated that growth would require augmenting the national staff, located outside Chicago; strengthening local spiritual assemblies; revamping the long-standing system of State Conventions (by which delegates were elected to the annual National Convention to elect the National Spiritual Assembly) to take into account a much larger electorate; and experimenting with new methods of communication and education for more children, youth, and adults than ever before. The "administration of the Cause in the United States," it wrote, was "entering a completely new phase."[8]

On the ground in South Carolina as well, it became quickly apparent that the response of the population to the spirit and teachings of the Bahá'í Faith had outstripped the community's capacity to respond. As one organizer put it, with the sheer number of new believers "there just weren't enough people to continue teaching and consolidating." In addition, the relative remoteness of many of the new Bahá'ís and the acute poverty and limited literacy that many of them faced made for serious logistical challenges. One observer noted:

> The problems of relocating rural people were very real. . . . Many of the people who had become Bahá'ís were illiterate, and their card had to be written out for them. Many of the cards were illegible. People had given their post office box number or general delivery as an address, and there is virtually no way to find a person using this information. They live on country roads which are not accurately mapped, several families using one post box which was located in town at the post office.

For example, in spring 1971, the beginning of the first Bahá'í administrative year after the Dillon project, the State Goals Committee (the statewide arm of the National Teaching Committee) deployed teams across South Carolina to supervise the election of 108 local spiritual assemblies, up from only 8 the previous year. As impressive as this accomplishment was, it was clear that simply holding elections for local assemblies was not enough to ensure that they began to function or, more broadly, to ensure that patterns of Bahá'í individual and collective life took root in dozens of localities across the state. Further growth in South Carolina, or, indeed, simply maintaining the community at its new, larger size, would depend on mobilizing many more Bahá'ís, both new and veteran, as teachers and organizers.[9]

In this context, the National Assembly made a number of major decisions aimed at involving more of the grassroots of the community in the planning and implementation of teaching activities and facilitating the Bahá'í education of vastly more people. Two of them had direct and significant effects on South Carolina. The first was to replace the State Goals Committees around the country with some eighty new District Teaching Committees that would mostly serve only portions of states. South Carolina was initially assigned four District Teaching Committees, responsible for approximately the northwestern, north-central, eastern, and southern portions of the state. Within a few months, the eastern district, which included most of the territory of the initial Dillon project and counted the largest number of Bahá'ís, was further divided, for a total of five District Teaching Committees. In addition to the committees, the National Assembly also assigned to South Carolina one of the five new Regional Teaching Committees to serve between the district and national levels. The regional and district committees were given enormous responsibilities: to plan and execute teaching projects and open new localities to the Bahá'í Faith; to foster the establishment and development of local spiritual assemblies; to coordinate the services of traveling teachers and recruit and settle pioneers; to enroll new believers in areas not served by a local assembly; and to maintain accurate membership lists for their respective territories[10] (see figure 5.1).

As the new teaching committee structure was being established, some of the leaders of the Dillon project asked the National Assembly to establish a permanent "teaching institute," one of the educational agencies that the Universal House of Justice had called for in areas of large-scale growth, and a radio station to reach new believers in isolated rural areas. While the question of the radio station was deferred for more than a decade, the National Assembly agreed on the need for a permanent training facility that could be open year-round. It purchased a 130-acre wooded tract, the family land of two white charismatic pastors who had recently become Bahá'ís, in rural Georgetown County outside the town of Hemingway. The Louis G. Gregory Bahá'í Institute, named for the son of former South Carolina slaves who had become an attorney and one of the most influential early teachers and administrators of the Bahá'í Faith in the United States, was opened in October 1972. Set amid farmland and pine forests, the modest facility quickly began offering

Figure 5.1 The Members of the 1974 Northern #1 District Teaching Committee Serving the Greenville-Anderson Area in the Upper Piedmont. *Source: South Carolina Regional Bahá'í Bulletin.*

classes on various topics and of various durations—weekend, five-day, and longer periods during the summer—for youth and adults.[11]

By the end of the Nine Year Plan, the District Teaching Committees, now numbering six with the division of the southern portion of the state into two districts, and the handful of strong local spiritual assemblies, had emerged as the principal means for consolidating new believers and communities, providing a structure through which veteran South Carolina Bahá'ís "pioneers," that is transplants from other parts of the country who came specifically to help the growth of the Bahá'í Faith, and new members worked to build the institutions and practices of Bahá'í community life in cities and towns across the state. For example, by the end of 1972 in the Piedmont city of Greenville, the state's oldest and largest local Bahá'í community, where Bahá'ís had defied opposition and violence since the late 1930s to build an interracial movement and where some three hundred people had embraced the religion during the Army of Light project earlier in the year, weekly activities included a study class on Wednesday in one home; a "fireside" (an introductory meeting on the Bahá'í Faith) on Thursdays and two on Fridays in three other homes; and four neighborhood children's classes in different locations. With some twenty local communities under its purview, the District Teaching Committee serving the Greenville area divided its territory into four sectors, each with its own consolidation team focused on home visits to new believers and nurturing new local spiritual assemblies. Other District Teaching Committees experimented with similar methods.[12]

Far beyond Greenville, by the end of the Nine Year Plan, there were weekly firesides, study groups, or children's classes in more than twenty-five localities in South Carolina, including hamlets of only a few hundred people such as Richburg (Chester County), Starr (Anderson County), and Van Wyck (Lancaster County). In many of the new rural Bahá'í communities, all or almost all of the believers were African American. Some of them depended on the assistance of more experienced Bahá'ís (black or white, or a combination), either pioneers who took up residence at the request of the Regional Teaching Committee or regular visitors from nearby established localities. A few, however, flourished with minimal outside assistance. One example was Aynor, a town of fewer than 600 people in rural Horry County, where an energetic group, all African Americans and mostly very new to the faith, ran the Local Spiritual Assembly, weekly children's classes, and ambitious teaching projects aimed at reaching all the residents of Aynor and two adjacent towns. In October 1972, at a statewide social event held at Santee State Park more than one hundred miles away, sixty-two of the approximately two hundred people in attendance were Bahá'ís and friends from Aynor, the largest group from a single local community, accounting for some 10 percent of the town's population.[13]

The gathering at Santee State Park was one of a number of occasions, formal and informal, that helped strengthen the social fabric and solidify religious identity for a statewide community that was spread across many localities and included so many new members. Even such long-standing events as summer and winter schools, long-weekend or week-long conferences that had been a tradition since the late 1950s, gained a new lease on life with more participants, especially young people. In August 1972, for example, Hand of the Cause of God (a senior international advisor) William Sears was the main speaker at the Carolinas Bahá'í Summer School, held at Kings Mountain State Park near Rock Hill. One report noted that nine black youth from Oakridge, an unincorporated hamlet in nearby York County, had returned home from the school "bubbling with enthusiasm." The following week, "when the pioneers for that area arrived for the regular meeting, they discovered that the school had inspired the young Bahá'ís to begin teaching. Seven of their friends became Bahá'ís that evening." The community quickly grew to more than thirty people, most of them teenagers.[14]

INTRODUCING THE FIVE-YEAR PLAN

Just before the close of the Nine-Year Plan in 1973, the Universal House of Justice announced that the next global teaching plan would not be launched until spring 1974, leaving an interim year during which National Spiritual Assemblies were encouraged to pursue their own plans, including those for "developing and enriching Bahá'í community life" and "fostering youth activity." The last months of the Nine-Year Plan and the interim year also included key decisions by the Universal House of Justice meant to enhance the global community's administrative capacity, from the grassroots to the World Center of the religion in Haifa, Israel. These included an increase around the world in the number of Auxiliary Board members, appointed regional advisors charged, among other duties, with nurturing local spiritual assemblies. This change had a direct effect on the South Carolina Bahá'í community.[15]

Early in 1974, the Universal House of Justice introduced a Five-Year Plan (1974–1979) with three broad objectives: "consolidation of the victories won" during the previous decade, a "vast and widespread expansion of the Bahá'í community," and "development of the distinctive character of Bahá'í life," particularly at the local level. Reflecting new needs for a faith that had seen the initial success of mass teaching in many countries, the House of Justice called national communities everywhere to give specific attention to the welfare of children and youth and to the development of local spiritual assemblies. The education and nurturing of the young, it wrote, was an "essential obligation" both of parents and communities that must become a "firmly established Bahá'í activity." As for the strengthening of local assemblies, the "basic administrative unit" of the religion operating "at the first levels of human society," the House of Justice indicated that success in this one area would "greatly enrich the quality of Bahá'í life" and better equip the Bahá'í communities to deal with large-scale growth. This dual emphasis strongly shaped the activities of South Carolina's Bahá'ís during the Five Year Plan and remained prominent in the community's culture and identity for decades.[16]

South Carolina and its new black-majority Bahá'í population also figured prominently in the specific goals that the Universal House of Justice assigned to the United States, albeit not by name. Echoing themes that it had outlined in a previous letter to the U.S. National Spiritual Assembly, the House of Justice assigned a set of domestic goals that indicated that large-scale growth should not be confined to the South or to people of African descent. For example, the number of local assemblies was to be increased to 1,400, including at least 25 on Indian reservations; the use of radio and television, both for proclaiming the religion to a larger portion of the population and for "deepening the faith of the believers, particularly in rural areas," was to be expanded; and specific teaching campaigns were to be conducted among the indigenous, Latino, Chinese, and Japanese populations as well as among such European immigrant communities as the Armenians, Basques, and Greeks. The House of Justice also directed the National Assembly to develop "intensive teaching and consolidation plans" in at least three of the states that 'Abdu'l-Bahá had visited in 1912, none of which, owing to the paucity of Bahá'ís there at the time, had been in the Deep South; the National Spiritual Assembly quickly chose New York, Illinois, and California for this purpose.[17] Essentially, the religion's supreme administrative body was asking the Bahá'ís across the United States to bring to additional regions and populations the new approaches to teaching that were already meeting with such success among black southerners. During the course of the plan, the National Assembly and its agencies, along with the religion's advisory institutions, including the Auxiliary Board members, expended a great deal of energy to rally the entire national Bahá'í community to the ambitious domestic teaching goals. However, despite small successes in a number of areas, it seemed impossible to achieve a breakthrough in mass teaching outside the Deep South.[18]

ADMINISTRATIVE ARRANGEMENTS

In preparation for the Five-Year Plan, the National Spiritual Assembly decided to reduce costs and administrative duplication by eliminating the Regional Teaching Committees, except for South Carolina's, which was, instead, augmented with additional members. Owing to the volume of work at the grassroots, near the beginning of the plan, the number of District Teaching Committees in the state was increased to eight. In addition to the formidable tasks associated with establishing and nurturing new local spiritual assemblies, District Teaching Committees experimented with a variety of expansion and consolidation activities, for example, training believers in the use of new materials; helping to start children's classes and youth clubs in high schools and colleges; hosting picnics, dances, and other opportunities for fellowship; and organizing teaching projects in specific localities over weekends or longer periods. Service on District Teaching Committees provided dozens of South Carolinians, new and veteran believers, long-time residents and pioneers, the opportunity to gain valuable experience in Bahá'í administration and become intimately familiar with communities beyond their own locality.[19]

In addition to being an arena for the organization of teaching, districts also served as the electoral units for choosing the delegates to the National Convention to elect the National Spiritual Assembly, and the District Teaching Committees planned and conducted annual district conventions that took the place of the state convention. With the distribution of the 171 delegates roughly proportional to Bahá'í population around the country, most districts elected only one, but in South Carolina, there were so many Bahá'ís that six of the eight districts elected three, four, five, or six delegates. Usually day-long affairs held in rented facilities, district conventions became important annual venues not only for community consultation, but also for social bonding and identity formation: most included children's programs and, reflecting strong elements of South Carolina culture, an outpouring of singing and communal meals. South Carolina's large number of delegates ensured that the state's Bahá'ís had a voice at the national level. In 1974, for example, twenty-seven of the twenty-nine delegates elected from South Carolina made the trip to the National Convention, the largest group ever to attend from a single state. In the Bahá'í Faith, there is no caucusing, nominations, or exit polling in elections, therefore, it is not possible to determine if the large number of delegates from South Carolina had any direct bearing on the membership of the National Spiritual Assembly. However, individuals with extensive experience in large-scale growth in the South did serve on the National Spiritual Assembly. Magdalene Carney, a young black Mississippian, who had been a member of the Deep South Committee, was elected every year from 1970 to 1982. Alberta Deas, an African American from the Charleston area, who had served as secretary of the South Carolina Regional Teaching Committee, was yearly a member from 1983 to 1997. Others elected from South Carolina were Jack McCants of Greenwood, who served from 1986 to 2001 and Tod Ewing of Columbia elected between 1992 and 1994. McCants was a white man originally from Texas who had been a strong advocate of Bahá'í interracial activities since the 1950s; Ewing was an African American pioneer originally from Minnesota.[20]

While the national and local spiritual assemblies and the teaching committee structure were prominent in the organization of the community in South Carolina, the advisory institutions that formed the other branch of the Bahá'í Faith's administrative order (the Hands of the Cause of God, the Continental Boards of Counselors, responsible for continental areas,[21] and the Auxiliary Board members) also played important roles in the planning and implementation of teaching, education, and the development of community identity. In late 1973, when the Universal House of Justice announced the increase in the number of Auxiliary Board members around the world, South Carolina was one of the areas that benefitted directly. Elizabeth Martin, a black high school English teacher who had moved with her husband and children as pioneers to Winnsboro, a county-seat town north of Columbia, in 1968, was appointed to the Auxiliary Board with responsibility for South Carolina. Previously, Auxiliary Board members in the Southeast had served a number of states; now one of them would have just South Carolina, the state with the largest Bahá'í population in the country, to focus on. During the rest of the decade Martin worked closely with the regional and district teaching committees and the staff of the Louis Gregory Institute; conducted training seminars and helped organize conferences; wrote frequently for the state newsletter; and corresponded with and traveled extensively to local Bahá'í communities large and small. More senior members of the Bahá'í Faith's advisory institutions, such as the Hands of the Cause of God and members of the Boards of

Counselors, came to South Carolina as well. Sarah Martin Pereira, an African American whose family in Cleveland had been taught the Bahá'í Faith by Louis Gregory early in the century and a member of the Continental Board of Counselors, was a frequent visitor during the rest of the decade. Several Hands of the Cause of God, including 'Alí-Akbar Furútan, Zikrullah Khadem, Rahmatu'lláh Muhájir, John Robarts, and William Sears, made trips to the state, some of them more than once. In addition to planning the teaching work and educating the community, the Hands of the Cause and Counselors who visited South Carolina played a more subtle but no less significant role in loving and encouraging those with whom they interacted. For example, a Bahá'í in Orangeburg, Emma Glover, recalled being visited in the hospital by Rahmatu'lláh Muhájir, a physician originally from Iran, after severely injuring her hand at work. Doctors had told her it would have to be amputated, but Muhájir sat by her bedside, stroked her hand, prayed with her, and assured her that it could be saved. Not only was the hand not amputated, but Glover regained its full use, an outcome she attributed in part to Muhájir's kind intervention. Moreover, the fact that she, a local black woman, had received a visit from a "white" foreign dignitary caused people in the hospital to inquire about her religion[22] (see figure 5.2).

Figure 5.2 To the Left Is Dr. Sarah Martin Pereira, Member of the Continental Board of Counselors. To the Right Is Alberta Deas, Secretary of the South Carolina Regional Teaching Committee, 1974. *Source: South Carolina Regional Bahá'í Bulletin.*

APPROACHES TO TRAINING

During the Five Year Plan, a variety of actors from around the state and elsewhere including the staff of the Louis Gregory Institute, various agencies of the National Spiritual Assembly, Auxiliary Board members, and the regional and district teaching committees, engaged in experimentation to try to discover the best ways to train large numbers of teachers and administrators for the South Carolina movement, to deepen the faith and strengthen the Bahá'í identity of thousands of believers, and to effectively deploy human resources in dozens of localities across the state. Their efforts were often thoughtful, energetic, and collaborative, and also sometimes chaotic and halting, resulting in a process that proved to be both immensely challenging and rewarding.

The center of experimentation with training and curriculum development was the Louis Gregory Institute. According to one early mission statement, its purpose was to "train Bahá'í teachers and administrators and to work with teaching committees in using these trained persons in their home communities and in the field." In his remarks at the Institute's dedication program, Harold Jackson, its first dean, called the facility a "gift to the people of the South" that would have "aims, goals, and objectives, curriculum, lesson plans, and methods" designed specifically for them. However, the Institute began its life with no ready-made curriculum or training methods, no particular approach for recruiting participants from across the state, no system for deploying trained individuals for service in their home communities, and no roadmap for its working relationship with regional and district teaching committees. Moreover, frequent changes in administration likely made it difficult to take a long-term approach to the Institute's development.[23]

In the middle of 1973, less than a year after the Institute's inauguration, its dean, Harold Jackson, stepped down to return to California to complete a graduate degree. Bransford Watson, a former member of the National Teaching Committee, was appointed to take his place. The following summer, Caswell Ellis, a former manager of the national Bahá'í House of Worship in suburban Chicago, was appointed assistant dean. In spring 1975, Allen Murray, a special education teacher and recent pioneer to the Charleston area, replaced Watson.[24]

In this context, the Institute experimented with a variety of programs, relying on volunteer instructors from around the state and elsewhere, and the results were somewhat haphazard. During 1974, the Institute began to offer, almost weekly, a new five-day course, the Gregory Institute Intensive Deepening Program. Designed by the National Teaching Committee, it was intended primarily for "new and undeepened believers" and focused on the Covenant and the Administrative Order. Other programs of seven and nine days' duration were also held. By the end of 1976, the longer-form programs had mostly been replaced by three-day deepening weekends for new believers. During 1975, the Institute began to offer programs for children. Previously, staff had discouraged participants from bringing children because the physical facilities were not large enough for separate children's programs. By early summer 1975, however, the construction of a new classroom-dining hall building, divisible by folding walls into three sections, allowed for the holding of multiple concurrent classes with larger groups. The Institute began regular weekly classes for local children, and during the summer it held four week-long sessions for children and two for youth, designed and supervised by Betty Morris, a Montessori teacher. The weekly class and the summer programs continued for several years[25] (see figures 5.3, 5.4, and 5.5).

In addition to regular programs, the Institute also hosted holy day observances, community dinners, and youth activities that usually drew from a smaller geographic area, as well as occasional courses and seminars and special programs with attendees from across the state and region. In January 1975, for example, before the completion of the new classrooms, some 140 participants gathered for a statewide youth conference that stretched the physical facilities to the limits. The highlight of the conference was splitting into five workshop groups for study and consultation on "dating, sexual behavior,

Figure 5.3 Early Participants in Programs at the Louis G. Gregory Bahá'í Institute.
Source: Louis G. Gregory Bahá'í Institute.

Figure 5.4 Early Participants in Programs at the Louis G. Gregory Bahá'í Institute.
Source: Louis G. Gregory Bahá'í Institute.

Figure 5.5 Early Participants in Programs at the Louis G. Gregory Bahá'í Institute.
Source: Louis G. Gregory Bahá'í Institute.

and preparation for marriage." There were also occasions that fostered an appreciation of the South Carolina Bahá'í community's history and global connections. In August 1973, for instance, Roy Williams, one of the first black pioneers to Greenville, spoke at the Institute about his teaching trips across the region with Louis Gregory from 1919 to 1921. The following year, Vivian Wesson, a black Chicagoan who had helped establish new Bahá'í communities in Togo and Liberia in the 1950s, spoke. In fall 1975, the Institute received its first visit by a member of the Universal House of Justice. Hugh Chance, the former attorney for Palmer College of Chiropractic in Iowa, and his wife Margaret taught the Bahá'í Faith to many students there, including white couples who had settled in Florence and Lake City and became early proponents of large-scale growth. The Chances were guests of honor for the largest weekend gathering at the Louis Gregory Institute since its opening, which included a campus work day and a fish fry.[26]

By the end of the Five Year Plan, more than five years after the Institute's inauguration, there seemed to be a widespread consensus that raising up ranks of confident protagonists of the Bahá'í Faith and promoting social and spiritual transformation of individuals and communities had proven much harder than anyone had imagined. Yet, the Institute had emerged as a vital center of learning, and a site for strengthening bonds of community across the state and region. During a nine-month period in 1975–1976 alone, after the completion of the new classroom building, the Institute served some 8,600 participants. Clearly it had begun to affect the lives of thousands of people, even if there were thousands more whom its programs were unable to effectively reach.[27]

THE FOLLY GROVE COMMUNITY AND OPPOSITION TO THE BAHÁ'Í FAITH

An indirect benefit of the establishment of the Louis Gregory Institute was the emergence of a vibrant local Bahá'í community in the immediate area, a part of rural Georgetown County called Folly Grove. Woodrow Jackson, an illiterate black farmer, was the first local resident to become a Bahá'í, having befriended members of the Institute staff while the facility was still under construction. He was followed by a number of his family members and neighbors. Jackson's adult daughter, Mary Beckmon, recalled investigating the Bahá'í Faith as a result of seeing the positive transformation of local children participating in classes at the Institute. Soon, members of the extended Jackson-Beckmon family were among the most active supporters of the religion in the state. For example, in 1975, Woodrow Jackson, who had never been outside the South, helped fulfill one of the U.S. Bahá'í community's international goals for the Five Year Plan when he participated in a teaching trip to the Turks and Caicos Islands. Similarly, Mary Beckmon and her best friend and neighbor, Elnetha Graham, who had also become a Bahá'í, made trips to Jamaica and Trinidad. Beckmon, who had a fifth-grade education, served on her Local Spiritual Assembly, on the District Teaching Committee, and as a delegate to National Convention. She became well known in the state and region as a singer and composer of Bahá'í songs, and as a cook at the Institute thanks to her traditional South Carolina cuisine[28] (see figure 5.6).

Mary Beckmon was also among those targeted for violence and intimidation by local whites. During the 1970s, the Institute frequently received threatening phone calls, and vandals destroyed the mailbox on several occasions. Once while Beckmon was walking to work at the Institute, a driver attempted to run her down, forcing her to jump in a roadside ditch to avoid being run down by a car. Across the state in the Piedmont county-seat town of York, pioneers Charles and Alice Nightingale, an interracial couple from Massachusetts, suffered a cross burned on their lawn, glass and nails scattered in their driveway, and "numerous obscene phone calls."[29]

The pattern of harassment was familiar. Since shortly after Louis Gregory's first teaching trip to South Carolina in 1910, Bahá'ís had been subjected

Figure 5.6 To the Left Is David Gordon of Greenville. To the Right Is Woodrow Jackson, the First Person from the Folly Grove Community to Become a Bahá'í, in the 1970s. *Source*: Louis G. Gregory Bahá'í Institute.

to surveillance, slander, intimidation, economic reprisals, and occasional violence at the hands of conservative ministers, the Ku Klux Klan, the FBI, local law enforcement, and government officials. The first person to become a Bahá'í in the state, an African American lawyer in Charleston named Alonzo Twine, had even been judged insane for "religious obsession" and committed to the insane asylum in Columbia, where he died in 1914. The incidents from Folly Grove and York indicate that even in the 1970s, well after the passage of the Civil Rights Act of 1964, in small-town South Carolina, the Bahá'ís' combination of unorthodox religious belief and racial unity continued to make them targets for upholders of white supremacy.[30]

APPROACHES TO TEACHING THE BAHÁ'Í FAITH

During the interim year and the Five Year Plan, Bahá'ís in South Carolina engaged in energetic experimentation in teaching the Bahá'í Faith to others. Sometimes their plans were grandiose and achieved much less than the desired results, with a measure of disappointment that the large-scale growth of the early part of the decade could not be replicated. For example, in June 1973 at a statewide conference at Penn Center, a former school for freed people on St. Helena Island, and a perennial site for Bahá'í conferences in South Carolina, the Regional Teaching Committee announced a five-month plan for the interim year that called for activating 3,000 of the state's Bahá'ís as teachers and enrolling 3,000 new members. Presenting no specific program, the committee simply suggested that the ambitious goals would be reached if each local assembly in the state pledged to bring in twenty-five new believers. Nevertheless, the conference participants decided to raise the goal to 6,000 enrollments.[31]

At Thanksgiving, when some 250 people, half the number the committee had planned for, probably in large part because of the recent dramatic spike in gas prices due to the Arab oil embargo, gathered at the Wade Hampton Hotel in downtown Columbia for a conference to conclude the campaign, it was clear that the 6,000 new believers had failed to materialize. Yet, a number of local initiatives had met with good results. For example, following a training seminar conducted by Helen Thomas, a veteran of the Dillon project, several summer youth programs had taken place, the most successful of which, in Rock Hill, had garnered 100 new believers, many of whom had arisen to help with the consolidation of others. In Greenwood and Saluda, the District Teaching Committee had experimented with a "Mobile Institute," a large van outfitted as a reading room, with materials for teaching, deepening, and holding children's classes, primarily to reach those who had become Bahá'ís in the area during the Army of Light project the previous year[32] (see figure 5.7).

Figure 5.7 Local Bahá'ís and Friends with Home-Front Pioneers, Black and White, Saluda, South Carolina, 1974. *Source*: National Bahá'í Archives.

Following the conference, a diverse range of local communities continued to pursue their own goals, illustrating a variety of approaches to expansion and consolidation. During late 1973 and early 1974 in Columbia, for example, the Local Spiritual Assembly planned a number of activities in Wheeler Hill, a mostly working-class black neighborhood adjacent to the University of South Carolina. Residents of the neighborhood were organizing in response to the unexpected news that Booker T. Washington High School, the first public high school for African Americans in the state and an anchor of neighborhood life (and where Louis Gregory had spoken decades before) was being closed and sold to the university without any plan for preservation or relocation of the historic structure. In this charged local environment, interracial groups of Bahá'ís spent time canvassing the neighborhood and becoming acquainted with the residents in preparation for a "tent revival" program in February. Posters with the title "Christ Has Returned" were placed throughout the city to advertise the event, and several radio and television interviews about the Bahá'í Faith reached an even larger audience. Some forty Bahá'ís from across the state came to support the effort, including a signing group from Rock Hill. Thirteen people embraced the Bahá'í religion as a result.[33]

In the coastal city of Georgetown, a weekend project in March 1974 also drew support from other local communities. The Georgetown Bahá'ís secured newspaper and radio publicity, and Bahá'í teachers canvassed the city, delivering hundreds of invitations to a public meeting at the local library that included a variety of musical performances. Some seventy people attended the meeting, and two people became Bahá'ís. In addition, during the course of the neighborhood canvassing, teachers met two people who had previously joined the religion, but whose addresses had been lost.[34]

Occasionally a local community received a boost to its teaching plans through no effort of its own. In January 1974, for example, the popular soft rock duo Seals and Crofts, consisting of two Bahá'ís originally from Texas, performed at Clemson University. They mentioned the Bahá'í Faith and its effect on their art both at a press conference and during their performance, inviting anyone who was interested to stay afterward to learn more about the Bahá'í Faith. Several hundred did so, and then a dozen or so came to a more intimate gathering at the home of some local believers. In the weeks after the performance the community noted an increase in the number of individuals at information meetings and other gatherings of the university's Bahá'í club.[35]

The pattern of successful local initiatives continued during the Five Year Plan. The statewide goals adopted by the Regional Teaching Committee included several items related to the expansion and the development of community life, including increasing the number of localities where Bahá'ís resided from 300 to 500; forming 80 new, strong local spiritual assemblies, with at least 1 in each county of the state; establishing children's classes in strong communities; and educating local assembly treasurers. However, there was no numerical goal for new believers, a tacit admission of the failure of the five-month campaign during the interim year. Many local communities responded energetically and creatively to the new statewide plan. For example, the Local Spiritual Assembly of Florence and the District Teaching Committee in its area worked together to coordinate a variety of teaching efforts in Florence and a number of surrounding towns. In July 1974, the Florence community put on an art show at the city's new indoor shopping mall, entitled "Keys to Harmony" that featured pieces on loan from Bahá'í artists across the state. The following November, young Bahá'ís from Florence opened Cash, a hamlet in Chesterfield County, to the Bahá'í religion with a day of canvassing homes, businesses, and public places. The day ended with a public meeting featuring a talk and music led by the Florence community's youth chorus. In January 1975, the Florence Bahá'ís organized a nineteen-day project that included donating Bahá'í books to local school libraries, making presentations to a number of civic organizations, and several days of propagation efforts at a shopping center.[36]

Another active community near Florence was Hartsville, a college town in Darlington County. Most of the Bahá'ís there lived near each other in one neighborhood, and for a time all the members of the Local Spiritual Assembly lived on the same street. Elizabeth Ellis, who had come from Vermont for the Dillon campaign as a new Bahá'í and stayed as a pioneer, recalled a tight-knit Hartsville community in which virtually every gathering included food, singing, and socializing. The social portion of the Nineteen-Day Feast (the central gathering in a local Bahá'í community, held every nineteen days) often included a fish fry and card games late into the night.[37]

In the Piedmont, the Spartanburg community pursued a number of initiatives, including the acquisition of its first Bahá'í Center, a converted house in a predominantly African American neighborhood, in early 1975. The dedication program was part of several days of publicity and propagation efforts, including radio advertisements and newspaper and television coverage, several public meetings, and at least one enrollment into the religion. A few months later the District Teaching Committee sponsored a summer youth project based in Spartanburg during which teams of teachers opened the neighboring towns of Boiling Springs and Inman to the Bahá'í Faith. In Union, where there was a list of believers but no organized activities, the Bahá'í teachers "were greeted by friends who had been Bahá'ís for years and asked, 'Where have you been all this time?'" The visitors helped them to organize a group and elect officers in preparation for forming their Local Spiritual Assembly. The capstone of the project was a weekend trip for fourteen Spartanburg young people, most of them relatively new Bahá'ís, to the House of Worship in Chicago, a powerful experience of cementing Bahá'í identity, strengthening bonds of community, and establishing spiritual and practical links with the national center of their faith.[38]

SOUTH CAROLINA AND THE NATIONAL PLAN

By the mid-point of the Five Year Plan, the Bahá'ís in South Carolina had made progress on a number of fronts. In South Carolina, and in the country as a whole, however, there were no signs of the rapid membership growth of the early years of the decade, and the lack of progress in achieving the plan's domestic goals caused the National Spiritual Assembly considerable alarm. A significant number of local spiritual assemblies formed late in the previous plan were now jeopardized due to low numbers, and the community was "lagging behind" its targets for the number of new localities opened and additional local assemblies established. Moreover, the "magnetic goal" of initiating large-scale growth in California, Illinois, and New York seemed nowhere close to realization.[39]

In this context, the National Spiritual Assembly asked Hand of the Cause of God Rahmatu'lláh Muhájir, who had been among the earliest advocates of propagating the Bahá'í Faith to rural peoples as a pioneer in Indonesia in the 1950s, to help plan a new teaching campaign in the South that would spark the necessary action across the country. The new initiative, which Muhájir announced at a large gathering at the Louis Gregory Institute in January 1976, called for teaching projects in the nine southern states that had nine or more local spiritual assemblies. The National Teaching Committee would provide additional assistance for projects in and around Atlanta, Georgia; College Station, Texas; and Columbia, South Carolina. The initial results in South Carolina were modest but encouraging. By April 1976, some fifty people had become Bahá'ís across the state, with a notable uptick in teaching activities in Rock Hill and York, in the Columbia area, in Orangeburg, in Charleston and Beaufort, and in Florence and nearby towns. Notably, the number of children being served in Bahá'í classes doubled to some two hundred.[40]

Perhaps the most welcome boost to the opening phase of the new campaign came entirely unexpectedly. In March 1976, the renowned jazz trumpeter John Birks "Dizzy" Gillespie, easily the most famous Bahá'í with South Carolina roots, was honored by the state government as part of its celebration of the national bicentennial. Born in Cheraw in 1917, Gillespie had moved with his family to Philadelphia in the 1930s, joining the stream of tens of thousands of black South Carolinians fleeing the devastation of the boll weevil and a fresh wave of anti-black violence led by government officials and the Ku Klux Klan. When he returned more than forty years later, Gillespie was an international star, having pioneered his own signature style, called "bebop," and collaborated with virtually all of the other leading jazz artists of his generation. Since becoming a Bahá'í in Los Angeles in 1968, he had been known for mentioning two points during his concerts: his hometown of Cheraw (which he often jokingly pronounced "CHEE-raw") and the Bahá'í Faith. On March 9, Gillespie and his band performed for a joint session of the General Assembly, which had only welcomed its first African American members since Reconstruction in 1971, and guests, including Gov. James B. Edwards and the mayor of Cheraw. During the ceremony, the South Carolina Arts Commission presented Gillespie with a plaque commending his contribution "to the world of music and the state of South Carolina." For his part, Gillespie said that he was "full of hope for America," quoting a short passage from 'Abdu'l-Bahá:

> The continent of America is in the eyes of the one true God the land wherein the splendors of His light shall be revealed, where the mysteries of His Faith shall be unveiled, where the righteous will abide and the free assemble.

Then he read the entire text of an editorial, "Two Hundred Years of Imperishable Hope," from the bicentennial issue of *World Order*, the National Spiritual Assembly's journal of ideas. Afterward, Gov. Edwards hosted a reception for 300 people at a building in the Governor's Mansion complex, followed by a private dinner for Gillespie, his band, and members of the Arts Commission. It seemed a remarkable reversal of fortune for a black man who had been forced to become a refugee from his home state, and a striking symbol of the extent to which the civil rights movement had revolutionized public life in South Carolina. Moreover, for a faith community whose theological unorthodoxy and interracial commitment had left it struggling to achieve basic civil protections, much less public acceptance, since its arrival in the state more than six decades earlier, the occasion represented unprecedented recognition by South Carolina's government[41] (see figure 5.8).

The Regional Teaching Committee's goals for the Five Year Plan in South Carolina envisioned the District Teaching Committees and stronger local spiritual assemblies as the primary organizers of teaching, an approach that appeared only to be enhanced in the first few months of the new regional campaign. In June 1976, however, the staff of the Louis Gregory Institute proposed their own initiative to the Regional Teaching Committee. Named "Project Outreach," it called for teams of local and visiting teachers housed at the Institute to work full time for the summer. Their goal was to inform

Figure 5.8 John Birks "Dizzy" Gillespie (1917–1993), a Native of Cheraw, Performing for Gov. Edwards and a Joint Session of the General Assembly as Part of South Carolina's National Bicentennial Celebrations, State House, Columbia, March 1976. *Source*: Bahá'í News.

everyone within a thirty-mile radius of the campus about the Bahá'í Faith. A number of nearby towns and hamlets—Stuckey, Donnelly, Nesmith in Williamsburg County, Gresham and Friendship in Marion County, and Andrews and Plantersville in Georgetown County, all of which had very large African American populations—received special attention with a view to establishing a local spiritual assembly in each. For the first several weeks, about a dozen mostly young Bahá'ís went out in teams to the focus communities every day. "We would walk down a road," one participant recalled, "and stop at each house, knocking on the door and handing the person an invitation" to activities at the Institute. If people asked questions, the teachers told them more about the religion. According to another participant, they "set up firesides in interested persons' homes as well as in new believers' homes," and sometimes they held classes for children. By focusing on a few small, rural neighborhoods over an extended period, the teachers were able to tap rich local networks of kinship and friendship to identify new interested people in the religion and to reestablish contact with people who had embraced the Bahá'í Faith during previous campaigns.[42]

Unfortunately, the project soon fell prey to the same grandiosity that had led to the failure of the Regional Teaching Committee's five-month campaign in 1973. In mid-July, the secretary of the Regional Teaching Committee and a member of the National Teaching Committee came to the Institute to announce an entirely new approach. They said that the National Spiritual Assembly had decided to "give Project Outreach its unlimited support and an open-ended budget." The effort was to be broadened to a series of nine-week campaigns, with a goal to enroll 10,000 people in the first nine weeks. Soon the group was plagued by disagreements about leadership, goals, and methods, which even a visit by the secretary of the National Spiritual Assembly seemed unable to resolve. By the fall, most of the young volunteers had left to return to school, and Project Outreach quickly dwindled. Altogether only about 110 people became Bahá'ís in the area during the summer, far short of the revised project's goal.[43] Further research is required to understand the reasons for the lack of success.

After the failure of Operation Outreach, the locus of planning shifted back to the regional and district teaching committees. At a January 1977 meeting, the National Spiritual Assembly encouraged the South Carolina Bahá'ís to "initiate plans of their own and rely less on the National Center for guidance," a somewhat strange directive given that it was the national agencies' imposition of Operation Outreach that had taken the initiative away from the District Teaching Committees. A new program planned by the Regional Teaching Committee called "Operation Grassroots" envisioned expansion and consolidation work in each of the state's districts plus a concerted statewide media campaign including radio, television, newspaper ads, and direct mail. The results were modest, with a small number of enrollments around the state and the initiation of activities in a few new areas such as Cowpens and Gaffney, small towns near Spartanburg.[44]

In January 1978, the National Teaching Committee was back with representatives at a meeting of some three hundred Bahá'ís from around the state, including one hundred youth, to adopt a strategy for the remaining months of the Five Year Plan. Called simply "1000 + 80," it included goals of having 1,000 believers participating in community activities and 80 functioning local assemblies. The Universal House of Justice had announced that lapsed local spiritual assemblies around the world could be reformed any time during the final year of the plan, and not just on the first day of the Ridván Festival in April as in most years. This strategy called for teams to visit every such locality in South Carolina. By the fall, dozens of towns had received multiple visits, resulting in the enrolment of new believers as well as reconnecting with older ones. In Marion, for example, where no teachers had visited in at least two years, one team reported finding that the believers were keeping up with national and international news in the *American Bahá'í*, the National Spiritual Assembly's monthly newspaper. Trudy White, the secretary of the Regional Teaching Committee, noted that many communities would gladly receive more visits, but there were too few teachers and too few cars available.

Figure 5.9 Home Visit with Bahá'í Family, Eastern South Carolina, 1979. *Source*: Personal Collection of Sandy Hoover.

All of the state's districts but one exceeded their goals for the formation of local assemblies and the opening of new localities, some by wide margins. In November, the National Spiritual Assembly announced that the national community had reached its Five Year Plan goal of 1,400 Local Assemblies, aided in no small part by the effort in South Carolina[45] (see figure 5.9).

CONCLUSION

During the 1970s, the Bahá'ís in South Carolina were among the many individuals and organizations that were addressing themselves to the unfinished business of the civil rights movement. Having achieved the dismantling of the Jim Crow legal regime with the landmark federal legislation of the previous decade, the challenges of bringing blacks and whites together at the local level across the South and beginning to redress the social, economic, educational, and political effects of generations' worth of white supremacy remained formidable. In short, there were few working models, religious or secular, for what Martin Luther King, Jr. had famously termed the "beloved community": a spiritualized polity characterized by justice, love, and the "total interrelatedness" of all people.[46] South Carolina's Bahá'ís—white, black, and indigenous—made concerted efforts during the 1970s to discover some aspects of what that ideal society might look like in practice. Having experienced unprecedented membership growth from 1970 to 1972, during the interim year and the Five Year Plan, a South Carolina Bahá'í community that had already accumulated significant experience in overcoming barriers of race, class, and gender, and, by extension, the national Bahá'í movement of which it now formed the largest state-level component, responded to a new set of challenges. With energy and creativity and in a spirit of experimentation and learning, they attempted to develop methods and approaches that would allow vastly more people from a variety of social backgrounds to become confident protagonists of the religion's development and, as a united body, contribute to the spiritual, social, and intellectual transformation of their neighborhoods and communities.

By the end of the 1970s, the statewide South Carolina Bahá'í community was undoubtedly stronger, more capable, and more experienced at meeting the needs of its members of all ages than it had been at the outset. Further, the influx of so many rural black southerners had permanently changed the identity and priorities of the national Bahá'í movement. Yet, in some respects, the results were disappointing: the surges of enrollments that had taken place early in the 1970s could not be replicated, either in South Carolina or anywhere else, and the painstaking work of consolidation resulted in too few local communities, especially in rural areas, where the members could take charge of their own affairs and be self-sustaining. In the context of Bahá'í experiences around the world, South Carolina was not alone. Surveying similar developments in a number of countries during the 1970s and 1980s, an analysis commissioned by the Universal House of Justice notes that large-scale growth "launched the Bahá'í world on a learning process that has proved to be as important as the expansion itself." It continues:

> It is safe to say that during these years there was virtually no type of teaching activity, no combination of expansion, consolidation and proclamation, no administrative option, no effort at cultural adaptation that was not being energetically tried in some part of the Bahá'í world. The net result of the experience was an intensive education of a great part of the Bahá'í community in the implications of the mass teaching work, an education that could have occurred in no other way. By its very nature, the process was largely local and regional in focus, qualitative rather than quantitative in its gains, and incremental rather than large-scale in the progress achieved.

While the results in South Carolina and other areas of the world were incomplete at best, they contributed directly to a body of knowledge which, during the late 1990s, resulted in the deployment of a new system of grassroots education designed to systematize large-scale growth of the faith and open its community-building processes to a broader cross section of society. It was a development that Bahá'ís in the state and around the country hoped would enable them to contribute afresh to the continuing work of dismantling "every instrument devised by humanity over the long period of its childhood for one group to oppress another."[47]

NOTES

1. The Bahá'í Faith does not have clergy, therefore, instead of using congregation, Bahá'ís call their local group of believers a community.

2. The data regarding the Bahá'í Faith as the second-largest religious group in South Carolina are from the U.S. Religion Census conducted by the Association of Statisticians of American Religious Bodies (ASARB), http://usreligioncensus.org. For examples of media treatment, see Gustav Niebuhr, "Hemingway Journal: A Little Bit of a Change from Old-Time Religion," *New York Times*, March 31, 2000; Stephanie Harvin, "The Ripple Effect: Influencing the Tide of History," *Charleston (SC) Post and Courier*, February 2, 2003; Paul Bowers, "How a 19th-Century Persian Faith Became the Second-Most Common Religion in Our State," *Charleston (SC) City Paper*, June 17, 2014; Jennifer Berry Hawes, "How the Bahá'í Faith Became South Carolina's Second-Largest Religion," *Charleston (SC) Post and Courier*, June 21, 2014; Linton Weeks, "The Runner-Up Religions of America," "The Protojournalist:

Very Original Reporting" blog, *National Public Radio*, June 22, 2014; Melissa Rollins, "Bahá'í Faith is Second Most Prevalent Religion in South Carolina," *Florence (SC) Morning News*, July 19, 2014. For more information on the Louis G. Gregory Bahá'í Museum, see www.louisgregorymuseum.org. For "Carolinian Pentecost," see Stephen W. Angell, review of *No Jim Crow Church: The Origins of South Carolina's Bahá'í Community*, by Louis Venters, *American Historical Review* 121, no. 4 (October 2016): 1301–1302. For Bahá'í membership in South Carolina, see Arthur Hampson, "Growth and Spread of the Bahá'í Faith," PhD diss., University of Hawaii, 1980, 281, and *Bahá'í News*, no. 492 (March 1972), 11. The Bahá'í Faith is also the second-largest religion in a number of counties across the country.

3. See, for example, Mark Newman, *Divine Agitators: The Delta Ministry and Civil Rights in Mississippi* (Athens: University of Georgia Press, 2004), and R. Wright Spears, *Journey toward Unity: The Christian Action Council in South Carolina* (Columbia, SC: Christian Action Council, 1983).

4. Universal House of Justice, *Messages from the Universal House of Justice, 1963–1986: The Third Epoch of the Formative Age*, comp. Geoffry Marks (Wilmette, IL: Bahá'í Publishing Trust, 1996), 18.6.

5. Universal House of Justice, *Messages, 1963–1986*, 14.4, 18.1–5.

6. Richard Hollinger, "Introduction: Bahá'í Communities in the West, 1897–1992," in *Community Histories*, ed. Richard Hollinger (Los Angeles: Kalimát Press, 1992), xxx; Hampson, "Growth and Spread," 233; "Southern Teaching Conference," *National Bahá'í Review*, no. 23 (November 1969): 1–4; "Baha'is Recruit Southern Blacks," *Greenville (S.C.) News*, June 28, 1970. The local spiritual assembly is the local governing body for Bahá'í communities.

7. *American Bahá'í*, January 1971, 1; Universal House of Justice, *Messages from the Universal House of Justice 1968–1973* (Wilmette, IL: Bahá'í Publishing Trust, 1976), 65; Hampson, "Growth and Spread" 281; Robert Stockman, "U.S. Bahá'í Community Membership: 1894–1996," *American Bahá'í*, November 23, 1996, 27; *Bahá'í News*, no. 492 (March 1972): 11.

8. "Operation 'Gabriel,'" *American Bahá'í*, January 1972, 3; Annual Report of the National Spiritual Assembly of the Bahá'ís of the United States, 1970–1971, n.p., National Bahá'í Archives.

9. Roger Roff, quoted in Annette Reynolds, *Trudy and the Bahá'ís' Spiritual Path in South Carolina* (Bloomington, IN: Xlibris, 2015), 51–2; Sandra Santolucito Kahn, "Encounter of Two Myths: Baha'i and Christian in the Rural American South—A Study in Transmythicization" (PhD diss., University of California, Santa Barbara, 1977), 262–3; *American Bahá'í*, May 1971, 4–5. The local spiritual assembly is the local governing body for Bahá'í communities.

10. Annual Report of the National Spiritual Assembly, printed in *National Bahá'í Review*, no. 53 (May 1972): 1–2; *American Bahá'í* (September 1971): 8; *American Bahá'í* (September 1971): 2; *American Bahá'í*, August 1971, 6–7.

11. Annette and Jordan Young, interview by the author, Easley, SC, September 25, 2003; Kahn, "Encounter of Two Myths: Baha'i and Christian in the Rural American South—A Study in Transmythicization," 268–73; *American Bahá'í*, March 1973, 7; *Baha'i Bulletin* 3, no. 5 (Summer 1973): 2.

12. *South Carolina Regional Bahá'í Bulletin*, 'Izzat 129 (September 1972): 4–5.

13. Reynolds, *Trudy*, 91; *South Carolina Regional Bahá'í Bulletin*, Qawl 129 (November 1972), 11; *South Carolina Regional Bahá'í Bulletin*, 'Izzat 129 (September 1972): 8; *South Carolina Regional Newsletter* 2, no. 4 (November 1972): 1.

14. *South Carolina Regional Bahá'í Bulletin*, 'Izzat 129 (September 1972): 6.

15. Universal House of Justice, *Messages 1963–1968*, 124.2.

16. Universal House of Justice, *Messages 1963–1968*, 124.2, 137.1–6, 141.4, 141.11, 141.13–14.

17. See the introduction for information on 'Abdu'l-Bahá. For a map and list of places in the United States that he visited, see "Travels of 'Abdu'l-Bahá by City," *Commemorating 'Abdu'l-Bahá in America, 1912–2012*, http://centenary.bahai.us/cities.

18. Universal House of Justice to the Bahá'ís of the United States, Naw-Rúz 1974, in *National Bahá'í Review*, no. 76 (May 1974): 3–4; National Spiritual Assembly of the Bahá'ís of the United States to the National Teaching Committee, May 17, 1974, in *National Bahá'í Review*, no. 82 (November 1974): 2–3; Universal House of Justice to the National Spiritual Assembly of the Bahá'ís of the United States, February 14, 1972, *National Bahá'í Review*, no. 51 (March 1972): 1, also published in Universal House of Justice, *Messages from the Universal House of Justice 1968–1973*, 85–6. The reasons it proved difficult to initiate large-scale growth in places outside the Deep South, including with other minority groups, are unclear; this is an area that calls for further research. Naw-Rúz means "new day" and is the Bahá'í New Year.

19. National Spiritual Assembly, December 13, 1973, quoted in Mike McMullen, *The Bahá'ís of America: The Growth of a Religious Movement* (New York: New York University Press, 2015), 156.

20. *South Carolina Regional Bahá'í Bulletin* 4, no. 3 (Fall 1974): 3; *South Carolina Regional Bahá'í Bulletin* 5, no. 1 (Fall 1975): 2; *South Carolina Regional Bahá'í Bulletin* 4, no. 1 (Spring 1974): 1.

21. When Shoghi Effendi died, as per 'Abdu'l-Bahá's Will and Testament, no more Hands of the Cause of God could be appointed. The Universal House of Justice created the institution of the Continental Boards of Counselors to serve a similar function.

22. *South Carolina Regional Bahá'í Bulletin* 3, no. 6 (January 1974): 8. Reynolds, *Trudy*, 86.

23. *South Carolina Regional Bahá'í Bulletin* 3 (April 1973): 1; *South Carolina Regional Newsletter* 1, no. 3 (December 1972): 1; *South Carolina Regional Bahá'í Bulletin* 3, no. 5 (Summer 1973): 4; *South Carolina Regional Bahá'í Bulletin* 4, no. 2 (summer 1974): 4–5; *South Carolina Regional Bahá'í Bulletin* 5, no. 1 (fall 1975): 7.

24. *South Carolina Regional Bahá'í Bulletin* 3 (April 1973): 1; *South Carolina Regional Newsletter* 1, no. 3 (December 1972): 1; *South Carolina Regional Bahá'í Bulletin* 3, no. 5 (Summer 1973): 4; *South Carolina Regional Bahá'í Bulletin* 4, no. 2 (summer 1974): 4–5; *South Carolina Regional Bahá'í Bulletin* 5, no. 1 (fall 1975): 7. Beginning in 1909 under the direction of 'Abdu'l-Bahá, the project to build the Bahá'í House of Worship in Wilmette, Illinois (just outside Chicago where the first local Bahá'í community in the country emerged in the mid-1890s) was the

impetus for the development of the religion's first national body in the United States. Constructed over the course of decades that included two world wars and the Great Depression, it was completed in 1953 and listed on the National Register of Historic Places in 1978. See Bruce Whitmore, *Dawning Place*, 2nd ed. (Wilmette, IL: Bahá'í Publishing Trust, 2015).

25. *South Carolina Regional Bahá'í Bulletin* 4, no. 1 (Spring 1974): 6; *South Carolina Regional Bahá'í Bulletin* 5, no. 1 (Spring 1975): 3; *South Carolina Regional Bahá'í Bulletin* 5, no. 3 (Fall 1975): 7; *South Carolina Regional Bahá'í Bulletin* 4, no. 3 (Fall 1974): 2; *Bahá'í News* 52, no. 7 (July 1975): 19; miscellaneous programs and calendars, 1975–1977, author's personal collection.

26. *South Carolina Regional Bahá'í Bulletin* 4, no. 3 (Fall 1974): 2; *South Carolina Regional Bahá'í Bulletin* 3, no. 5 (Summer 1973): 3; *South Carolina Regional Bahá'í Bulletin* 5, no. 1 (Spring 1975): 3; *South Carolina Regional Bahá'í Bulletin* 5, no. 3 (Fall 1975): 1.

27. *Southern Bahá'í Bulletin* (April 1976): 4.

28. Kahn, "Encounter of Two Myths: Baha'i and Christian in the Rural American South—A Study in Transmythicization," 374–376, 386–392; *South Carolina Regional Bahá'í Bulletin* 5, no. 3 (Fall 1975), 4; Reynolds, *Trudy*, 127.

29. *Weekly Observer (Hemingway, S.C.)*, August 28, 1975; Charles Nightingale, quoted in Reynolds, *Trudy*, 78–79; "Alonzo Twine," South Carolina State Hospital Commitment Files, South Carolina Department of Archives and History, Columbia. For accounts of earlier opposition, see Louis Venters, *No Jim Crow Church: The Origins of South Carolina's Bahá'í Community* (Gainesville: University of Florida Press, 2015).

30. *Weekly Observer (Hemingway, S.C.)*, August 28, 1975; Charles Nightingale, quoted in Reynolds, *Trudy*, 78–79; "Alonzo Twine," South Carolina State Hospital Commitment Files, South Carolina Department of Archives and History, Columbia. For accounts of earlier opposition, see Venters, *No Jim Crow Church*.

31. South Carolina Regional Teaching Committee to all local spiritual assemblies in *South Carolina Regional Bahá'í Bulletin* 2, no. 9 (June 1973): 4.

32. *American Bahá'í*, December 1973, 3–5, 12; *American Bahá'í*, October 1973, 15; *South Carolina Regional Bahá'í Bulletin* 3, no. 6 (January 1974): 4; *South Carolina Regional Bahá'í Bulletin* 3, no. 5 (Summer 1973): 8; *South Carolina Regional Newsletter* (October 1973): 1; *American Bahá'í*, December 1973, 12.

33. Booker T. Washington High School Foundation, "History," http://bookertwashingtonfoundationsc.org/BTWHistory.htm; *South Carolina Regional Bahá'í Bulletin* 4, no. 1 (spring 1974): 7; *South Carolina Regional Bahá'í Bulletin* 3, no. 6 (January 1974): 6.

34. *South Carolina Regional Bahá'í Bulletin* 4, no. 1 (Spring 1974): 7; *South Carolina Regional Bahá'í Bulletin* 3, no. 6 (January 1974): 6.

35. Ibid.

36. *South Carolina Regional Bahá'í Bulletin* 4, no. 2 (Summer 1974): 1, 7; *South Carolina Regional Bahá'í Bulletin* 4, no. 3 (Fall 1974): 6, 8; *South Carolina Regional Bahá'í Bulletin* 5, no. 1 (Spring 1975): 4; Elizabeth Ellis, personal conversation with author, 2016.

37. Elizabeth Ellis, personal conversation with author, 2016.

38. *South Carolina Regional Bahá'í Bulletin* 5, no. 1 (Spring 1975): 2; *Bahá'í News* 52, no. 8 (August 1975): 20; *South Carolina Regional Bahá'í Bulletin* 5, no. 3 (Fall 1975): 3, 5.

39. *National Bahá'í Review*, no. 99 (April 1976): 1.

40. *Bahá'í News*, no. 539 (February 1976): 11–12; *Bahá'í News*, no. 540 (March 1976): 28–29; *Southern Bahá'í Bulletin*, April 1976, 1. While the number nine holds symbolic meaning in the Bahá'í Faith as the numerical equivalent of the word *bahá*, the choice of states seems to have reflected a perceived need for a strong enough local administrative base to sustain large-scale growth.

41. *Bahá'í News*, no. 542 (May 1976): 17.

42. Kahn, "Encounter of Two Myths: Baha'i and Christian in the Rural American South—A Study in Transmythicization," 276, 295–296.

43. Kahn, "Encounter of Two Myths: Baha'i and Christian in the Rural American South—A Study in Transmythicization," 315–316, 318, 328–332, 338–340; Bahá'í National Information Office, "Study at Louis G. Gregory Bahá'í Institute, Hemingway, South Carolina, December 26, 1976–January 2, 1977," 1977, Office of the Secretary Records, National Bahá'í Archives.

44. *American Bahá'í*, September 1977, 4.

45. *American Bahá'í* (March 1978): 6; *American Bahá'í* (March 1979): 7, 9; *Bahá'í News,* no. 575 (February 1979), 11.

46. Martin Luther King, Jr., *Why We Can't Wait* (New York: Harper and Row, 1963), 128.

47. *Century of Light* (Wilmette, IL: Bahá'í Publishing Trust, 2000), 102–103, http://www.bahai.org/library/other-literature/official-statements-commentaries/century-light/; Universal House of Justice to the Conference of the Continental Boards of Counsellors, December 28, 2010, http://www.bahai.org/library/authoritative-texts/the-universal-house-of-justice/messages/#d=20101228_001&f=f1.

BIBLIOGRAPHY

American Bahá'í. January 1971, 1.
American Bahá'í. May 1971, 4–5.
American Bahá'í. August 1971, 6–7.
American Bahá'í. September 1971, 2, 8.
American Bahá'í. March 1973, 7.
American Bahá'í. October 1973, 15.
American Bahá'í. December 1973, 3–5, 12.
American Bahá'í. September 1977, 4.
American Bahá'í. March 1978, 6.
American Bahá'í. March 1979, 7, 9.
American Bahá'í. November 23, 1996, 27.

Angell, Stephen W. Review of *No Jim Crow Church: The Origins of South Carolina's Bahá'í Community*, by Louis Venters. *American Historical Review* 121, no. 4 (October 2016): 1301–1302.

Annual Report of the National Spiritual Assembly, *National Bahá'í Review*, no. 53 (May 1972), 1–2.

"Around the World: United States." *Bahá'í News*, no. 575 (February 1979), 11. Also available at https://bahai.works/Baha%27i_News.

Association of Statisticians of American Religious Bodies. Accessed December 30, 2017. http://usreligioncensus.org.

Baha'i Bulletin 3, no. 5 (Summer 1973), 2.

"Bahá'ís Recruit Southern Blacks." *Greenville (SC) News*, June 28, 1970.

Booker T. Washington High School Foundation. "History." http://bookertwashingtonfoundationsc.org/BTWHistory.htm.

Bowers, Paul. "How a 19th-Century Persian Faith Became the Second-Most Common Religion in Our State." *Charleston (SC) City Paper*, June 17, 2014.

Century of Light. Wilmette, IL: Bahá'í Publishing Trust, 2000. Also available at http://www.bahai.org/library/other-literature/official-statements-commentaries/century-light.

Commemorating 'Abdu'l-Bahá in America, 1912–2012. http://centenary.bahai.us/cities.

"Expansion Completed at Gregory Institute." *Bahá'í News* 52, no. 7 (July 1975), 19. Also available at https://bahai.works/Baha%27i_News.

Hampson, Arthur. "Growth and Spread of the Bahá'í Faith." PhD diss., University of Hawaii, 1980.

Harvin, Stephanie. "The Ripple Effect: Influencing the Tide of History." *Charleston (SC) Post and Courier*, February 2, 2003.

Hawes, Jennifer Berry. "How the Bahá'í Faith Became South Carolina's Second-Largest Religion." *Charleston (SC) Post and Courier*, June 21, 2014.

Hollinger, Richard. "Introduction: Bahá'í Communities in the West, 1897–1992." In *Community Histories*, edited by Richard Hollinger, vii–xlix. Los Angeles: Kalimát Press, 1992.

Kahn, Sandra Santolucito. "Encounter of Two Myths: Baha'i and Christian in the Rural American South—A Study in Transmythicization." PhD diss., University of California, Santa Barbara, 1977.

King, Martin Luther, Jr. *Why We Can't Wait*. New York: Harper and Row, 1963.

Louis G. Gregory Baha'i Museum. https://www.louisgregorymuseum.org.

"Louis G. Gregory Institute, Hemingway, South Carolina" *Bahá'í News*, no. 492 (March 1972), 11. Also available at https://bahai.works/Baha%27i_News.

McMullen, Mike. *The Bahá'ís of America: The Growth of a Religious Movement*. New York: New York University Press, 2015.

"Mr. Gillespie Honored by South Carolina." *Bahá'í News*, no. 542 (May 1976), 17. Also available at https://bahai.works/Baha%27i_News.

National Bahá'í Archives. Wilmette, IL.

National Bahá'í Archives. Office of the Secretary Records. Wilmette, IL.

National Bahá'í Review no. 99 (April 1976), 1.

National Spiritual Assembly of the Bahá'ís of the United States to the National Teaching Committee, May 17, 1974. *National Bahá'í Review*, no. 82 (November 1974), 2–3.

Newman, Mark. *Divine Agitators: The Delta Ministry and Civil Rights in Mississippi*. Athens: University of Georgia Press, 2004.

"New Teaching Projects Begin." *Bahá'í News*, no. 539 (February 1976), 11–12. Also available at https://bahai.works/Baha%27i_News.

Nieburh, Gustav. "Hemingway Journal: A Little Bit of Change from Old-Time Religion." *New York Times*, March 31, 2000.

"Operation 'Gabriel.'" *American Bahá'í*, January 1972, 3.

Reynolds, Annette. *Trudy and the Bahá'ís' Spiritual Path in South Carolina*. Bloomington, IN: Xlibris, 2015.

Rollins, Melissa. "Bahá'í Faith Is Second Most Prevalent Religion in South Carolina." *Florence (SC) Morning News*, July 19, 2014.

South Carolina Regional Bahá'í Bulletin. September 1972, 4–8.

South Carolina Regional Bahá'í Bulletin. November 1972, 11.

South Carolina Regional Bahá'í Bulletin. April 1973, 1.

South Carolina Regional Bahá'í Bulletin 2, no. 9 (June 1973), 4.

South Carolina Regional Bahá'í Bulletin 3, no. 5 (Summer 1973), 3–8.

South Carolina Regional Bahá'í Bulletin, October 1973, 1.

South Carolina Regional Bahá'í Bulletin 3, no. 6 (January 1974), 1–8.

South Carolina Regional Bahá'í Bulletin 4, no. 1 (Spring 1974), 1–7.

South Carolina Regional Bahá'í Bulletin 4, no. 2 (Summer 1974), 4–5.

South Carolina Regional Bahá'í Bulletin 4, no. 3 (Fall 1974), 2–8.

South Carolina Regional Bahá'í Bulletin 5, no. 1 (Spring 1975), 2–4.

South Carolina Regional Bahá'í Bulletin 5, no. 1 (Fall 1975), 2–7.

South Carolina Regional Newsletter 2, no. 4 (November 1972), 1.

South Carolina Regional Newsletter 1, no. 3 (December 1972), 1.

South Carolina Regional Newsletter, October 1973, 1.

South Carolina Regional Newsletter 5, no. 3 (Fall 1975), 1–7.

South Carolina State Hospital Commitment Files, South Carolina Department of Archives and History, Columbia.

Southern Bahá'í Bulletin. April 1976, 1, 4.

"Southern Teaching Conference." *National Bahá'í Review*, no. 23 (November 1969), 1–4.

Spears, R. Wright. *Journey toward Unity: The Christian Action Council in South Carolina*. Columbia, SC: Christian Action Council, 1983.

"Teaching Program Launched in South." *Bahá'í News*, no. 540 (March 1976), 28–29. Also available at https://bahai.works/Baha%27i_News.

Universal House of Justice. *Messages from the Universal House of Justice, 1963–1986: The Third Epoch of the Formative Age*. Compiled by Geoffry Marks. Wilmette, IL: Bahá'í Publishing Trust, 1996. Also available at https://bahai.works/Messages_from_the_Universal_House_of_Justice,_1963-1986.

———. *Messages from the Universal House of Justice 1968–1973*. Wilmette, IL: Bahá'í Publishing Trust, 1976. Also available at https://bahai-library.com/uhj_messages_1968_1973.

———. Universal House of Justice to the Conference of the Continental Boards of Counselors, December 28, 2010. http://www.bahai.org/library/authoritative-texts/the-universal-house-of-justice/messages/#d=20101228_001&f=f1.

Venters, Louis. *No Jim Crow Church: The Origins of South Carolina's Bahá'í Community*. Gainesville: University of Florida Press, 2015.

Weekly Observer (Hemingway, SC), August 28, 1975.

Weeks, Linton. "The Runner-Up Religions of America." "The Protojournalist: Very Original Reporting" blog, *National Public Radio*, June 22, 2014.

Whitmore, Bruce. *The Dawning*-Place. 2nd ed. Wilmette, IL: Bahá'í Publishing Trust, 2015.

"Youth Participate in 9 Special Projects." *Bahá'í News* 52, no. 8 (August 1975), 20. Also available at https://bahai.works/Baha%27i_News.

Chapter 6

Race Unity Efforts among American Bahá'ís

Institutionalized Tools and Empirical Evidence

Mike McMullen

> The world is at present in an exceedingly dark condition spiritually; hatred and prejudice, of every sort, are literally tearing it to pieces. We, on the other hand, are the custodians of the opposite forces, the forces of love, of unity, of peace and integration, and we must constantly be on our guard, whether as individuals or as an Assembly or Community,[1] lest through us these destructive, negative forces enter into our midst . . . must constantly animate our Bahá'í lives, and we must pray to be protected from the contamination of society which is so diseased with prejudice.[2]

Over the last thirty years, there has been increasing scholarly interest in racially and ethnically diverse communities. Fueled in part by a desire to understand how American religious organizations are dealing with immigrant diversity since the changes in the immigration law of 1965 and concomitant sociodemographic changes,[3] these studies have highlighted the fact that multiracial religious organizations continue to be rare, face unique challenges, and are filled with unique people who dedicate a great deal of work toward not only building these communities, but maintaining them.[4] Often, the challenge within multiethnic communities is effectively negotiating ethnic identity with a religious identity, all the while fostering "unity in diversity" in a diverse community.[5] This chapter examines the unique success the American Bahá'í community has enjoyed in fostering racially mixed communities.

This chapter focuses on African American diversity within the American Bahá'í community. However, I will also introduce another ethnic group that makes up a significant minority community among American

Bahá'ís—Persian Bahá'ís. While cultivating African American converts has been of unique concern since the earliest years of the American Bahá'í community (as will be seen below), the fostering of a multiracial religious community has created a new dynamic since the influx of Persians from their native Iran prior to and after the Iranian Islamic revolution in 1979. Understanding the racial and ethnic interaction among the white majority and African American and Persian minorities helps us understand the challenges that Bahá'ís face in living out their vision of "unity in diversity." While this chapter provides the context for understanding this level of diversity in the American Bahá'í community, future research will be necessary to analyze the dynamics of culture and race in this multiracial religious faith.

RACE AND RELIGION IN THE UNITED STATES

The intersection of religion and race has a long history in the United States.[6] Martin Luther King, Jr. famously said that "11:00 on Sunday morning . . . [is] the most segregated hour of Christian America."[7] Divided by faith and struggling with an increasingly diversified nation, religious communities across the ideological spectrum have had to deal with the issue of race. Race and ethnic identity play a significant role in the United States, shaping where people live, whom they make friends with, how they are able to access power and resources, and where they worship.[8] While some congregations[9] have recently taken steps to address the challenges diversity presents, others continue to ignore the issue. Emerson and Smith point out that the United States is in its third period of racial division, what they call a "racialized" society.[10] This is different from the earlier periods of slavery or Jim Crow segregation in that rather than racism being overt, it becomes more unconscious and indirect.[11] This change has been characterized as the shift from "old-fashioned racism" to "symbolic racism."[12] While some individuals still harbor prejudiced attitudes, a racialized society is reflected in the structural inequalities found in healthcare, law enforcement and the criminal justice system, housing, jobs, educational opportunities, and financial resources.

PREJUDICE AND CONTACT THEORY IN RELIGIOUS ORGANIZATIONS

Despite continuing levels of individual prejudice as well as systemic discrimination, research shows that the development of intimate, warm, and supportive relationships with members of different racial and ethnic groups reduces the level of prejudice, stereotyping, and overt discrimination—what is known as "Contact Theory."[13]

Emerson, Kimbro, and Yancey extend Contact Theory to interaction in religious organizations, examining whether prior contact with members of interracial groups leads to contemporary multiracial social ties, thereby improving race relations in general.[14] These ties are important both for what Robert Putnam called "bonding" and "bridging" social capital.[15] Bonding social capital creates ties of reciprocity and trust between in-group members, while bridging social capital creates relationships between members of potentially different social groups, expanding networks of trust. For N. Wadsworth, at multiracial church settings, the bonding incentives demand "difficult kinds of bridging or reaching across deep historical and identity-based differences, in order to create trust based networks where they have not existed. When successful, however, such networks can open new paths to race-related political engagement."[16] Emerson, Kimbro, and Yancey's results show that interracial relationships early in one's lifecycle (such as in schools or churches) have significant effects on the likelihood that one will foster and maintain a multiracial circle of friends as an adult.[17] Yancey elsewhere concludes:

> Those who have both previously lived in a mixed neighborhood and attended a mixed school [both of which are defined as having at least 20 percent non-white membership] are 5.5 times more likely to be in a racially-mixed religious congregation when compared to those who had neither experience. . . . [F]or those who had no prior interracial contact, just 4% of whites and 7% of African Americans are in mixed congregations. For those with both types of prior contact, these figures jump to 24 and 28%, respectively.[18]

Despite the abovementioned success of Contact Theory, there is consensus among researchers that mere contact does not necessarily lead to better race relations. Yancey summarizes the proposed conditions that aid the development of more tolerant and positive outcomes:

- Contact must be relatively egalitarian.
- Contact must be noncompetitive and nonthreatening.
- Contact must be of an intimate nature, as opposed to superficial.
- Contact receiving support from relevant authority figures can improve harmonious relations.[19]

Yancey maintains that religious organizations are more likely to meet all four criteria (because of the greater likelihood of developing primary bonds) and are, thus, a better source of promoting racial reconciliation than are neighborhoods, educational settings, or the workplace. The *primary* relationships (close friendships and marriages) developed in a congregational setting are more conducive to advancing racial harmony than *secondary* relationships developed in educational or neighborhood contexts, which tend to be more superficial.[20] He points out that after controlling for demographic variables, the most powerful outcomes of attending an integrated church for whites is that they on average engage in less stereotyping and have lower levels of social distance (desire to avoid contact with minority group members); thus, the Contact Hypothesis is at least partially supported by research in religious organizations.[21] He concludes:

> One may argue that primary interracial relationships formed within religious institutions are most effective in altering informal racial society myths, somewhat effective in altering overt racism in whites and their attitudes toward governmental policies that benefit African Americans, but have little or no effect in shaping modern racism.[22]

THE DEARTH AND IMPORTANCE OF MULTIRACIAL CONGREGATIONS

Despite the research cited above that shows churches are promising incubators of racial reconciliation, the reality is that most congregations are monoracial. More sociological research on multiracial churches has appeared in the last fifteen years.[23] Much of this work is pursued in the hope that understanding what makes successful multiracial churches (and the primary interracial relationships developed there) can be expanded to improve race relations throughout society. While the post-civil rights era has done a great deal to break down segregation in our secondary institutions, for the majority of Americans, our primary contacts remain fairly homogenous. This underscores why those few multiracial religious congregations that exist (both Christian and non-Christian) are all the more important to understand.

While we have seen U.S. society become dramatically more multiracial and multiethnic in the last forty years, we have not witnessed a concomitant integration of our religious organizations; hence the applicability of King's assertion that Sunday morning continues to be a bastion of segregation. Just since 1980, the African American population in the United States grew by nearly 30 percent, the Hispanic population by 142 percent, the Native American population by 75 percent, and the Asian population by 185 percent.[24] The 2015 population estimates of the U.S. Census Bureau indicated that 73.6 percent of the American population was white, 12.6 percent was African American, 0.8 percent was American Indian or Alaska Native, 5.1 percent was Asian, 0.2 percent was Native Hawaiian or Pacific Islander, 3.0 percent marked more than one race, and 4.7 percent were Other.[25] In addition, 17.1 percent specified that they were of Hispanic ethnicity. Sociology of religion scholars define racially mixed congregations as having no more than 80 percent of a congregation comprised of one racial or ethnic group. Using this standard, only about 7.5 percent of the approximately 300,000 congregations in the United States are racially mixed. Just looking at Christian churches, which consist of 90 percent of all religious congregations, only 5.5 percent are multiracial; and half of these, they estimate, are in transition from one racially dominant group to another, or are mixed only temporarily.[26] The academically defined threshold (20 percent) is well above people's inflated perception about diversity. For example, Marti states that some church officials call their congregations "diverse" when in reality only 5 percent to 10 percent of their congregations are multiracial.[27] Additionally, the National Congregations Study found that nearly 90 percent of American congregations are at least 90 percent one racial group, and nearly 80 percent are at least 95 percent one racial group.[28]

STRUCTURAL AND IDEOLOGICAL BARRIERS TO MULTIRACIAL CONGREGATIONS

The reason that society's diversity is reflected in relatively few religious organizations, despite no legal prohibition against interracial worship, is the effect of two forces: (1) the ideological resources found in evangelical Protestantism as practiced in the United States; and (2) the structure of religious organizations themselves—a consequence of the way our society has institutionalized the division of church and state.[29] As for the first, Emerson and Smith utilize the concept of a "cultural tool kit" (from Ann Swidler) to identify the set of ideas and worldviews that give meaning to the world and establish strategies for acting and solving problems in the world. It implies modes of reasoning, value commitments, and vocabularies and menus for action. The white evangelical Protestant ideological tool kit is dominated by the concept of freewill individualism, whereby the sin of racism is seen primarily as a result of *prejudiced individuals* who have yet to develop the proper relationship with Christ. Once an individual matures in a relationship with Jesus, prejudice supposedly declines.[30]

The second cause for Emerson and Smith of mono-racial religious congregations is the structure of American religion. Because of the separation of church and state, religion in the United States is a voluntary association. In fact, it is the most important voluntary sector of civil society in terms of numbers of people involved, money donated, symbolic meaning derived, and social capital accrued.[31] Therefore, religion operates as a "marketplace," whereby religious groups compete for membership and affiliation from individuals, who themselves are making individual choices based on "consumer preference."[32] The cost of marketing one's religious product (i.e., salvation, belonging, meaning) to a diverse society is quite high; thus, churches tend to "niche market," or appeal to a more homogenous racial or ethnic group, class background, nationality, or language. This is reflected in the style of preaching or leadership; the style of worship and music; the social services provided; the theological orientation; where a congregation is located; programs, such as for singles groups or youth; social justice mobilization, and so on.[33] Thus, the combination of individualistic values, a diverse religious marketplace, and the costs of mass appeal tend to keep religion in the United States segmented and segregated. In addition, Emerson and Smith point out that the sociological principle of "homophily" operates at the individual level, whereby people tend to *voluntarily* associate with those with whom they share similar characteristics. The result is homogeneous religious organizations, leaving members of society isolated from each other and without the propinquity to develop diverse primary relationships.[34]

EFFORTS TO INTEGRATE SEGREGATED CHURCHES

The checkered record of American Christian churches with respect to racial segregation goes back to the earliest history of the United States. Despite this, there are historical instances, as well as contemporary examples, of churches making efforts to overcome racial divisions. The biblical injunction requires that adherents "love thy neighbor as thyself" (Matt. 19:22). To this end, there have been serious attempts, especially since World War II, for American churches to reconcile with their racist and segregated past. This has taken at least four forms:

1. Mainline and Evangelical churches reuniting after their mid-nineteenth-century splits over the issue of slavery and divisions within national denominational structures over Jim Crow segregation.[35]
2. The parachurch movement, such as Promise Keepers[36] and the megachurch and nondenominational movements, for example, the Vineyard.[37]
3. New Religious Movements, especially of the last forty years that stress racial reconciliation, such as Koinonia[38] and Oneida.[39]
4. Local congregational efforts (outlined below and in Yancy and Emerson; and Becker)[40] that are generally clergy-led and focused on a particular local community or neighborhood. Those advocating increasing inclusiveness in churches are appearing from both the left and right; from Mainline *and* Evangelical Christianity.[41]

Despite these uncoordinated and intermittent efforts, institutionalized religion in the United States remains a voluntary organization, beyond the legal requirement to desegregate as has happened in other public institutions. Compounded with the unique separation of church and state institutionalized in the United States, social class segregation and divided residential patterns in the United States meant that religious congregations perpetuated racial divisions.[42]

HOW DO CHURCHES ATTEMPT TO OVERCOME RACIAL DIVISIONS?

Given the cultural, ideological, structural, and demographic forces, especially the long-standing strength of African American churches and denominational organizations[43] that are thwarting the development of multiracial religious congregations, what contributes to the existence of the small proportion of those that have developed and grown? Yancey and Emerson determined four pathways that are "used to create racially integrated congregations: leadership, evangelical, demographic, and network":[44]

- Leadership Multiracial Churches develop because of the vision of the leadership (clergy or laity) at the local level who convince followers of the legitimacy of the integrated vision, which usually requires charismatic leadership;
- Demographic Multiracial Churches arise because of the changing demographic composition of the neighborhood surrounding the church. Efforts are made to recruit minorities who move into the surrounding area, although many of these churches end up transforming from black to white or vice versa, rather than becoming truly multiracial;
- Evangelical Multiracial Churches emerge because a congregation, possibly due to declining enrollment, decides to proselytize members of all races (desire to "win all people to Christ"); and
- Network Multiracial Churches appear when two churches—one black and one white, for example—merge because of declining numbers in both, and then begin growth through the personal integrated networks from the combined membership.[45]

None of these types can explain the prevalence of Bahá'í multiracial communities. The Bahá'í case represents a unique combination of institutional and ideological mechanisms that foster multiracial communities. In fact, Yancey and Emerson incorrectly state that "the power of charisma to overcome previous societal barriers against racial integration can be seen in the multiracial nature of several religious organizations (the Unification Church and the Bahá'í Faith) driven by charismatic leadership."[46] In the Bahá'í case, although early revered, charismatic successive heads of the Faith ('Abdu'l-Bahá and Shoghi Effendi) emphasized racial reconciliation and the unity of humanity as the primary Bahá'í value or goal, it is *not* current charismatic leadership that motivates the development of multiracial communities.[47] In addition, Bahá'ís highlight the need to "teach the Faith" to their neighbors, friends and family, and often times are encouraged by national leaders to *intentionally* seek racial and ethnic minorities as part of this teaching work (thus conforming to Yancy and Emerson's "Evangelical" model above).[48] However, as will be discussed below, Bahá'í multiracial communities are the result of a *unique* cultural "tool kit" and institutional structures that reflect the Bahá'í worldview.[49]

THE CASE OF THE BAHÁ'Í FAITH

By some accounts, the highest levels of diversity in American communities are in non-Christian groups.[50] Among these lesser studied groups is the Bahá'í Faith, whose approximately 1,100 American communities are 53 percent multiracial or multiethnic compared to only about 5 percent of Christian congregations.[51]

While many non-Judeo-Christian faiths such as Buddhism have historically followed waves of new immigrants into the United States and found their homes in ethnically based enclaves, a new religious movement,[52] the Bahá'í Faith, came into the complex American racial landscape without the support of a majority ethnic population (nearly 70 percent of American Bahá'ís are converts).[53] How has the Bahá'í Faith, although numerically small in the United States, managed to become one the most diverse American religious communities? Bahá'ís have other ideological and institutional mechanisms that are unique in understanding its growth in American religious history.[54]

There are four sociological and theological mechanisms in the Bahá'í "tool kit"[55] that foster this multiracial identity: (1) core ideological and theological principles; (2) historical examples of key figures in Bahá'í history ('Abdu'l-Bahá and Shoghi Effendi especially); (3) consistent guidance from the Universal House of Justice and the National Spiritual Assembly (NSA), respectively the international and national governing councils of the Bahá'í Faith,[56] in the context of systematic plans for growth of the religion; and (4) institutional laws and practices that promote multiracial communities, especially at the primary worship experience and in electing Bahá'í leadership.

After surveying these four mechanisms of racial unity, this chapter will make use of ten years of empirical data to demonstrate the current reality of multiracial Bahá'í communities. As mentioned earlier, an astounding 53 percent of local Bahá'í communities in the United States are multiracial, meaning that in over half of all Bahá'í communities in the United States at least 20 percent of their membership is not of the majority ethnic or racial group.[57] This compares with only roughly 7 percent of all American religious congregations (and about 5 percent of American churches) that are multiracial.[58]

1. Core Ideological and Theological Principles

The Bahá'í Faith's teachings rest upon three major tenets: the oneness of God, the oneness of religion, and the oneness of humankind.[59] Thus, for Bahá'ís, there is only one God who has revealed all of the world's religious scripture through various historical messengers called "Manifestations of God," which include, but are not limited to: Buddha, Moses, Zoroaster, Christ, Muhammad, and Bahá'u'lláh. The spiritual truths of each Manifestation remain constant, but the social teachings vary with each new Manifestation of God in conformity with the moral and social development of humanity, what Bahá'ís call "progressive revelation." Although each Manifestation of God reveals a comprehensive set of teachings, there is a special message emphasized by each of them; Bahá'ís believe that Bahá'u'lláh's unique mission was to unite all of humankind, eliminate all forms of prejudice, and establish a global civilization. This religion's administrative order functions to promote its basic principles: the independent investigation of truth, the abandonment of all forms of superstition, the recognition of the unity of religion and science, the promotion of the equality of women and men, the advancement of universal education and economic justice, and the need for a spiritual foundation for society. For Bahá'ís, this will lead to the establishment of the "Most Great Peace," that is, the Kingdom of God on earth.[60]

The primary social value in the Bahá'í Faith is the unity of humanity. This means that Bahá'ís try to live out the vision in their scripture: "It is not for him to pride himself who loveth his own country, but rather for him who loveth the whole world. The earth is but one country, and mankind its citizens."[61] Thus, Bahá'ís are enjoined by their scripture to eliminate all forms of prejudice: racial, gender, national, and religious. There are administrative laws in the Bahá'í writings that require that minorities should be given preference in the case of a tie vote. A future global civilization will also require a universal auxiliary language to be taught in every school throughout the planet in conjunction with indigenous languages to help unite the whole human family. This theme of the unity of humankind and "unity in diversity" pervades most Bahá'í scripture study groups, administrative meetings, and worship experiences.[62]

2. Historical Examples of Key Figures in Bahá'í History (Especially 'Abdu'l-Bahá and Shoghi Effendi)

THE EXAMPLE OF 'ABDU'L-BAHÁ AND LOUIS GREGORY

When Baha'u'llah (1817–1892), founder of the Bahá'í Faith, died, his son 'Abdu'l-Bahá (1844–1921) became the head of the Bahá'í Faith based on Bahá'u'lláh's written instructions. By1908, the political situation in Palestine had changed, allowing the small group of Bahá'ís there to be released from house arrest. 'Abdu'l-Bahá decided to travel to the West in order to help educate the nascent band of Bahá'ís, who at this point had limited understanding about the administrative order, Bahá'í theology, and the Bahá'í worldview.[63] 'Abdu'l-Bahá made a trip throughout Europe and North America in 1911–1912. While in the United States, he traveled from New York to San Francisco, teaching his father's religion and preaching about the desperate need for Bahá'ís to practice racial unity among themselves.[64]

During his time in Washington, DC, 'Abdu'l-Bahá upset Washington's racially segregated protocol by inviting a young black lawyer, Louis Gregory, to sit at 'Abdu'l-Bahá's right hand in the seat of honor at a dinner reception. Louis Gregory, then a new Bahá'í, went on to become one of the most prominent traveling teachers of the Bahá'í Faith in U.S. history. Gregory frequently traveled throughout the South, spreading the message of racial unity.[65] It was through the encouragement of 'Abdu'l-Bahá during his 1912 trip that Louis Gregory and a British woman, Louisa Mathew, married after a long friendship, becoming the U.S. Bahá'í community's first interracial couple. Throughout 'Abdu'l-Bahá's trip, he frequently spoke about the positive influence interracial couples would have on the elimination of racism in the United States. He said:

> If it be possible, gather together these two races, black and white, into one assembly and put such love into their hearts that they shall not only unite but even intermarry. Be sure that the result of this will abolish differences and disputes between black and white. . . . This is a great service to the world of humanity.[66]

Louis Gregory went on to become a member of the NSA of the United States, a pioneer[67] to Haiti, and was appointed as a Hand of the Cause of God before his death in 1951,[68] remaining married to Louisa Mathew for thirty-nine years. The Louis Gregory Bahá'í Institute in South Carolina, an educational center, was named after him. Bahá'ís frequently make references to developing the same type of faithfulness and commitment to teaching the Bahá'í Faith as Louis Gregory had.[69] Bahá'ís also point out that while in the United States, 'Abdu'l-Bahá spoke to the fourth annual meeting of the NAACP about racial unity, undoubtedly because of the influence that Louis Gregory had within black intellectual circles.[70]

The examples of 'Abdu'l-Bahá and Louis Gregory are important for two reasons. First, they establish a record of Bahá'í activity promoting racial unity well before the modern civil rights era. 'Abdu'l-Bahá's visit to North America and Louis Gregory's teaching activity were all taking place less than fifty years after the end of the Civil War. Race riots occurred in the South, and the postbellum racial divisions led to the rebirth of the Ku Klux Klan in 1915.[71] In this era, nearly all Protestant Christian denominations were still divided over the issue of race and slavery, and remained so well into the 1950s.[72] Into this cultural context came Persian and African American traveling teachers (and others) with a message of racial reconciliation, forty years before *Brown v. Board of Education*, lunch counter sit-ins, and the Civil Rights Act of 1964. The second reason is that these acts of social and spiritual courage remain important for Bahá'ís today. The importance of 'Abdu'l-Bahá as the "exemplar" of the Bahá'í Faith, in part, stems from his willingness to take a stand for racial unity against the opposition of social norms and laws. Bahá'ís, thus, turn to 'Abdu'l-Bahá as a model for behavior in their local communities, although they do not always live up to that high standard. Bahá'ís state that they have had the courage to speak out against racist slurs or jokes because they feel 'Abdu'l-Bahá would have done so. Louis Gregory remains a role model (especially for African American Bahá'ís) in his ground-breaking roles as first African American member of the NSA, only African American Hand of the Cause of God, traveling Bahá'í teacher in the United States and overseas, and pioneer of Bahá'í interracial marriage.[73]

THE GUIDANCE OF SHOGHI EFFENDI

The second resource in a historical tool kit from which Bahá'ís draw guidance is Shoghi Effendi. He wrote a lengthy epistle to the U.S. Bahá'í community in 1938, reminding them of the absolute necessity for Bahá'ís to embrace racial unity, and which was immediately published by the NSA in book form under the title *The Advent of Divine Justice*. Shoghi Effendi uses bold language to set high expectations for the American Bahá'í community, in contrast to the prevailing cultural standards throughout the United States:

> Freedom from racial prejudice, in any of its forms, should, at such a time as this when an increasingly large section of the human race is falling a victim to its devastating ferocity, be adopted as the watchword of the entire body of the American believers, in whichever state they reside, in whatever circles they move, whatever their age, traditions, tastes, and habits. It should be consistently demonstrated in every phase of their activity and life, whether in the Bahá'í community or outside it, in public or in private, formally as well as informally,

> individually as well as in their official capacity as organized groups, committees and Assemblies. It should be deliberately cultivated through the various and everyday opportunities, no matter how insignificant, that present themselves, whether in their homes, their business offices, their schools and colleges, their social parties and recreation grounds, their Bahá'í meetings, conferences, conventions, summer schools and Assemblies.[74]

The sentiment expressed by Shoghi Effendi in this letter has left an indelible impression on a U.S. Bahá'í identity, and still challenges Bahá'ís almost eighty years after its initial writing, especially in light of the American NSA citing Shoghi Effendi's guidance on racial unity to this day.[75]

One section of *The Advent of Divine Justice*, entitled "The Most Challenging Issue," has frequently been the topic of discussions at firesides (meetings to inform Bahá'ís' friends and acquaintances about the Bahá'í Faith) and deepenings (scripture study) that this researcher has attended. In it, Shoghi Effendi said, "As to racial prejudice, the corrosion of which, for well nigh a century, has bitten into the fiber, and attacked the whole social structure of American society, it should be regarded as constituting the most vital and challenging issue confronting the Bahá'í community at the present stage of its evolution."[76] He sent this message during a period in U.S. Bahá'í history when Bahá'ís themselves were making accommodations, especially in the South, to Jim Crow segregation laws.[77] Shoghi Effendi censured the American community, calling it to a different standard. After forewarning them that "a long and thorny road, beset with pitfalls, still remains untraveled, both by the white and the Negro exponents of the redeeming Faith of Bahá'u'lláh,"[78] and recalling the example set by 'Abdu'l-Bahá when in America, Shoghi Effendi wrote:

> To discriminate against any race, on the ground of its being socially backward, politically immature, and numerically in a minority, is a flagrant violation of the spirit that animates the Faith of Bahá'u'lláh. The consciousness of any division or cleavage in its ranks is alien to its very purpose, principles, and ideals. . . . If any discrimination is at all to be tolerated, it should be a discrimination not against, but rather in favor of the minority, be it racial or otherwise.[79]

Thus, the Bahá'í Faith advocates a form of "affirmative action" in promoting the diversity of its committees and assemblies. Bahá'í administrative law requires that if a tie exists for the ninth spot in the election of a spiritual assembly between someone from a majority group and another from a minority in that society, then the minority is elected to the position, in order "to further the interests of the community."[80]

In addition, Shoghi Effendi explained that both whites and blacks have responsibilities in eradicating prejudice:

> Let the white make a supreme effort in their resolve to contribute their share to the solution of this problem, to abandon once for all their usually inherent and at times subconscious sense of superiority, to correct their tendency towards revealing a patronizing attitude towards the members of the other race, to persuade them through their intimate, spontaneous and informal association with them of the genuineness of their friendship and the sincerity of their intentions, and to master their impatience of any lack of responsiveness on the part of a people who have received, for so long a period, such grievous and slow-healing wounds. Let the Negroes, through a corresponding effort on their part, show by every means in their power the warmth of their response, their readiness to forget the past, and their ability to wipe out every trace of suspicion that may still linger in their hearts and minds. . . . Let neither think that anything short of genuine love, extreme patience, true humility, consummate tact, sound initiative, mature wisdom, and deliberate, persistent, and prayerful effort, can succeed in blotting out the stain which this patent evil has left on the fair name of their common country.[81]

3. Consistent Guidance from the Universal House of Justice and NSA in the Context of Systematic Plans for Growth of the Bahá'í Faith

Shortly after 'Abdu'l-Bahá visited the United States, he wrote a series of fourteen letters to the North American Bahá'í community that have subsequently been published in book form entitled *Tablets of the Divine Plan*. In them, 'Abdu'l-Bahá provided the direction for, initially American Bahá'ís, and then all Bahá'ís everywhere, to systematically travel throughout the world teaching the Bahá'í Faith, with the aim of advancing social justice and unifying patterns of community life. Shoghi Effendi initiated two Seven Year Plans (in 1937 and 1946) and a Ten Year Plan (1953) that culminated in the election of the Universal House of Justice in 1963, now the governing body of the world's Bahá'ís and architect of ongoing Bahá'í plans for growth and expansion.[82] From these Plans developed by the Universal House of Justice, the U.S. NSA consults with continental and regional Bahá'í institutions and a national plan of action is developed, frequently with numerical benchmarks. As discussed below, racial unity and the elimination of racial and ethnic prejudice has been a constant theme over the last half century, serving as yet another tool by which Bahá'ís have built multiracial communities in the United States.[83]

When the Universal House of Justice first began issuing systematic plans, the United States was in the midst of the modern civil rights movement. In the decade prior to the Nine Year Plan (1964–1973), Rosa Parks refused to move to the back of her bus, which triggered the Montgomery Bus Boycott and vaulted a young Dr. Martin Luther King, Jr. to national prominence in 1955; Arkansas Gov. Orval Faubus used the National Guard to block nine black students from attending Little Rock High School in 1957; the nonviolent lunch counter sit-in movement began in Greensboro, North Carolina, in 1960, which was concomitant with the social protest activities of civil rights organizations such as CORE, SNCC, and SCLC; Freedom Rides began in 1961 challenging states to uphold a ruling that declared segregation on interstate public buses to be unconstitutional; President Kennedy sent federal troops to the University of Mississippi to end riots, allowing James Meredith, the university's first black student, to attend classes in 1962; civil rights leader Medgar Evers was killed in 1963 by a sniper; and that same year, four elementary school girls were killed in a church bombing in Birmingham, Alabama. While the Nine Year Plan was in effect, the Civil Rights Act of 1964, and the Voting Rights Act of 1965, were both passed by Congress; the Black Power movement gained adherents; Malcolm X, a leader in the Nation of Islam, was assassinated on February 21, 1965; and Martin Luther King, Jr. on April 4, 1968.[84]

This was the historical context of the efforts of American Bahá'ís during the Nine Year Plan to promote their vision of racial unity based on the teachings of Bahá'u'lláh and the example and guidance of 'Abdu'l-Bahá and Shoghi Effendi.[85] The National Assembly insisted that Bahá'ís not allow racial prejudice to creep into Bahá'í administrative functions or processes. In an April 11, 1968, letter, right before the annual vote for local spiritual assemblies, the NSA reminded Bahá'ís of administrative laws related to Bahá'í elections, including age requirements, and the solemn spiritual atmosphere that should be cultivated during the actual election process. The longest part of the letter was about the "flagrant violation" of Bahá'í administrative law were any prejudice or discrimination in electing representatives to the Assembly to be tolerated. The letter quoted extensively from Shoghi Effendi's writings:

> Every organized community, enlisted under the banner of Bahá'u'lláh should feel it to be its first and inescapable obligation to nurture, encourage, and safe-guard every minority belonging to any faith, race, class, or nation within it. So great and vital is this principle that in such circumstances, as when an equal number of ballots have been cast in an election, or where the qualifications for any office are balanced as between the various races, faiths or nationalities within the community, priority should unhesitatingly be accorded the party representing the minority.[86]

In 1968, the NSA established several programs to address racial prejudice. This was in the aftermath of the assassination of Martin Luther King, Jr. in

April 1968 and the subsequent riots. A booklet was published in summer 1968 entitled "Why Our Cities Burn," and looked at the solution from a Bahá'í perspective. The NSA reported in a June 25 letter that the Universal House of Justice had seen the publication and "commented on its excellence and suggested that it may be a model for the presentation of the Bahá'í view on other controversial issues."[87] The booklet warned that "the violence and destruction inflicted upon this nation as a result of its failure to remove the various forms of discrimination and unjust restrictions against persons of minority and racial groups is an outward sign of a grave spiritual sickness. . . . Many progressive steps, including legislation on civil rights, have been taken, but the nation still faces the specter of burning cities. Why? Because remedial actions must be based on spiritual principles and this has yet to be done."[88] The booklet "Why Our Cities Burn" was part of proclamation activities[89] for the rest of the year, and the NSA encouraged its distribution by local spiritual assembly (LSA) representatives to all local mayors, government and school officials, local human and civil rights organizations, as well as local media. The NSA distributed the booklet to members of Congress, members of the U.S. Supreme Court, and the national media.[90]

Because of the focus on race unity during the late 1960s and early 1970s, and the progressive nature of Bahá'í attitudes toward race relations, there was a massive influx of African Americans into the Bahá'í Faith, mostly in the South. This influx was facilitated by "mass teaching" whereby teams of Bahá'ís traveled on foot through neighborhoods knocking on doors and telling willing listeners about Bahá'u'lláh and the oneness of humanity. Sometimes, new adherents signed up to be Bahá'ís on the spot. At one point during this period, South Carolina became the state with the largest Bahá'í population in the United States. The NSA recognized this development in a letter dated April 1, 1970, when it stated "The flame of mass teaching which was kindled in the Deep South a few months ago is spreading rapidly throughout that part of the country."[91] The NSA attributed this growth, at least in part, to a conference held in March 1970 at Frogmore, South Carolina, attended by 250 Bahá'ís, who then engaged in teaching the Bahá'í Faith by going door to door and talking to whoever answered. This resulted in forty mini-conferences throughout the United States on mass teaching and fund-raising to meet the needs of the national financial debt of the NSA. This activity led to the establishment of a Deep South Teaching Committee.[92]

For the next several months, NSA communications enumerated the mass enrollments that were occurring throughout the South, as reported by the Deep South Teaching Committee. It reached a peak in early 1971. In a six-week period in January-February 1971, over 8,000 new believers enrolled as Bahá'ís in South Carolina, most of them African Americans. The NSA congratulated the American Bahá'í community for rising to the challenge of the Nine Year Plan and initiating the process of "mass conversion" or "entry by troops," which they hoped would inevitably envelop the entire country.[93] However, this mass growth, which has always been a goal of the Bahá'í Faith since Shoghi Effendi began drafting Plans for Bahá'í advancement, has not yet been replicated elsewhere in the United States.

The Universal House of Justice encouraged the American NSA to broaden the teaching efforts to other minority groups toward the end of the Nine Year Plan, emphasizing the importance of the minority teaching committees formed in 1970. In a letter dated February 14, 1972, the Universal House of Justice stated, "Efforts to reach the minorities should be increased and broadened to include all minority groups such as the [American] Indians, Spanish-speaking people, Japanese and Chinese. Indeed, every stratum of American society must be reached and can be reached with the healing Message, if the believers will but arise and go forth with the spirit which is conquering the citadels of the southern states. Such a program, coupled as it must be with continuous consolidation, can be effectively carried out by universal participation on the part of every lover of Bahá'u'lláh."[94]

In order to prepare for the upcoming Five Year Plan (1973–1979), the National Teaching Committee re-appointed four Minority Teaching Committees: American Indian, Asian American, Spanish-speaking, and Black Teaching committees. A letter dated February 6, 1974, from the National Teaching Committee, right before the launch of the Five-Year Plan, asked for recommendations for the various Minority Teaching Committees, reminding the LSA members that "your recommendations should include, whenever possible, representatives of minority peoples and youth. Only through the application of the principle of unity in diversity can we find the fullest expression of our God-given potential."[95]

Toward the end of the Five-Year Plan, the NSA reminded Bahá'ís, in a letter dated February 22, 1978, that "in the United States, racial prejudice stands out as the most damaging blight upon society."[96] It reiterated the example of 'Abdu'l-Bahá during his visit to North America, and Shoghi Effendi's message in 1938 that "placed the responsibility squarely upon the Bahá'í community to root out racial prejudice" and that it is the "most vital and challenging issue confronting the Bahá'í community at the present stage of its evolution." The NSA, thus, felt impelled to "once again to bring to the attention of the entire American Bahá'í community this vital question which, despite the strenuous attempts already made, has not yet been satisfactorily resolved. The success of our teaching work depends very largely on the progress we make on this question, because it involves the central principle and primary objective of the Revelation of Bahá'u'lláh, namely, the oneness of mankind."[97]

IRANIAN PERSECUTION AND CULTURAL CHANGES FOR AMERICAN BAHÁ'ÍS

From a sociological point of view, race and ethnicity are often analyzed together, since both represent socially constructed identities, and hence both manifest cultural habits, practices, and worldviews that may differ from the majority group in a society. Ethnic diversity, then, poses similar challenges sociologically to creating a unified community as does racial diversity.[98] This is certainly true of Iranian American Bahá'ís, who came to the United States from Iran in waves prior to the 1979 Islamic Revolution, as well as in subsequent years to escape heightened persecution. Thus, it is instructive to look at the resulting influx of Persians into the American Bahá'í community as adding to its ethnic diversity, and creating additional opportunities for Bahá'ís to practice unity in diversity.[99] The significant increase in the Persian Bahá'í population calls for further research to see how this influx affected the implementation of racial diversity in the Bahá'í population and in Bahá'í communities.

Bahá'ís have faced persecution in Iran since the mid-nineteenth century. Momen identified at least four periods of Bábí and Bahá'í persecution that began when the Báb declared his mission in 1844.[100] The earliest phase was clearly the most violent, where it is estimated that around 20,000 believers were killed both prior to 1850 when the Báb was executed, as well as in the chaotic aftermath. The most recent intensification of Bahá'í persecution marks a new and ongoing period of harassment, death sentences, prison time, and humiliation of the Iranian Bahá'ís. It began with Iran's Islamic revolution led by the Supreme Leader Ayatollah Khomeini who returned from exile in Paris to Tehran on February 1, 1979 (and led to the taking of American Embassy hostages for 444 days). In the chaotic aftermath of the Islamic Revolution, organizations such as the Hojjatiyeh Society (an Iranian anti-Bahá'í organization formed in the 1950s) "would play an important role in the persecution of the Bahá'ís," and its activities "included publication of anti-Bahá'í pamphlets, denunciation of Bahá'ís to the authorities, and the disruption of Bahá'í gatherings by gangs of toughs."[101]

On August 21, 1980, all nine members of the NSA of Iran were arrested and never heard from again. This was the first of three purges of national leadership, and successive waves of mass persecution. Over the next several years, the leading mujtahids (mulláhs empowered to issue legal rulings) legitimated the expropriation of all Bahá'í community property, as well as private property of individuals, including agricultural land, businesses, and homes. Bahá'ís were fired from jobs explicitly for membership in the "misguided sect." All Bahá'ís in the civil service (professors, government bureaucrats, doctors, army officers) were fired—some ten thousand Bahá'ís in all.[102] Momen has concluded that it would be more appropriate to call the situation in Iran a "suspended genocide" or possibly an "arrested genocide" since international pressure, as well as the consciousness raising efforts of the Bahá'í International Community (a United Nations NGO) and the American NSA, forced the Iranian government to change tactics while still trying to pursue the goal of eliminating the Bahá'í community from Iranian society.[103]

This persecution led to thousands of Bahá'ís fleeing Iran, many ending up in the United States. A Persian Affairs Committee was set up in 1980 at the U.S. Bahá'í National Center to handle the various tasks of issuing credentials, assisting with housing or jobs, and helping out refugees with their immigration status. Local spiritual assemblies that had questions about integrating members of the Persian community into U.S. society and the Bahá'í community were asked to contact the Bahá'í National Center and the Persian Affairs Committee. The NSA facilitated Congressional hearings in which U.S. lawmakers condemned the ongoing persecution of the 300,000 Bahá'í minority in Iran. In 1982, the first of at least two-dozen Congressional resolutions were passed in an attempt to mitigate Persian Bahá'í oppression by the Iranian government.[104]

Kazemzadeh estimates that since 1979, over 30,000 Bahá'ís have left Iran. It is estimated that between 12,000 and 15,000 Iranian Bahá'ís came to the United States as immigrants or refugees.[105] The influx of Iranian Bahá'í refugees into the United States added to the ethnic and cultural diversity of the U.S. Bahá'í community. More Bahá'í prayers were chanted in the Persian language at the Nineteen-Day Feasts (see below); more *tadeeg*, *ghormeh sabzi*, *ash* and other traditional Persian food were served at Bahá'í holy day festivities; and more personal stories of family members tortured and martyred were told during a variety of meetings. In March 1984, for the first time in American Bahá'í community history, the monthly Feast letter mailed to all local spiritual assemblies included a Persian translation in an attempt to integrate the rising number of Iranian immigrants into the community.[106] All these changes produced a profound effect on American Bahá'í culture, as approximately 20 percent of the American community is now ethnically Persian.[107]

THE VISION OF RACE UNITY

In 1991, the U.S. NSA further highlighted the commitment of the Bahá'í community to racial and ethnic unity with the publication of *The Vision of Race Unity: America's Most Challenging Issue*, a twelve-page pamphlet that outlines the "spiritual solution" to racism in this country. It invites Americans to investigate the Bahá'í Faith as a "model"[108] for bringing about social change. It has been used widely by Bahá'ís in teaching efforts, becoming one of the most popular pamphlets given to others to promote awareness of the Bahá'í Faith.[109]

The document began with the assertion that "racism is the most challenging issue confronting America. A nation whose ancestry includes every people on earth, whose motto is *E pluribus unum*, whose ideals of freedom under the law have inspired millions throughout the world, cannot continue to harbor prejudice against any racial or ethnic group without betraying itself. Racism is an affront to human dignity, a cause of hatred and division, a disease that devastates society."[110] The NSA laments the rise of racist incidences in the United States, and claims, "The recent resurgence of divisive racial attitudes, the increased number of racial incidents, and the deepening despair of minorities and the poor make the need for solutions ever more pressing and urgent. To ignore the problem is to expose the country to physical, moral and spiritual danger."[111] The NSA then called on Bahá'ís and all people of goodwill to boldly address the problem. In the document, it offers the Bahá'í Faith's global experience of racial unity within their own community as a model for others to examine.[112]

The statement goes on to discuss the importance of reforming the educational system and curricula in this country to reflect the biological, social, and spiritual oneness of humanity. It decries the "grim doctrine" of racial separation on the part of both blacks and whites, and offers the Bahá'í Faith as a model for the future: "We mention the experience of the Bahá'í community not from any feeling of pride and ultimate victory, because that which we have accomplished still falls short of that to which we aspire; nonetheless, the results to date are most encouraging, and it is as a means of encouragement that we call attention to them."[113] Approximately 200,000 copies of the *Vision of Race Unity: America's Most Challenging Issue* were distributed nationally in subsequent years.[114]

During the Three Year Plan (1993–1996), the NSA developed the stated goal of striving "to become leaders in the movement for race unity and have Bahá'í communities be models of race unity" and that through Bahá'í educational efforts, that Bahá'í children will "become the first generation of Americans free of racial prejudice."[115] During the Four Year Plan (1996–2000), race unity activities were again emphasized. Task forces to reach the African American, Chinese, Latin American, and American Indian populations were revived. A National Persian Integration Committee was formed in 1997 to mobilize Persian believers who continued to arrive in the United States to escape persecution in Iran. The NSA again warned the American believers toward the end of the Four Year Plan that: "For a Bahá'í, racial prejudice is a negation of faith. Freedom from prejudice is the supreme injunction of

Bahá'u'lláh and the 'hallmark of a true Bahá'í character.' . . . As the Bahá'í Writings clearly state, the fundamental solution to racial conflict rests ultimately in recognition of Bahá'u'lláh, obedience to His commandments and acceptance of the principle of the oneness of humankind."[116]

Since 2001, the Universal House of Justice and NSA of the United States have developed plans that have increasingly focused on what are known as "core activities," which include children's classes, junior youth (middle schoolers) groups, interfaith devotional gatherings, and study circles which follow a well-organized curriculum endorsed by the Universal House of Justice that explores various themes from Bahá'í scripture for the purpose of cultivating spiritual insight, knowledge, qualities, and abilities to serve one's community. Race unity activities continue to be an important theme, but other emphases have become as significant. However, throughout all periods of growth discussed in this chapter, the American NSA has consistently encouraged outreach to minority communities to expand the religion and manifest the goals for the unity of all humanity.[117] While race unity efforts remain implicitly highlighted in communications from the Universal House of Justice and the NSA, further research is required to see how effectively race unity activities have been infused throughout the core activities.

The most recent example of NSA guidance about the problem of racism and the need for racial unity came in a letter from the NSA to the American Bahá'í community, dated February 25, 2017.[118] This letter underscored the various racial, ethnic, ideological, and religious divisions in American society. In it, the NSA declares that "at this pivotal juncture in our nation's history, our foremost responsibility is to everywhere affirm—in the name of Bahá'u'lláh—the truth of the oneness of humanity in a manner that will have an impact for decades to come. We must accelerate our efforts to remove the stains of prejudice and injustice from the fabric of our society." They go on to say that "the nation is afflicted with a deep spiritual disorder, manifest in rampant materialism, widespread moral decay, and a deeply ingrained racial prejudice. . . . The resolution to these challenges lies in recognizing and embracing the truth at the heart of Bahá'u'lláh's Revelation—the incontrovertible truth that humanity is one. Ignorance of this truth—which embodies the very spirit of the Age—is itself a form of oppression, for without it, it is impossible to build a truly just and peaceful world."[119]

The letter continues, that during the current Five Year Plan, Bahá'ís have a twofold mission: one, to shape the inner workings of local Bahá'í communities to reflect unity in diversity; and two, to engage with other likeminded groups and individuals to address the problems of modern society. While not being blind to "the harsh realities that exist in the world," Bahá'ís should appeal to the spiritual truths that are also part of human consciousness. The National Assembly then invokes the example of 'Abdu'l-Bahá, who laid the groundwork for all subsequent plans for the growth and development of the Bahá'í Faith, and also demonstrated the practical applicability of the spiritual truth of the oneness of humanity during his visit to the United States over 100 years ago. The letter states, "He unhesitatingly warned of the dire consequences to American society and to the cause of world peace if her peoples failed to live up to the truth of the oneness of humanity—especially in the relations between black and white."[120]

In this letter, the NSA shares the three ways that the Bahá'í community should be engaged in social change.[121] The first is to continue the process of expansion and consolidation of the Bahá'í community. This is done mostly through outreach to friends, neighbors, family members, and coworkers to invite them to participate in core activities. In these core activities, Bahá'ís and others learn to "create an atmosphere of reverence and devotion to God in the community, to foster a spirit of friendship and intimacy that transcends the barriers of race and class, [and]to provide spiritual and moral education for young people." The second is to engage in social action, and the NSA letter "highlight[ed] those which tackle, directly or indirectly, situations with a bearing on race relations." The third is to participate in the "discourses of society," or in other words, bring the Bahá'í perspective to bear on discussions of social issues, such that Bahá'ís can "assist our fellow citizens to abandon the language and practices in society that have resulted in an intractable divide, unite on the basis of commonly held ideals and principles, and work together for a social order free of prejudice and characterized by unity in diversity."[122]

This is one of the strongest statements about racial unity produced by the NSA since the 1991 publication of *The Vision of Race Unity*. It emphasizes that the unity of humanity has to be at the core of all Bahá'í teaching and consolidation activities throughout the rest of the current Five Year Plan and beyond. The letter states, "The task of transforming an entire society will require a many-faceted approach through which a pattern of life can emerge demonstrating the rich possibilities inherent in walking the spiritual path of love and service. The Universal House of Justice, without attempting to strictly define them, has stated that these possibilities can be considered as falling into the three broad categories of expansion and consolidation, social action, and engagement in the discourses of society."[123] Thus, the NSA's message integrates race unity issues with the thrust of the Plans for the development and growth of the Bahá'í Faith since approximately 2001.[124]

4. Institutional Laws and Practices That Promote Multiracial Communities, Especially at the Primary Worship Experience and in Electing Bahá'í Leadership

As Durkheim pointed out, ritual enacts the values and solidarity of a religious community.[125] This is certainly true of Bahá'ís, as their ritual practices reinforce the global worldview of the Bahá'í Faith, and links them to the global centre of their administrative order. While Bahá'í scripture discourages overly formalized ceremonies or dogmatic rites, "ritual" is being used in the sociological sense, where Bahá'í worship and administrative procedures dramatizes its global doctrine and reinforces its multiracial, mutiethnic community life.[126]

THE BAHÁ'Í CALENDAR AND NINETEEN-DAY FEASTS

Bahá'í theology states that whenever a new manifestation of God appears to humanity, they bring with them a new calendar to institutionalize a new pattern of worship, festivals, and sacred holidays.[127] The Bahá'í year is divided into nineteen months, each with nineteen days (totaling 361), with the insertion of "Intercalary Days" (four or five days which constitute the religious holiday of Ayyam-i-Há) between the eighteenth and nineteenth months to adjust the calendar to the solar year. Each month (and each day of the week) is named after an "attribute of God," virtues that Bahá'ís are supposed to acquire throughout their lives.[128]

On the first day of each Bahá'í month, Bahá'ís gather for the Nineteen-Day Feast, which is the central communal worship experience in the Bahá'í Faith. The Nineteen-Day Feast consists of three loosely structured parts: (1) a devotional period, during which the writings and prayers of the Báb, Bahá'u'lláh and 'Abdu'l-Bahá are read (also readings from some of the other world religion's scriptures can be read, such as from the Bible or Qur'án), and prayers might be read or sung in a variety of languages depending on the community. There can be recorded music (for example, from Iranian Bahá'í singer Narges Houhneján Fání, Leonor Dely and Millero Congo, and Bahá'í gospel music); or Bahá'í songs sung in a variety of languages. These are all examples of the flexibility of the devotional portion of the Feast, which can be adapted to the local culture; (2) an administrative period, usually chaired by a member of the LSA, that focuses on community-wide consultation on important issues facing the community; and finally, (3) a social portion, involving fellowship and refreshments.[129]

The administrative portion is in some ways sociologically the most important aspect of a Feast. Participants might discuss the progress of the community's efforts to expand and consolidate the local growth of the Bahá'í Faith, or organize a new service project. A treasurer's report informs members on the financial health of the community. Someone usually updates the community on future activities or social events. Sometimes, individuals will give reports on teaching trips they have recently taken, or relate a story they heard concerning successful teaching taking place in other parts of the world. Recommendations are referred to the LSA for consideration. In a sense, each

Feast represents a mini-Town Hall meeting where Bahá'ís can have input into community governance and exchange information. Bahá'ís visiting from another area or country are recognized, and news read from the NSA, and also the Universal House of Justice. All communications from the National Assembly are key to linking the local community to the national and international levels of the Bahá'í Administrative Order.[130]

Thus, for Bahá'ís, the Nineteen-Day Feasts are also part of their institutional tools that reinforce their multiracial and multiethnic communities. The Feast format (devotions, administration, socializing) is flexible enough to incorporate the cultural expressions of the various community members. Since 91 percent of American Bahá'í communities (according to FACT data) hold this activity in members' local homes, primary ties of friendship across racial lines develop at least every nineteen days in the intimacy of Bahá'í homes (not to mention weekly meetings that also happen in the home, such as study circles, children's classes, junior youth groups, or interfaith devotional meetings). The Universal House of Justice, in a 1989 letter giving guidance to Bahá'í communities on the Nineteen-Day Feast, encouraged the introduction of music and "uplifting talks," the use of "quality consultation," and said this of the diversity possible in the Feast experience: "The effects of different cultures in all these respects are welcome factors which can lend the Feast a salutary diversity, representative of the unique characteristics of the various societies in which it is held, and therefore conducive to the upliftment and enjoyment of its participants."[131]

In 1987 the Universal House of Justice further warned about the temptation to racially or ethnically segregate, even unconsciously, the Feast: "The sub-division of the city should be seen merely as an administrative necessity meant to serve the good of the whole community. . . . Given the racial and social stratification of large cities, the Spiritual Assembly would also have to exert the utmost care not to allow the Bahá'í community. . . to become, in effect, racially or socially fragmented, even though one race or stratum of society may be dominant in a sub-unit of the city. [The LSA should] uphold at all times . . . the primary principle and goal of our Faith, namely, the unity of the human race."[132] Bahá'ís overcome this fragmentation as discussed above by conscientiously pursuing unity in diversity in all of its study circles, devotional programs, children's classes, junior youth groups, and Nineteen-Day Feasts.

FACT DATA ON BAHÁ'Í MULTIRACIAL EFFORTS

Data[133] from the various Faith Communities Today (FACT) surveys since 2000 indicate that local Bahá'í communities over the last fifteen years have had relatively more success in promoting racial unity than other religious communities in the United States (as measured by the importance given to race unity efforts, as well as the fact that Bahá'í communities are ten times more likely to be multiracial than local churches). In the 2000 FACT survey, just under 57 percent of Bahá'í respondents said that their local community was "trying to increase racial/ethnic/national diversity" within their community. Another 63 percent said that new members "are easily incorporated into the life of the community." Nearly one-third of respondents indicated that "our community is working for social justice" which in the Bahá'í case most often translates into programs that promote racial unity.[134]

Two-thirds of Bahá'í communities (67 percent) said that they had community deepenings (scripture study) or special programs that explicitly focused on race unity, and respondents ranked those programs as the most important that the Bahá'í community offered to the wider non-Bahá'í world (Bahá'í service to the wider community tended to cluster around educational programs, with race unity events by far the most likely, as compared to churches which had the resources to be able to offer more material support to the community in the form of food pantries and clothing and thrift stores).[135]

The 2000, 2005, and 2010 FACT surveys indicated that in 33.2 percent, 41 percent, and 58.3 percent of Bahá'í communities "quite a bit" or "a lot" of effort is spent on working for social and racial justice, respectively. Concomitantly, the same surveys showed that "very serious" or "moderately serious" ethnic conflict occurred in 6.2 percent of communities in 2000, but only 4.4 percent of communities in 2010. The 2008 FACT survey found that 48.9 percent of Bahá'í communities state that racial and ethnic unity was the greatest community strength in the previous year (far outranking other options). In the 2010 FACT data, 93.1 percent of respondents in Bahá'í communities specified they "agreed" or "strongly agreed" that they want their community to "be racially and culturally diverse" (including 62.5 percent alone who said "strongly agree").[136]

One strength of the primary communal worship experience of the Bahá'í Faith—the Nineteen-Day Feast—is its institutional flexibility. Bahá'í writings state that devotions, community business, and social fellowship are the only requirements for the Feasts. Beyond this simple structure, Bahá'ís are free to customize Feast for their local communities. This can include prayers in multiple languages, songs from all musical styles, and translations of letters from the NSA or Universal House of Justice read in Persian for the first-generation Iranian believers. Spanish translations are also distributed monthly as well. This flexibility allows for new cultural expressions to find a home in Bahá'í worship, which overcomes a significant barrier to diversifying the religious community.[137]

When asked about the racial and ethnic composition of the local Bahá'í communities, the data consistently show (from the 2000 to 2008 to 2010 surveys) that on average about 23 percent or 40 percent of the community is non-white, depending on how you classify Persian believers (the Census Bureau considers people from Iran to be racially "white" or "Caucasian;" however if Persians are grouped with other racial and ethnic minorities, the average percentage of non-white community membership increases to at least 40 percent). When analyzing the data collected from a sample drawn from the approximately 1,100 Bahá'í LSA secretaries in the United States, the data show that 53 percent are multiracial as defined by sociological researchers (meaning that there are at least 20 percent minority membership, excluding Persians as minorities). As already noted, this is far above the 7.5 percent of all religious congregations, and about 5.5 percent of churches, which are multiracial. In addition, statistical analysis was performed on Feast attendance by race, ethnicity, and gender, and it was found that all races and ethnicities and both men and women are *equally likely* to attend the Nineteen-Day Feast.[138]

LOCAL GOVERNANCE: THE LSA

The decision-making branch of the Bahá'í Administrative Order is a series of democratically elected assemblies or councils at the local, regional, national, and international levels of social life. Each year, wherever there are at least nine adult Bahá'ís (age twenty-one and older) within a recognized municipal boundary, an election is held to form a LSA of nine members, which constitutes the governing body of local Bahá'í community life. Every community member votes for nine individuals, and the nine receiving the most votes become LSA members. If there is a tie for the ninth spot, administrative law dictates that the position goes to the individual who is a "minority" in the community—a form of electoral "affirmative action" (however, Bahá'í administrative guidelines do not consider Persians a minority group). Local elections take place the first day of the twelve-day Festival of Ridván held in late April.[139]

The role of the LSA includes overseeing the spiritual and financial health of the local Bahá'í community; encouraging community members to take initiative in carrying out the current plans and activities of the Bahá'í Faith (more recently, in localities with Area Teaching Committees, teaching plans fall to that body);[140] ensuring the spiritual education of children and youth and socioeconomic projects for the local area; and providing firm but loving guidance for a Bahá'í who is having difficulty adhering to Bahá'í law. Bahá'í LSAs attempt to always use "consultation" and consensus-based decision-making after discussion of any issue; but if necessary, a majority-vote is used to make decisions. This scripturally encouraged value to seek consensus also promotes unity among the nine-member LSA.[141]

Statistical analyses were performed on leadership data from the FACT surveys, and it was found that there is no statistical association between gender and likelihood of serving on the LSA, nor was there an association between race and ethnicity and the probability of being elected to the LSA. In other words, men and women, as well as whites, blacks, Hispanics, and Persians, were all equally likely to serve in elected LSA leadership positions in Bahá'í communities throughout the United States. Thus, the average proportion of minority members on the LSA reflects the average national proportion of racial and ethnic minorities in the wider Bahá'í community. Similar to overall community membership data, when comparing the FACT 2000 and 2010 data (the only years where detailed race and ethnic data were collected on LSA membership), we find striking levels of racial and ethnic inclusion. In the FACT 2000 survey, on average, LSA membership was 24.4 percent non-white (excluding Persians); and the FACT 2010 survey showed that the average LSA membership was 30.8 percent non-white (thus minority representation at leadership levels of the average local community actually increased over the decade from 2000–2010).[142]

The above is important for at least two reasons: (1) Since there is no clergy in the Bahá'í Faith, community leadership is *elected* from among the *local* community (not appointed from above at a national level). This means that Bahá'ís take seriously their desire to promote racial unity at the local level. (2) Many Bahá'í communities are not only multiracial in their membership, but also in their leadership. This is unique among American religious organizations, based on the FACT data analyzed for this chapter and when making comparisons between Bahá'í communities and churches.

CONCLUSION

This chapter has reviewed some of the ideological and institutional tools in a Bahá'í "tool kit" that over the last century of Bahá'í development in the United States has made it the most racially and ethnically diverse religious group in America. Special attention was given to (1) Core ideological and theological principles; (2) Historical examples of key figures in Bahá'í history ('Abdu'l-Bahá and Shoghi Effendi especially); (3) Consistent guidance from the Universal House of Justice and NSA in the context of systematic plans for growth of the Bahá'í Faith; and (4) Institutional laws and practices that promote multiracial communities, especially at the primary communal worship experience and in electing Bahá'í leadership.

As we have seen in this chapter, the American Bahá'í community has been persistent in tackling racism, the "most challenging issue," as declared by Shoghi Effendi.[143] Promoting racial unity has been an ongoing focus of the guidance communicated from the Universal House of Justice and NSA. The frequent references to the examples of 'Abdu'l-Bahá during his trip to America in 1912, and the guidance from 1938 by Shoghi Effendi (and still quoted by the NSA to this day), attest to their importance in building this multiracial religious community. Bahá'ís are engaged in this work despite the constraints of few material resources and its relatively small size in the America religious marketplace (FACT data show that most Bahá'í communities have on average fewer than twenty-five members, and a yearly average budget of $18,000. There are only about 150,000 Bahá'ís in the United States). In fact, it might be their small size and intimate worship experience in each other's homes that helps facilitate the primary relationships pointed to in Contact Theory that develops racial unity. Compared to other religious communities in the United States, Bahá'ís have been relatively more successful in promoting multiracial religious community life.

FACT data showed that 53 percent of Bahá'í communities meet the sociological definition of a multiracial organization (where at least 20 percent of members are of a non-majority racial and ethnic group).[144] This compares to churches in the United States, where only 5–7 percent are considered multiracial.[145] Even more noteworthy is that not only are most Bahá'í communities multiracial, but that on average, this diversity is reflected in their locally elected leadership (the nine-member LSA).

NOTES

1. In using the term local "Bahá'í community," I am referring to the organization of local Bahá'í groups by municipal geographic boundary (usually at the city or county level) where membership is not chosen on a "voluntary" basis as is the structure of most American religious congregations (see R. Stephen Warner, "Work in Progress Toward a New Paradigm for the Sociological Study of Religion in the United States," *American Journal of Sociology*, 98, no. 5 (1993): 1059). In other words, Bahá'ís cannot choose their worship group based on demographic or theological affinity, but find themselves living in a geographic "community." This has enormous implications for living out the primary Bahá'í value of "unity in diversity," as Bahá'í communities must confront existing diversity in their municipal boundary, but also overcome residential segregation that comes with American residential life.

2. Letter dated February 5, 1947 from Shoghi Effendi's secretary to the Local Spiritual Assembly of Atlanta, Georgia, quoted in *Bahá'í News*, no. 210 (August 1948): 2; reprinted in *Living the Life: A Compilation* (London: Bahá'í Publishing Trust, 1984), 26.

3. See Stephen L. Klineberg, *The Houston Area Survey (1982–2005): Public Perceptions in Remarkable Times* (Houston: Rice University Press, 2005).

4. See Penny Edgell Becker, *Congregations in Conflict: Cultural Models of Local Religious Life* (New York: Cambridge University Press, 1999).

5. Ibid., 43.

6. See, for example, Eugene D. Genovese, *Roll, Jordan, Roll: The World the Slaves Made* (New York: Vintage, 1976); and Dee Brown, *Bury My Heart at Wounded Knee: An Indian History of the American West* (New York: Holt, 2007).

7. Stewart Burns, Susan Carson, Peter Holloran, and Dana L. H. Powell, eds., *The Papers of Martin Luther King, Jr.*, vol. 3 (Berkeley, CA: University of California Press), 417. See also Michael O. Emerson and Rodney M. Woo, *People of the Dream: Multiracial Congregations in the United States* (Princeton, NJ: Princeton University Press, 2006); Troy C. Blanchard, "Conservative Protestant Congregations and Racial Residential Segregation: Evaluating the Closed Community Thesis in Metropolitan and Nonmetropolitan Counties," *American Sociological Review* 72: 416–433; and Brad Christerson, Korie L. Edwards, and Michael O. Emerson, *Against All Odds: The Struggle for Racial Integration in Religious Organizations* (New York: New York University Press, 2005).

8. See Curtiss Paul DeYoung, Michael O Emerson, George Yancey, and Daren Chai Kim, *United by Faith: The Multiracial Congregation as an Answer to the Problem of Race* (New York: Oxford University Press, 2003); and Michael Emerson and Christian Smith, *Divided by Faith: Evangelical Religion and the Problem of Race in America* (New York: Oxford University Press, 2000).

9. American Christianity is organized along denominational and congregational lines. Thus, when referring to churches, the term "congregations" will be used. The Bahá'í Faith is organized into jurisdictional "communities," hence that term will be used to refer to local Bahá'í communities.

10. Emerson and Smith, *Divided by Faith*, 7.

11. Martha Augoustinos and Katherine Reynolds, *Understanding Prejudice, Racism, and Social Conflict* (Newbury Park, CA: Sage, 2001), 25.

12. Sears et al. point out that "symbolic" or "new" racism is part of a family of concepts of negative attitudes toward an "Other," such as "symbolic racism"; "modern racism"; "subtle racism"; and "racial resentments." David O. Sears, Colette Van Laar, Mary Carriollo, and Rick Kosterman, "Is It Really Racism?: The Origins of White Americans' Opposition to Race-Targeted Policies," *The Public Opinion Quarterly* 61, no. 1 (1977): 16; David O. Sears, "Symbolic Racism," in *Eliminating Racism: Profiles in Controversy*, eds. Phyllis A. Katz and Dalmas A. Taylor (New York: Plenum, 1988), 55; Lawrence Bobo, "Race, Public Opinion, and the Social Sphere," *The Public Opinion Quarterly* 61, no. 1 (1997): 4; Donald R. Kinder and David O. Sears, "Prejudice and Politics: Symbolic Racism Versus Racial Threats to the Good Life," *Journal of Personality and Social Psychology* 40 (1981): 414; J. B. McConahay, "Modern Racism, Ambivalence, and the Modern Racism Scale," in *Prejudice, Discrimination and Racism*, eds. John F. Dovidio and Samuel L. Gaertner (Orlando: Academic Press, 1986), 91; T. F. Pettigrew and R. W. Meertens, "Subtle and Blatant Prejudice in Western Europe," *European Journal of Social Psychology* 25 (1995): 58.

13. See Gordon W. Allport, *The Nature of Prejudice* (Cambridge, MA: Addison-Wesley, 1954); Lee Sigelman and Susan Welch, "The Contact Hypothesis Revisited: Black-White Interaction and Positive Racial Attitudes," *Social Forces* 71 (1993): 781–95; J. Allen Williams, "Reduction of Tension through Intergroup Contact: A Social Psychological Interpretation," *Pacific Sociological Review* 7 (1964): 81–88; George Yancey and Michael Emerson, "Integrated Sundays: An Exploratory Study into the Formation of Multiracial Churches," *Sociological Focus* 36, no. 2: 111–126; George Yancey, "An Examination of the Effects of Residential and Church Integration on Racial Attitudes of Whites," *Sociological Perspectives* 42, no. 2 (1999): 279–304; W. A. Barnard and M. S. Benn, "Belief Congruence and Prejudice Reduction in an Interracial Contact Setting," *Journal of Social Psychology* 128 (February 1988): 125–134; M. Hewston, "Contact Is Not Enough: An Intergroup Perspective on the 'Contact Hypotheses,'" in *Contact and Conflict in Intergroup Encounters*, eds. M. Hewstone and R. Brown (Oxford: Basil Blackwell, 1986), 1–44; and Y. Amir, "The Role of Intergroup Contact in Change and Prejudice and Ethnic Relations," in *Towards the Eliminiation of Racism*, ed. P. A. Katz (New York: Pergamon Press, 1976), 245–398.

14. See Michael O. Emerson, Rachel Tolbert Kimbro, and George Yancey, "Contact Theory Extended: The Effects of Prior Racial Contact on Current Social Ties," *Social Science Quarterly* 83, no. 3 (2002): 745–761.

15. Robert Putnam, *Bowling Alone: The Collapse and Revival of American Community* (New York: Simon and Schuster, 2000), 22.

16. N. Wadsworth, "Bridging Racial Change: Political Organizations in the United States Evangelical Multiracial Church Movement," *Politics & Religion* 3, no. 3 (2010): 439.

17. Michael O. Emerson, Rachel Tolbert Kimbro, and George Yancy.

18. George Yancey, "An Examination of the Effects of Residential and Church Integration on Racial Attitudes of Whites," 283.

19. Ibid., 282. See also Daniel A. Powers and Christoher G. Ellison, "Interracial Contact and Black Racial Attitudes: The Contact Hypothesis and Selectivity Bias," *Social Forces* 74, no. 1 (1995): 205–226.

20. Yancey, "An Examination of the Effects of Residential and Church Integration on Racial Attitudes of Whites," 284.

21. Yancey, "An Examination of the Effects of Residential and Church Integration on Racial Attitudes of Whites," 297–298.

22. Ibid., 297. Part of the changing levels of prejudice in the United States can be attributed to the growing demographic diversity of the U.S. racial and ethnic population, the shift to the Sunbelt and exurbs, refocusing analysis on hypersegregation or macro-segregation, as well as the changing nature of ethnic enclaves of recent immigrants. See Daneil T. Lichter, Domenico Parisi, and Michael C. Taquino, "Toward a New Macro-Segregation? Decomposing Segregation within and between Metropolitan Cities and Suburbs," *American Sociological Review* 80, no. 4 (2015): 843–873; Chad R. Farrell, "Immigrant Suburbanization and the Shifting Geographic Structure of Metropolitan Segregation in the United States," *Urban Studies* 53, no. 1 (2016): 57–76; Douglas S. Massey, "Residential Segregation is the Linchpin of Racial

Stratification," *City & Community* 15, no. 1 (2016): 4–7; and Chenoa A. Flippen, "The More Things Change the More They Stay the Same: The Future of Residential Segregation in America," *City & Community* 15, no. 1 (2016): 14–17.Neighborhoods in American cities, however, remain as segregated by class as they have always been. See, for example, Matthew Hall, Matthew, Kyle Crowder and Amy Spring, "Neighborhood Foreclosures, Racial/Ethnic Transitions, and Residential Segregation," *American Sociological Review* 80, no. 3 (2015): 526–549; Jake Intrator, Jonathan Tannen, and Douglas S. Massey, "Segregation by Race and Income in the United States 1970–2010," *Social Science Research* 60 (2016): 45–60. Without a doubt, as neighborhoods become more integrated, then this will have a concomitant impact on interracial neighborhood and public school friendships. There is substantial research on how reducing "social distance" between racial groups in various social settings has a positive impact on race relations. See, for example, E. S. Bogardus, *Social Distance* (Yellow Springs, OH: Antiochh Press, 1959); Kate Strolly, "Racially and Ethnically Diverse Schools and Adolescent Romantic Relationships," *American Journal of Sociology* 120, no. 3 (2014): 750–797; and Vincent N. Parrillo and Christopher Donoghue, "The National Social Distance Study: Ten Years Later," *Sociological Forum* 28, no. 3 (2013): 597–614. A full review of this research is beyond the scope of this chapter. I will instead focus on the importance of relationships developed within voluntary religious organizations on improving race relations.

23. See Emerson and Woo; Emerson and Smith; DeYoung et al., *United by Faith*; K. D. Dougherty and K. R. Huyser, "Racially Diverse Congregations: Organizational Identity and the Accommodation of Differences," *Journal for the Scientific Study of Religion* 47, no. 1 (2008): 23–43; G. Ganiel, "Is the Multiracial Congregation the Answer to the Problem of Race? Comparative Perspectives from South Africa and the USA," *Journal of Religion in Africa* 38, no. 3 (2008): 263–283; K. Garces-Foley, "Comparing Catholic and Evangelical Integration Efforts," *Journal for the Scientific Study of Religion* 47, no. 1 (2008): 17–22; G. Marti, "Fluid Ethnicity and Ethnic Transcendence in Multiracial Churches," *Journal for the Scientific Study of Religion* 47, no. 1 (2008): 11–16; G. Marti, "Affinity, Identity, and Transcendence: The Experience of Religious Racial Integration in Diverse Congregations," *Journal for the Scientific Study of Religion* 48, no. 1 (2009): 53–68; S. L. Perry, "Racial Diversity, Religion, and Morality: Examining the Moral Views of Multiracial Church Attendees," *Review of Religious Research* 55, no. 2 (2013): 355–376; G. C. Stanczak, "Strategic Ethnicity: The Construction of Multi-Racial/Multi-Ethnic Religious Community," *Ethnic and Racial Studies* 29, no. 5 (2006): 856–881; Wadsworth; Yancey, "An Examination of the Effects of Residential and Church Integration on Racial Attitudes of Whites"; Yancey and Emerson; G. Yancey and Y. Kim, "Racial Diversity, Gender Equality, and SES Diversity in Christian Congregations: Exploring the Connections of Racism, Sexism, and Classism in Multiracial and Nonmultiracial Churches," *Journal for the Scientific Study of Religion* 47, no. 1 (2008): 103–111; and K. M. Gushiken, "Cultivating Healthy Discipleship Settings in Multi-Ethnic Churches," *Transformation: An International Journal of Holistic Mission Studies* 32, no. 1 (2015): 17–26.

24. Curtiss Paul DeYoung, Michael O. Emerson, George Yancey, and Karen Chai Kim, "All Churches Should Be Multiracial," *Christianity Today* (April 2005): 33.

25. Sandra L. Colby and Jennifer M. Ortman, "Projections of the Size and Composition of the U.S. Population: 2014 to 2060, Current Population Reports," U.S. Census Bureau, Washington, DC, 2014, https://www.census.gov/content/dam/Census/library/publications/2015/demo/p25-1143.pdf.

26. DeYoung et al., "All Churches Should Be Multiracial," 34.

27. G. Marti, "When Does Religious Racial Integration 'Count'? A Caution about Seeking Ideal Ethnographic Cases," *Journal for the Scientific Study of Religion* 48, no. 1: 227.

28. Michael O. Emerson and Karen Chai Kim, "Multiracial Congregations: An Analysis of Their Development and a Typology," *Journal for the Scientific Study of Religion* 42, no. 2 (2003): 217.

29. See Emerson and Woo; Emerson and Smith; DeYoung et al., *United by Faith*; DeYoung et al., "All Churches Should Be Multiracial"; Garces-Foley; R. Pitt, "Fear of a Black Pulpit? Real Racial Transcendance Versus Cultural Assimilation in Multiracial Churches," *Journal for the Scientific Study of Religion* 49, no. 2 (2010): 218–223; Yancey and Emerson; Emerson and Kim; and Blanchard.

30. Emerson and Smith, *Divided by Faith,* 132.

31. See Putnam; David Knoke and Randall Thomson, "Voluntary Association Membership: Trends and the Family Life Cycle," *Social Forces* 56, no. 1 (1977): 48–65; James G. Hougland and James R. Wood, "Control in Organizations and the Commitment of Members," *Social Forces* 59, no. 1 (1992): 153–170; Evan Schofer and Marion Foucade-Gourinchas, "The Structural Contexts of Civil Engagement: Voluntary Association Membership in Comparative Perspective," *American Sociological Review* 66, no. 6 (2001): 806–828; James E. Curtis, Edward G. Grabb and Douglas E. Baer, "Voluntary Association Membership in Fifteen Countries: A Comparative Analysis," *American Sociological Review* 57, no. 2 (1992): 139–152; James E. Curtis, Douglas E. Baer and Edward G. Grabb, "Nations of Joiners: Explaining Voluntary Association Membership in Democratic Societies," *American Sociological Review* 66, no. 6 (2001): 783–805.

32. See Peter Berger, *The Sacred Canopy* (New York: Doubleday, 1967), 145; Laurence R. Iannaccone, "Sacrifice and Stigma: Reducing Free Riding in Cults, Communes, and Other Collectives," *Journal of Political Economy* (April 1992): 272; and R. Stephen Warner, "Work in Progress toward a New Paradigm for the Sociological Study of Religion in the United States," 1044.

33. See Nancy Tatom Ammerman, *Congregation and Community* (New Brunswick, NJ: Rutgers University Press, 1997).

34. There is a burgeoning scholarship on steady, albeit slight, declines in residential racial segregation over the last twenty years. Despite these decreases, housing segregation, and the voluntary nature of religion in the United States, help foster segregated churches. See Ingrid Gould Ellen, Justin P. Steil and Jorge De la Roca, "The Significance of Segregation in the Twenty-First Century," *City & Community* 15, no. 1 (2016): 8–13; and Douglas S. Massey, "Residential Segregation Is the Linchpin of Racial Stratification," 4–7.

35. See Robert Wuthnow, *The Restructuring of American Religion: Society and Faith since World War II* (Princeton: Princeton University Press, 1988); Elna C.

Green, "Vale of Tears: New Essays on Religion and Reconstruction," *Church History* 76, no. 1 (2007): 210–211; Henry Y. Warnock, "Southern Methodists, the Negro, and Unification: The First Phase," *The Journal of Negro History* 52, no. 4 (1967): 287–304; David M. Reimers, "The Race Problem and Presbyterian Union," *Church History* 31, no. 2 (1962): 203–215.

36. See Wuthnow, *The Restructuring of American Religion: Society and Faith since World War II*; Dean Allen, "Promise Keepers and Racism: Frame Resonance as an Indicator of Organizational Vitality," *Sociology of Religion* 61, no. 1 (2000): 55–72; and Sean F. Everton, "The Promise Keepers: Religious Revival or Third Wave of the Religious Right?" *Review of Religious Research* 43, no. 1 (2001): 51–69.

37. See Scott Thumma and Dave Travis, *Beyond Megachurch Myths: What We Can Learn from America's Biggest Churches* (San Francisco: Jossey-Bass, 2007); Robin D. Perrin and Armand L. Mauss, "Saints and Seekers: Sources of Recruitment to the Vineyard Christian Fellowship," *Review of Religious Research* 33, no. 2 (1991): 97–111; and Robin D. Perrin and Armand L. Mauss, "Strictly Speaking . . . : Kelley's Quandary and the Vineyard Christian Fellowship," *Journal for the Scientific Study of Religion* 32, no. 2 (1993): 125–135.

38. See Clarance Jordan, *Cotton Patch Gospel* (Macon, GA: Smyth and Helnys, 1973).

39. See Lyman Tower Sargent, "The Social and Political Ideas of the American Communitarians: A Comparison of Religious and Secular Communes Founded before 1850," *Utopian Studies* 2, no. 3 (1991): 37–58.

40. See Yancey and Emerson, "Integrated Sundays: An Exploratory Study into the Formation of Multiracial Churches," 111–126; Becker, "Making Inclusive Communities: Congregations and the 'Problem' of Race," 451–472.

41. Of course, there were movements prior to World War II in American Christianity to promote racial reconciliation, such as the Quakers, who were anti-slavery advocates back in the eighteenth century. See J. William Frost, "Quaker Antislavery: From Dissidence to Sense of the Meeting," *Quaker History* 101, no. 1 (2012): 12–33. There were also the Jehovah's Witnesses from the late nineteenth century, see R. Stark and L. R. Iannaconne "Why the Jehovah's Witnesses Grow So Rapidly: A Theoretical Application," *Journal of Contemporary Religion* (1997): 133–157. One should also look at the Pentecostal movement from the early twentieth century. See K. D. Dougherty, "How Monochromatic Is Church Membership? Racial Ethnic Diversity in Religious Community, *Sociology of Religion* 64, no. 1 (2003): 65–85; Harvey Gallagher Cox, *Fire from Heaven: The Rise of Pentecostal Spirituality and the Reshaping of Religion in the Twenty-First Century* (Reading, MA: Addison-Wesley, 1995); H. Elinson, "The Implications for Pentecostal Religion for Intellectualism, Politics, and Race Relations," *American Journal of Sociology* 70, no. 4 (1965): 403–415.

42. See Carl S. Dudley and David A. Roozen, *Faith Communities Today: A Report on Religion in the United States Today* (Hartford, CT: Hartford Seminary, 2001); and Blanchard.

43. See C. Eric Lincoln and Lawrence H. Mamiya, *The Black Church in the African-American Experience* (Durham, NC: Duke University Press, 1990).

44. Yancey and Emerson, "Integrated Sundays," 111.

45. Ibid., 118.

46. Ibid., 123.

47. I am using the term "charisma" or "charismatic leadership" the way that Max Weber used the term in sociological theory. See Max Weber, *From Max Weber: Essays in Sociology*, eds. H. H. Gerth and C. Wright Mills (New York: Oxford University Press, 1946). Charismatic leadership is defined as "someone who claims power on the basis of personal characteristics." H. Paul Chalfant, Robert E. Beckley, and C. Eddie Palmer, *Religion in Contemporary Society*, 3rd ed. (Itasca, IL: F. E. Peacock, 1994), 122. Gerth and Mills state that for Weber, "The founders of world religions and the prophets as well as military and political heroes are the archetypes of the charismatic leader." Weber, *From Max Weber,* 52. Bahá'ís also insist that although the authority of Bahá'u'lláh, 'Abdu'l-Bahá, and Shoghi Effendi has charismatic characteristics, it is also grounded in a written Will and Testament establishing a covenant that passed authority from Bahá'u'lláh to 'Abdu'l-Bahá to Shoghi Effendi and then to the Universal House of Justice. From a sociological point of view, the authority of these founding figures of Bahá'í history are based both on an adheret's love and reverence for them personally (i.e., charisma), as well as the recognition that there is a covenantal authority passed down through written, legal documents. See also Peter Smith, "Motif Research: Peter Berger and the Bahá'í Faith," *Religion* 8 (1978): 210–234. For an explanation of the Universal House of Justice, see below.

48. Yancey and Emerson, "Integrated Sundays," 117.

49. In a similar analysis to Yancey and Emerson, Emerson and Kim posit that there are three primary causal factors that propel a Christian congregation to foster diversity: (1) Mission or theological and cultural orientation; (2) Resource calculation (a change in a congregation's resources, new budget constraints, etc.); and (3) External authority structures (denominational leaders who champion multiracial congregations). Emerson and Kim state that multiracial congregations that are strongest and most likely to survive are those that are motivated by a sense of mission or theology, and those that are least likely to survive are those that result from mergers or bureaucratic mandate. Emerson, "Multiracial Congregations," 224–225. The Bahá'í Faith does utilize the mission and theological orientation as the primary motivation for pursing multiracial congregations, as will be seen below.

50. See Dougherty and Huyser, "Racially Diverse Congregations."

51. FACT 2010 data. Emerson, *Divided by Faith*, 16. Also see Dudley, *Faith Communities Today: A Report on Religion in the United States Today.*

52. I am using the term "new religious movements" in the sociological sense, whereby a religious tradition may be decades or centuries old, but relatively innovative or unknown to a new host society. See Chalfant, *Religion in Contemporary Society*, 240.

53. Mike McMullen, *The Bahá'í: The Religious Construction of a Global Identity* (New Brunswick, NJ: Rutgers University Press, 2000), 18. The growing literature on ethnic and immigrant congregations point out that some ethnic congregations either are uniracial or combine multiple ethnic groups in one mosque or temple but who worship at different times. See Helen Rose Ebaugh and Janet Saltzman Chafetz, *Religion and the New Immigrants: Continuities and Adaptions in Immigrant*

Congregations (Walnut Creek, CA: AltaMira Press, 2000); Warner and Wittner, *Gatherings in Diaspora*; Fenggang Yang and Helen Rose Ebaugh, "Transformations in New Immigrant Religions and Their Global Implications," *American Sociological Review* 66, no. 2 (2001): 269–288. Although the issue of multiracial ethnic congregations is mentioned, there is no in-depth analysis of race and ethnic relations in those congregations.

54. For more information, see McMullen, *The Bahá'í.*

55. See Ann Swindler, "Culture in Action: Symbols and Strategies," *American Sociological Review* 51, no. 2 (1986): 273–286.

56. Democratically elected institutions now oversee the proper functioning of Bahá'í communities. All Bahá'ís twenty-one and older are eligible to both vote in Bahá'í elections and be elected to office. Elections are held without nominations or campaigning. These are, at the international level, the Universal House of Justice; nationally, the National Spiritual Assembly; regionally, the Regional Bahá'í Council; and locally, the local spiritual assembly. There is also an advisory branch of the Bahá'í administrative order composed of Counselors, auxiliary board members, and assistants to the auxiliary board members. For more on this, see "The Bahá'í Administrative Order," *Bahai.org*, http://www.bahai.org/beliefs/essential-relationships/administrative-order.

57. FACT 2000 and 2010 data.

58. Emerson, "Multiracial Congregations," 217.

59. For information on basic Bahá'í doctrine and history, see J. E. Esslemont, *Bahá'u'lláh and the New Era* (Wilmette, IL: Bahá'í Publishing Trust, 2006).

60. See Esslemont; and William S. Hatcher and J. Douglas Martin, *The Bahá'í Faith: The Emerging Global Religion* (Wilmette, IL: Bahá'í Publishing, 2002).

61. Bahá'u'lláh, *Gleanings from the Writings of Bahá'ulláh*, trans. Shoghi Effendi (Wilmette, IL: Bahá'í Publishing, 2005), 250.

62. This assertion about the ubiquity of "unity in diversity" themes at Bahá'í meetings is based on my years of participatory observation field research in the American Bahá'í community. See Mike McMullen, *The Bahá'í: The Religious Construction of a Global Identity* (New Brunswick: Rutgers University Press, 2000); Mike McMullen, *The Bahá'ís of America: The Growth of a Religious Movement* (New York: New York University Press, 2015); Mike McMullen, "The Atlanta Bahá'í Community and Race Unity: 1909–1950," *World Order*, 26, no. 4 (1995): 27–43.

63. See, for example, Robert H. Stockman, *'Abdu'l-Bahá in America* (Wilmette, IL: Bahá'í Publishing, 2012).

64. See, for example, Stockman, *'Abdu'l-Bahá in America*, and Esslemont.

65. For more on Louis Gregory, see Morrison, *To Move the World: Louis G. Gregory and the Advancement of Racial Unity* (Wilmette, IL: Bahá'í Publishing Trust, 1982).

66. 'Abdu'l-Bahá, quoted in Morrison, *To Move the World: Louis G,* 45–46. At the time `Abdu'l-Bahá was saying this, miscegenation was illegal in most of the U.S. South. It was not until 1967 (in *Loving v. Virginia*) that the U.S. Supreme Court declared that the prohibition against miscegenation is unconstitutional.

67. "Pioneer" is the term that Bahá'ís use for an individual who voluntarily moves to another country with the goal of spreading the Bahá'í Faith.

68. A Hand of the Cause of God was an elevated advisory administrative position last appointed by Shoghi Effendi. There are no longer any living Hands of the Cause of God.

69. This assertion about frequent references to the faithfulness of Louis Gregory at Bahá'í meetings is based on my years of participatory observation field research in the American Bahá'í community. See endnote 62.

70. For more information, see Stockman, *'Abdu'l-Bahá in America*; Morrison, *To Move the World: Louis G*; and Gwendolyn Etter-Lewis and Richard Thomas, *Lights of the Spirit: Historical Portraits of Black Bahá'ís in North America, 1898–2000* (Wilmette, IL: Bahá'í Publishing, 2006), 33.

71. See, for example, George Brown Tindall, *The Emergence of the New South, 1913–1945* (Baton Rouge: Louisiana State University Press, 1967), 152–156, 187.

72. See Emerson and Smith, *Divided by Faith*.

73. This assertion about frequent references to Louis Gregory being a role model, especially among African American Bahá'ís, is based on my years of participatory observation field research in the American Bahá'í community. See endnote 62.

74. Shoghi Effendi, *The Advent of Divine Justice,* 36.

75. For example, Letter dated December 31, 1995 to the American Bahá'í Community for the Feast of Sharaf (National Bahá'í Archives, Evanston, IL, Box 12, Folder October-December 1995); National Bahá'í Archives is hereafter cited as NBA; Letter dated December 17, 1997 to the American Bahá'í Community (NBA, Box 12, Folder September-December 1997); Letter dated December 27, 1999 to the American Bahá'í Community (NBA, Box 13, Folder October–December 1999); National Spiritual Assembly of the Bahá'ís of the United States, Letter to the American Bahá'í Community dated February 25, 2017, https://www.bahai.us/static/assets/20170225-NSA-on-America-and-the-Five-Year-Plan.pdf and attachments to a Letter dated January 17, 2017 (personal papers).

76. Shoghi Effendi, *The Advent of Divine Justice,* 33–34.

77. See McMullen, *The Bahá'í,* 154.

78. Shoghi Effendi, *The Advent of Divine Justice,* 34.

79. Ibid., 35.

80. Ibid.

81. Ibid., 40.

82. McMullen, *The Bahá'ís of America,* 41–43.

83. The subsequent account of how the U.S. Bahá'í community implemented Plans for growth from the Universal House of Justice and the National Spiritual Assembly is significant in the history of African Americans because of the consistent way in which all racial and ethnic minorities, but especially African Americans, were the target of teaching activities. Although not always successfully carried out, the analysis of Bahá'í attempts to welcome African Americans is rare in American religious history, either in Bahá'í efforts to recruit or actual enrollments and integration of African Americans into the community. See Wade Clark Roof and William

McKinney, *American Mainline Religion: Its Changing Shape and Future* (New Brunswick, NJ: Rutgers University Press, 1987), 138–144.

84. For more historical context see Aldon D. Morris, *The Origins of the Civil Rights Movement: Black Communities Organizing for Change* (New York: Free Press, 1984); and Doug McAdam, *Political Process and the Development of Black Insurgency, 1930–1970* (Chicago: University of Chicago Press, 1982).

85. McMullen, *The Bahá'í*, 153–156.

86. Houston, TX Bahá'í Center Archives (hereafter: HBCA), 1968.

87. HBCA, 1968.

88. NBA, General Correspondence, Box 4, 1968.

89. A proclamation activity is a presentation given by Bahá'ís at a public venue (often using media to announce the event) to teach the Bahá'í Faith or educate the public about Bahá'í principles and values.

90. NBA, General Correspondence, Box 4, 1968.

91. NBA, General Correspondence, Box 5, 1970.

92. HBCA, April 1, 1970.

93. NBA, General Correspondence, Box 5, February 19, 1971.

94. NBA, General Correspondence, Box 5, 1972.

95. NBA, General Correspondence, Box 5, 1974.

96. NBA, General Correspondence, Box 7, 1978.

97. NBA, General Correspondence, Box 7, February 22, 1978.

98. See, for instance, Martin Marger, *Race and Ethnic Relations: American and Global Perspectives*, 10th ed. (Belmont, CA: Wadsworth, 2014).

99. The U.S. Census Bureau has historically considered people from the Middle East, including both Arabs and Persians, to be "white" in America's racial classification system. Advocacy groups have pressured the Census Bureau to create a separate geographic category for people of Middle Eastern or North African (MENA) descent for the 2020 census. NPR News, "For Some Americans of MENA Descent, Checking a Census Box Is Complicated," https://www.npr.org/sections/codeswitch/2017/03/11/519548276/for-some-arab-americans-checking-a-census-box-is-complicated.

100. See Moojan Momen, "The Babi and Bahá'í community of Iran: A Case of 'Suspended Genocide,'" *Journal of Genocide Research* 7, no. 2 (2005): 221–241.

101. Firuz Kazemzadeh, "The Bahá'ís of Iran: Twenty Years of Repression," *Social Research* 67, no. 2 (2000): 540. For more on Bahá'í persecution, see Center for Human Rights in Iran and Bahá'í International Community, "Documents and News."

102. Kazemzadeh, "The Bahá'ís of Iran," 544.

103. Momen, "The Babi and Bahá'í community of Iran," 239.

104. McMullen, *The Bahá'ís of America*, 177–179. See also: *Summary Record of U.S. Congressional Resolutions on the Bahá'ís of Iran*, http://publicaffairs.bahai.us/wp-content/uploads/2017/02/Summary-and-Table-of-Congressional-Resolutions.pdf.

105. McMullen, *The Bahá'ís of America*, 174.

106. McMullen, *The Bahá'ís of America*, 179.

107. FACT 2010 data.

108. National Spiritual Assembly of the Bahá'ís of the United States, *The Vision of Race Unity: America's Most Challenging Issue* (Wilmette, IL: Bahá'í Publishing

Trust, 1991), 4, 11–12. The NSA wrote: "We mention the experience of the Bahá'í community not from any feeling of pride and ultimate victory, because that which we have accomplished still falls short of that to which we aspire; nonetheless, the results to date are most encouraging, and it is as a means of encouragement that we call attention to them. . . . Guided and inspired by such principles, the Bahá'í community has accumulated more than a century of experience in creating models of unity that transcend race, culture, nationality, class, and the differences of sex and religion, providing empirical evidence that humanity in all its diversity can live as a unified global society. . . . Therefore, the Bahá'ís offer the teachings of their Faith and the example of their community for examination, convinced that these can make a contribution toward the eradication of racism endemic in American society." National Spiritual Assembly of the Bahá'ís of the United States, *The Vision of Race Unity*, 5.

109. This assertion about the popularity of *The Vision of Race Unity* as a teaching tool is based on my years of participatory observation field research in the American Bahá'í community. See endnote 62.

110. Ibid., 1.

111. Ibid., 1.

112. Ibid., 12.

113. National Spiritual Assembly, 11.

114. McMullen, *The Bahá'ís of America*, 201.

115. Ibid., 211.

116. *American Bahá'í* 24, no. 14 (1999): 1.

117. McMullen, *The Bahá'ís of America*, 158.

118. National Spiritual Assembly of the Bahá'ís of the United States to the American Bahá'í Community, February 25, 2017.

119. Ibid.

120. Ibid.

121. The term "Bahá'í community" refers to not only registered members of the Faith but also others who participate in Bahá'í activities who share the Bahá'í vision and are collaborating to achieve those goals.

122. National Spiritual Assembly of the Bahá'ís of the United States to the American Bahá'í Community, February 25, 2017.

123. Ibid.

124. See McMullen, *The Bahá'ís of America*, 249–258.

125. Emile Durkheim, *The Elementary Forms of the Religious Life* (New York: Free Press, 1965), 51–52.

126. For more information on this aspect of ritual, see Robert Wuthnow, *Meaning and Moral Order: Explorations in Cultural Analysis* (Berkeley, CA: University of California Press, 1987), 99–101, 107–109; see also McMullen, *The Bahá'í*, 76–77.

127. J. E. Esslemont, *Bahá'u'lláh and the New Era* (Wilmette, IL: Bahá'í Publishing Trust, 1970), 18. "Manifestation of God" is the term Bahá'ís use to refer to the divinely-inspired founders of the world's major faith traditions, including, but not limited to, Buddha, Moses, Zoroaster, Jesus, Muhammad, and, the most recent, Bahá'u'lláh.

128. Esslemont, *Bahá'u'lláh and the New Era,* 185.

129. See McMullen, *The Bahá'í*, 84.

130. See McMullen, *The Bahá'í*, 85–86.

131. Universal House of Justice, quoted in *Bahá'í News*, no. 702 (November 1989): 1.

132. Universal House of Justice, quoted in *Bahá'í News*, no. 702, 1.

133. Since 1998, I have been the lead researcher for Bahá'í data collection for Faith Communities Today (FACT), a research project studying most major religious groups in America. This consortium of forty different denominations and faith traditions was initially funded through a Lily Foundation grant, and is headquartered at Hartford Seminary's Institute for Religious Research in Connecticut. FACT surveyed more than forty thousand American congregations (over 12 percent of all religious congregations in the United States). It is the longest-running, most comprehensive survey of religious groups in the United States, and the participating religious groups represent 90 percent of all worshipers in America (see http://faithcommunitiestoday.org/). Questionnaires were fielded in surveys in 2000, 2005, 2008, and 2010. The result is a one-of-a-kind longitudinal Bahá'í dataset describing its members, growth, and community characteristics, from which selected empirical data for this chapter were drawn. The FACT surveys used the methodology of a "key informant" survey. See Earl Babbie, *The Practice of Social Research*, 13th ed. (Belmont, CA: Wadsworth Cengage Learning, 2007). For most religious groups, this meant that the lead clergy of the congregation received the survey. However, because the Bahá'í Faith has no clergy, it was decided to send the questionnaire to the secretary of the local spiritual assembly for each community. With the help of the Research Office of the Bahá'í National Center in Wilmette, Illinois, all 1,100 secretaries were sent questionnaires in 2000, 2005, 2008, and 2010, giving respondents the option of filling out a paper copy of the survey, or providing a link to complete it online. The response rate for the 2000 FACT survey was 52 percent, and the 2010 FACT survey had a response rate of 36 percent (with the 2005 and 2008 surveys each having about a one-third response rate).

134. FACT 2000 data.

135. FACT 2000 data.

136. FACT 2000, 2005, 2010 data.

137. See McMullen, *The Bahá'í*, 91–93.

138. FACT surveys tended to focus on four large racial and ethnic groups in the United States: African Americans, Hispanics or Latinos, Asians, and Whites (which are categories that the U.S. Census Bureau uses). When I report on non-white minority groups, I am referring to these three large communities. FACT surveys did not uniformly ask about additional ethnic groups that the Census Bureau might use such as American Indian and Alaska Native, or Native Hawaiian and Pacific Islander.

139. Ridván (meaning "paradise" in Arabic) commemorates the public declaration in 1863 of Bahá'u'lláh as a Manifestation of God in a garden outside Baghdad, Iraq, during his exile.

140. In 2001, the Universal House of Justice began aggregating LSA jurisdictions into geographic "clusters" to facilitate planning for systematic growth and large teaching campaigns. Cluster agencies have developed to coordinate Bahá'í activity in the cluster; in more mature clusters, the Area Teaching Committee has taken over

systematic teaching plans from the Local Spiritual Assembly (see McMullen, *The Bahá'ís of America*, 99). As such, the LSA role in these clusters has shifted as Bahá'ís learn to expand core activities to more and more people: The goal is for the LSA to seek "to create an environment in which all feel encouraged to contribute to the community's common enterprise. It is eager to see the cluster agencies succeed in their plans, and its intimate familiarity with the conditions in its area enables it to foster the development of interacting processes at the local level. With this in mind, it urges the wholehearted participation of the friends in campaigns and meetings for reflection, and it provides material resources and other assistance for initiatives and events being organized in the locality" (Universal House of Justice, letter dated December 29, 2015, http://www.bahai.org/library/authoritative-texts/the-universal-house-of-justice/messages/20151229_001/20151229_001.pdf).

141. Hatcher and Martin, *The Bahá'í Faith,* 144–147.
142. FACT 2000, 2010 data.
143. Shoghi Effendi, *The Advent of Divine Justice,* 62.
144. See Yancey, "Integrated Sundays," 112.
145. Emerson, *Divided by Faith*, 16.

BIBLIOGRAPHY

'Abdu'l-Bahá. *Tablets of the Divine Plan.* Wilmette, IL: Bahá'í Publishing Trust, 1993. Also available at http://www.bahai.org/library/authoritative-texts/abdul-baha/tablets-divine-plan/.

Allen, L. Dean. "Promise Keepers and Racism: Frame Resonance as an Indicator of Organizational Vitality." *Sociology of Religion* 61, no. 1 (2000): 55–72.

Allport, Gordon W. *The Nature of Prejudice.* Cambridge, MA: Addison-Wesley, 1954.

Amir, Y. "The Role of Intergroup Contact in Change of Prejudice and Ethnic Relations." In *Towards the Elimination of Racism*, edited by P. A. Katz, 245–308. New York: Pergamon Press, 1976.

American Bahá'í 24, no. 14 (1999), 1.

Ammerman, Nancy Tatom. *Congregation and Community.* New Brunswick, NJ: Rutgers University Press, 1997.

Augoustinos, Martha and Katherine Reynolds. *Understanding Prejudice, Racism, and Social Conflict.* Newbury Park, CA: Sage, 2001.

Babbie, Earl. *The Practice of Social Research.* 13th ed. Belmont, CA: Wadsworth Cengage Learning, 2012.

"Bahá'í Administrative Order." *Bahai.org.* http://www.bahai.org/beliefs/essential-relationships/administrative-order.

Bahá'í International Community. "Documents and News." Also available at https://www.bic.org/documents-and-news-s.

Bahá'u'lláh. *Gleanings from the Writings of Bahá'u'lláh.* Translated by Shoghi Effendi. Wilmette, IL: Bahá'í Publishing Trust, 1976. Also available at http://www.bahai.org/library/authoritative-texts/bahaullah/gleanings-writings-bahaullah.

Barnard, W. A., and M. S. Benn. "Belief Congruence and Prejudice Reduction in an Interracial Contact Setting." *Journal of Social Psychology* 128 (February 1988): 125–134.

Becker, Penny Edgell. "Making Inclusive Communities: Congregations and the 'Problem' of Race." *Social Problems* 45, no. 4 (1998): 451–472.

Becker, Penny Edgell. *Congregations in Conflict: Cultural Models of Local Religious Life*. New York: Cambridge University Press, 1999.

Berger, Peter L. *The Sacred Canopy*. New York: Doubleday, 1967.

Blanchard, Troy C. "Conservative Protestant Congregations and Racial Residential Segregation: Evaluating the Closed Community Thesis in Metropolitan and Nonmetropolitan Counties." *American Sociological Review* 72 (2007): 416–433.

Bobo, Lawrence. "Race, Public Opinion, and the Social Sphere." *The Public Opinion Quarterly* 61, no. 1 (1997): 1–15.

Bogardus, E. S. *Social Distance*. Yellow Springs, OH: Antioch Press, 1959.

Brown, Dee. *Bury My Heart at Wounded Knee: An Indian History of the American West*. New York: Holt, 2007.

Burns, Stewart, Susan Carson, Peter Holloran, and Dana L. H. Powell, eds. *The Papers of Martin Luther King, Jr.* Vol. 3. Berkeley: University of California Press, 1997.

Center for Human Rights in Iran. https://www.iranhumanrights.org.

Chalfant, H. Paul, Robert E. Beckley, and C. Eddie Palmer. *Religion in Contemporary Society*. 3rd ed. Itasca, IL: F. E. Peacock Publishers, 1994.

Christerson, Brad, Korie L. Edwards, and Michael O. Emerson. *Against All Odds: The Struggle for Racial Integration in Religious Organizations*. New York: New York University Press, 2005.

Colby, Sandra L., and Jennifer M. Ortman. "Projections of the Size and Composition of the U.S. Population: 2014 to 2060, Current Population Reports," US Census Bureau, Washington, DC, 2014. https://www.census.gov/content/dam/Census/library/publications/2015/demo/p25-1143.pdf.

Cox, Harvey Gallagher. *Fire from Heaven: The Rise of Pentecostal Spirituality and the Reshaping of Religion in the Twenty-first Century*. Reading, MA: Addison-Wesley, 1995.

Curtis, James E., Edward G. Grabb, and Douglas E. Baer. "Voluntary Association Membership in Fifteen Countries: A Comparative Analysis" *American Sociological Review* 57, no. 2 (1992): 139–152.

Curtis, James E., Douglas E. Baer, and Edward G. Grabb. "Nations of Joiners: Explaining Voluntary Association Membership in Democratic Societies." *American Sociological Review* 66, no. 6 (2001): 783–805.

DeYoung, Curtiss Paul, Michael O. Emerson, George Yancey, and Karen Chai Kim. *United by Faith: The Multicultural Congregation as an Answer to the Problem of Race*. New York: Oxford University Press, 2003.

DeYoung, Curtiss Paul, Michael O. Emerson, George Yancey, and Karen Chai Kim. "All Churches Should Be Multiracial." *Christianity Today* (April 2005): 32–35.

Dougherty, K. D. "How Monochromatic Is Church Membership? Racial Ethnic Diversity in Religious Community, *Sociology of Religion* 64, no. 1 (2003): 65–85.

Dougherty, K. D., and K. R. Huyser. "Racially Diverse Congregations: Organizational Identity and the Accommodation of Differences." *Journal for the Scientific Study of Religion* 47, no. 1 (2008): 23–43.

Dudley, Carl S., and David A. Roozen. *Faith Communities Today: A Report on Religion in the United States Today*. Hartford, CT: Hartford Seminary, 2001.

Durkheim, Emile. *The Elementary Forms of the Religious Life*. New York: Free Press, 1965.

Ebaugh, Helen Rose, and Janet Saltzman Chafez. *Religion and the New Immigrants: Continuities and Adaptations in Immigrant Congregations*. Walnut Creek, CA: AltaMira Press, 2000.

Elinson, H. "The Implications of Pentecostal Religion for Intellectualism, Politics, and Race Relations." *American Journal of Sociology* 70, no. 1 (1965): 403–415.

Ellen, Ingrid Gould, Justin P. Steil, and Jorge De la Roca. "The Significance of Segregation in the Twenty-First Century." *City & Community*. 15, no. 1 (2016): 8–13.

Emerson, Michael O., and Karen Chai Kim. "Multiracial Congregations: An Analysis of Their Development and a Typology." *Journal for the Scientific Study of Religion* 42, no. 1 (2003): 217–227.

Emerson, Michael O., and Christian Smith. *Divided by Faith: Evangelical Religion and the Problem of Race in America*. New York: Oxford University Press, 2000.

Emerson, Michael O., and Rodney M. Woo. *People of the Dream: Multiracial Congregations in the United States*. Princeton, NJ: Princeton University Press, 2006.

Emerson, Michael O., Rachel Tolbert Kimbro, and George Yancey. "Contact Theory Extended: The Effects of Prior Racial Contact on Current Social Ties." *Social Science Quarterly* 83, no. 1 (2002): 745–761.

Esslemont, J. E. *Bahá'u'lláh and the New Era*. Wilmette, IL: Bahá'í Publishing Trust, 2006.

Etter-Lewis, Gwendolyn, and Richard Thomas. *Lights of the Spirit: Historical Portraits of Black Bahá'ís in North America, 1898–2000*. Wilmette, IL: Bahá'í Publishing, 2006.

Everton, Sean F. "The Promise Keepers: Religious Revival or Third Wave of the Religious Right?" *Review of Religious Research* 43, no. 1 (2001): 51–69.

FACT 2000. http://faithcommunitiestoday.org/faith-communities-today-2000-study.

FACT 2005. http://faithcommunitiestoday.org/faith-communities-today-2005-study.

FACT 2008. http://faithcommunitiestoday.org/faith-communities-today-2008-study.

FACT 2010. http://faithcommunitiestoday.org/fact-2010.

Farrell, Chad R. "Immigrant Suburbanization and the Shifting Geographic Structure of Metropolitan Segregation in the United States." *Urban Studies* 53, no. 1 (2016): 57–76.

Flippen, Chenoa A. "The More Things Change the More They Stay the Same: The Future of Residential Segregation in America." *City & Community* 15, no. 1 (2016): 14–17.

Frost, J. William. "Quaker Antislavery: From Dissidence to Sense of the Meeting." *Quaker History* 101, no. 1 (2012): 12–33.

Ganiel, G. "Is the Multiracial Congregation an Answer to the Problem of Race?" *Comparative Perspectives from South Africa and the USA. Journal of Religion in Africa* 38, no. 3 (2008): 263–283.

Garces-Foley, K. "Comparing Catholic and Evangelical Integration Efforts." *Journal for the Scientific Study of Religion* 47, no. 1 (2008): 17–22.

Genovese, Eugene D. *Roll, Jordan, Roll: The World the Slaves Made*. New York: Vintage, 1976.

Green, Elna C. "Vale of Tears: New Essays on Religion and Reconstruction." *Church History* 76, no. 1 (2007): 210–211.

Gushiken, K. M. "Cultivating Healthy Discipleship Settings in Multi-Ethnic Churches." *Transformation* 32, no. 1 (2015): 17–26.

Hall, Matthew, Kyle Crowder, and Amy Spring. "Neighborhood Foreclosures, Racial/Ethnic Transitions, and Residential Segregation." *American Sociological Review* 80, no. 3 (2015): 526–549.

Hatcher, William S., and David Martin. *The Bahá'í World Faith: An Emerging World Religion*. Wilmette, IL: Bahá'í Publishing Trust, 2002.

Hewston, M. "Contact Is Not Enough: An Intergroup Perspective on the 'Contact Hypotheses.'" In *Contact and Conflict in Intergroup Encounters*, edited by M. Hewstone and R. Brown, 1–44. Oxford: Basil Blackwell, 1986.

Hougland, James G., and James R. Wood. "Control in Organizations and the Commitment of Members." *Social Forces* 59, no. 1 (1992): 153–170.

Houston, TX Bahá'í Center Archives.

Iannaccone, Laurence R. "Sacrifice and Stigma: Reducing Free Riding in Cults, Communes, and Other Collectives." *Journal of Political Economy* (April 1992): 271–291.

Intrator, Jake, Jonathan Tannen, and Douglas S. Massey. "Segregation by Race and Income in the United States 1970–2010." *Social Science Research* 60 (2016): 45–60.

Jordan, Clarance. *Cotton Patch Gospel*. Macon, GA: Smyth and Helnys, 1973.

Kazemzadeh, Firuz. "The Bahá'ís of Iran: Twenty Years of Repression." *Social Research* 67, no. 2 (2000): 537–558.

Kinder, Donald R., and David O. Sears. "Prejudice and Politics: Symbolic Racism Versus Racial Threats to the Good Life." *Journal of Personality and Social Psychology* 40 (1981): 414–31.

Klineberg, Stephen L. *The Houston Area Survey (1982-2005): Public Perceptions in Remarkable Times*. Houston: Rice University Press, 2005.

Knoke, David, and Randall Thomson. "Voluntary Association Membership: Trends and the Family Life Cycle." *Social Forces* 56, no. 1 (1977): 48–65.

Lichter, Daneil T., Domenico Parisi, and Michael C. Taquino. "Toward a New Macro-Segregation? Decomposing Segregation within and between Metropolitan Cities and Suburbs." *American Sociological Review* 80, no. 1 (2015): 843–873.

Lincoln, C. Eric, and Lawrence H. Mamiya. *The Black Church in the African-American Experience*. Durham: Duke University Press, 1990.

Living the Life: A Compilation. London: Bahá'í Publishing Trust, 1984. Also available at https://bahai-library.com/compilation_living_the_life.

Marger, Martin N. *Race and Ethnic Relations: American and Global Perspectives*. 10th ed. Belmont, CA: Wadsworth, 2014.

Marti, G. "Fluid Ethnicity and Ethnic Transcendence in Multiracial Churches." *Journal for the Scientific Study of Religion* 47, no. 1 (2008): 11–16.

Marti, G. "Affinity, Identity, and Transcendence: The Experience of Religious Racial Integration in Diverse Congregations." *Journal for the Scientific Study of Religion* 48, no. 1 (2009): 53–68.

Marti, G. "When Does Religious Racial Integration 'Count?' A Caution about Seeking Ideal Ethnographic Cases." *Journal for the Scientific Study of Religion* 49, no. 2 (2010): 224–230.

Massey, Douglas S. "Residential Segregation Is the Linchpin of Racial Stratification." *City & Community* 15, no. 1 (2016): 4–7.

McConahay, J. B. "Modern Racism, Ambivalence, and the Modern Racism Scale." In *Prejudice, Discrimination and Racism*, edited by John F. Dovidio and Samuel L. Gaertner, 91–126. Orlando: Academic Press, 1986.

McAdam, Doug. *Political Process and the Development of Black Insurgency, 1930–1970*. Chicago: University of Chicago Press, 1982.

McMullen, Mike. "The Atlanta Bahá'í Community and Race Unity: 1909–1950." *World Order* 26, no. 4 (1995): 27–43. Also available at https://bahai.works/World_Order.

McMullen, Mike. *The Bahá'í: The Religious Construction of a Global Identity*. New Brunswick: Rutgers University Press, 2000.

McMullen, Mike. *The Bahá'ís of America: The Growth of a Religious Movement*. New York: New York University Press, 2015.

Momen, Moojan. "The Babi and Bahá'í Community of Iran: A Case of 'Suspended Genocide'?" *Journal of Genocide Research* 7, no. 2 (2005): 221–241.

Morris, Aldon D. *The Origins of the Civil Rights Movement: Black Communities Organizing for Change*. New York: Free Press, 1984.

Morrison, Gayle. *To Move the World: Louis G. Gregory and the Advancement of Racial Unity*. Wilmette, IL: Bahá'í Publishing Trust, 1982.

National Bahá'í Archives. Wilmette, IL. Box 12, Folder October-December 1995.

National Bahá'í Archives. Wilmette, IL. Box 13, Folder October-December 1999.

National Bahá'í Archives. Wilmette, IL. General Correspondence, Box 5, 1970.

National Bahá'í Archives. Wilmette, IL. General Correspondence, Box 5, February 19, 1971.

National Bahá'í Archives. Wilmette, IL. General Correspondence, Box 5, 1972.

National Bahá'í Archives. Wilmette, IL. General Correspondence, Box 5, 1974.

National Bahá'í Archives. Wilmette, IL. General Correspondence, Box 7, 1978.

National Bahá'í Archives. Wilmette, IL. General Correspondence, Box 7, February 22, 1978.

National Spiritual Assembly of the Bahá'ís of the United States. *The Vision of Race Unity: America's Most Challenging Issue*. Wilmette, IL: Bahá'í Publishing Trust, 1991.

———. To the American Bahá'í Community. February 25, 2017. https://www.bahai.us/static/assets/20170225-NSA-on-America-and-the-Five-Year-Plan.pdf.

NPR News. March 11, 2017. "For Some Americans of MENA Descent, Checking A Census Box Is Complicated." http://www.npr.org.

Parrillo, Vincent N., and Christopher Donoghue. "The National Social Distance Study: Ten Years Later." *Sociological Forum* 28, no. 3 (2013): 597–614.

Perrin, Robin D., and Armand L. Mauss. "Saints and Seekers: Sources of Recruitment to the Vineyard Christian Fellowship." *Review of Religious Research* 33, no. 2 (1991): 97–111.

Perrin, Robin D., and Armand L. Mauss. "Strictly Speaking . . . : Kelley's Quandary and the Vineyard Christian Fellowship." *Journal for the Scientific Study of Religion* 32, no. 2 (1993): 125–135.

Perry, S. L. "Racial Diversity, Religion, and Morality: Examining the Moral Views of Multiracial Church Attendees." *Review of Religious Research* 55, no. 2 (2013): 355–376.

Pettigrew, T. F., and R. W. Meertens. "Subtle and Blatant Prejudice in Western Europe." *European Journal of Social Psychology* 25 (1995): 57–75.

Pitt, R. "Fear of a Black Pulpit? Real Racial Transcendence Versus Cultural Assimilation in Multiracial Churches." *Journal for the Scientific Study of Religion* 49, no. 2 (2010): 218–223.

Powers, Daniel A., and Christopher G. Ellison. "Interracial Contact and Black Racial Attitudes: The Contact Hypothesis and Selectivity Bias." *Social Forces* 74, no. 1 (1995): 205–226.

Public Affairs Office, National Spiritual Assembly of the Bahá'ís of the United States. "Summary Record of U.S. Congressional Resolutions on the Bahá'ís of Iran." http://publicaffairs.bahai.us/wp-content/uploads/2017/02/Summary-and-Table-of-Congressional-Resolutions.pdf.

Putnam, Robert. *Bowling Alone: The Collapse and Revival of American Community*. New York: Simon and Schuster, 2000.

Reimers, David M. "The Race Problem and Presbyterian Union." *Church History* 31, no. 2 (1962): 203–215.

Roof, Wade Clark, and William McKinney. *American Mainline Religion: Its Changing Shape and Future*. New Brunswick, NJ: Rutgers University Press, 1987.

Sargent, Lyman Tower. "The Social and Political Ideas of the American Communitarians: A Comparison of Religious and Secular Communes Founded Before 1850." *Utopian Studies* 2, no. 3 (1991): 37–58.

Schofer, Evan, and Marion Fourcade-Gourinchas. "The Structural Contexts of Civic Engagement: Voluntary Association Membership in Comparative Perspective." *American Sociological Review* 66, no. 6 (2001): 806–828.

Sears, David O. "Symbolic Racism." In *Eliminating Racism: Profiles in Controversy*, edited by Phyllis A. Katz and Dalmas A. Taylor, 53–84. New York: Plenum, 1988.

Sears, David O., Colette Van Laar, Mary Carriollo, and Rick Kosterman. "Is It Really Racism?: The Origins of White Americans' Opposition To Race-Targeted Policies." *The Public Opinion Quarterly* 61, no. 1 (1997): 16–53.

Shoghi, Effendi. *The Advent of Divine Justice*. Wilmette, IL: Bahá'í Publishing Trust, 1963. Also available at http://www.bahai.org/library/authoritative-texts/shoghi-effendi/advent-divine-justice.

Sigelman, Lee, and Susan Welch. "The Contact Hypothesis Revisited: Black-White Interaction and Positive Racial Attitudes." *Social Forces*, no. 71 (1993): 781–795.

Smith, Peter. "Motif Research: Peter Berger and the Bahá'í Faith." *Religion*, no. 8 (1978): 210–234.

Stanczak, G. C. "Strategic ethnicity: The Construction of Multi-Racial/Multi-Ethnic Religious Community." *Ethnic and Racial Studies* 29, no. 5 (2006): 856–881.

Stark, R., and L. R. Iannaccone. "Why the Jehovah's Witnesses Grow So Rapidly: A Theoretical Application." *Journal of Contemporary Religion* 12, no. 2 (1997): 133–157.

Stockman, Robert. *'Abdu'l-Bahá in America*. Wilmette, IL: Bahá'í Publishing, 2012.

Strolly, Kate. "Racially and Ethnically Diverse Schools and Adolescent Romantic Relationships." *American Journal of Sociology* 120, no. 3 (2014): 750–797.

Swidler, Ann. "Culture in Action: Symbols and Strategies." *American Sociological Review* 51, no. 2 (1986): 273–286.

Thumma, Scott, and Dave Travis. *Beyond Megachurch Myths: What We Can Learn from America's Biggest Churches.* San Francisco: Jossey-Bass, 2007.

Tindall, George Brown. *The Emergence of the New South, 1913–1945*. Baton Rouge: Louisiana State University Press, 1967.

Universal House of Justice. Letter to the Followers of Bahá'u'lláh. August 27, 1989. In *Bahá'í News*, no. 702 (November 1989), 1–14. Also available at https://bahai.works/Baha%27i_News.

Universal House of Justice to the Conference of the Continental Boards of Counselors, December 29, 2015. http://www.bahai.org/library/authoritative-texts/the-universal-house-of-justice/messages/20151229_001/20151229_001.pdf.

Wadsworth, N. "Bridging Racial Change: Political Orientations in the United States Evangelical Multiracial Church Movement." *Politics & Religion* 3, no. 3 (2010): 439–468.

Warner, R. Stephen. "Work in Progress Toward a New Paradigm for the Sociological Study of Religion in the United States." *American Journal of Sociology* 98, no. 5 (1993): 1044–1093.

Warner, R. Stephen, and Judith G. Wittner. *Gatherings in Diaspora: Religious Communities and the New Immigration.* Philadelphia: Temple University Press, 1998.

Warnock, Henry Y. "Southern Methodists, the Negro, and Unification: The First Phase." *The Journal of Negro History* 52, no. 2 (1967): 287–304.

Weber, Max. *From Max Weber: Essays in Sociology*. Edited by H. H. Gerth and C. Wright Mills. New York: Oxford University Press, 1946.

Williams, J. Allen. "Reduction of Tension through Intergroup Contact: A Social Psychological Interpretation." *Pacific Sociological Review* 7 (1964): 81–88.

Wuthnow, Robert. *The Restructuring of American Religion: Society and Faith since World War II.* Princeton: Princeton University Press, 1988.

Wuthnow, Robert. *Meaning and Moral Order: Explorations in Cultural Analysis.* Berkeley: University of California Press, 1987.

Yancey, George. "An Examination of the Effects of Residential and Church Integration on Racial Attitudes of Whites." *Sociological Perspectives* 42, no. 2 (1999): 279–304.

Yancey, G., and Y. Kim. "Racial Diversity, Gender Equality, and SES Diversity in Christian Congregations: Exploring the Connections of Racism, Sexism, and Classism in Multiracial and Nonmultiracial Churches." *Journal for the Scientific Study of Religion* 47, no. 1 (2008): 103–111.

Yancey, George, and Michael Emerson. "Integrated Sundays: An Exploratory Study into the Formation of Multiracial Churches." *Sociological Focus* 36, no. 2 (2003): 111–126.

Yang, Fenggang, and Helen Rose Ebaugh. "Transformations in New Immigrant Religions and Their Global Implications." *American Sociological Review* 66, no. 2 (2001): 269–288.

Chapter 7

Race, Place, and Clusters

Current Vision and Possible Strategies

June Manning Thomas

Division of people of various races, ethnicities, and classes coupled with estrangement and oppression in many forms continue to be problematic aspects of human society. In North America, the cause of division related to race is partially the result of persistent prejudice and discrimination, but also of structural inequalities that reduce the potential of human life and threaten the stability of society. Therefore, continuing to think about racial unity in terms of individual relationships or personal prejudice, while important, is not a sufficient response to the need for cultural unity. Structural issues of inequality are essential as well, but these are complex and not easily resolved.

Since its birth in Iran in the mid-nineteenth century, the Bahá'í Faith has emerged as a religious community with significant capacity to unite people across traditional barriers of race, class, nationality, gender, and creed. The cardinal teaching of the Bahá'í Faith, in fact, is the oneness of all humanity. Bahá'í institutions have paid special attention to the issue of racial disunity in North America ever since 'Abdu'l-Bahá's visit to the American shores in 1912, when, through both word and deed, He pointedly encouraged interracial fellowship and the disavowal of traditional norms of racial segregation and discrimination. He urged people to overcome all racial barriers through means such as intermarriage, and to worship together as one; these were remarkable exhortations for a time when even casual social mixture of the races was uncommon and when racially segregated religious congregations were the norm.[1]

More than a century after 'Abdu'l-Bahá's visit to North America and a half century after the civil rights era yielded major legislative accomplishments that lessened overt racial discrimination, substantial differences of access and opportunity still linger. This suggests that it is timely to reexamine how to overcome problems of racial disunity, prejudice, and unequal opportunity in the present day. Of the many ways we could look at this—spiritually, psychologically, legally, socially, spatially, and so on—this chapter focuses on the interaction between "place" (meaning spatial geographic location) and the institute process (meaning the system of education, expansion, and consolidation currently guiding worldwide plans of the Bahá'í community). Place is important to consider because many social and economic attributes are spatially arranged: lack of access to opportunity is highly associated with place of residence, such as in high-poverty neighborhoods. The institute process is important because of its great potential to address this problem and because at present it is the major tool for the expansion and consolidation of the Bahá'í community, which has a solid record of positive work in building unity among diverse peoples. Indeed, the current Bahá'í planning agenda is but the latest stage in a long line of multi-year expansion plans dating back to the 1930s and, conceptually, dating back even further to 'Abdu'l-Bahá's letters written from 1916 to 1917 and collected in the volume *Tablets of the Divine Plan.*[2] *Tablets of the Divine Plan* and subsequent plan-related documents focused on expanding the global reach of the Bahá'í Faith. With the latest planning phase, particularly since 2001, the Bahá'í community's planning process entered a new era. The global community, building on previous experience, began to deepen its presence in (and service to) villages and neighborhoods throughout the world. Such deepened presence was possible only because of the evolution of particular tools and strategies related to expansion, consolidation, and social action.

This paper will look at how the Bahá'í vision concerning matters related to racial prejudice and unequal opportunity is proposed to operate in an era of geographic clusters, with a focus on neighborhoods and villages. Clusters are the spatial configuration framing the current expansion and consolidation work of the Bahá'í Faith, and both neighborhoods and villages are the places, or levels of action, in which much current Bahá'í expansion and consolidation takes place. To begin, we will describe the place-based strategies that the Universal House of Justice has advised Bahá'ís around the world to use as they build communities and human resources in a wide range of places, whether rural or urban. We will explore briefly as well how any place-based strategy in certain urban areas of the United States has the potential to encounter the lingering effects of racial disunity, structural oppression, and prejudice that have existed for generations and have abated only somewhat since the legislative civil rights victories in the 1960s. We will then return to a closer examination of how the Universal House of Justice sees the current Bahá'í global plans as eventually leading to the ability of societies to overcome the effects of ills such as entrenched racial prejudice. To do this, we will draw in particular on the guidance of the Universal House of Justice from 2010 to 2016, a period of time that covers the launching of two consecutive five-year plans (2011 to 2016 and 2016 to 2021). We will end by suggesting potential strategies for addressing the issue of place-based racial disunity, building on those that have been advanced by the Universal House of Justice, which counsels at a broad level with full expectation of adaptation to specific circumstances. Specifically, we will describe how those strategies might work in challenging urban settings, such as metropolitan Detroit, which, by several creditable metrics, is one of the most racially segregated areas in the United States and is plagued with high rates of central-city poverty. Of particular importance will be our discussion of how these strategies could help overcome its social and economic divisions. For this last part of the paper, the strategies indicated will be merely a visionary exercise. What actually evolves in the future will be determined by the actions of people living in this area, forces of social integration and disintegration, and the passage of time.

PLACE-BASED PLANNING STRATEGIES

The matter of place has always been important in the expansion plans of the Bahá'í Faith. 'Abdu'l-Bahá's letters written to the North American believers, compiled in *Tablets of the Divine Plan*, mention specific states, countries, and other places in North America, South America, and the world at large to which Bahá'ís should travel in order to spread the teachings of the Faith. His instructions were couched in spiritual exhortations and practical advice, but they were very place specific. The series of plans initiated and led by His grandson, Shoghi Effendi, were also unambiguous, often naming the countries, regions, and territories to which Bahá'ís should travel in order to expand the reach and influence of the Bahá'í Faith; it was Shoghi Effendi who began the practice of naming specific multi-year timeframes for national or global plans, but he built these upon exhortations given in *Tablets of the Divine Plan*.

Many subsequent plans generated by the Faith's worldwide governing body, the Universal House of Justice, and by various National Spiritual Assemblies, have asked for Bahá'ís to travel to specific places in order either to assist local Bahá'í communities or to establish them. In a new series of global plans initiated in 1996 with the call for creation of a worldwide "network of training institutes," however, the concept of place became important in the expansion plans of this global religion in a different way—as an organizational construct allowing communities to shape their teaching and consolidation efforts (Ridvan 1996, par. 29). The most important aspect of this effort was the continued evolution of training institutes, which are Bahá'í-sponsored "centers of learning" (Ridvan 1996, par. 28) designed to build human resources and improve communities through training for such purposes as enhancing devotional meetings and conversational skills on meaningful topics as well as facilitating the spiritual education of children and junior youth. Out of several potential curricula, the Universal House of Justice chose those developed by the Ruhi Institute in Colombia as the most effective ones available for use throughout the world.

In 2001, after a short period of experimentation in a few countries, the Universal House of Justice announced that the primary locus of planning and action—the venue for plan-related activities employing Ruhi Institute materials—would move from the national level to that of the "cluster." Clusters were defined by the Universal House of Justice as "smaller geographic areas" composed of "a cluster of villages and towns, but, sometimes, a large city and its suburbs" or other similar groupings (letter dated January 9, 2001, par. 10). Boundaries were not to be set with regard to the presence of Bahá'í communities or jurisdictions, but rather the cluster would derive from existing secular social constructs as determined by "culture, language, patterns of transport, infrastructure, and the social and economic life of the inhabitants" (par. 10).

In North America, the division of American and Canadian geographic terrain into clusters was placed largely in the hands of Regional Bahá'í Councils—subnational bodies that the Universal House of Justice had brought into existence in 1997 to advance the work of expansion and consolidation, and to decentralize certain administrative functions previously handled at the national level (letter dated May 30, 1997, par. 3, 4). These councils, in consultation with various parties, carved North America into geographic clusters. In southeast Michigan and the Midwest, these clusters were often single counties or nearby groups of counties. The 2001–2002 decision of that particular Regional Bahá'í Council to use existing counties met the criteria set forth and also enabled the use of available census information.[3] Throughout the world, because of the aforementioned criteria, some clusters actually had no resident Bahá'ís at the time of the clustering process but became possible places for future communities of believers, as they were "virgin areas" (Universal House of Justice, letter dated January 9, 2001, par. 11).

As the Universal House of Justice and its agencies learned more about the process of increasing Bahá'í membership and consolidating new believers through the institute process and as the Ruhi Institute materials gained a strong footing, the Universal House of Justice began to place great emphasis on urging Bahá'ís to focus their efforts at the level of neighborhoods or villages within their own or nearby clusters. Messages sent between 2010 and 2016 repeatedly mention the value of working within receptive neighborhoods and villages because it was in such settings that positive results emerged in response to efforts to expand the scope of the Bahá'í Faith's influence. In 2010, Bahá'ís were advised to continue focusing on conversations with everyday coworkers and acquaintances, meaning existing social networks, but also to look for "smaller pockets of the population" that could become the center of a variety of efforts utilizing the institute process beyond Bahá'ís' existing social networks. The Universal House of Justice defined where these pockets might be: "in an urban cluster, such a centre of activity might best be defined by the boundaries of a neighbourhood; in a cluster that is primarily rural in character, a small village would offer a suitable social space for this purpose" (Ridván Message 2010, par. 5).

In such places, the task would be to nurture children and youth and to advance spiritually based discussions, but also to "enable people of varied backgrounds to advance on equal footing and explore the application of the teachings to their individual and collective lives" (Universal House of Justice, Ridván Message 2010, par. 5). Later, in the same letter, the power of increasing numbers of children enrolled in Bahá'í children's classes was referred to as "a requisite of the community building process gathering momentum in neighbourhoods and villages" (par. 14). The Universal House of Justice expanded on this theme in 2013 as well, noting that its hopes had been exceeded concerning the power of "community building by developing centers of intense activity in neighbourhoods and villages," and they assured the worldwide community that "where this approach has advanced for some years in a neighbourhood or village and the friends have sustained their focus, remarkable results are becoming gradually but unmistakably evident" (Ridván Message 2013, par. 6). The same theme emerged in 2015 and 2016, when the Universal House of Justice continued to refer to "neighbourhoods and villages that show promise," stating that "a pattern of action that is able to embrace large numbers comes chiefly from working to bring more neighbourhoods and villages . . . to the point where they can sustain intense activity" and counseling that because of such strategies the Faith was being shared in many different venues, including "crowded urban quarters and villages along rivers and jungle paths" (letter dated December 29, 2015, par. 17; letter dated March 26, 2016, par. 5).

All of this was in service to a specific vision pursued by the Universal House of Justice as part of its efforts to set in place an alternative to a faltering world order. What this body was beginning to see in locations where its advice about the institute process was taking hold was a salutary transformation in the lives and fortunes of the people being influenced by that process. In several of its messages, the Universal House of Justice describes this transformation:

> A broader cross section of the population is being engaged in conversations, and activities are being opened up to whole groups at once—bands of friends and neighbours, troops of youth, entire families—enabling them to realize how society around them can be refashioned. The practice of gathering for collective

> worship, sometimes for dawn prayers, nurtures within all a much deeper connection with the Revelation of Bahá'u'lláh. Prevailing habits, customs, and modes of expression all become susceptible to change—outward manifestations of an even more profound inner transformation, affecting many souls. The ties that bind them together grow more affectionate. Qualities of mutual support, reciprocity, and service to one another begin to stand out as features of an emerging, vibrant culture among those involved in activities. (letter dated December 29, 2015, par. 24)

In some parts of the world, such activities transformed the life of entire communities, including members of diverse faiths and creeds, as whole villages began to benefit from and turn toward new ways of educating children and youth and both individuals and local institutions rectified their conduct in response to moral teachings about human virtues. The effects of the Bahá'ís' activities in the future, therefore, would not be limited to the Bahá'í community. As the Universal House of Justice promised in a letter to the believers in the United States and Canada, "the movement of your clusters to the farthest frontiers of learning will usher in the time anticipated by Shoghi Effendi . . . when the communities you build will directly combat and eventually eradicate the forces of corruption, of moral laxity, and of ingrained prejudice eating away at the vitals of society" (letter March 26, 2016, par. 3). This was in direct reference to Shoghi Effendi's 1938 book-length letter, *The Advent of Divine Justice*, which urged North American believers to wield a "double crusade" by regenerating first their own community and then attacking the "evils" of the larger society such as corruption, moral laxity, and racial prejudice (41). The Universal House of Justice's 2016 letter thus harkened back to historical roots well known to its Baha'i audience, as it promised that results from their contemporary efforts would extend beyond the obvious, affecting even the problem of "ingrained prejudice" in the larger community. We will discuss this subject further, but first let us consider the reality of racial division and severely uneven opportunity in some geographic places, such as in many U.S. metropolitan areas.

PLACE, RACE, AND DIVISION

The abovementioned benefits associated with the systematic promulgation of the institute process potentially apply, as we have noted, to a wide variety of places, both rural and urban, and to a variety of peoples around the world. Such a process, however, may confront conditions in society at large that are shaped by social, economic, and political forces beyond the control of the Bahá'ís. This is the case with contemporary metropolitan areas, such as those in the postindustrial Midwest.

Each metropolitan area has its own story that includes facets such as which indigenous populations originally lived there, which transportation systems became firmly established, how industrialization and postindustrialization affected the local economy, what determined the nature of political boundaries, which races and ethnic populations and nationalities arrived and when, and many more. We can, however, summarize some of the factors that have influenced patterns of race, ethnicity, and socioeconomic status in many older, postindustrial U.S. cities and then go on to describe the results in at least one specific metropolitan area, Detroit.

The social division in many metropolitan areas in the United States is so long-standing that people may mistakenly see it as the natural order of things, or they may hold to simplistic notions about the cause of such phenomena as what some have called "chocolate cities" and "white suburbs." This too is a simplistic characterization, of course, because suburbanization has become more integrated racially over the last decade and because central cities and their metropolitan areas are often composed of several major groupings of people, including Latino/Latina, Asian, Indigenous, African American (black), white, and many other configurations. Biologically and spiritually, all races are one, but socially and politically the concept of race has a distinct reality, and the federal government's census measures it for various geographic settings.

The reasons the main issue of concern is often one of race, and specifically one of black-white relations, are manifold. One is that for some time now, statistical measurements of U.S. metropolitan areas have recorded much higher levels of segregation between blacks and whites than between whites and other groups of people or between other groups of people as categorized by race. One particularly popular tool among scholars who measure segregation is known as the index of dissimilarity. This metric shows that the level of spatial segregation between blacks and whites has declined over the decades between 1970 and 2010 in some metropolitan areas, such as in Boulder and Fort Collins, Colorado, but remained high in others, such as Detroit, Gary, Chicago, Newark, and New York City (Rugh and Massey p. 221).

In Detroit, the unusually high index of dissimilarity score of 86.7 means that in 2010, close to 86.7 percent of blacks would have had to move in order to disperse the black population throughout the metropolitan area (Rugh and Massey, p. 207, Social Science Data Analysis Network). Surveys in several key cities including Detroit have shown that such segregation is not due to voluntary action on the part of blacks, who actually prefer mixed-race neighborhoods and generally see no advantage to living close together in enclaves.[4] Whites in the same surveys, on the other hand, reported being mostly comfortable with one or a few black neighbors but became increasingly uncomfortable moving into or remaining in a neighborhood if a rising percentage of blacks lived there. However, in many circumstances, a rising percentage of blacks was almost inevitable since those whites least comfortable with racial integration continued to avoid the neighborhood or leave, thereby increasing the proportion of the black population and making other whites increasingly uncomfortable. Because of this predictable cycle, some mixed-race situations were inherently imbalanced, as blacks sought racial integration while some whites sought to avoid it, or, at least, too much of it (Charles; Farley, Danziger, and Holzer).[5] Rather than a benign characterization of place, high levels of racial segregation may mean possible neighborhood instability (at least temporarily, during periods of racial change) as well as markedly different access to transportation, high-quality schools, jobs, and other social benefits, especially if the area has become mostly black and is also poor.

Among the factors that led to such residential segregation by race were federal housing policy, federal urban policy, the history of race riots, the process of suburbanization itself, and a host of other formal and informal agents. The roots of residential segregation of blacks date back to the nineteenth century and before, but it was with successive waves of black migrants from the South during the two world wars that patterns of residential segregation in northern (Midwest and Northeast) states began to be calcified.

These patterns were first held in place by custom and by the resistance of some members of the white working class, which in the industrial North sometimes perpetrated violent reigns of terror that included some of the bloodiest race riots in American history, such as the East St. Louis race riot in 1917 and the Detroit race riot of 1943. Both of those events saw white mobs indiscriminately attacking black residents because of perceived intrusion into employment venues or white residential neighborhoods.[6]

Even more effective, if much tamer, tools of residential segregation were federal policies that essentially codified racially segregated neighborhoods; these included loans supported by the federal Home Owners' Loan Corporation, established during the New Deal in 1933; the subsequent Federal Housing Administration, or FHA (1934); and the Veterans Administration, or VA (1944). These federal mortgage insurance programs initially made it easy for white working-class and middle-class families to obtain mortgages in order to buy new houses, but their provisions classified any neighborhoods with black residents as inherently inferior, and they actively discouraged whites from moving to neighborhoods into which intrusion by blacks had already taken place or could take place. Blacks were therefore barred from obtaining such loans, except in certain carefully isolated sites located in various pockets of the metropolitan area (Thomas and Ritzdorf, pp. 282–4; Thomas, *Redevelopment,* pp. 84–86).

Long after the FHA and VA stopped actively discriminating against people and families of color, and long after the Civil Rights Act of 1964 and the

Fair Housing Act of 1968 outlawed such outright discriminatory practices in housing sales and rentals, other actors (such as financial institutions and real estate agents, as well as political leaders in some cities and suburbs) sought to skirt the spirit and letter of the law by maintaining segregated racial lines. Lax federal enforcement of civil rights laws further weakened the legislative gains of the 1960s.

The U.S. Department of Housing and Urban Development systematically documented active discrimination in housing over many years, extending well into the 2000s, and nonprofit fair housing centers were established in several metropolitan areas to document and litigate against such informal means of exclusion. However, such documentation and litigation did not actually solve the problem, for testing showed continued racial prejudice and discrimination in housing well after 2012 (Oh and Yinger, pp. 30–36). Meanwhile, because of the private real estate market and federally supported public housing, many opportunities were lost for children from low-income families to grow up in less distressed, more racially and economically integrated settings, which, studies showed, could have greatly enhanced their life chances (Massey et al., pp. 186–196).

The federal urban renewal program, initiated in 1949 and nicknamed "Negro removal," destroyed many black (as well as other racial minority and white ethnic) central-city neighborhoods and small-business commercial areas over the next two decades without fair compensation or humane relocation, sometimes leaving racially segregated neighborhoods more crowded or marginalized than they were before and severely dampening both community life and the spirit of black entrepreneurship (Thomas, *Redevelopment,* chapters 3, 5). Federal income tax and transportation policies facilitated decentralization, but that process was, for reasons described above, racially discriminatory and left marginalized people farther behind in the race for livable environments, at least until select areas in many central cities became popular again (though unaffordable for some) due to a process of gentrification. The end results were staunch barriers of exclusion and encircling strands of oppression that created a moral dilemma: an interlocking web of social, economic, and political constraints severely limited life opportunities for some, even as society at large refused to take social responsibility for this situation but rather blamed oppressed individuals for their personal circumstances (Young, pp. 393–98).

All of the above characteristics existed in metropolitan Detroit, as elsewhere, with variations in the strength with which various trends manifested themselves. Racially selective suburbanization was a strong factor, as well as selective clearance of black neighborhoods, unwillingness of whites to live in increasingly black neighborhoods, prejudice against black residents, growing poverty in an abandoned central city, and lessening entrepreneurship, particularly among blacks. On the other hand, a process of gentrification—wherein well-to-do professionals, often white, move back into the central city—has taken place since 2012 only to a limited extent (and in a very limited area) in Detroit, and that process is still minimal compared to experiences in other major cities in the North.[7]

Although definitions of metropolitan Detroit differ, the core of the region includes the three counties of Wayne, Oakland, and Macomb. Among these, the most economically distressed is Wayne County, which includes the city of Detroit and just over forty other municipalities. The wealthiest is Oakland County, which includes some of the richest census tracts in the United States. For recent regional transportation and planning purposes, one could expand the parameters of the region by adding Washtenaw County (Ann Arbor) and possibly several other counties as well.

Even if we talk just about the core three-county area—Wayne, Oakland, and Macomb—we can see fairly well the problematic trends that we've described. Some of the cities in these counties in which the population dropped between 2000 and 2010 include Highland Park (down by 29.7 percent) and Detroit (down by 25 percent), both in Wayne County, and Pontiac (down by 10.3 percent) in Oakland County. At the same time, however, several suburban municipalities grew, fueled by new subdivisions and commercial growth (Thomas, "Redesigning" 195).

Not surprisingly, levels of poverty also vary greatly among these municipalities, as does the presence of blacks, foreign-born populations, and Latinos/Latinas. Detroit, Wayne County's largest city, had 35.5 percent of its families—a solid one-third—living below the poverty line in the Census Bureau's 2011–2015 estimates; Troy, Oakland County's largest city, had only 5.4 percent of its families living below the poverty line for that same span of years. The population of Macomb County was estimated to be 10.3 percent black in 2011–2015 (up slightly from 8.5 percent in 2010), but the neighboring Wayne County was 40.5 percent black and Oakland County was 13.9 percent black. Blacks comprised 83 percent of the city of Detroit's population in both the 2010 census and in 2011–2015 estimates (*American FactFinder II*).[8]

Michigan's political situation has led to an unusual degree of municipal fragmentation in the Detroit metropolitan region, creating winners and losers. In this state it is very easy to incorporate as a municipality and very difficult for one municipality to annex another (Jacobs, "Embedded," pp. 161–163). This has allowed collections of subdivisions and subsets of counties to incorporate and protect their boundaries, leading to increasing numbers of municipalities and establishing a process of exclusion, sometimes by encircling geographic territory and then setting up land use regulations designed to favor commercial development and large lots or houses. This fragmenting phenomenon aggravates racial and socioeconomic divisions and deviates markedly from the policies in Canada, where several consolidations have reduced the number of municipalities in any one metropolitan area. The comparison is all the more stark because Canada is located directly across the Detroit River, in plain sight of Detroit's central business district, and because metropolitan Toronto, with a less fragmented, more consolidated governance system, yet with a population size comparable to metropolitan Detroit, is a mere four hours' drive away. More efficient metropolitan governance and less fragmentation have helped bring many benefits to Toronto, including strong, diverse economic development (Jacobs, "Embedded," pp. 147–148, Jacobs, "The Impact," pp. 353–354).

Detroit's transportation system has relied upon private automobiles and an unusually extensive interstate highway system within the city boundaries, a situation that has also affected racial and class segregation. Unlike other major American cities, Detroit has no light rail or commuter rail system of any substantial length; extensive streetcar lines were taken out in the 1950s, a three-mile loop of monorail surrounds the central business district, and a new three-mile-long light rail extends only from the central business to New Center, an office/commercial hub northward.

Confirming trends that have been in place since Henry Ford's invention of the automobile assembly line in a factory located in metropolitan Detroit's city of Highland Park, a series of proposals for some form of regional mass transit died over the years, either because of legislative opposition, the failure of ballot proposals, or, in one case, a governor's veto. Instead, two separate bus systems, one for the suburbs and one for the central city, were poorly connected so that inner-city residents, predominately black, could not get to major job centers in the suburbs and suburbanites, predominately white, had no reason to continue to live in the central city. As is the case in other cities such as Chicago, wealthy suburbanites who still had jobs in the central city (which they increasingly did not) could commute easily by car. As recently as fall 2016, voters in the core three-county region, plus Washtenaw County, failed yet again to approve funding for an integrated regional transit system.

Other problematic circumstances that are specific to metropolitan Detroit include a historically heavy reliance on the automobile industry, which made the metropolitan area particularly vulnerable when deindustrialization took jobs away; the fiscal distress of Detroit's city government—the largest U.S. city to ever declare bankruptcy—accompanied by a major plummet in the quality of public services; and a high rate of housing vacancy, abandonment, and ultimately demolition.[9] Aggravating the housing crisis was the Great Recession, which began in 2007; this led to a rash of mortgage foreclosures and then, a few years later, increased property tax foreclosures, which hit southeastern Michigan cities such as Detroit, Hamtramck, and Highland Park particularly hard. These predominately minority-race cities had been especially vulnerable to foreclosure because of a history of subprime mortgages and predatory lending targeted at minority-race neighborhoods; in addition, their housing prices failed to rebound nearly as much as did markets in other cities (e.g., Deng et al.). Each of these three circumstances—economic downturn, municipal fiscal distress, and decline in the housing market—has had major implications.

Deindustrialization means that the foundations of the area's working class have been severely undermined, as tens of thousands of blue-collar jobs have simply vanished, leaving in their wake men and women ill-equipped to earn a livelihood in an increasingly sophisticated world economy and neighborhoods and subareas of distressed central cities with high levels of unemployment and poverty.

The fiscal collapse and the decline in public services in Detroit and in other distressed cities have affected certain neighborhoods, rendering them undesirable to young families, who might not move there because of poor public services and troubled school systems. The foreclosure crisis has been particularly devastating because it has led to a high number of vacant structures, which have brought down surrounding property values even more and chased away families and individuals (except those with significantly fewer choices), and waves of both mortgage and tax foreclosures in Wayne County, which have further jeopardized the social viability of many neighborhoods. This combination of circumstances has had serious social repercussions and may make sole reliance on a neighborhood-based strategy, for any purpose, challenging.

SEARCHING FOR GUIDANCE

After the above discussion, it will be especially salutary to think about how actors in this stage of development of the Bahá'í Faith, a worldwide community involved in a visionary global plan, might operate in such settings. Revisiting the messages of the Universal House of Justice, we now note that this body has made very specific suggestions that are relevant to this discussion of race and place. Likewise, it is useful in this context to review several relevant Bahá'í principles: the importance of teaching minority races and ethnic populations, the imperative of overcoming prejudice; the necessary strategies for allowing focus neighborhoods or villages to develop capacity and local leadership, and the crucial roles of both social action and discourse in accomplishing such tasks.

As the Universal House of Justice itself has noted, the *Tablets of the Divine Plan* were very clear that Bahá'u'lláh's message should be brought to all the world's peoples. While 'Abdu'l-Bahá particularly mentioned the importance of teaching people indigenous to the Americas, He also strove to show how people of all races, including blacks, should become a part of the Bahá'í community. In a letter to the National Spiritual Assembly (NSA) of the Bahá'ís of the United States, the Universal House of Justice underscores "the importance of giving due attention to historically significant populations in the United States" (par. 9). This is a clear reference to Bahá'í documents talking about the significance of teaching blacks as well as whites. The letter also calls American Bahá'ís' attention to the growing relevance of immigrants of all races:

> Today, the remarkable phenomenon of immigration that has accelerated in recent decades must also claim a major share of your attention. After all, immigrants—whether from the Latin regions of your own continent, across the Pacific from Asia or the Atlantic from Africa—constitute a sizeable proportion of the American population. Their sons and daughters now apparently number almost one in four of the children in your country. Among these families whose origins lie beyond your borders a vibrant sense of community is often more pronounced. Raising capacity within these populations to conduct classes for their children, and particularly to implement the program for the spiritual empowerment of their junior youth, will enhance the vitality of community-building endeavors in many clusters. (letter dated August 9, 2012, par. 9)

Similarly, in a letter dated December 29, 2015, the Universal House of Justice refers yet again to the importance of including all populations in community-building efforts in places around the world:

> In the course of their endeavours, the believers encounter receptivity within distinct populations who represent a particular ethnic, tribal, or other group and who may be concentrated in a small setting or present throughout the cluster and well beyond it. There is much to be learned about the dynamics involved when a population of this kind embraces the Faith and is galvanized through its edifying influence. We stress the importance of this work for advancing the Cause of God: every people has a share in the World Order of Bahá'u'lláh, and all must be gathered together under the banner of the oneness of humanity. (par. 25)

Prejudice enters the picture for several reasons. The Universal House of Justice recalled Shoghi Effendi's counsel concerning the importance of "freedom from prejudice" and pointed out that prejudice "still permeates the structures of society," even though negative preconceptions about race, class, ethnicity, gender, and/or religious belief cannot be defended or tolerated (letter dated December 28, 2010, par. 34). Like Shoghi Effendi, who wrote extensively about prejudice concerning blacks and whites in his book *The Advent of Divine Justice*, the Universal House of Justice noted that it was important for anyone who hoped to attract people of different backgrounds, or "distinct populations," to display absolute love and no prejudice against them; otherwise those contacts would not be attracted to the Faith. Furthermore, any division in the Bahá'í Faith would threaten to rend it asunder, and this too is not to be tolerated. Prejudicial behavior or attitudes toward race would be a sure way to build deep division (letter dated December 28, 2010, par. 34).

As noted in a letter to an individual believer, however, the nature of racial prejudice has changed in the years since the publication of *The Advent of Divine Justice*, and members of the Bahá'í Faith need to rethink their approach to racial issues. One aspect of that change is the increasing racial and ethnic diversity of America, meaning that it is no longer possible to talk about race relations just between blacks and whites. Another difference is that racial prejudice has become "less blatant," meaning that it is more ingrained and difficult to confront (Universal House of Justice, letter dated April 10, 2011, par. 5). Therefore, strategies that Bahá'ís have been using for many years to address racial concerns are no longer effective.[10] The Universal House of Justice observes that the individual believer to whose letter it is responding has said much the same thing:

> In your letter, you observe that the many activities carried out in the past by the American Bahá'í community to address racial concerns, despite their obvious merit and the results achieved to date, have been limited in their effect and have not been systematic in nature. Your review of such efforts suggests a cyclical pattern, with fits and starts, in which a certain course of action is presented with fanfare by the institutions, many believers take part although others remain on the sidelines, activities reach a peak, and then, after months or perhaps years, attention wanes, and the community is drawn to other areas until some incident occurs or a new heartfelt appeal is uttered, thus beginning the cycle anew. Simply to repeat the approaches implemented in the past, then, will surely not produce a satisfactory result. (par. 2)

As an alternative to this approach and a new framework for action, the Universal House of Justice offered the institute process. It suggested that issues of prejudice of various kinds would certainly arise as Bahá'ís reach out in "the closely knit context of neighborhoods," but that at the same time, activities would adjust to the needs of that particular population and new believers would be "confirmed in a nurturing and familiar environment" (par. 4). It also pointed out that the institute process suitably raises the human resources needed to address the problem of prejudice and marginalization. This is likely true because those who study the institute materials gain grounding in the essentially spiritual nature of human existence, thus helping to overcome prejudices based on artificial barriers such as race.

As for marginalization, institute process participants are expected to create paths of service and, after perhaps receiving short-term outside support from local or visiting tutors, arise to tutor others themselves, becoming in essence indigenous teachers and community leaders. Therefore the institute process is "not a process that some carry out on behalf of others who are passive recipients—the mere extension of the congregation and invitation to paternalism—but one in which an ever-increasing number of souls recognize and take responsibility for the transformation of humanity" (Universal House of Justice, letter dated April 10, 2011, par. 4). Thus fortified, the letter goes on to note, a growing number of new and veteran believers would be more able through practice and spiritual upliftment to address effectively issues of racial prejudice in a wide variety of settings, in their neighborhoods but also in their workplaces and other social venues (par. 4). Other letters offered similar comments, noting that the destiny of people living in a particular place would have to be in their own hands, a requirement fulfilled by deep engagement in, and ownership of, the institute process (Ridván Message 2010, par. 5; letter dated December 29, 2015, par. 5).

A particularly compelling example of the Universal House of Justice's faith in the institute process is its interaction with the Black Men's Gathering. Nicknamed the BMG, this national group was composed of black men, largely based in the United States, who had, under the leadership of Dr. William Roberts, formed a mutual support community that met at least once a year as a whole (and sometimes in smaller regional meetings), studied guidance, and offered coordinated service projects, existing in that way for over twenty-five years. Although it's highly unusual for any group purposefully homogeneous by race or gender to exist in the Bahá'í Faith, the Universal House of Justice supported the BMG in response to a distinct pattern of disengagement or estrangement that had emerged for a number of black male Bahá'ís. In 2007, the Secretariat of the Universal House of Justice said that this group was inspired to help "overcome the crippling effects of a long history of oppression" and that "what the Gathering does so well is to instill in its participants the desire to strive to realize the potentialities they possess" for contributing to the effort to "accomplish the Master's scheme for world redemption" (letter dated June 3, 2007, par. 10).

The many services carried out by members of the BMG during its existence included teaching trips to the continent of Africa, where they were able to interact with numerous indigenous communities. BMG members also encouraged each other to participate in community-building activities at the local level in the United States and engaged in deep reflection about spiritual guidance when they gathered together. But in part, this was a self-healing group that provided social and emotional support for black male Bahá'ís, "creating an environment in which injuries could be tended" (Universal House of Justice, letter dated August 28, 2011, par. 2; see for history of BMG Landry, McMurray, and Thomas).[11] This quote came from a remarkable letter dated August 28, 2011, and addressed to the participants of the Black Men's Gathering, in care of Dr. William Roberts. In it, the Universal House of Justice gave a much fuller description of several purposes for the BMG; it had served "as a bulwark against the forces of racial prejudice afflicting your nation, and, indeed, attacking the Bahá'í community itself, creating an environment in which injuries could be tended, bonds of unity strengthened, sparks of spirituality fanned into flames, and the capacity for assuming the responsibility for the work of the Cause gradually developed through the experience in the field of action" (par. 2). It then explained the importance of fuller engagement in the institute process and went on to suggest that it was time to end the BMG. It cited the fact that several clusters in Africa, using the institute process, had not only expanded the membership of their Bahá'í communities to a remarkable degree, but also transformed the fortunes and spirits of countless children and junior youth and thrown off "the burdensome yoke of social ills such as tribalism" (par. 3). The letter mentions in particular a certain cluster in Kenya, Tiriki West, an area lacking in urban or rural centers, implying that it contains at most villages, and yet that cluster was using the institute process to facilitate community development for thousands of people, only a tenth of whom were Bahá'ís (Simwa 71). This was a particularly remarkable reference because during previous periods of time, American believers of African descent would have been expected to travel abroad and help "teach" Africans; now African villages were being held up as examples for African American men. The Universal House of Justice followed that letter with another dated December 4, 2011, also addressed to the BMG, praising past accomplishments but noting that "new possibilities and new spaces for thought and action have been created" and that members' attention should focus on those (par. 2). The letter encouraged the holding of a series of final regional meetings in which BMG members could reflect upon this development and rise to new challenges.

What, then, is so special about the institute process that it can be presented as solution for so many different kinds of problems and situations? Inherent in the teachings of the Bahá'í Faith, we should note, is the assumption that its message has the power to solve many social problems. Specifically concerning problems associated with the legacy of American slavery and oppression of blacks, for example, the Universal House of Justice pointed out that Bahá'u'lláh "has given us the prescription for a new World Order, declaring that 'mankind's ordered life hath been revolutionized through the agency of this unique, this wondrous System'" (letter dated June 3, 2007, par. 4). We've already mentioned the very specific benefits that would come from full engagement in the institute process, including the expansion of the Bahá'í community, the elevation of the spiritual dialogue taking place in a locality, the education of children, the nurturing of junior youth, the raising up of natural leaders, and the promotion of moral conduct, but it's also important to note that all of this leads to various forms of social action. Built into the institute process is the idea that groups of people, such as junior youth, will actually develop service projects that can address any kind of community problem, ranging from health and welfare to water safety, provision of food, or neighborhood beautification.

The study circles that are at the basis of the institute process, therefore, are only the first step in what the Universal House of Justice sees as a serious process of community development starting with spiritual empowerment and moral education, extending to social action at a small scale, and ultimately expanding to include progressively complex community-building projects. Eventually, it would also be possible to see greater influence by the Bahá'í community in matters of public discourse, such as race relations—a topic to which the Universal House of Justice has given considerable thought, as evidenced in its missives to individual believers and elsewhere—and other important areas of discussion. In this way, Bahá'u'lláh's vision, furthered by His descendants and by the institutions of His Faith, would be realized.[12] The following is one such passage, which addresses how the current Bahá'í strategy challenges prejudice and oppression:

> While it is true that, at the level of public discourse, great strides have been taken in refuting the falsehoods that give rise to prejudice in whatever form, it still permeates the structures of society and is systematically impressed on the individual consciousness. It should be apparent to all that the process set in motion by the current series of global Plans seeks, in the approaches it takes and the methods it employs, to build capacity in every human group, with no regard for class or religious background, with no concern for ethnicity or race, irrespective of gender or social status, to arise and contribute to the advancement of civilization. We pray that, as it steadily unfolds, its potential to disable every instrument devised by humanity over the long period of its childhood for one group to oppress another may be realized. (letter dated December 28, 2010, par. 34)

The Universal House of Justice focuses in large part on expanding human resources because, in its opinion, the size of the Bahá'í Faith is currently too small to make a difference in the world at large. It stated this clearly in its December 28, 2010, letter when it proposed that the numbers of Bahá'ís worldwide would need to rise significantly in order for the faith of Bahá'u'lláh to have any effect on the general population. As it notes there, a small community "can never hope to serve as a pattern for restructuring the whole of society" (par. 14). Therefore, in addition to its many other benefits, the institute process serves to help make the impact of the Baha'i Faith larger.

We should note here that in its communications, the NSA of the Bahá'ís of the United States clearly reflects the guidance of the Universal House of Justice concerning strategies necessary to address such dilemmas as racial disunity. In a letter dated February 25 2017, written after its representatives met with several members of the Universal House of Justice in Haifa in late fall 2016, the NSA writes at some length about America's challenges of materialism, moral decay, and "a deeply ingrained racial prejudice" (par. 3).[13] It assures its members that current Bahá'í institute-related activities would help undo the negative effects of America's racial prejudice and injustice through a process of working in neighborhoods to increase salutary activities involving inclusive interracial fellowship, but also through promotion of community-directed social action and associated discourse in the greater society.

THINKING ABOUT DETROIT

Now we return to the question of how this overall scheme might operate for areas with major place- and race-related problems, such as metropolitan Detroit. We have outlined several difficulties concerning race for this severely fragmented region, and of course segmentation by socioeconomic status, present although not described in comparable detail, is a part of that dilemma as well.[14] At the same time, we have reviewed a remarkable vision and tool for the implementation of strategies that, the worldwide Bahá'í community has been assured, could help resolve some deeply entrenched problems—not just prejudice, but also the need for the education of young people and other social action. How might this set of strategies potentially work in a place like metropolitan Detroit? Could distressed central cities indeed function as healthy venues for the institute process?

Although we can only speculate as to possibilities and constraints, let us undertake a somewhat visionary approach to these questions, but one grounded in the realities of this area. First, a matter of context: there are people living in even the most distressed municipalities in the metropolitan area, and many of those people are in desperate need of a better life. Although Detroit's population dropped markedly in the period after World War II, the Census Bureau estimated in 2016 that 673,000 people lived there. In 2011–2015, an estimated 80.1 percent of city residents identified themselves as African American only, and 7.7 percent identified themselves as Hispanic or Latino/Latina of any race. Yet the existing active Bahá'í community is extremely small in numbers.

The Bahá'í-generated clusters are organized by county in this metropolitan area, and so Bahá'ís live in the three clusters of Wayne, Macomb, and Oakland counties, as well as in Washtenaw County, which is located just to the west of Wayne County. Communities with various numbers of Bahá'ís exist in each of these counties, but those who are actively involved in the institute process are largely concentrated in Oakland and Washtenaw counties, with other counties and communities having initiated activities as well. As we have noted, metropolitan Detroit mirrors the pattern of the "chocolate city" and "white suburbs," although the Bahá'í communities surrounding the city of Detroit are somewhat racially diverse. In their home localities, these Bahá'ís are carrying out the charge of attempting to build up the institute process by creating, within their own clusters and selected neighborhoods, a more outward orientation to involve more and more people who are not declared Bahá'ís in a spiritually based community-building process.

In past decades, the Bahá'ís of metropolitan Detroit promoted racial unity through many of the devices used throughout the twentieth century by the American Bahá'í community, including race unity picnics, conferences, radio broadcasts, and other public programs. Their maintenance of interracial communities in different parts of these counties is a testament to their tenacity and belief in the vision of racial unity. Holy Day celebrations commonly bring together different communities, and people in Bahá'í communities throughout the region interact on various occasions. But given this new era that focuses on community building as described above, strategies would have to change to maintain and build racial diversity. As this area's neighborhoods and localities are some of the most segregated in the country, purposeful action is needed in order to build communities free of racial boundaries. The neighborhood level in these places, that is, could be a segregation trap.

One simple strategy in keeping with the above guidance would be to select neighborhoods with some presence of certain minority populations and begin developing the institute process in the way it is unfolding in other places around the world. This could happen in all counties listed because each contains, even if only to a limited degree, some minority-race or immigrant populations, as census data clearly documents. Much attention could be paid, therefore, to finding such diverse elements and enfolding them into the institute process. But if this process ultimately is to help overcome the social ills associated with disadvantaged places, it would also be necessary to build up functioning neighborhood-based communities within distressed central cities, and much benefit could stem from creating strong linkages among those urban and suburban communities. This approach ties in with the suggestion contained in the Universal House of Justice's December 29, 2015, letter that stronger clusters should serve as reservoirs, or helpers, for nearby clusters that are not as advanced in the institute process (par. 21).

So let us consider the possible implications of this. Wayne County, which contains Detroit and quite a few other postindustrial cities, as well as more prosperous municipalities (but without a critical mass of Bahá'ís), may not yet have abundant Bahá'í human resources for any portion of its cluster, but might draw from human resources (such as visiting tutors) in more suburban clusters, such as Washtenaw, Oakland, or Macomb counties. The tricky part, if enhanced activities were envisioned for the city of Detroit or other possible localities, would be to consider potential receptive neighborhoods, and to help initiate engagement that is both sustainable and not imposed from the outside.

Again focusing on the city of Detroit, outside of the gentrified Greater Downtown—which includes the central business district, portions of the riverfront, and Midtown—broad swaths of formerly healthy neighborhoods are in severe distress, some with only a few houses left standing where many once stood. The series of foreclosures and other economic crises have led to considerable depopulation and quite a number of vacant homes. So it would be necessary to consult carefully with knowledgeable people in order to decide which neighborhoods might be receptive and intact enough to benefit from the community building that the institute process entails. Possible areas within city limits might include majority-black west-side locations that are largely intact physically and socially, such as Minock Park or North Rosedale Park; largely Hispanic southwest locations, such as the Vernor-Springwells district; or east-side locations, such as the predominantly Muslim immigrant "Banglatown" neighborhood, located just north of the small enclave city of Hamtramck but within Detroit's city limits.[15]

The Universal House of Justice suggests that visiting tutors or homefront pioneers who reach out to a receptive local population, "youth in particular," can help generate initial impetus in an area's community-building process (letter dated December 29, 2015, par. 5). In a city such as Detroit, visiting tutors could help in this manner, but so too could a few pioneer individuals or families moving into specific neighborhoods and committing to community building in collaboration with local residents, particularly youth. Because a major drawback for families considering moving to Detroit is the public school system—although in some cases Detroit neighborhoods still retain access to good public or charter schools—it might be easier for people without school-age (or with home-schooled) children to make such a place-specific commitment, although the Ruhi Institute's children's classes and junior youth curriculum provide an important and salutary supplement in such a context, as well as opportunities for engagement. Deep integration into the local culture would be necessary to enable people to live safely and to join in ongoing efforts to uphold the neighborhood and protect it from destructive elements. North Rosedale Park, for example, has strong community-based organizations that do just that.

Who would make such inroads? Returning to the Universal House of Justice's explanation of the need to increase the number of Bahá'ís, at the present time even stable suburban localities within the Detroit metropolitan area do not have the critical mass of Bahá'ís necessary to undertake a major campaign of settlement or visitation in a city neighborhood like Detroit's. Nevertheless, the institute process has in some places in the world started successfully with a very few people and then blossomed. For example, in one of the aforementioned Detroit city neighborhoods it would be possible to recruit youth for initial training and then expand through junior youth activities, children's classes, and home visits to engage whole families, slowly enabling neighborhood-based people to lead such activities and then to shape their own community development in some way, however modest. Furthermore, helpers such as visiting youth or adult tutors could carry out service activities for a summer or a year, on a sequential basis, until local resources arise to carry forth the process.

Even without such numbers and resources, however, it would be useful for metropolitan-area Bahá'ís to begin to think about potential neighborhood centers of activity, to consider how to approach possibly receptive youth or households, make friends, and think seriously about the racial dynamics inherent in such a context. The main one is that in a city that is over 80 percent black, certain mixed-race or predominantly black neighborhoods would benefit from white or other ethnic visitors or pioneers as a visible demonstration of a lack of prejudice and an openness to others.

Such action would also help break the back of continuing forms of residential segregation, prejudice, and distancing. The same areas might also benefit from black visitors or new residents as a show of cultural affinity and affirmation and a means of promoting trust. Equally careful consideration would need to be made for predominately Hispanic, immigrant Middle Eastern, and other such neighborhoods. All action would have to be determined according to local circumstances in an organic manner free of artifice or patriarchy, without prejudice, and with full understanding of the potential for human advancement.

Motivation for such actions could be recognition of the isolation and relative deprivation experienced by many inner-city residents and the need to pursue racial unity in a new way. With the public school system in turmoil and multiple public and charter school closings a fact of life, many Detroit city children are in major danger of growing up without a good elementary or high school education. This has enormous implications for their future well-being, as well as that of their future families. And so, rather than trying to reform a public school system that is ridden with conflict, controversy, and failure, Bahá'í children's classes and junior youth programs may help provide educational benefits that outweigh those of public schools, as has happened in many African communities, according to the Universal House of Justice. Similarly, with few employment opportunities available for blue-collar workers or for high school students, early engagement in a Ruhi junior youth curriculum—which covers such topics as science and math, character-building, and service—and attachment to a wider community with many majority-race members favored with material means could open many doors in a process sometimes labeled "bridging social capital." This means simply that people in disadvantaged circumstances need to be able to access resources outside of their limited frames of reference or neighborhoods. Family friends in more prosperous or stable neighborhoods would be able to offer many benefits for youth who are not in secure or healthy environments.

As for the suburbs and other small localities or rural areas within these counties, it would also be important to think about how to build a base at the neighborhood level that is not racially exclusionary or homogeneous, particularly not all white. In the local history of this region, it has happened that a white family took in a black inner-city youth in order to have enough Bahá'ís to form a spiritual assembly or otherwise assist that person to advance economically.

Local Bahá'í lore tells of prosperous residents who, starting over fifty years ago, would gather youth together, of all races or specifically blacks, to meet in their homes or to travel to the grounds of the Flint area's Louhelen Bahá'í School for retreats or gatherings.[16] The same spirit of reaching across racial barriers would need to inform this new era of reservoir clusters and neighborhood-based activities because informal association between high-minority city neighborhoods and largely white suburban subdivisions does not always happen and in fact can be actively discouraged, particularly for the poor, because of lack of public transportation and consequent limited access to jobs or affordable housing. Bahá'í communities could consider ways to cross bridges into areas of the region that are normally ignored by residents of more prosperous areas. Assisting in the establishment of the institute process is part of that task, but also simple social association and interaction would also be important in order to build a foundation upon which expansion of human resources could thrive. Bahá'ís have made such efforts in the past, but now the institutional framework exists that would allow them to make their attempts at outreach and inclusion more focused and effective.

With such support and growth in neighborhood activities, in the future it would not be difficult to envision practical social action that helps provide basic needs for those facing material deprivation, in a way that honors self-determination and avoids paternalism. These actions would have to be modest, at least in the beginning, because social action may not be able to confront some major dilemmas such as lack of affordable public transportation in a city where perhaps one-fourth of the households do not have a car in 2010 (Grengs 103). But social action undertaken in the context of suburban support could indeed begin to improve the life chances for at least the younger members of the community.

Activities that have emerged recently in Detroit neighborhoods on their own, out of simple desperation or persistent unemployment, have included small-scale entrepreneurialism such as barbershops and beauty shops set up in living rooms; gardening that has sometimes grown to approach small-scale urban farming; a food cooperative that has evolved into a market with home delivery systems; home-based social services such as elder care or child care; a community-supported coffee shop that serves as a neighborhood venue for informal and formal gatherings; and other related efforts. Such activities could be built upon and enhanced with a more consolidated process of social action once a neighborhood was affected by the kind of vision-building possible with deep engagement in the institute process.

The following is just one possible example of social action: Central-city Detroit has a dearth of major grocery stores selling both fresh and affordable vegetables and fruits. Because of the high number of vacant lots and low incomes, and because of the educational efforts of various citywide urban gardening proponents, some city residents have in response created small urban gardens. These can supplement diets (reducing grocery bills) as well as improve the quality of health and well-being. Opportunities for building on such action, however, are limited. Some residential blocks have gardens; others don't. Many people are afraid of gardening because of historic contaminants in the soil or because of the work involved. Others have been trained to overcome such barriers (through soil infill, raised beds, and cooperation) but have no venue in which to share such knowledge and action more widely. Some gardening residents wish to sell their products at small farmer's markets, but those venues are limited (and sometimes exclusionary to amateur gardeners). The list continues in ways both large and small. Conceivably, a neighborhood that was spiritually uplifted by the institute process—and consequently more unified, deliberative, with active spiritual education for all ages of children and adults, affirmed by character-building and training in ways of serving humanity, connected to the outside world, and with an enhanced sense of empowerment—could choose to make of such efforts a coherent and powerful form of social action.

Furthermore, with enough neighborhoods affected in this and other comparable ways, it would be easy for Bahá'í communities to become involved in a necessary dialogue at the city, state, and national levels about realistic solutions for central cities such as Detroit and for such issues as deeply ingrained racial prejudice and marginalization. The discourse newly emboldened by human resources and activities described above could then tackle the larger public issues, such as economic development, transportation, quality of local schools, and social justice.

This strategy is actually the reverse of previous approaches. In this model, the discourse about race, poverty, and social justice would take place organically, with demonstrated action at the level of the neighborhood, not in the realm of abstraction and dialogue that seems to lead nowhere or moves in fits and starts.

CONCLUDING THOUGHTS

The above thought experiment envisioning possible Detroit-specific strategies, which is simply one individual's perspective about a hypothetical application of the Universal House of Justice's vision and strategies, would still be demonstrably superior to current trends, programs, and practices. Although some advances have been made in improving the physical aspects of life in Detroit's neighborhoods—for example, streetlights have been turned back on and a small but important number of the vacant houses have been torn down—significant improvements in neighborhood stability, public safety, child welfare, and economic opportunity are still a long way off. Furthermore, typical approaches to neighborhood development, with few exceptions, are limited. For example, although community-based organizations exist, they are largely dependent on outside funding from vanishing public coffers or from foundations, which typically require them to undertake narrow agendas such as construction or rehabilitation of housing, counseling services for home owners, or job training. Nonprofits that attempt to carry out specific actions such as helping feed the poor, a laudable endeavor to be sure, do so in a way that does not empower the poor to take control of their own destinies.

High-level panels and organizations that purport to consult about improving Detroit or enhancing race relations hardly touch the lives of the households where they reside. Proponents of improving the education of children continue to fight over charter schools versus public schools and seem to offer very few solutions for the failure of both kinds of educational institutions. A grassroots movement that builds on values-driven education of the young, moral and spiritual training for adults, service-related activities, and transformative social action would take time and patience but would in many ways be superior to the business-as-usual approach to social reform that currently exists.

The difficulty, of course, comes with implementation. What is needed are not theoretical ruminations—these are easily conceived and presented—but real-world actions that actually carry out the proposed process on the ground. Such an endeavor thus requires not only vision, but also tenacity, organization, leadership, systematization, perseverance, creativity, and any number of additional attributes. However, the potential for applying key principles is enormous, and the need, gargantuan. The promise of bringing about human society's positive evolution must in some way be fulfilled while time remains for the utilization of underlying strengths of a community that may appear—especially to those without an optimistic vision and salutary tools for reformation—as a hopelessly dysfunctional environment. The Universal House of Justice assures us that the people in every neighborhood have the inherent talents and capacities needed to transform society.

NOTES

1. Racial segregation of religious congregations has lessened, but recent surveys show that it still exists. In a 1998 survey, 72 percent of non-Hispanic whites belonged to congregations that were at least 80 percent white. When the survey was repeated in 2012, this racial isolation had dropped to 57 percent of non-Hispanic whites. Yet as of 2012, the majority of congregations in America, 86 percent, were composed mostly (at least 80 percent) of one race or another (Chaves and Eagle 21). This chapter was previously published, June Manning Thomas, "Race, Place, and Clusters: Current Vision and Possible Strategies," *Journal of Bahá'í Studies* 27, no. 3 (fall 2017): 85–114.

2. For a discussion of the role of planning in the Bahá'í Faith, see 'Abdu'l-Bahá tablets, referenced in text, but also others in works cited (Smith and Lample; Thomas, *Planning Progress*).

3. The "Midwest" was actually labeled the "Central States" during this period of boundary setting for the Regional Council. The twelve Central States had been named over eighty years before by 'Abdu'l-Bahá as a framework for action: Michigan, Indiana, Ohio, Minnesota, South Dakota, North Dakota, Wisconsin, Illinois, Missouri, Iowa, Nebraska, and Kansas. I participated in the creation of such cluster configurations in the Central States during this 2001–2002 period. Two years are listed because this and other Councils began to make decisions about cluster boundaries after receiving the Universal House of Justice's January 9, 2001, letter, and after considering input from Auxiliary Board members, but needed to make a few adjustments in the months just after receiving definitional clarification about cluster boundaries from the Department of the Secretariat, the Universal House of Justice, December 12, 2001, letter.

4. This is in contrast to some communities of foreign language-speaking immigrants, who may seek to live together in ethnic enclaves in order to facilitate shared housing, job-seeking, and other forms of mutual support.

5. The Charles article is a multi-faceted study of this "racial preference hierarchy," complete with quantitative data taken from surveys conducted in four

metropolitan areas and analyzed in several tables; her study clearly establishes white preference concerning race and residence but also notes changes over time and many variations concerning different racial and ethnic groups. For those who wish a short summary of this work, please see her discussion/ conclusion, pp. 401–403. For the Farley reference, refer especially to chapters 6 and 7; these provide fuller context and report on surveys conducted earlier than those by Charles, but using a similar methodology. These authors also found considerable complexity and variation over time.

6. Later, the term "race riot" became associated with the black community, when, after years of oppression, some of its members arose in several cities (particularly in the 1960s) to protest heavy-handed or violent police tactics and segregated/overcrowded housing, turning at times to looting and setting fires as attention-getting but ineffective approaches.

7. In 2010, Dan Gilbert moved his company, Quicken Loans, to downtown Detroit, and a year later he began to buy dozens of office and retail buildings and rehabilitate them. His initial 2010 staff of 1,700 downtown workers expanded over the next 7 years to over 14,000, and the number of buildings purchased may have approached eighty. By 2012, the pattern of employee and building expansion was clear, and lack of housing opportunities for new professional employees had become evident. In that year, Rock Ventures, the umbrella company that includes Quicken Loans, launched a program called Opportunity Detroit that was designed to systematize the promotion and corporate-driven redevelopment of Detroit's central business district, complete with attraction of new residents.

8. Except when otherwise cited, all census data for this paper is available through *American FactFinder II*, an online tool provided by the Census Bureau.

9. Detroit's economy was unusually dependent on one industry, automobile manufacturing, in the mid-twentieth century. Even then, however, firms were beginning to move to suburban locations in metropolitan Detroit, and this exodus escalated as years passed because, contemporary surveys showed, manufacturers sought large, contiguous plots of land and escape from city taxes. Between 1947 and 1955, the Big Three—Chrysler, Ford, and General Motors—built twenty new plants in metropolitan Detroit, but not a single one was located in the central city (Thomas, *Redevelopment and Race,* 72–74). In the late twentieth century, automobile manufacturing moved to other regions of the country, and global competition escalated, especially from Japanese firms; such factors led to major declines in automobile employment in the city of Detroit and in metropolitan Detroit.

10. Those strategies are not mentioned in the letter but probably include race unity picnics, conferences, training or outreach programs, and so on. See Richard Thomas's *Racial Unity: An Imperative for Social Progress.*

11. A new edition of Landry, McMurray, and Thomas's book is in preparation. This will include information from surveys taken of BMG members and their families. According to direct information from the authors, survey results have confirmed both the service and the social support functions of BMG.

12. See, for example, letters to individuals dated June 3, 2007; April 10, 2011; December 28, 2010, par. 24–25; December 29, 2015, par. 2, 30.

13. This pivotal meeting is clearly described, at some length, in the verbal report given by Ken Bowers, the Secretary of the National Spiritual Assembly of the Bahá'ís of the United States, available in a videotape of remarks he gave during his Secretary's Report to the 109th Bahá'í National Convention held in April 2017. This video along with an audio version are both accessible online to U.S. members of the Bahá'í Faith through a password-protected site.

14. In Detroit, as in America as a whole, black and brown people are a minority of the poor; however, the rate of poverty among black and brown people is disproportionately high compared to whites for the perfectly intelligible historical reasons I have discussed in the section "Place, Race, and Division."

15. I have led projects for classes or for research in three of these four named communities, and they have potential as outlined here, although of course the actual communities would have to be chosen through some other process.

16. These stories are common among black Bahá'ís in the area who date back to the early 1960s. White or prosperous black families that were involved in reaching out included those of Harold Johnson, Richard and Sharonne Fogel, James and Naomi Oden, and Mary Wolters.

BIBLIOGRAPHY

'Abdu'l-Bahá. *Tablets of the Divine Plan. Wilmetter, IL: Bahá'í Publishing Trust, 1993.*

American FactFinder II. United States Census Bureau. http://factfinder.census.gov/faces/nav/jsf/pages/index.xhtml. Accessed February 15, 2017.

Charles, Camille Z. "Neighborhood Racial-Composition Preferences: Evidence from a Multiethnic Metropolis." *Social Problems*, vol. 47, no. 3, 2000, pp. 379–407, https://doi.org/10.2307/3097236. Accessed February 15, 2017.

Chaves, Mark, and Alison Eagle. *Religious Congregations in 21st Century America: National Congregations Study*. Duke University, 2015, http://www.soc.duke.edu/natcong/Docs/NCSIII_report_final.pdf. Accessed July 22, 2017.

Deng, Lan, et al. "Saving Strong Neighborhoods from the Destruction of Mortgage Foreclosures: The Impact of Community-Based Efforts in Detroit, Michigan." *Housing Policy Debate*, 2017, pp. 1–27.

Farley, Reynolds, Sheldon Danziger, and Harry J. Holzer. *Detroit Divided.* Russell Sage Foundation, 2000.

Grengs, Joe. "Comparing People and Places with Transportation Accessibility in Metropolitan Detroit." In *Mapping Detroit: Land, Community, and Shaping a City*, edited by June Thomas and Henco Bekkering, Wayne State University Press, 2015, pp. 101–14.

Jacobs, Andrew J. "Embedded Contrasts in Race, Municipal Fragmentation, and Planning: Divergent Outcomes in Detroit and Greater Toronto-Hamilton Regions 1990–2000." *Journal of Urban Affairs*, vol. 31, no. 2, 2009, pp. 147–72. *Taylor & Francis Online*, doi:10.1111/j.1467-9906.2009.00440.x. Accessed February 15, 2017.

———. "The Impacts of Variations in Development Context on Employment Growth: A Comparison of Central Cities in Michigan and Ontario, 1980–2006. *Economic Development Quarterly*, vol. 23, no. 4, 2009, pp. 351–71. DOI: 10.1177/0891242409343304. Accessed August 28, 2017.

Landry, Frederick, Harvey McMurray, and Richard Thomas. *The Story of the Black Men's Gathering: Celebrating Twenty-Five Years, 1987–2011*. US Bahá'í Publishing Trust, 2011.

Massey, Douglas S., et al. *Climbing Mount Laurel: The Struggle for Affordable Housing and Social Mobility in an American Suburb*. Princeton: Princeton University Press, 2013.

National Spiritual Assembly of the Bahá'ís of the United States. Letter to the American Bahá'í Community, February 23, 2017.

Oh, Sun Jung, and John Yinger. "What Have We Learned from Paired Testing in Housing Markets?" *Cityscape*, vol. 17, no. 3, 2015, pp. 15–59. https://search.proquest.com/docview/1774580507?accountid=35396. Accessed August 28, 2017.

Rugh, Jacob, and Douglas Massey. "Segregation in Post-Civil Rights America." *Du Bois Review: Social Science Research on Race*, vol. 11, no. 2, 2014, pp. 205–32. DOI: https://doi.org/10.1017/S1742058X13000180

Shoghi Effendi. *The Advent of Divine Justice*. US Bahá'í Publishing Trust, 1984.

Simwa, Linus P. Iposhe. *The Establishment and Impact of Friends Church among the Tiriki of Western Kenya*. MA thesis, University of Nairobi, 2015. http://erepository.uonbi.ac.ke/handle/11295/93892.

Smith, Melanie, and Paul Lample. *The Spiritual Conquest of the Planet: Our Response to Global Plans*. Palabra Press, 1993. *Bahá'í Library Online*, http://bahai-library.com/pdf/s/smith_lample_spiritual_conquest.pdf.

Social Science Data Analysis Network. CensusScope. http://www.censusscope.org/us/rank_dissimilarity_white_black.html. Accessed August 28, 2017.

Thomas, June M. *Planning Progress: Lessons from Shoghi Effendi*. Association for Bahá'í Studies, 1999.

———. "Redesigning Community with Propinquity: Fragments of Detroit's Region." In *Mapping Detroit: Land, Community, and Shaping a City*, edited by June Thomas and Henco Bekkering, Wayne State University Press, 2015, pp. 189–207.

———. *Redevelopment and Race: Planning a Finer City in Postwar Detroit*. 2nd ed., Wayne State University Press, 2013.

Thomas, June M., and Marsha Ritzdorf, editors. *Urban Planning and the African-American Community: In the Shadows*. London: SAGE, 1997.

Thomas, Richard W. *Racial Unity: An Imperative for Social Progress*. Association for Bahá'í Studies, 1993.

Universal House of Justice. Letter written by the Department of the Secretariat on behalf of the Universal House of Justice to the National Spiritual Assembly of the Bahá'ís of the United States, December 12, 2001.

———. Letter written by the Department of the Secretariat on behalf of the Universal House of Justice to an Individual Believer, June 3, 2007.

———. Letter written by the Department of the Secretariat on behalf of the Universal House of Justice to an Individual Believer, April 10, 2011.

———. Letter written by the Department of the Secretariat on behalf of the Universal House of Justice to Participants of the Black Men's Gathering, August 28, 2011.

———. Letter written by the Department of the Secretariat on behalf of the Universal House of Justice to Participants of the Black Men's Gathering, December 4, 2011.

———. Letter written by the Department of the Secretariat on behalf of the Universal House of Justice to the National Spiritual Assembly of the Baha'is of the United States, August 9, 2012.

———. Letter to the Bahá'ís of the World acting under the Mandate of 'Abdu'l-Bahá, March 26, 2016.

———. Letter to the Conference of the Continental Board of Counsellors, January 9, 2001.

———. Letter to the Conference of the Continental Board of Counsellors, December 28, 2010.

———. Letter to the Conference of the Continental Board of Counsellors, December 29, 2015.

———. Letter to National Spiritual Assemblies, May 30, 1997.

———. Ridván Message 1996.

———. Ridván Message 2010.

———. Ridván Message 2013.

Young, Iris Marion, "Inclusion and Democracy." In *Readings in Planning Theory,* edited by Susan S. Fainstein and James Defilippis, Wiley Blackwell, 2016, pp. 389–406.

Conclusion

Multiple Authors of the Chapters in This Book

At the time of this writing, fifty years since the Orangeburg Massacre, the assassination of Martin Luther King, Jr., and the other unprecedented social and political upheavals of 1968, America's racial dilemma often appears to be worsening. Indeed, in the midst of a rapidly deteriorating situation, vital questions of who is or ought to be an American, of how we define prosperity and good governance and who deserves them, and of our country's role and place on the global stage press themselves on the conscience of the nation with relentless and bewildering urgency. While any honest assessment will acknowledge the important strides that the country has taken in the half century since the heyday of the civil rights movement, the changes still required of Americans and their institutions at all levels in order to establish a just and peaceful multiracial society are momentous and challenging. As one notable work has pointed out, history provides no guarantees of success, and it is no surprise that many Americans look to the immediate future with foreboding.[1] By adding to the scholarship about one American religious community's historic efforts to promote interracial harmony, this volume attempts to contribute in some way to contemporary public discourses, both inside and outside the academy, about our country's way forward.

While hardly a perfect record, the experience of the American Bahá'í community since the turn of the twentieth century should be a source of optimism. It is the story of a virtual cross section of the American population choosing, on the basis of shared values alone, to create and embrace a new collective identity that both champions diversity and transcends racial divisions. For Bahá'ís, the concept of the oneness of humanity has been far more than a cosmopolitan ideal; it has been a principled platform on which they have striven to build their religious communities and affect the historical course of their society. At every step of the way, the international authorities of the Bahá'í Faith, 'Abdu'l-Bahá, Shoghi Effendi, and the Universal House of Justice have insisted that the American Bahá'í community develop along soundly interracial lines. As such, to be a Bahá'í in the United States has meant an obligation to work for interracial harmony, regardless of one's race, class, social position, or inclination to activism. Their efforts have proceeded along two complementary lines: internally, to build an ever more diverse and cohesive interracial fellowship within their own community, and externally, to confront the disease of racism in the country at large as their resources and circumstances allowed. As the chapters in this volume indicate, pursuit of this "double crusade," as Shoghi Effendi termed it, has never been easy. At any given point, the American Bahá'í community's internal efforts might seem halting or incomplete and its membership and material resources too small to affect significant social change. Nevertheless, the aggregate of the last 120 years of work, both individual and collective, has produced one of the country's most diverse religious bodies, with a distinct administrative system that is multiracial, democratic, and non-partisan and, particularly with the recent implementation of the training institute system, increasingly capable to engage issues of race at the levels of public discourse and social action. Early experience in several parts of the country indicates that this training institute system may represent a significant step forward in the ability of the American Bahá'í community to engage larger numbers of people from diverse backgrounds, and to contribute more effectively in a wide range of collaborative efforts aimed at the social, economic, intellectual, and spiritual development of neighborhoods and towns.

A particularly interesting area of future research is how effective the current Bahá'í community-building effort through the training institute process grounded in the Ruhi sequence of courses is in improving race relations. In this case, depending on the area of the nation, race relations might involve other groups such as Hispanics and South Asian Indians. As it did in the past, as described in chapters in this book, the National Spiritual Assembly (NSA) of the Bahá'ís of the United States is actively working with local Bahá'í communities to specifically reach out to African Americans, American Indians, and immigrant groups. Reminiscent of the calls of Shoghi Effendi, the NSA is asking the Bahá'ís to move into the centers where these populations live. Every American Bahá'í is encouraged, in order to achieve this, to recognize the importance of the training institute process and to study Shoghi Effendi's *The Advent of Divine Justice* and *The World Order of Bahá'u'lláh*. The vision of the NSA is that systematic action will "steadily build the capacity to form deep, loving friendships inclusive of all peoples, as we pray and socialize together as true friends, provide spiritual education to our children and junior youth, consult about the conditions of our communities and act together for our common benefit."[2]

Race relations are often benchmarked by material success, political advancements, public policy, and demographic changes. The chapters in this book demonstrate that long-lasting change comes from individuals and institutions taking up the challenge of coming head-to-head with racial prejudices and striving to eliminate them in their lives and in their religious communities. These chapters contribute what the authors hope will be a continuing dialog among scholars of race and religion, at conferences and in other venues, about the Bahá'í Faith in the United States and the ways it has influenced African Americans and vice versa. In this respect, we stand on the shoulders of Gayle Morrison, whose seminal biography of Louis G. Gregory nearly forty years ago opened the way to thinking about the many previously unexplored connections between African American and Bahá'í history. Gregory was the "father" of Bahá'í race amity efforts in the early twentieth century. He was one of the architects of the Bahá'í Faith's unique interracial democracy and an intellectual who attempted to bridge African American and Bahá'í experiences. Probably more than anyone else, Gregory, a tireless teacher of the Bahá'í Faith, was responsible for introducing the Bahá'í message to the black public. Many other Bahá'ís worked with him. Yet, he unfortunately remains on the periphery of scholarly discourse. Further, the Bahá'í influences on more well-known African Americans, not only Alain Locke, but other adherents to this religion, including *Chicago Defender* publisher Robert S. Abbott, jazz trumpeter John Birks "Dizzy" Gillespie, poet laureate Robert Hayden, physicist and astronaut Ronald McNair, dancer Fayard Nicholas, and civil rights plaintiff Herman Sweatt, are seldom acknowledged, much less adequately explored.

More challenging still, the Bahá'í teachings seem to have influenced African American social, religious, and political visions in ways that are not always easy to trace. There is still much to be done exploring relationships between the Bahá'í Faith and the civil rights movement in all its dimensions, from the work of the Commission on Interracial Cooperation and the NAACP in the early twentieth century to the Black Power era of the 1970s. In this regard, the extensive archives of such national organizations as the NAACP, the Urban League, and the SCLC remain virtually untapped, while the possibilities at the local level around the country are almost endless.

In the realms of social and intellectual history, the Bahá'í phenomenon encourages an examination of the nature of religion itself, and particularly of African American religion. As historian Guy Emerson Mount has pointed out, the fifty-year connection between W. E. B. Du Bois and the Bahá'í Faith, for example, raises important questions about "the fluidity of religious identities . . . and how black thought specifically often blurs the lines between a congregation, a movement, a religion, politics, and philosophy." To what extent did Du Bois see himself as part of a Bahá'í "movement" or influenced by Bahá'í "philosophy"? To return to an example in this book, in the same vein but on a different scale, what were the effects on thousands of black South Carolinians of participation in Bahá'í classes for children beginning in the 1970s? How did they conceive of the Bahá'í Faith and their relationship to it? How did their early Bahá'í experience shape their lives and those of their own children? As Mount notes, proper analysis of these ideas and relationships will require a "deep recovery project" involving extensive scholarly collaboration over many years. The authors of this volume welcome such a development.[3]

NOTES

1. See Steven Levitsky and Daniel Ziblatt, *How Democracies Die* (New York: Crown, 2018).

2. National Spiritual Assembly of the Bahá'ís of the United States to the American Bahá'í community, January 31, 2018, https://app.box.com/s/vmd6rgniscz3zyq8lj4rk4np9n70ow7h. Shoghi Effendi, *The Advent of Divine Justice*; Shoghi Effendi, *The World Order of Bahá'u'lláh*, 2nd ed. (Wilmette, IL: Bahá'í Publishing Trust, 1974).

3. Guy Emerson Mount, "W. E. B. Du Bois and the Bahá'í Faith," *Black Perspectives* blog, October 16, 2016, https://www.aaihs.org/w-e-b-du-bois-and-the-bahai-faith.

BIBLIOGRAPHY

Levitsky, Steven, and Daniel Ziblatt. *How Democracies Die*. New York: Crown, 2018.

Morrison, Gayle. *To Move the World: Louis G. Gregory and the Advancement of Racial Unity in America*. Wilmette, IL: Bahá'í Publishing Trust, 1982.

Mount, Guy Emerson. "W. E. B. Du Bois and the Bahá'í Faith." *Black Perspectives* blog. October 16, 2016. https://www.aaihs.org/w-e-b-du-bois-and-the-bahai-faith.

National Spiritual Assembly of the Bahá'ís of the United States. Letter to the American Bahá'í community. January 31, 2018. https://app.box.com/s/vmd6rgniscz3zyq8lj4rk4np9n70ow7h.

Shoghi Effendi. *The Advent of Divine Justice*. Wilmette, IL: Bahá'í Publishing Trust, 1984. Also available at http://www.bahai.org/library/authoritative-texts/shoghi-effendi/advent-divine-justice/advent-divine-justice.pdf?80ffc30c.

Shoghi Effendi. *The World Order of Bahá'u'lláh*. 2nd ed. Wilmette, IL: Bahá'í Publishing Trust, 1974. Also available at http://www.bahai.org/library/authoritative-texts/shoghi-effendi/world-order-bahaullah.

Index

Page numbers in italics denote figures; page numbers followed by "n" refer to notes.

About the Contributors

Loni Bramson's doctorate is in contemporary history and history of religion from the Université Catholique de Louvain. She has taught at universities in Africa, Europe, and the United States. Currently she is an associate professor at the American Public University System. She teaches courses in modern United States and European history, history of religion, women's history, African American history, and American Indian history. Her publications include chapters in books, articles, and encyclopedia entries on the Bahá'í Faith, and a human rights monograph. She is an editor for the *Journal of International Women's Studies.*

Christopher Buck, PhD (University of Toronto), JD (Cooley Law School), is an independent scholar, Pittsburgh attorney, and online faculty member at the Wilmette Institute. He previously taught at Michigan State University, Central Michigan University, Quincy University, Millikin University, and Carleton University. Dr. Buck publishes broadly in Bahá'í studies, American studies, African American studies, Native American studies, Islamic studies, religious studies, Syriac Studies, and legal studies (constitutional law). His books include *Baha'i Faith: A Quick Reference*, *God and Apple Pie: Religious Myths and Visions of America*, *Alain Locke: Faith and Philosophy*, *Paradise and Paradigm: Key Symbols in Persian Christianity and the Bahá'í Faith*, *Symbol and Secret: Qur'an Commentary in Bahá'u'lláh's Kitáb-i Íqán*, *Religious Celebrations* (co-author), and *Generation Y Speaks Out: A Policy Guide* (coeditor).

Gwendolyn Etter-Lewis is professor of English, black world studies, women's, gender, and sexuality studies at Miami University in Oxford, Ohio. She earned her PhD in linguistics from the University of Michigan,

Ann Arbor. Dr. Etter-Lewis teaches a variety of interdisciplinary courses. Most recently she taught a course on black British writers at the Miami University John E. Dolibois European Center in Luxembourg, which included a five-day study tour in London. In 2007, she founded a college readiness program (Project REACH, now known as Dream Keepers) for underrepresented high school students in the greater Cincinnati area. The program was awarded an internal grant ($150,000) in 2015 and has become a university practicum offered each semester. Dr. Etter-Lewis' interest in women of color and education has taken her to various countries for research: Zambia, Zimbabwe, Ethiopia, Eritrea, Lesotho, Ghana, South Africa, and Kenya. She is the author of several books and articles including:

Lights of the Spirit: Historical Portraits of Black Bahá'is in North America. Coedited with Richard Thomas. Wilmette, IL: Bahá'í Publishing Trust, 2006.

Unrelated Kin: Race and Gender in Women's Personal Narratives. Coedited with Michele Foster. New York: Routledge, 1996.

My Soul Is My Own: Oral Narratives of African American Women in the Professions. New York: Routledge, 1993.

Mike McMullen is a professor of sociology and cross cultural studies at the University of Houston-Clear Lake in Houston, Texas. He received his doctorate from Emory University. His first book is *The Bahá'í: The Religious Construction of a Global Identity*. His areas of interest include Bahá'í studies, the sociology of religion, the Middle East, organizational development and change, and conflict resolution and mediation. Recently, he lived for a year in Cairo, Egypt, as a Fulbright Scholar, teaching at the American University in Cairo. He continues to research the American Bahá'í community, and recently published a book entitled *The Bahá'ís of America: The Growth and Change of a Religious Movement*. He is currently working on a book on the history of conflict resolution in the United States.

June Manning Thomas is Berry Distinguished University Professor at the University of Michigan, teaching in the Urban and Regional Planning Program. Some of her books include *Redevelopment and Race: Planning a Finer City in Postwar Detroit* (1997, 2013); *Planning Progress: Lessons from Shoghi Effendi* (1999); and the coedited *Mapping Detroit: Evolving Land Use Patterns and Connections* (2015). She currently serves on the Regional Baha'i Council of the Midwestern States. Her full biography can be accessed at http://taubmancollege.umich.edu/urbanplanning/faculty/directory/june-manning-thomas.

Louis Venters, PhD, teaches African and African diaspora history, southern history, and public history at Francis Marion University and is a consultant in the fields of historic preservation and cultural resource management. He is the author or coauthor of several site studies, public history reports, and exhibits, and is a member of the board of directors of Preservation South Carolina and of the South Carolina African American Heritage Commission. He is currently working on a sequel to his book, *No Jim Crow Church: The Origins of South Carolina's Bahá'í Community*. He blogs on issues related to race, religion, history, and culture at www.louisventers.com.

CPSIA information can be obtained
at www.ICGtesting.com
Printed in the USA
LVHW020039090921
697356LV00026B/524